The History of Galilee,
47 BCE to 1260 CE

The History of Galilee, 47 BCE to 1260 CE

From Josephus and Jesus to the Crusades

M. M. Silver

LEXINGTON BOOKS
Lanham • Boulder • New York • London

Published by Lexington Books
An imprint of The Rowman & Littlefield Publishing Group, Inc.
4501 Forbes Boulevard, Suite 200, Lanham, Maryland 20706
www.rowman.com

6 Tinworth Street, London SE11 5AL, United Kingdom

Copyright © 2021 The Rowman & Littlefield Publishing Group, Inc.

All rights reserved. No part of this book may be reproduced in any form or by any electronic or mechanical means, including information storage and retrieval systems, without written permission from the publisher, except by a reviewer who may quote passages in a review.

British Library Cataloguing in Publication Information Available

Library of Congress Cataloging-in-Publication Data

Names: Silver, M. M. (Matthew Mark), 1961- author.
Title: The history of Galilee, 47 BCE to 1260 CE : from Josephus and Jesus to the crusades / M. M. Silver.
Description: Lanham, Maryland : Lexington Books, 2021. | Includes bibliographical references and index.
Identifiers: LCCN 2021032541 (print) | LCCN 2021032542 (ebook) | ISBN 9781793649454 (cloth) | ISBN 9781793649478 (paperback) | ISBN 9781793649461 (ebook)
Subjects: LCSH: Galilee (Israel)—History. | Galilee (Israel)—Church history. | Galilee (Israel)—Religion.
Classification: LCC DS110.G2 S59 2021 (print) | LCC DS110.G2 (ebook) | DDC 956.94/5—dc23
LC record available at https://lccn.loc.gov/2021032541
LC ebook record available at https://lccn.loc.gov/2021032542

Dedicated to a future university in Galilee

Contents

List of Figures — ix

Introduction — 1

1 Josephus and Galilee — 9

2 Jesus and Galilee — 51

3 Mishnaic Galilee — 95

4 Byzantine Galilee — 163

5 Early Islamic Galilee — 209

6 Crusader Galilee — 239

Bibliography — 321

Index — 331

About the Author — 343

List of Figures

Cover: View from possible site of the Sermon on the Mount—Mount of Beatitudes. Courtesy of Adi Lam

Figure 0.1	1840 Map of Galilee, based on work of E. Robinson and E. Smith. *Source*: Courtesy of Tel-Hai College Historical Maps Archive	7
Figure 1.1	View of Arbela Caves. *Source*: Courtesy of Adi Lam	16
Figure 1.2	Map of Galilee in Roman Times, based on work of M. Avi-Yonah. *Source*: Courtesy of Tel-Hai College Historical Maps Archive	21
Figure 2.1	Map of Galilee in Jesus' Time. *Source*: From Henry Ward Beecher's 1871 volume, Life of Jesus, the Christ. (Beecher, 1871, 254)	56
Figure 2.2	View from possible site of the Sermon on the Mount—Mount of Beatitudes. *Source*: Courtesy of Adi Lam	75
Figure 2.3	Archaeological Remains at Caesarea Philippi (Banias). *Source*: Courtesy of Adi Lam	85
Figure 3.1	Necropolis at Beit She'arim. *Source*: Courtesy of Adi Lam	116
Figure 6.1	Map of Galilee in Crusader Times, based on work of J. Prawer and M. Benvenisti. *Source*: Courtesy of Tel-Hai College Historical Maps Archive	241
Figure 6.2	View of Acre Today. *Source*: Courtesy of Adi Lam	275
Figure 6.3	Crusader Acre. *Source*: Courtesy of Adi Lam	278

Introduction

A number of world cities are held in reverence by some or all three monotheistic faiths, but no world *region* has allure to all three on a level matched by Galilee, in northern Israel. As the region where Jesus came of age, Galilee is where Christianity came into being as a communal faith. Galilee was where monotheism first fractured into different religions, and so its history raises vexing questions about the relationship between place and belief, the character of religious experience, and the meaning of monotheism. How did it come about that faith in one God found expression pluralistically, in competing religious cultures? Questions of this sort are addressed on different levels by different people, and inspiring multiple answers, they probably yield as much confusion as clarity. Still, as the bedrock of interfaith dialogue, the questions are fascinating and compelling—and, if there is one region in the world where scholarly history can richly contribute to their discussion, it is Galilee.

In Galilee, Christianity broke away from Judaism. Concurrently, Judaism refashioned itself, pivoting away from a Temple-based cult in Jerusalem and becoming a rabbinical faith based on study of the Oral Law, the Talmud, in Galilee. Emerging from Arabia, Islam, like its two monotheistic rivals, staked sacred claims on Jerusalem's Temple Mount, but its battlefield in the country was Galilee. Just as had happened with Judaism and Christianity, Islam's staying power as a world religion was tested in Galilee. Three decisive military battles in world history, one marking the end of the Byzantine era in the Holy Land, another decisively weakening the Crusader kingdom in the country, and a third repulsing Mongol incursion in the region, were all fought in the heart of Galilee, or on its northern and southern rims, and, in each, Islam consolidated its position as the majority religion in the Middle East, and as a viable contender for, or keeper of, political power in Palestine. Thus, on different levels, spiritual, political, military, Galilee is where the resilience and durability of all three monotheistic faiths became undeniable.

Centuries down the road from the period of Jesus and the Jewish revolts against Rome, Galilee played host to intriguing and impactful developments in these three religious cultures. Galilee, including its coastal gateway, the city of Acre, is largely where the fate of the Crusaders' experiments in holy warfare, and rural settlement, was decided. Galilee is also where Jewish mysticism found its fullest expression. This happened in the sixteenth century, in the mountain town of Safed; and despite, or perhaps because of, its remote esotericism, Kabbalistic Safed has exuded, through the present, magnetic appeal to Jews and non-Jews. Medieval Islam experienced a small but significant fissure in Galilee; one people of faith, the Druze, who broke away from Islam, also excited the imagination of Holy Land visitors, explorers and commentators.

Just as the Crusades can be seen, for better or worse, as the pinnacle of the Middle Ages, so too is the French Revolution typically seen as the entryway to modernity—and, uniquely, Galilee is the place where these two historical turnstiles spin together. The two phenomena converge in Acre, Galilee's coastal edge, where the Crusaders established the capital of their second kingdom, and where, centuries later, Napoleon's invasion in the Middle East came to an inglorious end.

From the mid-eighteenth century through the present, two national movements, each buoyed on religious tradition, consolidated and fought for survival in Galilee. As had happened with the monotheistic faiths in late antiquity, Galilee, in the modern era of nationalism, became the testing ground of these movements' staying power. A patriarch of Palestinian nationalism, Zahir al-Umar, sponsored an underappreciated period of socioeconomic growth in Galilee toward the end of the eighteenth century, and while Palestinian national consciousness did not find fully identifiable expression until the World War I period, important transitional points in its development, following Zahir's career, were rooted in Galilee. These include Acre's resistance to Napoleon, led by Ahmad Pasha al-Jazzar, and rural uprisings in the 1830s.

Concurrently, Jewish nationalism defined its goals and refined its symbols in Galilee, decades before the late-nineteenth-century juncture when it gained formal status as Zionism. Jewish religious settlers came from Eastern Europe as early as the late eighteenth century. They created viable communities in Safed and Tiberias before political instability and natural disasters in the 1830s erased some of their achievements. Much more than the later, secular-minded, Jewish pioneers who belonged to Zionist organizations wanted to admit, these earlier, Orthodox Jewish, settlers in Galilee put down foundations of a future Jewish state. But to say this is not to denigrate the drama and significance of early twentieth-century *halutz* (pioneering) Zionist work in communal settlements in Galilee—the kibbutz, the courageous defense of the doomed Tel-Hai commune in the region's panhandle, and many other Galilee symbols of Zionist fortitude inspired generations of Israelis, through the present.

The tragic conflict between these two, Jewish and Arab, national movements, came to a head in 1948 in Galilee. This was inevitable because Galilee was where they had each, independently, passed through crucial turnstiles in the past. As happened many times before in differing contexts, and with regard to many sorts of phenomena, Jerusalem grabs headlines today in discussions of the continuing Jewish-Arab conflict, but the "grass roots" venue of its most complicated manifestations, the place where its intractability became incontrovertibly manifest, is Galilee.

Palestinians are thinking of many places in the country when they talk about a "right of return" to pre-1948 locales, but the focal point of this political claim, and of the 1948 Palestinian *Nakba* (catastrophe), is Galilee. Conversely, for Israel, the locale where Palestinian national claims are most untenable, because their application would spell the end of the Jewish state project, is not the post-1967 disputed territories of the West Bank and Gaza, which are subject to continuing negotiation and are currently under partial Palestinian autonomy, but rather Galilee. Galilee is "Ground Zero" in the Palestinian-Israeli conflict.

To recapitulate in a nutshell, here are milestones in Galilee's history: the rise of Christianity; the birth of Talmudic Judaism; Islam's consolidation in military battle; the later Crusader capital and the prime ground of the Franks' experiments in rural settlement; Kabbalah's capital; the Middle East border of Napoleonic warfare; and the most complicated and consequential flash point in the Israel-Arab 1948 war.

Galilee history is the Greatest Story Never Told.

A few anthologies relating to particular eras in Galilee history have been produced, typically under the auspices of publishers that had special interest in topics such as the New Testament landscape, or Zionist pioneering.[1] These volumes are extremely useful, but they suffer from thematic discontinuity issues which arise in collections of articles written by different authors. Nowhere to be found is a study of Galilee whose scope spans from antiquity to modernity, whose method is avowedly multicultural, and whose authorial viewpoint is consistent. The question of whether this lacuna reflects religious and cultural bias, or merely technical issues of research specialization, cannot concern us here. Instead, brief mention of my own calculations and intents in undertaking this first-of-its-kind Galilee history project will have to suffice.

Toward the end of the 1990s, I became engaged, mainly as a parent, in the establishment of a ground-breaking Arab-Jewish elementary school in Galilee. Preparatory meetings involving parents and the school's administration, and continuing discussions throughout the school's first years, hinged on the premise that national and religious tensions inherent in such a project might be overcome when participants are exposed to other "narratives" relevant to their own contemporary concerns. That is to say, we talked quite a bit about what the school ought to expect from its Muslim and Christian Palestinian pupils when their young Jewish peers celebrated Israel's Independence Day commemoration of the Zionist side's victory in the 1948 War, and also about how, and how much, Jewish pupils ought to hear about the Palestinian side's perception of 1948 as Nakba catastrophe.

Always interesting, these discussions were also sometimes productive. Yet, as a historian, I often reflected guiltily about how practitioners of my own craft had done very little to provide background and context to these debates. It was like being in a bar where zealous fans cheer or curse the basketball player who makes, or misses, the last shot in the game, responding to the event as though nothing had happened in its four quarters, before the final seconds.

Even though this well-spirited Galilee elementary school was intellectually unpretentious, and located very far from Broadway, there was percolating in it something pungent from the late-twentieth-century culture wars. What we were bringing to the school's classroom—that is, a "nationalist narratives" approach saturated in postmodernist relativism—may not have done justice to the depth and complexity of the children's heritages, in one of monotheism's three branches.

As it turned out, this elementary school was named "Galilee" in deference to the region's cherished landscape and history. In curriculum-oriented meetings held prior to the school's opening, its teachers and administrators discovered, astonishingly, that no history textbook could be found, as educational warrant for the school's name. This was because Galilee's history is unwritten.

Of all places in the world, Galilee is where young children can be taught to view history's seemingly irresoluble conflicts with discerning understanding, within a richly pluralistic frame of monotheistic history. Galilee is where they can learn that the flip side of violent confrontation between religious cultures is irrepressible belief in personal salvation and communal reconciliation. And the region's untold history ought to become a source of inspiration for educators, parents, and children in schools elsewhere in the world, as they struggle to understand what is (for them) exclusively appealing in their own faith, as opposed to what might enjoin interfaith dialogue and reconciliation.

Such were the thoughts and considerations that guided me when I began, belatedly, to collect Galilee memorabilia (travel books, posters, maps, memoirs, and other whatnots), years after three of my children finished their stints at this elementary school. I had, at this point, already spent some years teaching Jewish history to mixed groups of Arab and Jewish students in public college education in Galilee; and so, rather than a rarefied ideal, multiculturalist methodology had now become, for me, an issue of professional survival.

These colleges are publicly regulated by Israel's Council of Higher Education. Nonetheless, on many levels, they are budgeted and administered in a quite merciless spirit of privatization; and teachers who cannot fill classrooms do not last very long. So particularly as a youngish instructor teaching in fumble-mouthed Hebrew, I had to find a way to discuss Theodor Herzl, or the Holocaust, in a way that would not propel students (about 40% of them non-Jews) to walk down the hall and enroll in a course in business administration. By necessity, as some two decades of work went by, I became accustomed to thinking, teaching, and writing about history in frames comprehensible to different groups in Galilee's diverse population. If truth be told, I have had almost nothing to say about Galilee in my professional teaching work, as my course offerings and publications have pertained to rather different subjects; but this Galilee history project nonetheless took on a life of its own under the inspiration of my students. Much in Israel's current, ultranationalist, realities occludes such a vision, but I nonetheless view these students optimistically, as portents of a future of higher education development in Galilee undertaken in a spirit of liberal humanism, and constructive, interfaith, dialogue.

This volume explores Galilee's history from the period subsequent to Jesus' experiences and the fall of the Jews' Second Temple in Jerusalem (70 CE), through the Crusades. Its starting point, 47 BCE—the moment of Herod's ascent as the first in a colorful roster of princes of Galilee—might seem objectionable to some readers. In fact, one ambitious history of a phase of Galilean history, written by Sean Freyne, begins several centuries earlier, in 323 BCE, with Alexander the Great's conquest and the advent of Hellenism.[2] My own choice of a point of origin reflects an understanding that Galilee's indelible place in history is associated with fracture, crisis, and revitalization in monotheistic culture. This is a story whose roots lead discernibly to the Jews' calamitously failed revolt against Rome, and to the rise of Christianity, as chronicled monumentally in the gospels, and by Josephus.

Just as the designation of this starting line is debatable, the reader should be forewarned that this Galilee history project does not aspire to touch all the bases. I have followed themes of monotheistic fracture and rebirth over a long timeline, delved in religious, political, and military history, and furnished a fair measure of illustrative detail. Nonetheless, some periods in Galilee history (e.g., the Mamluk and British Mandate eras) receive little more than passing mention in this book, or in this project's second volume, and other omissions can be attributed to my own deficiencies of judgment, linguistic ability, or stamina. I will be gratified to see such gaps filled by others in future works, in conjunction with continuing debate about topics of Galilee history which are surveyed in these two volumes.

Following the discussions of Josephus' Galilee and Jesus' Galilee, chapters in this volume address the emergence of early Talmudic Judaism in the region, Byzantine Christianity in Galilee and the advent of Islam in the region, and Crusader warfare and settlement in Galilee. The next volume will survey Kabbalistic Safed, the eras of the Druze prince Fakhr al-Din and the Palestinian ruler Zahir al-Umar in Galilee, the Napoleonic invasion, Orthodox Jewish and early Zionist settlement in Galilee, and the 1948 war in the region.

Geographically, Galilee, today Israel's northern region, has complicatedly shifting borders in its various eras, and, in this short introduction, it would be overly burdensome to survey these demarcations, starting with Josephus' remarks and references in the gospels.[3] Throughout this volume, we have inserted some maps to help readers navigate this geography; and repeatedly the text discusses how key venues (such as Acre) have been marked within, or outside, of Galilee in different eras. I caution the reader by noting that in several instances this history elaborates on military events, or biographical episodes, which occurred on the region's edges, or even rather far from its borders—the rationale is that the full context of Galilee's incomparable contributions to monotheistic civilization cannot be appreciated without such a relatively creative grasp of its geography, as well as some of its other dimensions.

In these volumes, spellings of non-English terms and names do not derive from one specific transliteration system and are instead based on the way they have been standardized (more or less) in well-known or authoritative texts.

I gratefully acknowledge Lexington Press, an imprint of Rowman & Littlefield. My original thought was to publish with an outfit which sponsored critically engaged studies of Galilee produced by several remarkable New Testament scholars; Neil Elliot artfully directed this impulse to Lexington. At Lexington, Judith Lakamper, with assistance from Mikayla Mislak, arranged production of this volume.

I thank Adi Lam for her fine work photographing spring-season sites in Galilee. I also thank Shalom Termechy of Tel-Hai College's Historical Maps Archive for his knowledgeable assistance.

This book and its successor volume are dedicated hopefully to a future university in Galilee, an institution based on principles of liberal humanism and interfaith dialogue which I have tried to evoke and incorporate in this history project.

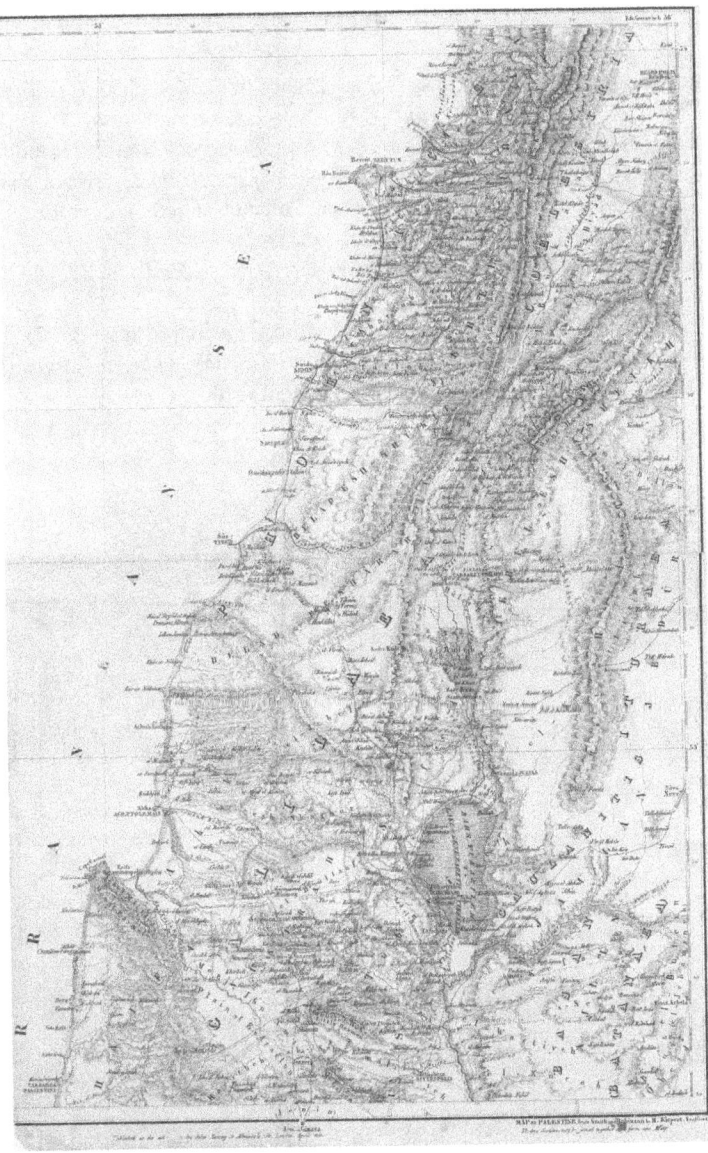

Figure 0.1 1840 Map of Galilee, based on work of E. Robinson and E. Smith. *Source*: Courtesy of Tel-Hai College Historical Maps Archive.

NOTES

1. For example: David A. Fiensy, James Riley Strange (eds.), *Galilee in the Late Second Temple and Mishnaic Periods* (Minneapolis: Fortress Press, 2014); Eric M. Myers (ed.), *Galilee Through the Centuries: Confluence of Cultures* (Winona Lake: Eisenbrauns, 1999); Lee Levine, *The Galilee in Late Antiquity* (New York: The Jewish Theological Seminary, 1992); Arnon Sofer et al (eds.), 2 volumes, *Ertzot Hagalil* (Haifa: Israel Ministry of Defense, 1983).

2. Sean Freyne, *Galilee: From Alexander the Great to Hadrian, 323 BCE to 135 CE* (Edinburgh: T&T Clark, 1980).

3. Josephus, *The Jewish War* (Oxford: Oxford University Press, 2017), 162–63; John M. Vonder Bruegge, *Mapping Galilee in Josephus, Luke and John* (Leiden: Brill, 2016); Freyne, *Galilee*, 3–21; Sofer, *Ertzot*, 43–200.

Chapter 1

Josephus and Galilee

HEROD AT THE ARBELA CAVES: THE OBSTREPEROUS GALILEANS

What brought about monotheism's multiplication as three religions was the obstreperously volatile, or pliantly sincere, character of residents in a particular region, Galilee, today the northern area of Israel. Core Jewish and Christian understandings over the past two thousand years, or a bit longer, were molded by the way their narrative-makers, Josephus in one case, the gospels in the other, related to the riddle of the Galileans, as an inherently rebellious and unworthy population, or as the sort of naturally discerning country folk who are endowed with the ability to recognize the messiah when they see him. Later, the rejuvenation and refashioning of these two faiths, in the early Talmudic Mishnah, in the Crusades, in Kabbalistic mysticism, would occur in Galilee. These reformatted faiths would also be determinatively influenced by the character of Galilee's population, just as the historical destiny of the third monotheistic faith, Islam, would, in some instances, from the era of Saladin and the Crusades, through the Napoleonic invasion and up through the 1948 war, hinge on peoples of Galilee, and we are devoting two volumes to the study of how all this happened, to a sustained reevaluation of Galilee's underappreciated history. But this is the place to begin at the beginning. For our purposes, that is, the study of pluralistic monotheism's origins in Galilee, our history must begin where we identify a real historical figure, one whose doings manifestly impacted the narratives of Josephus and Jesus, who struggled with the obstreperous Galileans. His name was Herod.

Herod's father, Antipater, gained effective power over Palestine in 48 BCE. Antipater appointed his eldest son, Phasael, to serve as governor in Jerusalem, and dispatched Herod to pacify affairs in Galilee. Galilee was now on its path: it would become the world's region where fundamental dilemmas of worldly striving versus other-worldly faith, of romantic politics verses pragmatic politics, found resolution in the emergence of Christianity, and in Judaism's transition from its cultic Jerusalem Temple mode to a rabbinic-based religion. The advent of Jesus, and of the Jews' exile from their own land, will ever be viewed in a multiplicity of causal contexts, both by believers and by skeptics. Still, however the necessity and implications of famed or controversial occurrences in the Jews' revolt against Rome, and in the life of Jesus, are weighed, it is undeniable that the one, indispensable element in all interpretations is the disposition of the village and town folk of Galilee. Had they been in a state of mind amenable to the imposition of Roman rule, none of what came after, neither the Vatican nor the Reformation, neither the diaspora nor the Holocaust, neither Muhammed nor Islam, would necessarily have come into being.

Galilee's Jewish character had been restored by the Hasmoneans, but the imposition of a new regime, closely aligned with Rome owing to the machinations of Antipater and Herod, would test the region's cultural bearing. There were many questions. Could Rome be trusted? How might tensions between Jewish identity retention and the maintenance of loyalty to Rome be resolved? Who, really, was Herod?

Both the gospels and Josephus concur that for a key stretch of time, this last question was determinative. Rather like the general situation of national-religious identity in Galilee, the length of Herod's Jewish roots was open to question. Herod's people, the Idumaeans, who were based in southern stretches of the country, were relative newcomers to Judaism; hence, Herod's rise to power both symbolized and instigated issues of identity ambiguity throughout the land. Both Idumaea (Edom) in the south and Galilee in the north were populated by new Jews or relocated Jews, descendants of converts or Jews whose forefathers had lived somewhere else. This circumstance of identity ambiguity encouraged dynamics of identity performance in the country's politics. Herod, a person of monumental energy and perverse character, would spend his years demonstrating how he was, concurrently, thoroughly Jewish and thoroughly Roman. He did so by rebuilding the Jews' splendid Second Temple in Jerusalem and by littering the country with new towns, like the impressive port Caesarea, which were built in effusive tribute to Rome. This hyped-up, two-tracked, identity strategy was not a good fit in Galilee. Demonstrating loyalty to Judaism and to Rome, Herod felt himself doubly blessed, but an indefinite number of residents in Galilee imagined themselves as being doubly burdened by him.

Throughout the century of Roman control, imposed by the client rulers of Herod's family, which culminated in the Jewish revolt and the decimation of the Second Temple (in 70 CE), residents in the Galilee subsisted in small-scale agriculture and trade. There is no evidence of prospering farmsteads in the region.[1] By and large, its residents did not belong to elite land-owning classes, nor were they subsistence-strafed tenant farmers. Most had a small stake in lands cultivated for their own needs, with a modest amount of farm surplus, products like olive oil, sent out in trade networks. Archaeological evidence points mostly to socioeconomic homogeneity among the region's residents: in Galilee and Golan Heights towns that have been extensively excavated, including Sepphoris, Jotapata, and Gamla, a few marginally wealthy private domiciles have been uncovered, but their opulence is not on a scale indicative of a rural class system among Jews. Wherever social stratification obtained, it was essentially extraregional, applying to relations between struggling Galileans and affluent priestly elites in Jerusalem, or framed as town-country conflicts, featuring the two hundred villages numbered by Josephus in opposition to the two or three venues in Galilee that might reasonably be termed cities (Tiberias, Sepphoris, and perhaps Gabara).

On this last point, archaeological and literary types of evidence are sometimes frustratingly incongruent. Josephus' writings, such as his autobiographical *Life*, project images of Galilee in outright town-country turbulence as the revolt against Rome erupted in 66 CE—this text calls the regular rural folk of the region "Galileans,"[2] and recurrently suggests that these rebellious elements were perpetually poised to attack and plunder urban Jewish compatriots from Sepphoris (who were, on the whole, opposed to revolt against Rome), and from Tiberias (where a significant number of Jewish elements withdrew support for the revolt). The text's confusing, and often amusing, character results from the unholy alliance between these insurrectionist, but easily manipulated, Galileans, and Josephus, a political moderate from Jerusalem's religious elite who secretly supported the pro-Roman disposition of the region's city-dwellers, but depended upon the Galileans for his own survival. It remains to be seen whether Josephus' political sociology can ever be corroborated by archaeological work. In past decades,[3] excavations at Sepphoris excited New Testament scholars, causing many to believe that evidence had been uncovered of Roman/cosmopolitan cultures in the city—this would mean that Jesus grew up in nearby Nazareth in proximity to non-Jewish value systems. However, this interpretation of the archaeological evidence at Sepphoris was over-drawn; in fact, the excavations have sometimes pointed to significant socioeconomic and cultural continuity between this town and Galilee's Jewish villages. So the fundamental issue remains: how was Galilee's relatively homogeneous, Jewish, society-oriented, overall, toward Rome, and toward compatriots who maintained the Temple cult in Jerusalem?

Herod's appointment as his father's emissary, and as ruler in Galilee, in 47 BCE is the starting point of the region's history as the cradle of monotheistic pluralism. Quick to demonstrate strength, he took up the cudgel against Ezekias (Hezekiah), defined by the class-biased Josephus as a "warlord" who commanded a "huge gang of bandits."[4] This gang had been raiding areas bordering Galilee; hoping to placate their gentile population ("Syrians," in Josephus' formulation), Herod killed Ezekias and several of his confederates. Herod's anti-bandit operations in Galilee blended in a broad diplomatic policy. Ever-solicitous about strengthening Roman patronage, Antipater and his prodigal son wanted to impress Syria's Roman governor, Sextus Caesar, a relative of Julius Caesar—in a complicated sequence, punctuated by Caesar's murder on the ides of March (44 BCE), Herod's initial pacification of social banditry in Galilee led to his being crowned client King of Judea.[5]

Specific information as to what Ezekias and his band were up to is lacking, but there are reasons to suppose that this Galilee rebel was popular among the region's rural Jewish folk. On one view, held by Religious Studies scholar Richard Horsley, Ezekias was a "Jewish Robin Hood" whose operations "symbolize[d] the Jewish peasants' basic sense of justice and their religious loyalties."[6] Eventually, the brutality of Herod's anti-bandit pacification caused Jews throughout the country to cry foul. Galilee supporters of Ezekias's rebel band pressed for justice in Jerusalem, appealing to the Sanhedrin for redress. Priestly elders, including the Pharisee Samaias, showed little concern about disorder that might have been caused by Ezekias' group, and focused instead on the tyrannical behavior of Herod and his father Antipater. Appealing to the high priest (Hyrcanus), these elders charged that Herod killed Ezekias and his comrades "in violation of our law, which forbids us to kill a man, even a malicious one, unless he has first been sentenced by the Sanhedrin."[7] Depicted by Josephus in his *Jewish Antiquities*, the scene brims with ironic familiarity. In the climactic scene in Josephus' autobiography, which is tacked on to the end of *Antiquities* as a kind of postscript (scholars argue about the exact status of Josephus' *Life*[8]), he himself, as the commander of the anti-Roman rebellion in Galilee, has to fend off precisely the same objection levelled by Sanhedrin-level Jerusalemites against Herod—these notables investigate whether Josephus has behaved as a bellicose "tyrant" in the region, and acted as a kind of latter-day Herod. Since Josephus' autobiographical writings about his exploits as a military commander in Galilee sometimes invoke this anti-killing proscription in a self-interested, rather duplicitous, fashion,[9] there is room to wonder about the rule's seriousness. Nonetheless, the anti-Herod protest waged by Galileans in Jerusalem is an unusually suggestive episode in Josephus' historical writing, implying that banditry was subsumed, on some level, within the frame of Jewish morality, and was amenable to protection afforded by Jewish institutions. The scene records a minimal level of political cooperation between aggrieved Galilee peasants and affluent Jerusalem priests (to be sure, it provides no assurance that this was a well-founded or lasting alliance). The scene demonstrates that Herod's ambition to serve as a client ruler, under Roman auspices, drove him to trespass past fundamental boundaries of Jewish ethics, religion, and society.

The story of Herod's pacification of Ezekias' banditry is thus an arresting portrait of proto-revolutionary volatility. It is, in fact, the starting point in the long, complicated story of monotheism's multiplication. What winds-up the gyroscope is the problem of Galilee's town and country peoples, their relationship to Jerusalem, their cultural orientations, and their political capabilities.

Herod was appointed king in Judea by Rome's senate, which acted at the behest of Mark Antony, in 40 BCE. For Herod, the sole remaining obstacle was the last trace of Hasmonean power, represented by Mattathiah Antigonus, a phlegmatic character whose claims kept some vitality for a few years due to his alliance with the Parthians.[10] Herod chased Antigonus up and down the country. In the south, the Parthian client king besieged Masada, where members of Herod's family were trapped, and Josephus' descriptions of these scuffles[11] not only foreshadows the climactic Masada scene in his masterwork, *The Jewish War* (henceforth, *JW*), but also reverses its political logic.

At first glance, far too much of *JW*, up to a quarter of its pages, is framed around Herod's monumental contributions to the country's landscapes and also to his numbingly brutal escapades in his domestic life. The most readily apparent justification for this extended treatment is that the salacious pathology of Herod's murders of bedmates and children excited readers, even in late-first-century Rome. Josephus, however, dwells on Herod for reasons that are deeper and more compelling than the subject's undeniable, perverse entertainment value, as the equivalent of a blood-stained twenty-first-century TV Reality Show whose curtains draw just as Jesus is born in Bethlehem (while this last occurrence was of no concern to Josephus, of all texts pertaining to the Jews' fateful late Second Temple period, his *Jewish War* probably survived because its graphic descriptions of Rome-produced debauchery among Jewish clients like Herod, and of Jewish self-defeating political fanaticism and in-fighting, well-suited then-evolving Christian narratives, including Jesus' prophecy about the Temple's impending destruction[12]). For Josephus, Herod's career positively demonstrated how politically prudent and morally flexible handling of an alliance with Roman power brokers, like Antony and Augustus, well-served Jewish interests. In subsequent parts of *JW*, when Josephus ridiculously exaggerates how he himself built-up fortifications in Galilee and commanded tens of thousands of locals, after he won appointment as general of the Jewish rebellion in the region, Josephus arrogates Herodian dimensions to his own career, and is essentially saying that he could have followed Herod's playbook and brought glory to the Jews (*JW*'s thesis is that the character of Palestine's Jews in Josephus' own generation preempted this outcome; their wanton extremism caused God to withdraw his covenantal patronage, and favor the Romans).

In terms of pedigree, Josephus presents Herod as a negative foil. The one, almost all-encompassing, explanation of the wretched depravity of Herod's family life is that as a newcomer Jew of Idumaean ancestry, Herod tried to burnish his status by marrying into the Hasmonean line, wedding Mariamne, a woman he loved beyond reason; Herod's murderous rampages stemmed from insecurity and vulnerability bred by this betrothal. Ironically, Herod's bid for Hasmonean gravitas was futile from the start: for decades, this clan's power claims in the Jews' Temple-based society had stirred resentment among elites, since the Hasmoneans lacked legitimate priestly roots in the Zadokite line. Even though he considered himself a genuine member of Jerusalem's priestly nobility, Josephus probably understood Herod's lineage-related compulsions—Josephus opened his own *Life* by rehashing his own pedigree, including its Hasmonean roots, but scholars notice discrepancies and apparent inaccuracies in this presentation of his family tree.[13] Setting aside these lineage considerations, and the appalling history of Herod's family life, Herod's course in *JW* basically reverses the arc Josephus followed a century later. Implicitly, Josephus' history presents this client king's career as a model he would like to have followed.

On Josephus' telling, in 40 BCE, Herod starts the consolidation of his rule by smashing away at Masada, and he finalizes his ascent by remorselessly and dexterously liquidating the remnants of Ezekias' band in Galilee. As such, this portrait of Herod's successful Jewish exploitation of Roman patronage exactly reverses the military geography of *JW*, which is a depiction of the Jews' calamitous rejection of Roman stewardship. Quite possibly, on a psychological level, Josephus' documentation of Herod's brutal pacification campaign in Galilee, at Arbela, constitutes a form of wish fulfillment: what Herod was able to do to bandit rebels at Arbela, was what Josephus would have needed to do as commander in Galilee, to stifle the peasants' insurrectionist behavior and control the Jewish rebellion in line with his well-placed Jerusalem elite's wishes (whether the elite wished to stifle the revolt altogether, or regulate its escalation in ways that would not provoke devastating Roman reprisals, cannot really be resolved on the basis of the ambiguous documentation in Josephus' two writings about the rebellion, *JW* and *Life*, which were composed in different periods, and, probably, with differing apologetic intents).

Arbela, a village located just north of Tiberias on the Sea of Galilee's west shore, was pocketed with caves.[14] After he rescued his mother and siblings from Masada, Herod headed furiously to Galilee, traveling, Josephus writes, through a "blizzard" en route to Sepphoris, where supplies awaited his weary army.[15] Meantime, "bandits" were "terrorizing a large area of the country"—the phrase connotes class warfare, but exactly what sort of Galilee *jacquerie* it refers to is left to the imagination. To hunt down the bandits, who hid in the Arbela Caves, Herod sent three infantry battalions, and one cavalry squadron, Josephus writes. Joined by the remainder of his army, Herod arrived at the caves forty days later. In the ensuing battle with Galilee's peasant rebels, Herod's army was, for a stretch, outflanked and endangered, and many of its soldiers fled. Herod, however, rallied his men, who then slaughtered the mass of the rebel fighters around the Jordan River, thereby pacifying Galilee, apart from a few bandits who remained in the caves.

Herod took his time before reconnoitering at these Arbela Caves, whose supposed impenetrability is described with great dramatic flair by Josephus, a writer who is always most memorable when dealing with suicides and sieges. "These were caves in precipitous mountain faces, utterly inaccessible except by zigzag and extremely narrow paths up, and the cliff they fronted stretched in a sheer fall to the torrents running in deep ravines far below," he wrote.[16] Hoisting ropes, Herod bungeed his best fighters up and down in crates; as they passed cave openings, these soldiers tossed in firebrands to "smoke out any who ordered resistance." In a sequence which foreshadows climactic episodes in Josephus' rendering of the Jewish rebellion, at Jotapata and Masada, the Jewish fighters choose to burn to death in the Arbela Caves, and not surrender.

In broad terms of power politics, there is no fundamental difference between this Arbela episode and the two, more familiar, mass suicide incidents which occurred over a century later, during the 66–70 CE Roman revolt. In all three incidents, the Jewish rebels directly or indirectly defied nominally Jewish client kings whom Josephus admired, Herod in the first case, Agrippa II (Herod's great-grandson, who corresponded extensively with Josephus during the production of *JW*) in the last two cases. Josephus' grisly description of what befalls the most zealous bandit hold-outs at Arbela typifies the way his prose becomes cunningly self-contradictory and suggestive when it applies to sieges and suicides: all at once, Josephus condemns the political imprudence of the Jewish fanatics, expresses sheer bewilderment at the sacrifice of family members, and pities and admires the religious-national fortitude and courage of the vanquished Jewish fighters. Arguably, the Arbela description most sharply reveals Josephus' own orientations, since the other two siege and suicide portrayals, particularly Jotapata (an incident in which Josephus himself was a major player), have shades of ambiguity accrued via the reader's much more prolonged exposure to the events' circumstances and personalities. Other than the allusion to their terrifying ways, the readers knows nothing about Ezekias' followers, ahead of the cave siege's most grisly sequence (which, interestingly, has parallels in the Second Book of Maccabees[17]). Josephus describes an old bandit who has seven sons. These

Figure 1.1 View of Arbela Caves. *Source*: Courtesy of Adi Lam.

boys and their mother beg the father to let them come out "under Herod's guarantee," but the bandit decides to kill each one. Each son presents himself at the mouth of the cave, where he is slain by this father. Herod, watching at some distance, is "appalled by the pity of it, and stretch[es] out his right arm towards the old man . . . who sneers at him for being so pathetic."[18] In the end, the aging bandit hurls his slain wife and children over the cliff, and then joins them in death, by diving after them, into the Galilee abyss.

At Arbela, Josephus' Herod appears as the moral inverse of the character multitudes of Christians came to know, thanks to the "Massacre of the Innocents" description in the Gospel of Matthew,[19] the scene where Herod responds to prophecy of Jesus' birth by ordering the execution of all small boys, under two years old, in the Bethlehem area. At Arbela, Herod, the King of the Jews, tries to *prevent* a massacre of the innocents. He motions toward the last rebel in the caves, imploring him not to slaughter his children. As a series of scholars have argued in past decades, the Gospel of Matthew was compiled more or less concurrently with the writing of Josephus' *JW*. Since both Matthew and Josephus are deeply engaged by the issue of social control in Galilee, the diametrically opposed images of Herod in these writings are thought-provoking. In the New Testament, Herod's pro-Roman orientation is villainous, a genuine threat that could potentially have precluded Jesus' miraculous, divine appearance in Galilee. Of course, Josephus' implicit endorsement of Herod's outlook and activities lacks the gospels' dynamics of messianic revelation, but, through Herod, Josephus' condemnation of anti-Roman rebellion in Galilee is nonetheless high-charged. Josephus' narrative at Arbela, and elsewhere, says that monotheism would not have fractured had there been "more Rome" in Galilee, whereas the gospels imply that had there been more Rome in Galilee, the messiah may not have come, or would have arrived in a different way.

Interestingly, Josephus' writing frames this core issue, "how much Rome," in gender terms: contrary to their posturing, bandits such as those in Ezekias' gang are unmanly. We turn now to this intriguing triangular issue of gender, Galilee politics, and monotheism's fracture.

JOSEPHUS AND THE UNMANLY JEWISH REVOLT

Did this last, aged, rebel at Arbela die a *manly* death? The question may not be completely resoluble, but it is important to pose because the topic of Jewish sovereignty, its preservation and extirpation, has a clear gender component. However pitiable, the aging bandit's suicide at Arbela could not, in Josephus, be a full expression of courageous manhood. One reason why involves genre and reader expectation. Readers in antiquity were more familiar with images of women throwing themselves from the heights, compared to men—one scholarly account claims that 13 percent of recorded male suicides in antiquity featured jumping, whereas in 22 percent of female suicides, the perpetrator/victim leaped to death.[20] More importantly, when thinking about prototypes of Jewish power and sovereignty, Josephus Romanized Jewish manhood. Herod becomes king via his alliance with Rome, whereas he ousts a failed Hasmonean, Antigonus, who had collaborated with Rome's enemy, the Parthians. When this last Hasmonean, King Antigonus, is finally seized, his Roman captor mocks his manhood, baiting him by using a female version of his name, Antigone.[21] Herod arranges affairs so that his Hasmonean rival is taken to Antioch, where Antony issues an extraordinary order mandating his decapitation.[22] Viewed through a Freudian prism, this lamentable end can be viewed as a castrating loss of manhood. Less debatably, the implication of Antigonus' career is that a Jew who is unable to forge some sort of intelligible accommodation with Rome is cast out of the political body, in all conceivable senses.

The most infamous exemplification of this principle in *JW* occurs in the setting of a Jerusalem famine that is induced by the anti-Rome revolt's catastrophic failure. Mary of Bethezuba, a Jewish woman from Transjordan, formerly of affluence and status, has, with her infant, fallen into starvation in Jerusalem. Josephus graphically describes her descent towards cannibalism:[23] when she offers Roman soldiers some portions of her own roasted child, the grotesque legalistic rhetoric ("This is my own lawful child, and this is my own doing, so eat! I have already eaten"), spooks them, and they flee from the scene. Josephus mentions that this is the only occurrence in the Romans' pacification of the Jewish rebellion when their soldiers lost nerve. Like Herod observing a rebel bandit slay his own wife and children at the Arbela cave, the soldiers in this infanticide/cannibalism vignette are witnessing a breach of nature, a setting wherein a Jew's appeal to law and morality ("This is my own lawful child") becomes incoherent. In the Gospel of Matthew, the polemical critique of Jewish law (personified by the Pharisees) proceeds mostly in spiritual terms; in contrast, in Josephus, Jewish law loses its natural basis as a result of gender and class politics.

Brigandage, if we are to use Josephus' nomenclature (others would call it class warfare), precipitates the Jews' fall from humanity. Much later, toward the end of the Jews' torturous experience of exile, they would discover that it was their ghettoized exclusion from the evolving nineteenth-century nation state which precluded their designation as rights-worthy human beings—much of the rhetoric in Jewish Enlightenment (*haskalah*) discourse refers to how a Jew is not a "man" unless he emancipates himself via some sort of assimilation into Europe's nineteenth-century body politic. Here, with the Temple erupting in flames, symbolizing the start of Jewish exile, the equivalent principle holds that a Jew is not human if he remains separated from Rome's body politic, and, functionally, under this equation, the equivalent of the late medieval ghetto is rural brigandage. Ancient banditry, like the late medieval ghetto, is "beyond the pale" of civilization. Just as a career in banditry propels the Arbela rebel toward the inhuman act of family massacre, so too does rural brigandage cast Mary of Bethezube toward the inhuman act of family cannibalism. Josephus writes that Mary reached Jerusalem in utter destitution because of rural bandits—day after day, taking orders from "warlords," country brigands plundered any possessions she had managed to bring with her from Peraea, the historian explains.[24]

In Josephus' writing, the Jews fall from God's grace, their kingdom falls from God's favor, and they are destined for exile in the diaspora, because Galilee peasants, unlike the author himself, reach an unmanly decision. By choosing Rome, as he himself did at the end of the failed rebellion in Galilee, or as he himself perhaps did from the very start, the Jews would have kept their sovereignty—which, by the hands of Josephus' gender compass, means they would have remained Jewish *men*.

A Jewish male who is unable to come to terms with the reality of Roman power will necessarily lose grips with his own manhood, Josephus insists. Metaphorically, by forging a necessary, prudent accommodation with Rome, a Jew demonstrates reasonable possession of his own powers, of his masculinity—political extremism, under this equation, is either the cause or effect of lost control in the realm of personal identity. Victorious Roman generals and emperors reinforced this point by throwing their most fierce, vanquished opponents in the ring with beasts. In this way, Rome withheld recognition of its enemies' humanity and refused to pay tribute to their courage. In *JW*, Josephus exploited these lines of thought so as to rationalize his own cravenly behavior at Jotapata, the village where his command of the Galilee rebellion came to an end: through mathematical trickery, he evades his role in a collective suicide agreement that had been forged with comrades under his command at the Jewish settlement who adulate him; Josephus then emerges from the cave where he had hidden with these forlorn comrades, and joins the Romans. On his own telling, Josephus' salvation is wrought in this episode by his talent for prophecy—he correctly predicts that Vespasian will become emperor.[25] This reference to prophecy in a context of Jewish accommodation with Rome is not a unique feature of Josephus' writing; in narratives generated by rabbinical Judaism, there is an obvious parallel in the life of Johanan ben Zakkai, the Tanna (religious scholar) who arranged for Judaism's rebirth following the disastrous rebellion by persuading the Romans to condone the reestablishment of the Sanhedrin at Yavne.[26] Ostensibly, what distinguishes the way Josephus showcases his own powers of divination is its manipulative class bias. Unlike his Jotapata comrades, whose dead bodies are strewn around the cave, Josephus has license not to take his life because he has prophetic access to God's will. Like many other things in Josephus, this claim to prophesy strains credulity, but is not outright mendacity. "It would be quite wrong," writes Josephus scholar Tessa Rajak, "to say that he [Josephus] is totally unwilling to recognize the claims of popular superstition." The catch, she explains, is that only characters such as Josephus himself who reach correct political decisions have prophetic power. "Only prophets who are on the right side are acceptable."[27] A less supernatural explanation of why Josephus imagined that readers would indulge his problematic behavior at the Jotapata cave features class and ego. Josephus, as the scholar Shaye Cohen mentions repeatedly, was notoriously vain.[28] As a member of Jerusalem's priestly class who lived a noble life, Josephus assumed that readers would understand why his life was more valuable than those of the Jotapata extremists who killed themselves in lieu of being captured by the Romans. Josephus, Cohen writes, "considered himself much too important for a death in a cave near an obscure fortress in the country district of a small province. He must have been born for greater things."[29]

Such explanations are perfectly reasonable, but they devalue the extent to which apologetic polemics in Josephus are inflected by gender. For Josephus, self-sacrifice at Jotapata was an *unmanly* choice. He underscores this point by caricaturing his primary Jewish rival in Galilee, John of Gischala, who ended up as the second-ranking Jewish rebel as the anti-Roman revolt reached its crescendo at the Jerusalem Temple (Simon, son of Gioras, was the preeminent rebel). Josephus, as we will see, depicts John of Gischala as a cross-dressing panzy in Jerusalem.

GALILEE IN JOSEPHUS' "THE JEWISH WAR," AND IN HIS "LIFE"

Josephus described his exploits in Jerusalem as designated military leader in Galilee for several months in 67 CE, until his surrender to the Romans at the ruinous end of their forty-seven day siege on Jotapata, in two texts, *JW* and *Life,* which he wrote in Greek (a language he never really mastered) at different times, under different circumstances, and with different intents. It suffices, at this point, to distinguish between these two accounts in terms of the quite different ways they relate to Josephus' basic purpose as military commander in Galilee of the Jews' anti-Roman revolt.

In *JW*, Josephus portrays himself more or less as a straight-shooting rebel commander. Presented to Roman readers, the text hews to their sensitivities and orientations—the scholar Martin Goodman observes that other histories in this period were written in a much more overtly fawning, pro-Roman, vein,[30] but *JW* was nonetheless crafted within the Roman mainstream. Its opening lines, following Thucydides, advertise the war as "the greatest of our time,"[31] but, confusingly, the title deflates this perception, hinting that the "Jewish War" rates as just another one of Rome's victorious campaigns;[32] both views of the event, as a singular triumph, or as another victorious feather in invincible Rome's series of conquests, flatter the target audience. By exaggeratedly boasting of his own achievements as the rebellion's military leader in Galilee, Josephus adds fuel to *JW*'s overall apologetic logic—Josephus' text enhances its reader's appreciation of Rome's triumph by showing them how the Jews, himself included, were worthy opponents. The siege at Jotapata, Josephus explains, conclusively demonstrated the futility of the Jews' uprising, and so it was natural for him to switch sides. The viciousness and obtuseness of the Jewish rebels are on full display in the text's subsequent, Jerusalem, parts; this expose reinforces the logic of Josephus' choice, and it assuages his Roman readers' sense of superiority, and their belief in the justice of the war's outcome.

Leaping into boats carefully moored at the Sea of Galilee,[33] forcing nefarious rivals to cut off their hands,[34] putting shell facades on the water at Tarichaeae so that masses of enemies in Tiberias imagine that a flotilla is approaching them,[35] Josephus decks himself up as a first-century, Jewish, James Bond. *JW*'s Galilee sections seep with examples of Josephus' own mental and physical dexterity. These, along with data provided by the author

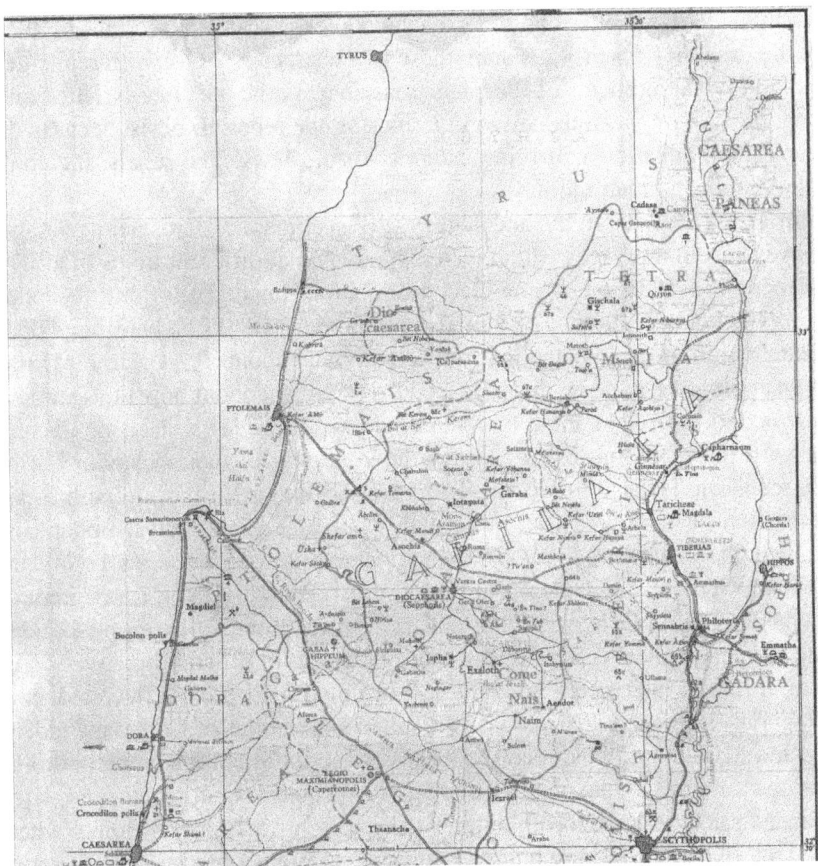

Figure 1.2 Map of Galilee in Roman Times, based on work of M. Avi-Yonah. *Source*: Courtesy of Tel-Hai College Historical Maps Archive.

about procurement and other matters of military organization or Galilean circumstances, are often outlandish. No scholar, for instance, has been able to make sense of the number of Galilee residents-cum-soldiers Josephus claims to have commanded (100,000).[36] On the other hand, scholars have published findings attesting to the veracity of several important claims Josephus makes about Galilee, including the handful of forts he says he revamped in anticipation of a Roman military invasion,[37] and also the large number of Jewish settlements (two hundred and four) he says existed in the region at the time.[38] However much *JW*'s Galilee sections promote the author's own supposed heroism, they are not inherently sectarian. Josephus has no motivation to dwell on his moral superiority, relative to other Jewish rebel leaders in the region—while they were, in various contexts, rivals,[39] they were also presumably fighting for the same cause. Josephus becomes unremittingly venomous toward a character like John of Gischala in later, Jerusalem, sections of *JW*—by the time they reach Jerusalem, these two characters are on different sides, and, in pivotal moments of Josephus' master-work, he operates as Titus' one-man, on-site, propaganda network, imploring the rebels to desist because the revolt's continuation will bring calamity to the Jews. The rebels, including John, mock and maim him.

In terms of receptivity and legacy, *JW*'s climactic, Jerusalem passages convey mixed messages which were appreciated at different times by different peoples. As Goodman has recently demonstrated, *JW*'s long reception history is not only impressive but also has bumps and twists, befitting a book written from a complicated, hybrid, identity standpoint.[40] As a Jew, writing as an apologist for the Romans, Josephus is adamant about how the Temple's destruction is brought about by the foolishness of the Jews' decision to carry on with the rebellion, as well as by the depravity of their behavior during the rebellion. He also insists that Titus and his father Vespasian (both future emperors) bear no moral burden for this outcome, since they emphatically warned the Jews and overlooked innumerable Jewish outrages before the Temple went up in flames (one dubiety in *JW* that relates to an item of monumental impact is the author's claim that the Temple fire erupted due to one Roman soldier's carelessness, and not owing to official directives). The overall line of interpretation could be welcomed by the text's intended, contemporary Roman audience, just as it suited generations of Christian readers, but Jews could hardly stomach Josephus' presentation of his emperors-to-be patrons as heroes, since they tortured and executed Jewish rebels, and, later, paraded sacked sacred Temple items in victory processions in Rome, where the arch of Titus would remain, its relief illustrations of these Temple spoils of victory an everlasting torment to Jewish consciousness. *JW*, in short, requires a reader to honor the leaders who precipitated the Jews' exile. Hence, it is no surprise that the Hebrew *Sefer Yosippon*, a bowdlerized text which altered *JW*'s interpretations of key events and trends in the revolt, and even changed the identity of the text's author, gained authority among Jewish readers after the tenth century, its popularity even lasting (in some cases) into the modern period. From the Jewish standpoint, *JW* provided precious few escape hatches to mitigate the agony produced by its core interpretation—but, in time, these two portals proved to be important.

First, *JW*'s concluding sequence of Jewish zealots' collective suicide at Masada, the indomitable Dead Sea fortress that had been built-up by Herod, could be seen as an awe-inspiring tribute to Jewish courage, to the Jews' national resolve to avoid surrender at all costs. In fact, Masada's placement at the end of *JW* raises vexing questions about narrative continuity and thematic coherence. Sicarii fanatics, who are, in Josephus view, culprits of the Jewish national tragedy, are depicted, more or less, as heroes at Masada, despite the fact that their choice and act is the exact opposite of the course taken by Josephus at Jotapata—the entire *JW* narrative up to the Masada sequence promotes the author's accommodation with Rome, including scenes in Jerusalem wherein Josephus pleads with rebels to ride on the road he has taken, to save the Jews. In fact, because of its thematic incongruity, apparent advocacy of political extremism, its sheer implausibility, and other factors, Jews ignored *JW's* Masada conclusion for about 1,900 years, until Jewish nationalists recouped the tale and framed it as Zionism's bedrock image. The use and abuse of Masada as an Israeli founding myth has been explored by a relatively recent wave of self-critical ("post-Zionist") scholarship in Israel.[41] These discussions sometimes fail to contextualize Masada in its most analytically apposite contexts, as a moral bookend to Josephus' Galilee narrative, particularly the Jotapata siege, as an outgrowth of an ethical discourse about suicide and honor that unfolded in Josephus' contemporary cultural setting, as exemplified by Seneca's writings, or Plutarch's rendering of the death of Cato the Younger, and as a variant of ways other historians in this period presented episodes of siege and collective suicide (this last aspect has been meticulously surveyed by Shaye Cohen[42]). Most broadly, Masada's long-delayed handling by Jews should be contextualized as one chapter in the wider saga of the inconsistent or ambivalent receptions afforded to Josephus by Jewish readers over the centuries. Goodman observes that in nineteenth-century settings, when Jews' integration in Europe's new civil spheres dominated communal agendas, Josephus "predicament," by which, of all possible political formulas, only accommodation with foreign power guaranteed survival, came to "seem to deserve sympathy more than condemnation."[43] At any event, however incongruous it might have been thematically, Josephus must have sensed that the image of Jewish Sicarii fighting bravely until the bitter end at Masada would provide some sort of consolation among readers sympathetic to the losers of the Jewish War story he told.

Second, *JW* does not hold Jews collectively to blame for the collapse of their Second Temple civilization. Josephus accentuates sectarianism in the Jews' religion and politics. In a famous, early section of the book, Josephus describes three Jewish religious sects, Essenes, Pharisees, and Sadducees,[44] and so the topic of Jewish sectarianism is embedded in a history whose main topic is the Jewish revolt against Rome—in *Life,* it bears mention, the discussion of the three sects is not embedded in this way, and instead flows from the author's quite interesting description of his youthful experiences, which, from the age of sixteen, featured three years of experimentation with these three Jewish lifestyle and belief options (his leisure to do so says something about his own relatively affluent socioeconomic status).[45] *JW's* section about the three sects is frustratingly uninformative, partly, it seems, because it is tailored to reader expectations (the sections portray the Jewish sects more as

Greek philosophical schools than as religious streams). Nonetheless, because of the dearth of other source materials about phenomena of interest to non-Jews, Josephus' writing won notoriety as "Jewish" documentation of items such as Pharisaical attitudes toward religious law which are highlighted in New Testament polemic.[46] Of course, in later *JW* sections relating to the rebellion and its developments, Josephus alluded, often in detail though not always with consistent precision, to important philosophical-political sects (Sicarii, Zealots) whose extremism tangibly fueled the rebellion, and, as Josephus saw things, generated its self-defeating irrationality. This subsequent discussion of political sectarianism has one well-known, perceptible connection to the earlier digression about the three spiritual sects. *JW* does not explicitly classify a fourth, politically militant, sect (such taxonomy arises in the later work by Josephus, *Jewish Antiquities*, which alludes to a "Fourth Jewish Philosophy"); nonetheless, in *JW*, Josephus introduces this group, the Zealots, directly ahead of his excursus about the three religious groups,[47] thereby implying that zealotry is indeed a fourth ideological possibility for Jews. The Fourth Philosophy is credited to a Galilean, Judas, and depicted as uncompromising resistance to non-Jewish expressions of power in the Jews' holy land: Judas preached "that it was cowardice to submit to Roman taxes and to tolerate mortal masters when God had been their only Lord."[48]

While Josephus' writings convey invaluable documentation about Jewish sectarianism in the late Second Temple period, the way Josephus links political extremism to religious sectarianism in this key passage (2:118) of *JW*'s second book creates considerable analytic confusion. Readers of his exposition about the three sects, particularly his depiction of the Essenes (which is much more detailed than the descriptions of the Pharisees and Sadducees), must have had trouble connecting dots on a trail leading to the grotesquerie of the political rebellion in Galilee and Jerusalem, and, needless to say, scholars have never stopped puzzling about the impact of messianic, end-of-days, thinking upon Jewish religious-political culture in this late Second Temple period in general, and in the three, or four, sects Josephus happened to describe (there might have been several other Jewish sects). One intriguing way of resolving some measure of the nonclarity clouding this subject is to posit, as did the prolific American-Jewish scholar Jacob Neusner, that there was simply no such thing as "Judaism" in this period—instead, there were several "Judaisms." Neusner's view continues to inspire debate.[49] This issue about the range and essence of Second Temple period Jewish sectarianism, it bears mention, has today powerful resonance in New Testament studies. Some New Testament scholars apply social science methodology and concepts (e.g., deviance theory) in discussions of the issue,[50] and recent publications contextualize core articles of Christian faith, such as the Book of Matthew, entirely within this frame of Jewish sectarianism.[51] At any event, for Jewish readers over the ages, who faced an excruciating report on the decimation of Second Temple life in Eretz Israel, Josephus' documentation of sectarianism, however elusive or polemical, alleviated burdens of collective responsibility. *JW* sweepingly laments the tragic failure of an entire generation of Jews in their land which lost God's favor, but its shifting foci suggest, more selectively, that some Jewish groups were responsible for the catastrophe, while others were not (a plausible reading of the evidence would conclude that a relatively small number of zealots caused the calamity, but Josephus is not really systematic on this point).

Josephus' other text about the Galilee rebellion, his *Life*, raises a different set of interpretive challenges. Produced at a later stage in his life, when he was no longer animated or restricted by considerations of patronage offered by the Vespasian-Titus combo, Josephus' *Life* circulated among readers for whom the issue of what had motivated this Jewish historian in his younger days, as a military commander in an anti-Rome revolt in Galilee, was not pertinent. *Life* is tacked onto Josephus' *Antiquities*, a ponderous and uninspired work compared to *JW*, and scholars have wondered whether *Life* was deliberately published as an organic part of *Antiquities*, and they have also been troubled by many other issues, including publication dates and numerous discrepancies of factual reportage yawning between this autobiographical text and Josephus' other works. Some have contended that *Life* is a later, much polished, version of an earlier war report composed by Josephus, possibly in a "Jewish" language (e.g., Aramaic), perhaps for his priestly colleagues in Jerusalem.[52] For our purposes, *Life* is a useful text in that it seems, relative to *JW*, to offer a less-varnished, more realistic, appraisal of Josephus' motivations in Galilee, and of his relations to its local power brokers and political culture.

Not mincing words, Josephus confesses in *Life* that he did not set off to Galilee with the intention of leading a rebellion against the Romans. His goal was the opposite, and if pro-rebellion sentiment among the region's masses, the Galileans, could not be defused, he would at least exert his military authority to moderate the Jews' rebellious activities so that they would not irreversibly antagonize the Romans. Josephus writes:

> The principal men of the Jerusalemites observed that the bandits, together with the revolutionaries, were well equipped with weapons. They became anxious that, standing unarmed themselves, they might be left to the mercy of their adversaries (which is what subsequently happened). And they discovered that the Galilee had not yet entirely defected from the Romans, but that a part of it was still peaceful. So they sent me and two other gentlemen who were priests, Ioazar and Judas, to persuade the wretches to put down their weapons and to instruct them that it was preferable to reserve these for the nation's elite. It was

agreed that these latter would hold the weapons constantly ready for the future, but would patiently learn what the Romans would do.[53]

Josephus sheds here any pretense of his being a true-blooded Jewish rebel in Galilee. Once it has exposed its author's real colors, *Life*'s account of Josephus' dealings with other prominent Jews in Galilee attains layers of complexity that are missing in the Galilee rebellion sections of *JW*—in *JW*, Josephus' quarrel with a rebel leader like John of Gischala is substantively outsourced to Jerusalem, where Josephus was aligned with Titus but John fought tenaciously against the Romans. Josephus' relations with like-minded moderates in Galilee, that is, with well-established Jews who, at some stage in the crisis, identified accommodation with Rome as the better bet for the Jews, are portrayed with higher reliability in *Life*.

In fact, one well-known account of the impetus of *Life*'s publication stresses Josephus' relationship with a Galilee moderate-accommodationist, Justus of Tiberias.[54] Writing in fluent Greek, Justus published an account of affairs in Galilee during the rebellion which was subsequently lost. This history apparently charged that Josephus' militant intemperance compromised the well-being of Tiberias, the Galilee city most akin to a polis where local groups vied against one another, some pro-revolt, others pro-Rome. Had Josephus demonstrated leadership and not excited the pro-rebellion radicals in Tiberias, the town would have been spared subsequent hardships, Justus presumably alleged. Among other things, Josephus' failed military command in Galilee left Tiberias at a competitive disadvantage with Sepphoris, a politically moderate settlement which never rebelled and which therefore was never damaged by Roman reprisals. Justus seems also to have charged Josephus with various improprieties in the field, including abusive treatment of women. Because Josephus devotes an extended digression to the refutation of Justus's allegations,[55] many scholars adduced that *Life*'s publication as a whole was prompted by Justus' history, but others have pointed to many other motivations and dynamics at play in Josephus' brief autobiography, and have dismissed sweeping conclusions regarding the impact of his dispute with Justus.[56] In fact, there are cogent reasons to believe that John of Gischala pressed on Josephus' mind as his main nemesis. This is because John, unlike Justus, evolved over time as a major player in the rebellion. Also, John's power base was in Upper Galilee, and he seems to have been the most powerful character in this area; his situation posed a threat, of sorts, to Josephus, who mostly operated as military commander in Lower Galilee.

Whatever prompted Josephus' confession about his identity as a kind of double agent in Galilee, as an anti-rebellion Jewish rebel leader, his frankness provides us with intriguing clues about the region's political culture. The overriding fact about Josephus' activity in Galilee is its failure. Class resentments and national enthusiasms were calibrated in the country's north in a fashion unsuited to the calculations and orientations of the Jerusalem Temple elite. Next to this issue, Josephus' failures to thwart the Roman siege at Jotapata seem not just preordained, in view of Rome's obvious military superiority, but also not entirely germane. Josephus' writings in *Life* and *JW* are not about Rome and Jerusalem. They are about Jerusalem and Galilee. They are not about an anti-colonial uprising. They are about a Jewish civil war. And Galilee functions in this Jewish narrative as a kind of negative mirror image to depictions of Jesus' wondrous popularity in Galilee in the Christian narrative. In Josephus' career, the negative disposition of the "Galileans" determined everything.

JOSEPHUS VERSUS JOHN OF GISCHALA

Gischala, then an isolated village in the middle of Upper Galilee, west of the Hula Valley, is today the site of an Arab town, Gish. The Hebrew name for the site, Gush Halav (block of milk—the reference apparently is to the soft white stone on a hilly peak in the area) is ancient nomenclature, but it remains today in use in common daily speech, even though no Israeli administrative entity is really called Gush Halav. Some Israeli researchers have termed Gush Halav "the [Jewish] capital of Upper Galilee" in the Second Temple period (two ancient synagogues have been excavated at the site).[57] In Second Temple times, Jewish residents in Upper Galilee apparently used Gush Halav as a launching base in ongoing conflicts with gentiles on the region's northern rim, spreading northwest, these disputes seem to have gone past another Jewish village (Kadesh), and reached Tyre, on the Lebanon coast.[58] Reporting on the period of the rebellion against Rome, Josephus refers to a wall in Gischala that was restored after having sustained damage in altercations with gentiles from Tyre. One passage in his *JW* alludes to "wealthy townspeople"[59]—this is a passing reference, and it is hard to identify any source of wealth for the ancient town other than its olive oil trade, but Israeli scholar Uriel Rappaport argues that there probably was substantive economic stratification among Jews in Upper Galilee in this late Second Temple era.[60] John, he explains, was a relatively wealthy resident who helped fund the rebuilding of the town wall.[61]

In sociopolitical terms, John should have consistently belonged, with Justus of Tiberias, to a Galilee elite whose members were not enthusiastic about the anti-Rome rebellion, fearing that its likely disastrous outcome would nullify their assets and social position.[62] Among members of this Galilee elite, John's declasse radicalism is unusual: Gischala was the last Galilee enclave to be conquered by the Romans, and John escaped, with a band of Galileans, and reemerged in Jerusalem as a major rebel leader, betraying his class roots. Depicting his rival's escape from Gischala as disgraceful desecration, Josephus highlights John's deceitful request from the Romans for a day of rest on Shabbat (according to Josephus, John fled on the Jewish Sabbath, leaving in the dust any Gischala townsfolk who could not keep pace with his cowardly sprint).[63] Rapaport, in contrast, does not see any reason why John, whom he designates at this stage as a political moderate, akin to Josephus, would need to flee. The Roman advance on Gischala occurred after the horrific siege at Gamala (Gamla), a town on the Golan Heights side of the Jordan River, but nonetheless part of a cultural-economic Galilee network in this era. Hilly Gamala witnessed the mass suicide of Jewish fighters on a scale unusual in antiquity (and surpassing the awful scene in Jotapata, which involved Josephus), thereby warranting its title as the "Masada of the north." *JW* reports that "4000 Gamala residents were slaughtered by the Romans, but the number throwing themselves over the cliff proved to be 5000."[64] With this gruesome recent scene in his mind as a fate to be avoided, John might simply have walked away from Gischala, giving the Romans no pretext to kill or capture him.[65]

John, Rapaport contends, underwent a political transformation. Skeptical about the revolt at first, he was moved by the courage and national resolve displayed by the pro-rebellion Galilean masses in his home region. John's political views were in tumult by the time he reached Jerusalem. In the holy city, he apparently hoped to join forces with a moderate camp led by High Priest Ananus ben Ananus, but the aim of such an alliance remains in the fog. What, exactly, would have been envisioned by John as the endpoint of moderate politics, in this period? A truce with Rome? A mini-revolt wherein Jews would save face by showing some military mettle but would also refrain from any act that might seriously antagonize the Romans? A moderate faction agenda is not really adducible. Nor does Rapaport really produce a convincing explanation of what John was trying to accomplish in an earlier episode in Galilee, detailed in *Life*, where he joined forces with Jerusalem moderates in a bid to depose (or kill) Josephus, and perhaps take in his own hands the reins of military command in Galilee.[66] Specifics in the political development and agenda of John of Gischala, a hero of the Jewish rebellion against Rome, remain elusive.

Josephus, of course, has a jaundiced, completely dissimilar, account of what brought John from Galilee to Jerusalem. He casts John as a war profiteer, political opportunist, and treacherous rebel responsible for a series of misdeeds in Galilee (in addition to alleged schemes to destroy Josephus, John supposedly price-gauged unsuspecting Jews in Syria, delivering to them religiously sanctioned olive oil from Eretz Israel[67]); then, in Jerusalem, no less than any other single individual in the rebellion, John brought ruin to his people in Jerusalem. John, in Josephus' account, is a nefarious double-dealer in Jerusalem—pretending to be a moderate in order to extract favors and information from High Priest Ananus, John surreptitiously aligns with the Zealots.[68] Indeed, John and his band of Galileans are a key causal lever around which the calamitous events of *JW*'s main, Jerusalem, sections rotate.

In Josephus' narration, Jewish racial bias complements anti-rural prejudice. The Second Temple's destruction is clinched when unruly elements who are on the ethnic and geography periphery of the Jews' body politic, John, from the north, and the Idumaeans from the south, begin to influence affairs in the holy city. The deadly combination of ideological zealotry, and the arrival of semi-foreign Jews, instigates the game-changing event in the Jewish tragedy, the murder of the High Priest Ananus. Josephus' account of this transformative assassination captures his own sociopolitical outlook in precis. The fall of Jerusalem, Josephus claimed, dated to the assassination of Ananus in the center of the city. This high priest had been revered as an impartial, judicious figure who dearly loved "democracy"—he always "set the common good before any private interests." Ananus knew Rome's might was "invincible"—when faced with no option other than to proceed with the war, "he took care that Jewish resistance . . . would at least be efficiently managed."[69]

What is Greek, what is Roman, what is Jewish, in this biographical description's blend of patrician elitism and democratic rhetoric? Was the assassination of the Jewish high priest an abomination because it was an act of religious desecration? Was the murder reprehensible because its perpetrators reached the wrong calculation regarding possible political options and scenarios? Did Ananus, and by extension, Josephus, uphold the proper position—Rome is invincible and should never be seriously provoked, but if the unruly Jewish masses leave Jerusalem's elite with no choice, make sure the revolt is "efficiently managed"—on account of their prestigious lineage, their proximity to God at the Temple, or something else? Parsing questions like the ones above, we encounter uncomfortable realities and paradoxes. Though they disagreed about tactics, Jewish political zealots and moderates in this period took up the preservation of the Temple's sanctity as their goal. Were moderate Jerusalemite spokesmen like Josephus self-conscious about how their agenda was influenced by their own class interest? This is an interesting, debatable, question. Less debatable is the fact that any confusion of ends and means, of substance and symbol, in their striving must have been opaque to them.

Of course, in its day, the Temple was seen as the ultimate symbol of Jewish authenticity, in opposition to foreign (Roman) power, and, as the moderates worked out the political mathematics, accommodation with Rome would preserve this symbol of Jewish independence. However, as scholars such as Seth Schwartz have shown, the Temple's special status never consolidated out of Jewish autonomy.[70] Instead, from the start, it depended upon recognition which only outside power, that is, Rome in this first-century CE setting, could confer. Accommodation with foreign powers is what has always *enabled* Jews to build symbols and institutions evocative of their sense of chosen-ness (including the modern state of Israel)—they do not forge ties with Rome, or America, to preserve, retroactively, sacrosanct symbols which came into being ex nihilo. For their part, Jews like John arose in rebellion from Galilee not necessarily because they revered the Temple; perhaps their revolt conveyed ambivalence. An impressive roster of scholars have insisted that Galilean Judaism in this late Second Temple period was substantively indistinguishable from the Jerusalemite version of the religion,[71] but I suspect that regionalism had impact in this ancient religious sphere comparable to its influence today in Israel in political affairs (Jewish residents on the country's northern and southern peripheries have patriotic, but nonetheless complicated, attitudes toward a state that has empowered them in some ways, but disadvantaged them in other senses). Economic-class dynamics enjoined in Temple cult observances might have caused many rural Galileans to have a love-hate relationship with the Second Temple. In other words, the rebelliousness of characters like John need not be seen as being expressive of religious devotion to the Temple, nor really as politically zealous dedication to the Temple as a symbol of Jewish national autonomy. Instead, characters like John might have been maddened by the Gordian knot of class exploitation and hypocritical subservience to Rome which tied up the Temple's claim of sanctity. Josephus obviously exaggerated and polemicized when he described the contemptuous desecration perpetrated by zealots within the Temple environs, but even when these hyperbolic, castigating depictions are pared down, they are suggestive not of partisans who are campaigning in the Temple to preserve its sanctity, or its semipolitical status of autonomy. They are instead suggestive of partisans who are in a state of insensate anger.

There is no reason for suspicion about the sincerity of Josephus' own pious devotion to the Temple, but I am suggesting that the ends and means of the moderate campaigns he wages in *JW* and *Life* can be seen on another level, one on which social control is the goal, and the Temple is a symbolic intermediary. Josephus' writing can be as a lament about the moderates' inability to hold the collective Jewish body together. A man who claimed to have found inner peace in his life and career by successively upholding Jewish and Roman standpoints, Josephus could not find a way to leverage either one of these identities, or the two twined together, so as to defuse the rebellious fury of the Galileans. His account of his dealings with them is a textbook illustration of the tail trying to wag the dog. In the end, his writing does to Galilee, to its people, to its leaders, what any partisan does when he realizes there is no way to win an argument: Josephus delegitimizes Galilee, picturing it as a region immersed in sheer banditry.

Bandits like John kidnapped Galilee, Josephus claims. He propounds this thesis when he describes what occurred in Gischala, following the fall of Jotapata and Gamala. Bandits took hold of the town's Jewish body, and "infect[ed]" it. The majority of the town's population, Josephus reports, wanted peace—these were "mainly" farmers who were preoccupied by the fate of their crops. This peace-leaning majority, however, was contaminated by bandits, led by John, "a specious rogue of infinite guile."[72]

In Jerusalem, John and his bandit gang fortify their rebel presence and forfeit their manly honor. Josephus' polemic about John's lost masculinity is acutely self-serving. He writes from a standpoint of insufferable anxiety about his own honor, following his turnabout at Jotapata: playing on the losing team, Josephus allowed his demoralized teammates to eliminate themselves, broke his promise to them, and then switched sides and joined the winner. To borrow from the lexicon of pop psychology, this rant about John and his Galilean pansies "projects" Josephus' own aching self-disappointment, but the passage's cultural suggestions stretch well beyond the author's own identity predicament:

> Among the Zealots the Galilean contingent took the invention and blatant practice of new atrocities to unrivalled extremes. It was they who had elevated John to power, and from the autocratic position he had won with their help he rewarded them with the licence to do whatever any of them wanted. Looting was their passion, and they could never get enough of it; they loved ransacking wealthy houses; they murdered men and raped women for amusement; and they boozed away the proceeds of the blood-stained spoils. Sated with all this, and with no one to stop them, they went effeminate, doing up their hair, wearing women's clothes, drenching themselves in scent, and applying eyeliner to make themselves pretty. And it was not just the adoption of female dress: they also played the female role in sex, and their total depravity had them inventing new and utterly obscene modes of intercourse. They treated the city as a brothel and wallowed in it, polluting every part with their contamination.[73]

Why is the sort of carnivalesque behavior described in this passage impossible to believe? The scene has some measure of credibility in view of its source—Josephus scholars acknowledge that he rarely invents scenes out of whole cloth, though he frequently exaggerates and distorts.[74]

Is it impossible to imagine subsistence farmers from Galilee going wild after resettling in the opulence of the Temple's environs, under conditions where their days were numbered, in view of the invincibility of the Roman army? Are there no comparable examples to be found among rebel bandit groups in other places and times? Why should we not examine Josephus' most disparaging comment—"they treated the city as a brothel"—with analytic rigor? After all, another monotheistic faith consolidated after another band of Galileans descended upon Jerusalem, and effectively reached the same exact conclusion, that the Temple was a prostituted arena. Jesus' group withdrew from Temple-urban depravity, but its leader, at least in the Book of Matthew, was merciless in his attack on Pharisees, arguably a "moderate" group. Unlike Jesus, the other Galilee rebel, John of Gischala, became irreversibly committed to the revolt against Rome; in his case, orgiastic crossdressing can also be seen as a revolutionary protest against the moderates, a way of demonstrating what Rome "really is about" for the edification of elite Jewish compatriots who imagined that the Temple could be kept holy under Roman patronage.

In such portraitures, Josephus posits that a Jew retains his honor and manhood by succumbing to the more powerful state outside of him. Subsequently, centuries of ghetto exclusion in the Diaspora wherein, as Daniel Boyarin provocatively argues, Jews willfully adopted models of "unheroic masculinity,"[75] can be seen as an extension of Josephus' premises, as though his polemicized presentation of gender politics in his Roman revolt narrative set the stage for diaspora sexuality.

John's Israeli biographer, Uriel Rappaport keeps Josephus' portrait of John's and the Galileans' homosexuality and transvestism in the closet. While he has cause to doubt the veracity of Josephus' polemical descriptions, the strategy of ignoring the argument conveyed in these depictions can be questioned, if only because this argument colors *all* the writing in Josephus text, including empirical-seeming passages which convey information about fundamental items on the late Second Temple period's landscape, such as the Jews' three sects, which won canonical status as common knowledge. The failure of the rebellion and the collapse of the Temple cult was, in the most fundamental sense, an identity trauma for Jews, and Josephus' defamatory portraiture of his rival captures this trauma's dimensions no less reliably than the empirical-seeming parts of his writing.

By the same logic, we will challenge the contemporary critical trends of overlooking anti-Pharisee, supersession-inflected, passages in the gospels, particularly Matthew, and of recasting Jesus as a Jew with presumptive taxonomic certainty that leads both academic and popular commentators to associate him firmly with one of the Jewish sects. In the case of New Testament criticism, I am deeply aware of the post-Holocaust sensitivities which have propelled commentators toward the adoption of creative arguments that refashion Jesus as a Jew, in a mood of interfaith communality. But, beyond moral objections regarding the conception of interfaith dialogue subsumed in this mood, this study insists that contemporary strategies in commentary on Josephus and Jesus are nothing more than that—analytic strategies. For Uriel Rappaport, John of Gischala is a Jewish national hero, presumably a forerunner of Yigal Allon and other Palmah fighters in Israel's 1948 statehood struggle in Galilee, just as for Reza Aslan, Jesus becomes a Jewish national hero, a zealot,[76] presumably a forerunner of Yigal Allon and other Palmah fighters in Israel's 1948 statehood struggle in Galilee. The counterintuitive suggestiveness in their commentary and its characterizations is enabled by hermeneutic agility, by a strategy of jettisoning much of what Josephus writes about Jewish groups he found unpalatable, and of what Matthew writes about Jewish groups he found unpalatable, as untrue polemic. By giving weight to such passages, despite their obvious exaggerations, we do not become committed to a reading of Josephus and the Gospels as "literature." Instead, we are suggesting that the sort of anachronistic partisanship which Albert Schweitzer identified in the search waged by critics for the "historical Jesus" from the start of the modern era in the late eighteenth century[77] extends to all commentary on all Second Temple writings, Josephus included (this point is borne out quite cogently in Martin Goodman's recent book on the reception of *The Jewish War* by Christians and Jews, over the centuries[78]). There are other considerations as well. One is that there is no way of proving that the kernel of Josephus' polemical descriptions, such as that of John of Gischala and his band on the Temple grounds, is fabrication.[79]

The sequel to *JW*'s Temple-area sexuality polemic is its enraged description[80] of the way John and the other Galileans deliberately vandalize and desecrate sacred Temple objects ("bowls, salvers, tables"), melting them away, or consuming wines and other delectables for their own pleasure, or distributing them to lift the spirit of rebel comrades. Speaking for his priestly class, Josephus' voice breaks in outrage. Hardly for the first or last time,[81] he trespasses the neat Greek forms of historical narrative, and apologizes for allowing emotion to carry his prose: "I believe that if the Romans had been slow to move against these sinners, either the earth would have opened up and swallowed the city . . . or the thunderbolts which struck Sodom would have struck again," he exclaims.[82] The passage's propagandistic lobbying for Titus is manifest. The Jewish rebels, Josephus writes, were the Temple vandals, not Vespasian, Titus, and the Romans.[83]

Fame being a cunning friend, the passage helps us understand how Josephus' writings survived due to dynamics that were out of the hands of this self-interested historian. The passage panders to Josephus' Roman patrons and readers, but along with comparable sections in *JW*, it was preserved and circulated over the centuries because of its usefulness to Christians, as a virtual blow-by-blow fulfillment of Jesus' prophecy recorded in Matthew (composed concurrently to *JW*): "'Do you see all these things?' he asked.

'Truly I tell you, not one stone here will be left on another; each one will be thrown down'"(Matthew: 24: 1–3; see also Mark 13:2).

In these Jewish and Christian narratives, the myth of rural Galilee plays multiple, moral and social, purposes. In Josephus, the obtusely radical Galileans are, owing to their heresy, the makers of the Temple's destruction. With Jesus, morally irreproachable, simple and sincere, rural Galileans are witness, via prophesy, to the Temple's impending destruction. In such Jewish-Christian convergences, Galilee functions as monotheism's critique of the Greek myth of the polis. Cultural meaning can never be institutionalized in the city. Yosef ben Matityahu (Josephus), and Matthew, attribute different character traits to the Galileans, but despite the differing intents in the presentations, both use them to deliver doubts about the myth of the sacred city. For Jews and Christians, Galilean Jews are makers and witnesses of the Temple's destruction. While (as we will see) there is a long-standing "Galilee of the Gentiles" interpretation by which Christianity is thought to have parted ways with Judaism because of Galilee's Hellenistic character, there are also senses in which the region's moral geography is evoked to explain how monotheism, as a whole, superseded Hellenistic norms and influences, one of them being the myth of the polis.

Tangential details in Josephus' account suggest that his project of delegitimizing Galilean rebels like John, as bandits not susceptible to norms of human morality, accorded with the victorious Romans' perceptions. In the Roman view, John remained a worthless bandit whose disposal after capture did not require ceremonial elaboration, whereas the other important Jewish rebel, Simon bar Giora, who cut a messianic role, as a self-sacrificing king of Jewish salvation, won notoriety among Romans. Simon, not the bandit John, was brought to Rome for the celebration of the triumph over the Jews, where he was publicly tortured and executed.[84]

SPEAKING TO THE GALILEANS

In *JW*, Josephus describes a war in Galilee, whereas his descriptions in *Life* highlight his own clever character. Incidents overlap in the two texts, but there are blatant discrepancies of detail, and the sequencing is sometimes dissimilar. Also, as mentioned, the motivational background is divergent since Josephus appears to be a genuine rebel commander in *JW*, whereas in *Life* he confesses openly to having functioned as a double agent, doing his utmost to stave off rebellion in the north or, if the Galileans could not be restrained, limiting its damages. The most consequential biographical sequence in Josephus' career, his command at Jotapata, his reneging of the suicide pact and his striking of an alliance with Vespasian as a prophetic adviser on Jewish affairs, is not described in the second, autobiographical, text. In this connection, *Life* simply corroborates the Galilee sections of *JW*. Josephus abruptly ends his *Life* after its dramatization of how he extricated himself from the plot hatched by Jerusalem priests and John of Gischala to revoke his Galilee command; he attests, at this juncture, that he "has reported with precision" the "things that happened to me in that place (Jotapata), and the way I was taken alive and chained" in *JW*.[85]

The key link between the two texts is the duplicitously cunning way Josephus, as a spokesman for the Jerusalem elite and the Temple cult, *speaks* to the Galileans, as in the Dabarittha affair and related incidents conveyed in detail in *Life* (discussed below), and in his disingenuous pleading against suicide, in *JW*, in the Jotapata cave.[86] He tells the people of Galilee anything that serves his passing interest. In *Life*, Josephus positively gloats about the way he dupes the gullible Galilean masses and their spineless elites, but *JW*'s Jotapata speech also features comic interpolation whereby Josephus makes promises to his doleful cave mates which his readers know will be betrayed by the end of the day. In both texts, Josephus speaks to Galilee's residents in the language of expediency and instrumentality, flashing rhetorical persuasiveness as a survival skill the way a cowboy flashes a six shooter in a Hollywood Western.

The way Josephus touts rhetorical finesse, not truth-telling, as a cardinal value in his account of how he managed affairs in Galilee raises issues about how his history ought to be read. Josephus wrote *JW* under imperial patronage, whereas *Antiquities* and *Life* were apparently composed under somewhat more tenuous circumstances, with some measure of protection afforded by Titus' brother Domitian, and patronage offered by a private individual, Epaphroditus,[87] "a freedman bibliophile of Alexandrian provenance."[88] These were not practically distressful circumstances, but Josephus clearly had an incentive to shape aspects of his historical narrative in line with his contemporary interests. Why shouldn't this mode of self-preservation and self-promotion via rhetorical finesse, which dominates Josephus' portraiture of himself, years before, as a military rebel commander in Galilee, be considered a lasting character trait, and a methodological pillar of his work as a historian?

Shaye Cohen, a skeptical-minded scholar who tends to present Josephus as a self-serving rhetorician, provides one thought-provoking example of how interests late in Josephus' career might have swayed the way he reported on his Galilee military activities. *Life*, unlike *JW*, furnishes an extended account of the military coup attempted by a Jerusalem elite and John of Gischala to oust Josephus in Galilee, and the report on this dramatic episode opens with words of praise for one of the Jerusalem notables, Simon, son of Gamiliel, and his fellow Pharisees, who "have the reputation of excelling others in their precision with respect to the traditional legal matters."[89] This modest encomium is thematically incongruous and jarring. The Jerusalem contingent, three of whose four members were Pharisees, subsequently appear in Josephus' autobiography as heartless power brokers, not as laudable religious jurists; they attempt to deceive, oust, and possibly harm him. Cohen speculates that Josephus threw this curveball of praise for Simon because of the Jews' post-Temple politics at the time he wrote *Life*—at the time, Pharisees were reconsolidating in the making of rabbinical Judaism at the Yavne academy. "We may conjecture that Josephus realized that they [Pharisees] would emerge as the leaders of the Jewish scene and imagined himself as their representative in Rome who would intercede on their behalf with emperors," hypothesizes Cohen.[90] Because Josephus' account in *Life* of the Jerusalem's contingent's cutthroat campaign to oust him is hardly a feel-good portrait for Pharisees, Cohen's conjecture is not accepted by all scholars.[91] Nonetheless, this example points to the challenge of understanding Josephus, and his Galilee, in their multilayered discursive contexts wherein rhetorical finesse, and clever promotion of self-interest, typically take precedence over sheer truth-telling.

Josephus' understanding of sophistry is pre-Talmudic, and essentially Greco-Roman. In these two texts, *JW* and *Life*, he pulls facts and truth expediently back-and-forth, not as an exegetical method of midrash to identify some spiritual principle, but rather in deference to sociological premises, and perceptions of heroism, which seem more Roman than Jewish. Josephus' manipulative attitude toward truth plays out on a semicolonial, metropole versus province, axis. Jerusalem, the Jewish metropole, owes no debt of transparency and probity in its dealings with its Jewish provinces; still, in the Roman colonial way, this Jewish metropole elite harbors certain anxieties about the childish impulsiveness of the Galileans. In fact, though *JW*'s report, unlike *Life*'s, does not elaborate on Josephus' own motivational doubledealing in Galilee, it is also formatted by this internalization of Roman colonial dynamics, a phenomenon much discussed by postcolonial theorists like Albert Memmi, in his *The Colonizer and the Colonized*.[92]

In both texts, *JW* and *Life*, Josephus' errand in Galilee is to impose social control in terms appreciable to his metropole Jerusalem elite. To be sure, *JW* is relatively cryptic on this point, but Josephus indirectly divulges the nature of his task when he writes that Jewish partisans who were responsible for the surprising defeat of Cestius Gallus, governor of Syria, in September–October 66 CE, descended upon the Jerusalem elite, and forced it to send generals to the provinces. Nothing in Josephus' phrasing suggests that the elite is invested in anything other than limiting damage likely to be wrought by the spread of the rebellion in Galilee: "When the Jews who had pursued Cestius returned to Jerusalem, they either forced or persuaded any remaining pro-Romans to join their movement, and held a mass meeting at the temple to appoint further generals to direct the war."[93] In Josephus, as in the gospels, the issue of social control in Galilee has clear causal interaction with the crisis of Temple Judaism. The respective heroes in these Jewish and Christian narratives, Josephus and Jesus, discharge this burden of control-imposition in Galilee, though neither in ways that mitigate the Temple crisis in the metropole.

Josephus' instrumental dealings with the rural Galileans can be instructively compared to Jesus' dealings with the same population. Cynics would argue that both protagonists were playing tricks on gullible peasants—in modern criticism, this line of argumentation regarding the gospels made its debut with Renan's remarkably popular *Life of Jesus*.[94] Viewing these narratives through the prism of postcolonial criticism helps us elucidate their varying levels of efficacy and determine why Christianity's "render unto Caesar" message of neutrality toward the Romans proved more manageable than the Chinese handcuffs slapped on by Josephus' more overtly proactive agenda of Roman accommodation. When Josephus' reached Galilee, why would his message of Roman accommodation make sense to embryonic rebels like John, if it translated as continued marginalization, on the periphery of the Jewish metropole?

Framed for Roman readers as a description of one of their wars, *JW* accentuates the dangerous volatility of Galilee as a military theater.[95] The Upper and Lower Galilee, Josephus writes, "have always stood firm against any attempt to fight them." Galileans, he adds, "are fighters virtually from birth." They have much to defend because Galilee features "rich arable soil, good pasturage, the production of every sort of tree"; "every acre" in the region is under cultivation. Straining credulity, he claims that Galilee teems with residents—of its two hundred and four settlements, even the smallest boasts at least 15,000 inhabitants (now and then, in modern times, a few commentators have taken these figures seriously,[96] but mostly they have been dismissed). Josephus' polyphonic style sometimes injects a measure of realism into these hyperbolic characterizations of Galilee. An example is Titus' pep talk to his troops, delivered before the assault on Tarichaeae, a town perched on the Sea of Galilee. Titus' motivational speech conveys the "real" Roman perception of Galilee as a provincial backwater, one which lurked beneath Josephus' bravura about the region's demographics and social zeal: "The Jews may be quite reckless fighters unafraid to die, but they have no discipline or experience in war, and are little more than a rabble," reveals Titus.[97] *JW*'s portrait of Josephus' experience of military command in Galilee exudes sublimated identification with the culture of Roman colonialism on many different levels, including its fictitiously inflated statistical dimensions, and its outright egoism. Not just the falsified data concerning the number of soldiers he commanded, 100,000 (60,000 are supposedly infantrymen[98]) but also Josephus' reports about his training methods, are tailored to the expectations, assumptions, and sensitivities of Roman readers. "Recognizing that Roman discipline depended on a multiplicity of links in the chain of command, he sectioned his army on the Roman army," Josephus writes, referring to himself.[99]

JW personalizes the fighting in Galilee to the point of megalomania. As Vespasian circles the wagons, a Jewish deserter informs the Roman commander that Josephus has moved to Jotapata. The fall of this Galilean settlement, and Josephus' capture, the Roman commander reasons, will beget "the fall of all Judea."[100] The historian thus informs the reader that the Jewish tragedy he is documenting hinged ultimately on his own personal fate.

None of these details and ego claims could fit within the frame of Josephus' *Life*. In this later text, Josephus discloses fascinating information about his early life, but none of the disclosures harmoniously cohere with the depictions in the earlier volume, *JW*, in which Josephus appears as a skilled military leader. Josephus' self-presentation in *Life* seems more compatibly identifiable with the upbringing of a suburban Jew in early twenty-first century America than the youthful preparedness for military greatness which can be extrapolated backwardly from *JW*'s Galilee depictions of Josephus. *Life* casts Josephus as an appealing, though mostly idle, young Jerusalemite who searches for himself through his early twenties. He is sufficiently ensconced socioeconomically to invest in a protracted examination of the three Jewish sects, and to scout them as possible outlets for his own spiritual career (this features a three year stretch of spiritual communion in the desert, under the tutelage of a kind of guru-mentor named Bannus[101]). The fact that Josephus belongs to an idle class whose leisure derives from growing revenue flowing from the provincial faithful to Jerusalem, as a result of the Jewish kingdom's expansion in the earlier Hasmonean period and also of Herod's monumental building projects on the Temple and elsewhere,[102] serves as background to the drama which enveloped his military leadership in the north. This drama is centered on the socioeconomic resentments harbored by the volatile "Galileans" and has nothing to do with the characterization of military know-how *JW* imaginatively imputes to its author. *Life*'s autobiographical record contains a detail which accounts for Josephus' pre-rebellion reputation in Rome: this is an account of his emissary work in Rome wherein, at the age of twenty-six, he maneuvered his way up corridors of power to reach Emperor Nero's wife Poppaea, so as to secure the release of two "excellent" members of Jerusalem's priestly caste who had been unjustly arrested by an imprudent Judean procurator, Felix.[103] This anecdote conveys a suggestion of how Josephus had acquired useful knowledge of Roman political culture not long before the rebellion; such experience buoyed Josephus when, after Jotapata's collapse, he finagled to secure a comfortable place on his new team, by the side of his new patrons, Vespasian and Titus. But none of the autobiographical background in *Life* makes explicable *JW*'s egotistical claim about how Josephus' stature in Galilee was so elevated in Rome's eyes that the conquest of the Jews' semi-autonomous state was presumed to hang on his capture.

Realism, tact, and common sense require us to scale down *JW*'s overblown statistics and self-promotional reports about Josephus' physical daring and military prowess in Galilee. Nonetheless, Josephus' *JW* narrative about Galilee can be, and should be, read as a disturbing account of a genuine Jewish tragedy in a real war. The Roman war in Galilee ended in a naval battle flowing out onto the Sea of Galilee from the siege on Taricheae—*something* happened on the same body of water where Jesus, decades before, serenely weathered storms, and reportedly worked miracles. For their own reasons of imperial ambition, Vespasian and Titus shared Josephus' incentive to dramatize the fighting in Galilee and Jerusalem, and, in this respect, Josephus' reportage on the Taricheae siege is right on cue (the whole lake was colored by blood and strewn with corpses, he writes, and for days a dreadful stench polluted the area[104]). This, however, does not make it unreasonable to conclude that the fight at Taricheae was fierce. In all likelihood, Vespasian was not telling fisherman's tales when he highlighted the naval battle of Taricheae, apparently via the issuance of commemorative coins, in Rome's celebration of his Jewish War campaign.[105] Josephus' incidental details, rather than his stylized presentation of supposed, major, facts, evoke the sheer lugubriousness of how the Galilee rebellion ended with Jews being poached mercilessly at sea, off Taricheae. Josephus offhandedly remarks that Jews on their woeful vessels had nowhere to disembark because all the land around the lake was in "enemy's hands."[106] For me, this remark suffices as an account of Rome's devastating conquest of Galilee. While writing drafts of this book, I spent several mornings kayaking around the Sea of Galilee and had occasion to ponder how Josephus' report attests to the crushing dimensions of the Jews' defeat. The Sea of Galilee is larger than life in reputation, and also, as Israel's main water source, it is not a small lake in reality—and here Josephus chillingly tells us there was no shoreline left for Jews to race to, out of the reach of Roman cavalry.

Even if we subtract one zero, or more, from Josephus' town-by-town body counts of fatalities in Galilee, his *JW* war report documents a bloodbath. Vespasian warms up his campaign at Gabara, where he avenges humiliations earlier perpetrated against Cestius and kills "all its people, whatever their age" (recall that in Josephus' demography, no Jewish settlement in Galilee hosted less than 15,000 residents).[107] At Japha, the Romans kill 15,000, and capture another 2,130, Josephus reports[108](he is talking about the village, or thereabouts, where Jesus grew up decades earlier). In the Taricheae siege, 6,700 Jews perish. Many flee from this siege and head for Tiberias, where they are deviously misled by Vespasian; elderly and infirm in this refugee group (1,200 persons) are slain in a gruesome stadium ceremony, at whose conclusion another 30,400 defeated Jews are sent into slavery.[109] Despite Josephus' self-professed military ingenuity and heroics at Jotapata, 40,000 Jews die in the town's collapse, *JW* discloses.[110]

The problem with processing these numbers goes beyond Josephus' own penchant for exaggeration and general issues about the reliability of reported body counts and statistics in antiquity. The rebellion's gruesome outcome in Galilee poses another aspect of the disconnect between *JW* and *Life*. The latter text focuses almost exclusively on internal Jewish power politics and feuds, and also on the doctored-up evidence of Josephus' laudable character traits—everything seems sheltered from terrifying details and images in *JW*. In *Life*'s climactic drama, the Jerusalem priestly junta, conspiring with John, desperately seeks evidence to incriminate Josephus, and so decides to send letters of inquiry to *all* Jewish settlements in Galilee (there were, recall, two hundred and four), reckoning that each must have a few residents who will find something unflattering to say about Josephus.[111] How could there have been leisure for such documentary fact-finding in a besieged community whose residents would soon by floating dead on the Sea of Galilee, or impaled on the walls in places like Jotapata?

BETWEEN DABARITTHA AND JOTAPATA: RECONSTRUCTING JOSEPHUS' APOLOGETIC

In Galilee, Josephus coopted social rebels ("bandits") by bribing them and shuffling them away as mercenaries. He tortured and mutilated antagonists. He cunningly operated to stifle rebellion in the region by causing Galileans to exhaust their passions in ineffectual, symbolic acts of protest against Roman vandalism of sacred objects. He dissimulated in front of angry crowds, either by telling outright lies, or by distorting and exaggerating the character of actions undertaken for their protection or for the prosecution of the anti-Roman rebellion. After championing the defense of Jotapata during the forty-seven-day siege, Josephus tricked partisans in the cave, capitulated to Vespasian, formally renounced the Jewish rebellion, and joined forces with the Romans in a last-ditch effort to forestall the revolt's continuance in Jerusalem. This activity roster emanates mostly from *Life*, though there is some overlap with details in *JW* (along with numerous inconsistencies between the texts). The only item on this activity list which exclusively appears in *JW*'s Galilee sections is the Jotapata suicide escape. As mentioned, scholars have explored an array of possible circumstances and motivations that may have prompted Josephus to append his autobiographical *Life* at the end of his ponderous *Antiquities*, ranging from the argument with Justus of Tiberias to speculation about circumstances in the composition of advanced drafts of these texts. On a thematic level, however, it makes most sense to read *Life* as an extension of, and implicit apologetic for, Josephus' suicide evasion at Jotapata.

In the context of *JW*, Josephus' behavior in the cave is inexplicable, both in terms of the fatuous spiritual arguments he concocts in the effort to dislodge his cave comrades from the suicide pact and also, more importantly, with regard to its outcome of sheer betrayal (from the partisan Jewish standpoint). In contrast, within *Life*'s moral-political parameters, the Jotapata scene loses much of its pungency. Why would Josephus have sacrificed his life in protest against Roman rule if he had, from the start, inwardly opposed the Jews' effort to overturn it? Why should his dissembling in and out of the Jotapata cave seem disturbing in view of *Life*'s premise that cleverly self-serving rhetoric, and cleverly self-serving acts of physical deception, are heroic traits?

Once Josephus' writing about Galilee is rearranged in this way, its larger themes can be usefully pondered in the broad context of Jewish history. For the Jews, over the ages, Josephus has been a chronic migraine, with discussions invariably fastening to the important, but ultimately limited, question of whether he ought to regarded as an outright traitor, or as a pragmatically subterranean Jewish loyalist. As Martin Goodman observes, this ping-pong match about Josephus, traitorous scoundrel or pragmatic patriot, was played by Jews with increasing intensity in periods when hopes of Jewish revitalization depended upon some sort of accommodation with outside patrons and superpowers, and it continued into the period of Israeli statehood, when, among other things, the country's state-sponsored television network staged in 1992 a mock trial about the issue of Josephus' loyalty.[112] Goodman cites an Israeli political scientist, Shlomo Avineri, who has recalled how, in the 1948 year of Israel's establishment, his youth movement sponsored a mock trial in which Josephus was one of the defendants accused of betraying Jerusalem.[113] The date cited in Avineri's recollection, I think, caps a setting in modern Jewish history when Josephus' dilemmas and choice had particular stringency: during the 1918–1948 period of British mandatory control in Palestine, when Jewish statehood dreams depended upon persuading English patrons to upgrade terms (e.g. Jewish "national home") that were incorporated in the 1917 Balfour Declaration, Zionist youth movements, and high school civics teachers in the "Yishuv" (the Jewish community in prestate Palestine), sponsored debates about whether Josephus subverted or supported Jewish national honor, and these had a handy reference point, with Britain's empire standing in for Rome (Hanoch Bartov, an Israeli writer who grew up in this mandatory period and served in British uniform during World War II, has vividly documented these Josephus controversies). As in a ping-pong match, where lots of spin and velocity can be put on the ball, but there is only so much that can be done on both sides of the table, this long-standing

Josephus debate can be stimulating, but it would have greater value were it to be played on a wider, multi-level, stage. Here, we come to another fundamental similarity between the Jewish and Christian narratives of Josephus and Jesus: both Josephus' writings and the gospels pivot on the self-sacrifice of the central figure, and how a symbolically fraught suicide, or nonsuicide, points to the transformation of Judaism in some new, post-Temple, form. That is to say, the enduring question raised by Josephus' career is not that of personal loyalty and honor, but rather how it serves as a broader symbol of cultural transition.

Josephus' audacious dissembling in Galilee (as opposed to Jesus' miracle working and moral earnestness) evokes Greco-Roman streams of individual honor and heroism. Striking this chord, Steve Mason, editor of a superbly produced translation of *Life*, alludes to Odysseus as one apt reference point for Josephus' presentation of his own exploits.[114] Equally true, the behavioral slyness and rhetorical opportunism Josephus displays in Galilee, all wrapped apologetically within an ethos of survival at all costs, can be associated with Jewish traits that evolved, either in myth or in reality, during the subsequent phase of Jewish experience in the diaspora—for the sake of this argument about Josephus as a transitional figure, it does not matter whether those traits are characterized pejoratively, a la anti-Semitism, or in a more sympathetic vein, a la the Boyarin brothers' reinterpretation of diaspora roles.[115] Nationally patriotic Jews of Galilee who appear in Josephus' writing—for example, John of Gischala, or Jesus son of Sapphias, a leader of Tiberias' radical, pro-rebellion faction—exercised little short-term impact in the region (Galilee did not participate in the next, and climactically final, rebellion against Rome, the Bar Kochba revolt, in 132–136). Over the long run, such nationally militant models were overlooked by Jews, until Zionism selectively celebrated zealous characters and images which appear in Josephus' works, particularly Masada. In contrast, the footprints of Josephus' calculations and choices in Galilee, including his heart-breaking maneuver at Jotapata, a kind of crucifixion of Jewish national honor comparable in some ways to Jesus on the Cross, can be readily followed into subsequent, Talmudic and Exilic, phases of Jewish experience. As a transformative figure, Josephus' life and writings must be measured in shifting moral and cultural frames of Temple-based, Jewish semi-sovereignty, in Eretz Israel, Greco-Roman civilization, and Diasporic Judaism. Harmonious reconciliation of these contrasting value systems could never be possible, of course, but the fact that Josephus' ongoing, egoistic, posturing keeps the reader's attention is significant. His sleight of hand turns horrific personal and national failure in Galilee into a triumph, of sorts. As in the case of the gospels, his history's magical attraction relies on its imaginatively creative, if not manipulative, presentation of Galilee's social landscape.

Before the climax at Jotapata, the Dabarittha incident most provocatively reveals the character of Josephus' engagement in Galilee. The culprits in this incident hail from Dabarittha, a village near Mt. Tabor; the occurrence's location remains a bit vague, but the crime happens in a Plain of Esdraelon area controlled by Agrippa II, on the edge of free Greek cities (called the Decapolis).[116] Dabarittean bandits plunder a convey headed by the wife of Agrippa's local administrator (named Ptolemy); they steal four mules and large stashes of silver and gold. When the loot is brought to Josephus in Tarichaeae on the assumption that the region's military leader will utilize it in the anti-Roman rebellion, he immediately resolves to double-cross the rebels and return the plunder to Agrippa via Ptolemy; Josephus pleads and rationalizes in *Life,* saying that he viewed Ptolemy as a compatriot, and also that Jewish law proscribes robbing adversaries.[117] With the revolt in full swing in Galilee, Josephus' double-cross naturally stirs suspicions—extemporizing in responses to questioners, he talks about putting the loot to use for the strengthening of defense walls in Jerusalem, or in Tarichaeae. Rumors continue to swirl about Josephus' alleged, traitorous agenda of surrendering Galilee to the Romans. Grabbing the stick at both ends, Josephus explains that the Dabarittha bandits stirred, in Tiberias, this innuendo about his character and intent because they did not receive commissions after they brought the spoils to him, and, concurrently, he informs the reader that the bandits' supposition about his intention to return the loot to the pro-Roman client king, Agrippa II, was entirely correct.[118] The looters' characterization of Josephus as a traitor makes headway and becomes perilous—seemingly unfazed, Josephus takes a nap in Tarichaeae. Even his bodyguards betray him and participate in a rally at the town's hippodrome; local anti-Roman militants, headed by Jesus son of Sapphias, excite the rally's crowd, demanding that revolutionary justice be exacted against Josephus. This Jesus exclaims that the laws of Moses enjoin swift punishment against Josephus.

The sequence finds mention in *JW*[119] where it is scaled in typical grandiosity (Josephus writes about a confrontation with 100,000 disappointed, anti-Roman rebels in the hippodrome, and also alludes to four guards counseling him to flee before they themselves abscond). As Mason mentions,[120] the twist in *Life,* where one loyal bodyguard, named Simon, stays with Josephus, and advises him to commit honorable suicide in the hippodrome, is tellingly significant. In fact, this detail links the Dabarittha incident to the Jotapata cave. In neither place can Josephus find cause to take his own life as putative honorable tribute to a Jewish rebellion he actually opposes. Both venues become carnival arenas where Josephus plays his hand as penitent, priestly ethicist, or as mathematical wizard, to save himself—the difference between the audiences is that the hippodrome peasant masses are illimitably susceptible to demagoguery, whereas the Jotapata cave holds forty persons from solid families who do not allow Josephus' situational ethics and egoism to affect their own choice.

In Tarichaeae's hippodrome, Josephus dons black clothing of repentance, drops his sword, falls prostrate to the ground and weeps. Sensing that the fickle crowd is now taking pity on him, in expectation of a moving confession of his pro-Roman double-dealing, he shifts the tide by duplicitously insisting that his intentions for the spoils of the Dabarittean heist were entirely pro-rebellion. This hippodrome speech, I believe, conveys valuable clues to Josephus' psychology and to the process of self-extenuation he experienced as the years passed and he became settled in his adopted Roman identity, and came to terms with his behavior at Jotapata. In tone and content, *Life*'s stylized version of the Dabarittha affair sequence is an assertive apologetic: Josephus is saying that it would have been rank stupidity for him to have sacrificed his life in solidarity with a Jewish rebellion which, he earnestly believed, lost God's favor, and which was, politically and militarily, monstrously foolish. The reader of his hippodrome speech understands that Josephus means the exact opposite of his pro-suicide avowal, and of his attestations to tell the truth ("I do want, before I should end my life, to indicate the truth to you"[121]). A biting exercise in sarcasm, the hippodrome speech's unstated, but nonetheless evident message is that the Galileans could never have staged an authentic and effective national revolt. Lacking breeding, discipline, and education, they are incapable of managing their own emotions, and sensibly assessing whatever they are told.

Josephus promises the hippodrome masses that he will use the Dabarittean loot to build a wall around Tarichaeae, so as to reward its citizens for being "so hospitable toward foreigners."[122] Of course, the comic turn here is the obeisance to the hospitality of a hippodrome full of raging discontents who were set to liquidate him and who are disposed to target other aliens in tune with demagoguery. In ensuing sequences, Josephus whips and mutilates antagonists in order to intimidate Tarichaeaen bandits who harbor lingering animosity toward him; when local radicals change focus, and plot the murder of notables from Galilee towns who were moderate about the rebellion or pro-Roman, Josephus maneuvers to shuttle these like-minded dignitaries out of Tarichaeae, right under the noses of the clueless radicals, and ship them across the Sea of Galilee to areas under Agrippa II's authority, where they are pardoned.[123] Later, Josephus uses the subterfuge of the fake flotilla to deter anti-Roman radicalism in Tiberias[124] and slyly decimates Tiberias' unreliable town council by finding pretexts to relocate its members to house arrest in Tarichaeae. This sequence affords Josephus leverage, as he moves to assert some measure of control in Tiberias, the Galilee locale of the greatest political volatility and unpredictability. As Josephus describes it, the town's residents, now a "mob," are in mortal fear about reprisals he might initiate to punish their sedition; so they offer to him one of their own, a certain Cleitus, an "audacious and reckless young man," for sacrifice as a kind of scapegoat.[125] As homage to Galilee witlessness, Josephus demands that Cleitus perform a physically improbable act of communal expiation by chopping off both of his own hands—scholars have wondered whether this request for a miracle of self-mutilation is meant to be taken seriously.[126]

The answer is probably "yes and no." Josephus' descriptions of Jewish radical hands being chopped off are metaphorical condemnations of the rebellion's status as an abominable and unnatural act of national Jewish self-mutilation. The Cleitus affair is the grotesquely comic climax of a sequence set off by the Dabarittha heist, and this chain of affairs has implicit and explicit linkages to Josephus' rendering of the Jotapata siege and suicide in *JW*. The hapless Cleitus becomes a tableaux vivant image of Josephus' condemnation of honor suicide in his cave peroration. In that Jotapata speech, after explaining (somewhat oddly) how Jewish tradition condemns suicide, Josephus adds that in some countries, the law requires that the right hand (presumably the agent of self-murder) be cut away from persons who have committed suicide. According to the thinking in such countries, suicide perpetrators have severed body from soul, and "so the hand that did it should be likewise be severed from the body."[127]

Particularly because, in *JW*, the Jotapata cave incident appears as a bookend to the semi-heroic presentation of mass Jewish suicide at Masada, it left loose ends about the author's character. Josephus could not have intended to present himself as a cravenly, self-interested, foil to the heroic, self-sacrificial, Sicarii militants at Masada, but the structure of his seminal work seems to convey this suggestion. Josephus' return to the Cleitus incident in *Life* completes the apologetic about the course of his career. Far from national betrayal, his handling of the Dabarittha heist was utterly justified, because the anti-Roman revolt was an act of national suicide. Cleitus' severed hands are coequal to the dead bodies of Josephus' erstwhile comrades in the Jotapata cave, symbolic tokens of how the deviant Jewish collective sinfully killed itself. From this standpoint, the black comedy of Cleitus makes perfect sense. The bizarrely entangling physicality of a man lopping off both his hands; the way his captor (Josephus) keeps a deliberately staged distance from the mutilation; the fact that the Jotapata speech had appealed to Hellenistic custom as the standard by which hand-severance has symbolic import,[128] implying that Jewish morality during the rebellion lost credibility—such details aptly attest to Josephus' plight, trapped as he was, the Galilee commander of a rebellion he knew to be a grotesque assault on the Jewish political body, on nature, and on God.

NOTES

1. A more detailed description of Galilee's socioeconomic circumstances (with citations), through the second-century CE, appears in this volume's third chapter.

2. The precise intention of this reference to "Galileans" has intrigued scholars. One effort to decipher the reference is Solomon Zeitlin, "Who were the Galileans? New Light on Josephus' Activities in Galilee," *Jewish Quarterly Review*, vol. 64, no. 3 (January 1974): 189–203.

3. We review this archaeological work in several subsequent sections of this study.

4. Josephus, *The Jewish War* (Oxford: Oxford University Press, 2017), 28.

5. Geza Vermas, *The True Herod* (London: Bloomsbury, 2014), 48–56.

6. Richard Horsley (with John Hanson), *Bandits, Prophets and Messiahs* (Harrisburg: Trinity Press, 1999), 75.

7. Horsley, 75, citing Josephus, *Jewish Antiquities* 14:167.

8. Steve Mason, *Flavius Josephus: Life of Josephus* (Leiden: Brill, 2003), xv–xix; Shaye Cohen, *Josephus in Galilee and Rome* (Leiden: Brill, 2002), xv–xix; Tessa Rajak, *Josephus* (London: Duckworth, 2004), 13.

9. As a general in Galilee, Josephus claims he was scrupulous about not executing conspiratorial enemies: *Jewish War*, 154–7.

10. Vermas, 36–7.

11. Josephus, *Jewish War*, 38–40.

12. Martin Goodman, *Josephus's The Jewish War* (Princeton: Princeton University Press, 2019), 18–26.

13. Cohen, 107–8, n. 33. Cohen declares that "Josephus' Hasmonean ties are probably bogus."

14. The possible location of the ancient Arbela village has sparked commentary since Samuel ben Samson and Nachmanides in the thirteenth century; apparently in the 1980s, Mordecai Aviam and other local archaeologists suggested that caves at Mount Nitai might be ones described by Josephus, albeit not necessarily in this Ezekias story. Zvi Eilan, Avraham Ezderkat, *Arbel* (Tel Aviv: Kibbutz Movement Yediat Haaretz Department, 1988), 11–13.

15. Josephus, *Jewish War*, 41.

16. Ibid, 41–2.

17. This story of the old bandit and his family at Arbela has parallels in 2 Maccabees 6, regarding the elderly Eleazar, and the woman with seven sons, 2 Maccabees 7.

18. Josephus, *Jewish War*, 42.

19. Matthew 2: 16–18.

20. Anton van Hoof, *From Autothanasia to Suicide: Self-Killing in Classical Antiquity* (London: Routledge, 1990), 44.

21. Josephus, *Jewish War*, 47.

22. Vermas, 37.

23. Josephus, *Jewish War*, 321–2.

24. Ibid, 321.

25. Ibid, 187–90.

26. Rajak, 188; Goodman, *Josephus's*, 18.

27. Rajak, 91.

28. Cohen, 139, 229–30.

29. Ibid, 230.
30. Goodman, *Josephus's*, 11–13.
31. Josephus, *Jewish War*, 3; Goodman, *Josephus's*, 13.
32. The title of the book "presupposed a non-Jewish perspective." Goodman, *Josephus's*, 11. Versions of Josephus' text prepared for Jewish readers tended to change the title; the new names, such as *The Wars of the Jews* in Kalman Schulman's 1862 translation, pointed to internal Jewish dynamics, and thus catered to the interests of a Jewish readership. Goodman, Josephus's 101.
33. Josephus, *Jewish War*, 154.
34. Ibid, 157.
35. Ibid, 156.
36. Ibid, 150. This edition's editor, Martin Goodman, deems this figure "wholly imaginary" (424).
37. M. Avi-Yonah, "The Missing Fortress of Flavius Josephus," *Israel Exploration Journal*, vol. 3, no. 2 (1953): 94–8.
38. For a detailed survey: Mordecai Aviam, Peter Richardson, "Josephus' Galilee in Archaeological Perspective," in Mason, *Flavius Josephus*, 177–200. These authors conclude that "the number of cities, towns and villages mentioned by JOSEPHUS is close to the number of Roman-period sites identified during the survey in the Galilee and the Golan." (199)
39. To be sure, the Galilee origins of the rivalry with the "treacherous" John of Gischala are presented in detail in *JW*: Josephus, *Jewish War*, 151–2.
40. Goodman, *Josephus's*.
41. Nachman Ben-Yehuda, *The Masada Myth: Collective Memory and Mythmaking in Israel* (Madison: University of Wisconsin Press, 1995). Another study, written in a different analytic vein by a former student of the premier Israeli Masada excavators, is: Jodi Magness, *Masada: From Jewish Revolt to Modern Myth* (Princeton: Princeton University Press, 2019).
42. Shaye J.D. Cohen, "Masada: Literary Tradition, Archaeological Remains and the Credibility of Josephus," *Journal of Jewish Studies* 33, nos. 1–2 (Spring–Autumn 1982): 385–405.
43. Josephus, *Jewish War*, xxxiii. See, generally, Goodman's *Josephus's*.
44. Josephus, *Jewish War*, 103–8.
45. Mason, *Flavius*, 15–20.
46. In *The Jewish War* Josephus wrote pithily that the Pharisees have "a reputation for precise interpretation of the law." (107)
47. Josephus, *Jewish War*, 103.
48. Ibid.
49. One critical survey of Neusner's claim about Judaisms, and its influence, is: Seth Schwartz, "How Many Judaisms Were There?," *Journal of Ancient Judaism*, vol. 2, no. 2 (May 2011): 208–38.
50. Anthony Saldarini, *Matthew's Christian-Jewish Community* (Chicago: University of Chicago Press, 1994).
51. John Kampen, *Matthew within Sectarian Judaism* (New Haven: Yale University Press, 2019).

52. See footnote 8 above.
53. Mason, *Flavius*, 28–30.
54. For Justus: Tessa Rajak, "Justus of Tiberias," *The Classical Quarterly*, vol. 23, no. 2 (Nov. 1973): 345–68.
55. Mason, *Flavius*, 135–50.
56. See Cohen's critical summary of these interpretations of Justus' impact on Josephus: Cohen, *Josephus*, 15–16, 238–9.
57. See the discussion in: Uriel Rappaport, *Yohanan mi-Gush halav: me-hare ha-Galil el homot Yerushalayim* (Jerusalem: Shazar Institute, 2006), 55–8.
58. Ibid, 57.
59. Josephus, *Jewish War*, 151.
60. Rappaport, 57–8.
61. Ibid, 66–8.
62. Ibid, 69–72.
63. Josephus, *Jewish War*, 210–11.
64. Ibid, 209.
65. Rappaport, 61–6.
66. Mason, *Flavius*, 107–20.
67. Josephus, *Jewish War*, 151.
68. Ibid, 219.
69. Ibid, 228.
70. Seth Schwartz, *Imperialism and Jewish Society: 200 B.C.E. to 640 C.E.* (Princeton: Princeton University Press, 2001).
71. Martin Goodman, "Galilean Judaism and Judean Judaism," in William Horbury, W. D. Davies, John Sturdy (eds.), *The Cambridge History of Judaism* (Cambridge: Cambridge University Press, 1999), 596–617; F.X. Malinowski, *Galilean Judaism in the Writings of Flavius Josephus* (PhD thesis), Ann Arbor, 1973, 99; Lawrence Schiffman, "Was there a Galilean Halakhah," in Lee Levine (ed.), *The Galilee in Late Antiquity* (Cambridge, MA: Harvard University Press, 1992), 143–56.
72. Josephus, *Jewish War*, 209. See the analysis in Horsley, 79.
73. Josephus, *Jewish War*, 246–7.
74. Cohen, a noticeably sober and skeptical commentator on Josephus, strikes this chord when he writes: "Josephus may have invented names occasionally, although no certain instance can be cited." Cohen, *Josephus*, 38. Goodman (Josephus, *Jewish War*, xxvii) is skeptical about the possibility of exposing untruths in Josephus' writing ("It will not always be possible to discover which parts of his narrative are fabrications . . .").
75. Daniel Boyarin, *Unheroic Conduct: The Rise of Heterosexuality and the Invention of the Jewish Man* (Berkeley: University of California Press, 1997).
76. Reza Aslan, *Zealot: The Life and Times of Jesus of Nazareth* (New York: Random House, 2013).
77. Albert Schweitzer, *The Quest of the Historical Jesus: A Critical Study of its Progress from Reimarus to Wrede* (London: Adam and Charles Black, 1910).
78. Goodman, *Josephus's*.
79. See footnote 74.

80. Josephus, *Jewish War*, 302–3.
81. Josephus "is a highly emotive writer, as he more than once tells himself," observes Tessa Rajak, *Josephus*, 79.
82. Josephus, *Jewish War*, 303.
83. Ibid.
84. Horsley, 126–7.
85. Mason, *Flavius*, 163–4.
86. Josephus, *Jewish War*, 187–8.
87. Mason, *Flavius*, 172–3.
88. Rajak, *Josephus*, 223.
89. Mason, *Flavius*, 198.
90. Cohen, *Josephus*, 237–8.
91. Mason, *Flavius*, 98 n. 853.
92. Albert Memmi, *The Colonizer and the Colonized* (Boston: Beacon Press, 1991).
93. Josephus, *Jewish War*, 148.
94. Ernest Renan, *The Life of Jesus* (London: Watts, 1935).
95. The following descriptions appear in Josephus, *Jewish War*, 162–3.
96. For example: Sellah Merrill, *Galilee in the Time of Christ* (London: The Religious Tract Society, 1885), 63.
97. Josephus, *Jewish War*, 195.
98. Ibid, 150.
99. Ibid.
100. Ibid, 170.
101. Mason, *Flavius*, 18.
102. Schwartz, *Imperialism*, 38–48.
103. Mason, *Flavius*, 21–7.
104. Josephus, *Jewish War*, 200.
105. Ibid, 436 (for the editor's comment on 3:522).
106. Ibid, 199.
107. Ibid, 169.
108. Ibid, 183.
109. Ibid, 201.
110. Ibid, 185.
111. Mason, *Flavius*, 113.
112. Goodman, *Josephus's*, 83.
113. Ibid, 82.
114. Mason, *Flavius*, xxxvii, 84 n. 671.
115. Jonathan Boyarin, Daniel Boyarin, *Powers of Diaspora* (Minneapolis: University of Minnesota Press, 2002).
116. Mason, *Flavius*, 80. Josephus' geographical reference here is confusing (see Mason's explanation, 80 n. 615).
117. Ibid.
118. Ibid, 81.
119. Josephus, *Jewish War*, 152.

120. Mason, *Flavius*, 83 n. 657.
121. Ibid, 84.
122. Ibid.
123. Ibid, 84–7.
124. There are some discrepancies between the two texts' descriptions of the fake flotilla ruse (Mason, *Flavius*, 89; Josephus, *Jewish War*, 156). In *JW* Josephus actually cites the number of boats, 230, each boarded by no more than four boatman. Scholars closely heed Josephus' details in light of the January 1986 discovery, by members of Kibbutz Ginosar, of an ancient wooden boat in an exposed area of the lake, close to the mouth of Nahal Salmon, not far from the ancient site of Tarichaeae—the discovery sparked speculation that the boat might have taken part in Josephus' trick. Shelley Wachsmann, "The Excavations of an Ancient Boat in the Sea of Galilee," *Atiqot*, vol. XIX (1990).
125. The portrayal in Mason, *Flavius*, 90–1, makes repeated use of this term, "mob." See also: Josephus, *Jewish War*, 156–7.
126. Cohen, *Josephus* (110) calls this self-mutilation incident "near nonsense." See also Mason, *Flavius*, 91 n. 768.
127. Josephus, *Jewish War*, 188.
128. Ibid, 433 n.3:378.

Chapter 2

Jesus and Galilee

MONOTHEISTIC FRACTURE AFTER THE DESTRUCTION OF THE JERUSALEM TEMPLE

Decades after the destruction of Jerusalem's Second Temple, monotheism became plural. Judaism, structured as a Temple cult, was gone forever, as was its monopoly over monotheism. Its new iteration as a rabbinic religion centered on oral law commentary on Torah could not be fully perceptible to Josephus, since the compilation of the Mishnah under Judah the Prince happened later, as a third-century phenomenon. Earlier, from the late first century, this reinvention of Judaism wherein Talmudic study replaced the Temple's sacrificial cult, took root in Galilee, and as we have seen, there is some evidence that Josephus, based far away in Rome, identified early elements in this process, reaching out to Pharisees who quite possibly initiated this process of forging a new, post-Temple, accommodation with the Romans, and of reconfiguring Judaism.

Exactly at this moment, perhaps a decade and a half, after the Temple's destruction, another group of Jews was establishing what would become a new, rival, monotheistic religion, Christianity. Differing views about the implications of the Temple's destruction fueled this competition. The Pharisees and others who created rabbinic Judaism imagined that "Jewish law," the composite of commandments and ritualistic practice whose most sacrosanct expression had occurred in the Temple, would be refined and perfected through continuing exegetical study, increasingly detached not just from the decimated Temple and Jerusalem, but from the Holy Land itself. This was partly a myth because Temple Judaism and Talmudic Judaism can be seen as two different dialects of the same language. But this idea holding that the rabbis were preserving the essence of Jewishness proved lasting and powerful, so much so that many groups in Israel today imagine that the fulfillment of the state's creation, and of centuries of messianic expectation, will be the establishment of a Third Temple in Jerusalem (only persons on their extreme fringes claim to be willing to carry out acts of repossession on the Temple Mount to actualize this premise). Alternatively, the group of incipient Christian Jews who put together the Gospel of Matthew held mounting doubts about the relevance of Jewish law in the aftermath of the Temple's destruction. Reflecting this group's lingering Jewish loyalty, and, probably, diversity of opinion within it about the normative and practical prospects of ongoing and future proselytizing missions among gentiles, the Book of Matthew famously features Jesus' proclamations about intentions to "fulfill" Jewish law, rather than replacing it.[1] But the precise meaning of "fulfill" in this context has always remained open to interpretation, whereas the overall thrust of Matthew, as a gospel announcing the advent of a new religious law, fundamentally superseding the Jews' old, Mosaic, law, is quite unmistakable.

Matthew is immersed in supersession imagery jettisoning the Jewish law of Moses and also polemical invective against Pharisaical adherence to Jewish law. Laden within the gospel's progression to the Passion and beyond, within the drama of Jesus' ministry to Jews and his post-Resurrection instruction, promulgated on a Galilee mountaintop, to "make disciples of all nations,"[2] is renunciation of Jewish law and a vision of a new religion whose adherents will be gentiles. Matthew is a book about the necessity of creating a new faith in view of the fact that the Temple's quite recent destruction rendered Judaism, as it had been practiced, untenable. What really was to be done with Jewish law once the place where it was most awesomely upheld and practiced was smashed to the ground by the Romans?

Josephus and Matthew shared the same diagnosis as to why the calamity had transpired. Both believed that an immoral generation of Jews had lost God's favor and the Temple's decimation was, consequently, punishment. In Christianity's case, the religion's evolution as a response to this specific tragedy was beclouded or disguised by the gospel's retrospective narrative structure, as the story of a divine life that unfolded a few decades before the Temple's destruction. This sorrowful Temple event is explicitly predicted by Jesus, and also evoked by the gospel's imagery, but, of course, it cannot be described in an account that ends some forty years too early. Contemporary explications of the Matthew group which produced this gospel assume that a large portion, if not the entirety, of actions and sayings it attributes to Jesus were really fashioned out of concerns and challenges it faced around 80 CE, as it distanced itself from Jewish groups who were resolved to preserve Jewish law—interestingly, this assumption remains firmly intact even in interpretations which insist that the Matthew group essentially remained "Jewish."[3] While their explication could be abrasive to Christian believers who fundamentalistically apprehend gospel content as documentation of what Jesus actually said and did, these commentators have strong grounds to regard Matthew as a retrospective account whose contents are colored, in some measure, by knowledge of events subsequent to the Crucifixion and Resurrection, including the Temple's destruction. Here Matthew puts its cards on the table in 28:15, when it accuses Temple priests of bribing Roman soldiers and of fabricating a denial of the Resurrection: the priests' concocted story, Matthew writes, "has been widely circulated among the Jews to this day." Is it possible to read these words without acknowledging that this gospel was written by a Jesus follower, or followers, who was or were directly concerned to distance his/their testimony from the sensibilities and beliefs of rival Jewish groups, at some moment relatively long after Jesus' Crucifixion?

The Gospel of Matthew reads as a constant juggling act between, on the one hand, present, or forward-looking anticipation of, "fulfillment" of prophecy, and, on the other hand, supersession of Jewish law warranted by the recent, apocalyptic fulfillment of prophecy.[4] Of all the balls juggled in the air, none rises higher and more formidably than the Temple. One revealing apocalyptic passage, 24:15–22, claims to look to the future, reiterating doomsday prophecy from Daniel. In fact, as Swiss theologian Ulrich Luz writes, these verses "clearly refer to the events of the Jewish War."[5] Using Jesus as its anachronistic spokesman, the Matthew group here laments the Temple's destruction as an event of "great distress, unequalled from the beginning of the world until now":

> So when you see standing in the holy place "the abomination that cause desolation," spoken of through the prophet Daniel—let the reader understand—then let those who are in Judea flee to the mountains. Let no one on the housetop go down to take anything out of the house. Let no one in the field go back to get their cloak. How dreadful it will be in those days for pregnant women and nursing mothers! Pray that your flight will not take place in winter or on the Sabbath. For then there will be great distress, unequaled from the beginning of the world until now—and never to be equaled again.

Such verses, scholars insist, "represent a backward glance," but there is no strong reason to believe that as time marched on, Matthew's readers grasped how this gospel uses and polemicizes historical events in a power struggle against rival Jewish leadership groups which was waged when the Temple rubble was seen or recollected quite vividly in everyone's eyes. As time moved on, most New Testament readers had little reason or incentive to reflect upon how they were perusing a text that presents one, innovative, solution to a problem shared by rival groups of persistent Jews, and withdrawers from Judaism, after the Temple's destruction in 70 CE. After all, in their express content, the gospels are about an experience undergone decades before. Analogously, if we imagine a book written in the 1870s about conflicts between Federalists and Republicans in the early years of American statehood, we can presume that its underlying agenda might "really" pertain to the Civil War, whereas many unassuming readers would quite reasonably believe that they were learning about Thomas Jefferson and John Adams.

Galilee was where Jewish and Christian responders to this shared problem of the Temple's destruction worked out their new solutions. Galilee was the region removed from the moral or political disfiguration in Jerusalem that produced the tragedy—from the rigid scholasticism and materialistic corruption of the priests and Pharisees, on the Christian view, or from the purblind anti-Roman zealots who congregated around the Temple in the climactic phases of the revolt, on Josephus' interpretation. Galilee was both prelude and aftermath to the Temple catastrophe. Both Jesus' disciples and Josephus prepare readers for their accounts' climactic moments in Jerusalem by elaborating on their heroes' Galilee prelude. In Matthew, resurrected Jesus and his disciples regather in Galilee after the Crucifixion, in preparation for Christianity's mission to the gentiles. In Judaism, by the second or third century, the codifiers of the Mishnah regathered in Galilee, paving the way for rabbinic Judaism. Galilee, in these and other senses, was the place in the world where monotheism became a pluralistic phenomenon, for better or worse. In the foundational texts of Jewish history, and of Christian faith, Galilee plays essentially the same function. If anything normatively worthwhile is to be accomplished, the hero, in both cases, must "win" Galilee.

In both cases, the hero cannot be a straight-talker. Both Josephus and Jesus have secret circles of true followers, comprised, in the first case, of Jewish pragmatists opposed to the anti-Roman revolt, and, with Jesus, of believers who recognize his uniqueness or divinity. Neither can address the Galileans, the region's masses, without ambiguity or perhaps even dissimulation. Josephus attests to having won the loyal support of the Galileans; to the extent that the claim is not simply specious, it is nevertheless problematic, since Josephus has consistently lied to Galilee's Jewish masses, and his military leadership cannot forestall devastating defeat at Jotapata and elsewhere. Jesus, in evident ways, wins a large following in Galilee, but these followers remain a crowd, differentiated from his true disciples. Jesus sometimes excoriates Galilee population groups, and there remain various doubts about the ethno-religious status of the region's crowds. Tellingly, the hero has no direct, unmediated relationship with masses in the Galilee, even though this is a placid region (at least compared to Judea) where the two religions will be established or resurrected. With Jesus, the Galilee crowd must be healed, or spoken to in parables, and its loyalty is not unquestionable. Galilee remains somehow inaccessible, and its population in nobody's pocket. In the broadest sense, the morally and politically ungovernable Galilee mass becomes a metaphor for monotheism's ultimate failure, for its inability to remain whole and universal. The region's core population made two monotheistic faiths possible, but this population's intractability also presaged limits in the reach of these religions.

Jesus, in Matthew, speaks to the Galilee crowds in parables because his message about the kingdom of heaven is incomprehensible to them. "Knowledge of the secrets of the kingdom of heaven has been given to you," Jesus tells the disciples, "but not to them [the Galilee crowds]."[6] The passage's reference to Isaiah 6:9 ("You will be ever hearing but never understanding; you will be ever seeing but never perceiving") problematizes Galilee's place in the gospels. Isaiah's prophesy was popular among early Christians as the foretelling of the way Jews would reject the Messiah.[7] So, arguably, its placement in Matthew suggests that Jesus healed and worked miracles in Galilee for naught. In the end, what he had to say to its population was unfathomable parable. It bears mention that the key point about Galilee, as the venue where monotheism multiplied, is that prophetic or divine knowledge always becomes segmented in it—the distinction in the gospels is not always between the disciples and the Galilee masses. Some passages in Matthew, for example, 11:25–30, contrasts the simple wisdom of "babes" (more precisely, *nepioi*, "simple ones") and the uncomprehending arrogance of Jewish intellectual-religious elites.[8]

In Josephus, the hero's message of pragmatic accommodation with Rome cannot be reasonably communicated to the obstreperous Galileans, whereas in Matthew Christianity's eschatology is opaque to the region's masses. Many in Galilee apprehend Jesus' uniqueness, and therefore follow him on his final journey to Jerusalem, but the failure of his message to penetrate seamlessly in the region is evidenced by how often the gospel returns to the division between Jesus' disciples who grasp the eschatology, albeit imperfectly, and the masses who mostly do not. The seating arrangement at the Sermon on the Mount demonstrates this problematic—Jesus preaches primarily to his disciples, but the Galilee masses are also there to hear him, comprehendingly or not.

THE GOSPEL OF MATTHEW AND GALILEE

Of the synoptic gospels, we focus on Matthew, rather than Mark or Luke, for identifiable reasons. Matthew is acknowledged as the most "Jewish" gospel owing to its continuing reference to the Hebrew Bible (*Tanakh*) and also to Jewish rituals and outlooks. Much of this referencing is critical or even (as in the case of Matthew: 23) virulently polemical, but the recent

Figure 2.1   Map of Galilee in Jesus' Time. *Source*: From Henry Ward Beecher's 1871 volume, *Life of Jesus, the Christ*. (Beecher, 1871, 254)

trend in scholarship is to claim that this negativity actually demonstrates how Matthew and his followers were still located, socially and emotionally, within Palestine's post-Temple Jewish society. As incipient Christians, they quarreled with Jewish compatriots about Jewish law, and they probably contemplated the possibility that Jesus' bequest to them ultimately was its annulment. But the dispute had characteristics of a family quarrel. In a sociological sense, Matthew's reference point is Jewry. Judaism was the religion/culture with which Matthew's group was still connected, and, at the time of the gospel's composition, the group could only have been imagining departure from Jewishness, the only identity it truly knew and had. Social science theory, claims Anthony Saldarini, supports this claim about how Matthew's negativity about Pharisees and other Jewish subjects reflects the group's continuing Jewishness. "Social science theory has established that nonconformity, resistance to social structures and deviance are, paradoxically, always part of a functioning society," he writes. To posit that Matthew's grievances reflect a true break with the Jewish community is "contrary to normal sociological processes."[9] Focusing on dynamics in Jewish culture between 165 BCE and 100 CE, J. Andrew Overman highlights phenomena of sectarianism, of tendencies of alienated, dissenting groups to castigate dominant groups, be they Pharisees or some other faction. Such groups, including Matthew's, remained within the Jewish frame, their dissent betokening its sectarianism, rather than actual departure from it, Overman suggests.[10] John Kampen makes much the same point, and also views sectarianism in this broad time frame, one which begins and ends decades before and after Jesus. As a specialist on the Dead Sea Scrolls, Kampen's strategy is to show how phrases in texts discovered in the Qumran caves, and dynamics reflected in these texts, show how a dissenting sectarian group like the Essenes remained within the fold of Judaism in a manner analogous to how Matthew's sectarian group remained Jewish. In actual fact, the question of whether Matthew (i.e., the individual or group responsible for the gospel's composition) was "Jewish" could be moot because the meaning of Judaism in the aftermath of the Temple's destruction was in flux (searching for a fixed identity label in the late first century CE, some scholars use the term "formative Judaism," meaning the precursor of rabbinic Judaism[11]). Whether the term "sectarian" is the label most evocatively suggestive of the Matthew group's lingering (albeit contentious) connection to whatever shape post-Temple Judaism had at the time is similarly inapposite. Matthew is interesting because of the intensity of its connection to Judaism: as testimonial to the interaction between Jews and Jesus' followers, prior to the formal establishment of a new monotheistic faith, it is the gospel of singular import, for our purposes.

Still more to our point: Matthew is profoundly interesting because of its suggestions as to how Galilee facilitated this interaction. Nothing definitive can be said about the status of Matthew's group, but in view of the gospel's evocations of urban culture, as well as its philippic against the Sanhedrin, some have concluded that it itself was Galilean, and resided in one of the region's two cities, Tiberias or Sepphoris, cited by Josephus as home to this Jewish assembly, the Sanhedrin, at times in the first century.[12]

Some scholars have wondered openly about Galilean locality in Matthew. "No distinctive Galilean point of view emerges in the Gospel of Matthew," proclaimed theology scholar Sean Freyne.[13] In the Gospel of Mark, Freyne believed, Galilee, studded with synagogues, comes across as being "thoroughly Jewish in character," and the region is not bordered by antagonistic religious cultures, meaning that Jesus travels freely into the Dekapolis, Tyre, and Sidon, thus bestowing upon this gospel an atmospheric sense of border crossing and fallen barriers (as evoked by the morally innovative table fellowship scene, Mark 2:13-17, where Jesus comingles with sinners and tax collectors).[14] I propose taking Freyne's suggestion in an unexpected direction: it seems to me that Matthew's Galilee viewpoint is interesting because it is not "thoroughly Jewish." We are living in an age wherein political correct homilies about how "Jesus was a Jew" are perceived as the solely appropriate response to the way late-nineteenth-century racial theories attempted to Aryanize Jesus by imagining that he was raised in a Galilee of the Gentiles (as Matthew 4:15 mentions, following Isaiah 9), and was therefore not really Jewish. This racist exploitation of Matthew's hints about gentile presence in Galilee reached its apotheosis in Nazi research and ideology, and its effort to eradicate Semitic roots of western civilization.[15] But when did it become wise to ignore a subject because very bad people murderously exploited and disfigured it? The intentions of people today who willfully overlook ambiguities in the New Testament about Galilee, and Jesus' life in it, are honorable, insofar as they are concerned about enhanced interfaith understanding, just several decades after the Holocaust. However, in addition to the fact that they are reading passages in Matthew, including Jesus' outbursts about Pharisees and other Jewish notables, in a way dissimilar to the way the gospel was beheld by readers for centuries, they are proceeding on a faulty spiritual theory. The most promising way to further interfaith understanding between Christians and Jews is for members of both groups to examine scrupulously how creative tensions are embedded in formative texts, without a presumption or policy of politically correct censorship—interfaith understanding that proceeds on the premise that members of one group ought to make concessions about its own scripture "because of history" is a misnomer, since it has nothing to do with understanding.

On this thinking, examination of Matthew's confusing Galilee, rather than Mark's manifestly Jewish region, constitutes a more enlightening exercise. The complexities of Jewish-Christian interaction will persist long beyond the early twenty-first century; they will not be defused because some scholars, theologians, and activists decided after the Holocaust to elevate a speculative postulate, "Jesus was a Jew," to the level of dogma. The postulate is problematic because it glosses a series of vexing questions. What would being Jewish in Galilee have meant, during the first three decades of the first century CE?

How might producers of a compilation, such as the Gospel of Matthew, been thinking about Jewishness in years following the Temple's destruction, when they themselves might have been living in Galilee?

Finally, it seems prudent to base a discussion of Galilee and Jesus on Matthew because this is the gospel which features the Sermon on the Mount as its centerpiece, and is thus the most morally impactful. The sermon's inclusion suggests that Matthew had at his command materials, and a wealth of accumulated interpretation and reflection, that is lacking in the other gospels. Not every commentator in the modern era has accepted the sequential premise that Matthew was written with Mark already in view, nor has everyone accepted the "Q" source theory holding that Matthew and Luke, but not Mark, had at their disposal some early church cataloguing of Jesus' sayings, but these, by and large, are the accepted views. Their implication is that Matthew is an edited and, morally, a farther-reaching, version of Mark. "One might view Matthew's Gospel as a new edition of Mark with an extended new introduction and a totally revised internal structure," Ulrich Luz authoritatively opined.[16]

The Gospel of Matthew is a triangle, with Jesus its apex, and its three sides consisting of Judaism, Christianity, and Galilee. If we imagine an isosceles configuration, with Judaism and Christianity claiming sides of equal length, the gospel's mystery is whether the third, unequal, Galilean side was long or short on Judaism.

More than a record of the tragedy and (from the Christian standpoint) miraculous resurrection of Jesus, Matthew's ambiguities do more than foretell the impending challenges and tragedies of Jewish-Christian relations. They make them necessary.

GALILEE OF THE GENTILES

"In the past he humbled the land of Zebulun and the land of Naphtali, but in the future he will honor Galilee of the gentiles" (Isaiah: 9:1).

Matthew's Galilee narrative begins after Jesus' baptism, when he returns to Galilee after hearing that John has been imprisoned. "Leaving Nazareth, he went and lived in Capernaum, which was by the lake in the area of Zebulun and Naphtali—to fulfill what was said through the prophet Isaiah."[17] Matthew's documentation of this sequence underscores this gospel's fundamental ambiguity: What does it mean when it announces that Jesus' pronouncements and experiences "fulfill" Jewish prophesy or law? Are they carrying out what Jews prayed and imagined for themselves, within their evolving religion's normative horizons? Or in this gospel's context, does the

Greek term for "fulfillment," *pleroma*, allude to a major abridgement or rearrangement of these Jewish prayers and expectations, essentially an overhaul? How often, in Matthew, does *pleroma* relate to the perfect consummation of Jewish laws and prophecies (either via their refinement, or their scrupulous actualization); alternatively, how often does fulfillment really mean "replacement," or in the theological idiom, their "supersession?" Where does "fulfillment" end and supersession begin? In this case, Matthew casts Jesus' return to his native Galilee as the fulfillment of Isaiah's prophecy (9:1–2): the quotation is not an accurate rendering of the Hebrew text,[18] and the parallel evoked by the key phrase in Isaiah's prophesy, "Galilee of the Gentiles," is troublingly imprecise. Isaiah prognosticated about the return of Jews to their land, starting from Galilee in the north, after the trauma of the Assyrian captivity—the prophet predicts the return of Jews to Galilee, a region whose population presumably became mostly gentile during this captivity episode. Jesus' ministry in Galilee does not appear to be dedicated to repopulating a gentile region with Jews, but Matthew depicts him as though he is carrying out acts which are literal reenactments of Isaiah's prophesy. Jesus leaves his native Nazareth, and moves to Capernaum, by the Sea of Galilee, and close to lands of Zebulun and Naphtali, in accord with Isaiah, whose prophesy refers to return to Zebulun and Naphtali.

What do we really know about the demography of Galilee in Jesus' time? To whom was he ministering in Galilee: Jews of well-rooted identity, relatively recently converted Jews of wavering commitment to Jewish law, or gentiles? In what way—metaphorical, literal, polemical—does Matthew refer to Galilee of the Gentiles? Was this a familiar turn of phrase?

We can start with the last question, because its assessment is easier, being grounded in textual evidence. Matthew 4:15 is an abrupt, hugely impactful reference. Beyond the aforementioned mention in Isaiah, referring to quite different circumstances of the Assyrian Captivity, there is a striking dearth of circulated references to Galilee of the Gentiles. That is to say, this phrase, one which profoundly influenced generations of preachers and believers whenever they thought about the character of Jesus' ministry, and the reasons underlying Christianity's rise out of Judaism, is primarily an invention of Matthew.

Mark Chancey, author of an argumentative study who insists that the image of a significant gentile presence in first-century CE Galilee is an outright myth, points out that of sixty-one references to Galilee in the gospels and Acts, only Matthew 4:15 alludes to the region as Galilee of the Gentiles. Moreover, he notes, this phrase "occurs only a handful of times out of hundreds of ancient pagan and Jewish references to the region." Incidentally, the term's earlier use in Isaiah could have arisen etymologically in description to Galilee's geopolitical circumstances, rather than its demography. "Galilee"

(גליל) apparently originated as a geometric term, referring to a cylinder or a circle, and then its meaning morphed, becoming "district." It is not a salient term in the Hebrew Bible, being found there just six times. "Galilee" might have found usage because of the region's circular-seeming shape, being surrounded by the Jordan rift, the coastal plain, mountains, and the Plain of Esdraelon. Or the term "Galilee" might have gained currency because of historical experiences, through the Second Temple period, in which the region's Israelites were encircled by gentile cities.[19]

The modifier "of the Gentiles" was clearly Matthew's editorial insertion, one which had scanty textual pedigree, apart from Isaiah. In view of this gospel's fixation with the fulfillment or supersession issue, it seems reasonable to suppose that Matthew's writers reclaimed the phrase, Galilee of the Gentiles, to underscore the *textual* continuity (on the fulfilment mode), or discontinuity (on the supersession mode), between Jesus' ministry in Galilee, on the one hand, and prophecy in what became known as the Jews' Old Testament, on the other hand. Considerations of textual congruity resurrected it from Isaiah—the phrase was not necessarily resuscitated as a bona fide description of Galilee's society a few decades into the first century, CE.

Nonetheless, the phrase's demographic implications had, over the ages, powerful theological and cultural consequences. In antiquity and then, via "ghetto" mythology through the nineteenth century, Jewish identity became associated with parochialism, as contrasted with the universal aspirations of Jesus' preaching and Christianity's practices. In this connection, "Galilee of the Gentiles" had a useful cosmopolitan ring. It implied that Christianity inherited, among other things, the philosophical-moral insights, and practical ingenuity, of Greco-Roman culture, whereas Judaism ghettoized owing to the obstinate legalism and superficial materialism which Matthew attributed to Jesus' pharisaical and priestly interlocutors. Yet more darkly, after the second half of the nineteenth century, pseudo-scientific racial categories grafted onto these distinctions. If first-century CE Galilee was significantly gentile, then Jesus, in his human iteration, could not really have been a Semite. In other words, the turn of phrase in Matthew 4:15 provided a safety hatch for influential anti-Semitic writers like Houston Stewart Chamberlain, whose racial theories of history would otherwise have been snagged and stalled by an obvious question: if Jesus were a Jew, how is it that the West's Christian Civilization had not been irretrievably damned and doomed by all the negative traits Chamberlain and others attributed, in their pathological rage and screed, to Semites?

Of course, not all commentators who upheld the Galilee of the Gentiles theory were motivated by such racist animus. On its most innocent level, the phrase poses one possible solution to a genuinely intriguing question, one which naturally arises on any serious reading of Matthew. Who were these people who became Jesus' early followers? Could they have been dyed-in-the-wool Jews whose dedication to their religion's evolving laws and rites, based on the Temple cult, was rooted in many decades of experience, in their own generation, and in those of their Galilee ancestors? If so, what happened to them? Was Jewish law, coupled to Roman tax obligations and other pressures, becoming too burdensome to them (Classics and Religion scholar Richard Horsley, who emphasizes not gentile populations, but rather Jewish banditry in Galilee, follows this economic line of analysis, referring to the yoke of "double taxation, Jewish and Roman"[20])? Is Matthew referring anachronistically to Jews in Galilee in his group's own era, following the collapse of the anti-Roman revolt, when disenchantment and trauma, and sudden liberation from Temple-centered pilgrimages and rites, possibly unhinged them from their religious law? Or were some of these people converts, not from Judaism, but from paganism to Judaism, meaning that their Jewish roots were relatively shallow?

However they answered such questions, or ignored them, an impressive roster of Christian theologians have taken literally the description, Galilee of the Gentiles. Liberal theologian Shirley Jackson Case, for instance, who in the early twentieth century published extensively on the rise of early Christianity and the historical Jesus, identified Sepphoris as the prime source of Galilean cosmopolitanism in Jesus' day. This town, within walking distance of Nazareth, was populated by "Jews and foreigners," Case believed. Anticipating claims that circulated later in the twentieth century, he reasoned that Sepphoris' non-Jewish strata deeply influenced the young Jesus. This encounter with Sepphoris, Case wrote in a 1926 article, explains the "unconventionality of Jesus in mingling freely with the common people, his generosity toward the stranger and the outcast, and his conviction of the equality of all classes before God."[21]

Chancey cites one quotation, the "Jesus Christ" entry in *The Interpreter's Dictionary of the Bible* written by F.C. Grant," which reads as a catchall synopsis of the "Galilee of the Gentiles" interpretation. "Jesus was a Galilean," wrote Grant. "This fact was of far-reaching significance for his whole career. For Galilee was the 'Circle of the Gentiles,' either because it was surrounded by foreign nations or because (in later times) the Jews there were surrounded by foreigners . . . [Galilee] had not always been Jewish territory. In the days of Jesus there were many non-Jews, especially Syrians, Phoenicians, Arameans, Greeks and Romans, living there."[22] Touching all the bases in this short, dense entry, Grant stressed eras when Jews reportedly evacuated Galilee, including the Assyrian episode, and the Maccabean War (when Jews were brought to Judea for their own safety). Galilee's cosmopolitan character in Jesus' day supported his creed's break with the Jews' view of themselves as a chosen, exceptional people: "How could a boy fail to be impressed with the vastness of the world, with the improbability of God's exclusive concern for one people only, when daily before his eyes came 'many from east and west' (Matthew 8:11), gentiles who might be seeking not only the riches of this world but also the kingdom of God!"[23]

Sifting through textual sources and archaeological findings, Chancey adamantly rejects speculation about a mixed Galilee population in Jesus' day. "For the most part," he concludes, "gentiles are low profile—even invisible—in the historical record of first-century Galilee." Galilee, as far as this scholar is concerned, was wholly Jewish, with the sole, known gentile minority being a Greek population sector in Tiberias which Josephus' claims was liquidated early in the anti-Rome revolt. The Book of Matthew's conspicuous gentile, the faithful centurion introduced at 8:5,[24] was probably not Roman, Chancey reasons; instead, he belonged to Herodian forces that were, at least nominally, ethnonational confederates with Galilee Jews. It is not until the second century CE when we find records of a significant gentile presence in Galilee, and this population is comprised mainly of Roman soldiers and their entourage.[25]

Chancey energetically musters evidence from archaeological excavations to support his contentions about an almost entirely gentile-free Galilee in Jesus' day, but his aggressively argued study only proves that there is little evidence of significant pagan sectors in the region at this time. Once it is shorn of its racial Aryanism, and of its less sinister variants whereby commentators, extrapolating on Matthew 4:15, made unsubstantiated demographic claims about the region, the "Galilee of the Gentiles" theory has meaningfully suggestive shades. Chancey and others are surely correct when they point out that archaeological findings of Greco-Roman influence upon decorative items or various utensils in excavated homes at key Galilee settlements, most notably Sepphoris, does not mean that Jews did not dwell in them. In all likelihood, Jews *did* live in such first century CE Galilee homes—yet, apart from fundamentalists who won't let any empirical facts bother their faith, and completely disinterested atheists, people would find it quite interesting to know (if it can be proven) that Jesus grew up in Galilee amidst, or next to, a complicated, somewhat eclectic, Jewish culture, one in which elite Jews in Sepphoris and elsewhere were demonstrating some sort of interest in outside culture, and possibly lacked deep-stretching roots in Judaism. What are we to make of contradictorily spirited passages in Matthew, one where Jesus seems personally at home, and mesmerizingly popular, in and around Capernaum,[26] as opposed to others where he curses the faithlessness of local residents?[27] Quite simply, the gospels read one way if we assume that Galilee was filled with devout, well-rooted Jews, and they read another way if we assume that *shades* of the Galilee of the Gentiles theory are plausible. Writing as a Jew, not as a Christian, I feel comfortable attributing a fair measure of historicity to Matthew, and the other synoptic Gospels. I *want* to believe that the Sermon on the Mount was delivered, but I find it impossible not to wonder about what sort of Jews listened to it. By the same token, as an academic specializing in Modern Jewish History, the *first* question I ask myself when hearing a report about how "Jews" have done this or that in America, or Israel, relates to whether these are Orthodox or modernized groups. This is because such categories, however, blunt and imperfect, are the best, readymade, measuring sticks of crucial attitudinal and motivational questions. Were the Jews who might have heard the Sermon two thousand years ago, on a hilly peak quite close to where I write these words, culturally inclusive and experimentally receptive types? Or were they strictly beholden to Jewish law, themselves and their ancestors having devoted time, resources, and spiritual energy to it?

What is Matthew saying when he repeatedly refers to how Jesus "withdraws" to and from Galilee? This happens because he is too popular, or because he is too unpopular, in the region? Galilee was almost certainly not "gentile," but isn't a shade of this theory, referring to its level of Jewishness, pertinent to such basic issues of gospels interpretation?

When he is not too busy deconstructing the "myth" of gentile Galilee, Chancey implicitly acknowledges that such shades are crucial and have never been sufficiently clarified. Isn't it significant that the place in the world where Judaism most momentously lost traction to a rival group, a group which went on to establish another monotheistic religion, was populated by persons whose *grandparents* or great-grandparents were not Jews by birth, and were perhaps instead Ituraeans, or, perhaps, Phoenicians? Chancey lends credence to this question when he writes about the Hasmonean conquest of Galilee in 104–103 BCE (led by Aristobulus)—following Josephus' reference in *Antiquities* (13: 318–19), scholars have reasoned that this conquest re-established Galilee's Jewish character, via the conversion of whoever was inhabiting it at the time.[28] Chancey underscores the import of this event: "Perhaps no event is as significant for understanding Galilee's subsequent population as Aristobulus's conquest."[29]

That is a coyly understated way of formulating an issue that has remained of utmost import in Christian-Jewish relations, in modern times—an issue which, in some contexts, has indeed defined modernity itself. As we will see in our next volume, following the eighteenth-century Enlightenment, when Jewish and Christian spokesmen became involved in a high-stakes quest for the historical Jesus, presumptions about the ethno-religious un-rootedness of first-century Galilean Jewry became a crucial component in the debate. Both Abraham Geiger, a founder of Reform Judaism and a Jewish communal leader who became deeply engaged by "was Jesus Jewish" sorts of debates,[30] and Heinrich Graetz, author of the first presumptively scientific history of the Jews, were thinking about this Hasmonean episode and its suggestion that Galilean Jews were the descendants of converts, when they staked out their apologetic positions in a debate where Christian theologians held the cards. Essentially, they stood upside down what twenty-first century archaeologists who talk about a Greco-Roman "overlay" at Jewish sites such as Sepphoris are suggesting: for Geiger and Graetz, Jewish listeners at the Sermon on the Mount were not cultural sophisticates who were receptive to new, stimulating ideas, but ignorant peasants with thin roots in Jewish culture, *amei ha'aretz*.[31] The original, "small band" of Jesus followers was comprised of the "low and vulgar," including tax collectors and other types of mercenaries who had formerly sold their souls to the Romans, Geiger wrote.[32] The provincial Galilee, Graetz wrote, "was far behind Judea in mental attainment and knowledge of the law." Proximate to the heathen Syrians, the Galileans had adopted innumerable superstitions, and in their ignorance, they attributed illness to demons, Graetz added.[33] Thus, in the modern period, as new forms of Biblical criticism took root, shades of the Galilee of the Gentiles theory preoccupied Jewish communal spokesmen. Preeminent figures like Geiger and Graetz were saying that Jesus was preaching to *amei ha'aretz*, not to Jews who were fully whole, in ethno-cultural senses.

What is ongoing archaeological research in Israel's north saying about the Galilee of the Gentiles hypothesis?

The answer to this question is quite a lot, but nothing that has been processed and disseminated with a kind of unifying logic that might stimulate intelligent interfaith dialogue between Jews and Christians. Archaeological research in the Galilee undertaken by foreign scholars has levels of coordination with an Israeli institutional framework, the country's Antiquities Authority. But this Authority has no connection to an Israeli university that is accountable to the past, present, and future of Galilee. One public college in Galilee (Kinneret College, on the Sea of Galilee) has developed a small "Galilean Archaeology" unit, but regional colleges in Israel's nondisputed peripheral regions lack laboratories and research infrastructure, and have no ability to sustain serious, long-term field research, or to disseminate research findings systematically in the global academic community (in contrast, for political reasons, an educational project catering to militant West Bank settlers, Ariel College in the disputed territories, was upgraded to university status over the past decade by Israel's right-wing governments, much to the benefit of its archaeology unit). Just a handful of Israelis researchers contributed importantly to the past generation of field research on Galilee in the Roman era, and the bulk of their work was conducted under the auspices of North American universities based in the United States. Just a few such Israeli archaeologists, most prominently Prof. Mordecai Aviam (who now heads Kinneret College's archaeology unit), actually managed to live in the region of their scholarly interest, and find employment in a public college in the Galilee. In other words, due to the absence of a university in Galilee, archaeological work in it is effectively outsourced, and it lacks the sort of analytic continuity of give-and-take refinement of hypotheses which occurs when local experts, solidly supported by a university framework, confer with outside authorities who bring their own perspectives.

These foreign excavators have reached exciting conclusions. Galilee in the time of Jesus' lifetime witnessed significant demographic growth and settlement expansion, this recent archaeological work suggests. During the rule of Herod's son, the tetrarch Antipas (who ruled from 4 BCE to 39 CE, a period spanning Jesus' lifetime) two towns took form in the region—Sepphoris was reconstructed and Tiberias was established, each reaching a population of about 10,000. Moreover, this research shows, between the late Hellenistic and early Roman periods there was a veritable explosion of small locales in Galilee—in eastern lower Galilee, a leap from nineteen to forty-one sites occurred in this period, and there was a jump from ten to thirty sites in the southern (Mount Tabor) end of the lower Galilee, along with a rise from 106 to 170 sites in Upper Galilee. Extrapolating on the basis of such evidence of settlement expansion, one scholar estimates that the population of Galilee probably doubled in the century that elapsed between 50 BCE to 50 CE.[34]

Such findings militate against the idea that Jesus grew up in crushing cultural isolation in Nazareth. Driving home this point, James Strange, a religious studies professor at the University of South Florida who for decades after 1969 participated in Galilee excavations, concluded that "there seems to be little reason to continue to insist that Galilee was isolated in any sense." In a 1997 publication, Strange claimed that forty Galilean villages were located within one day's walking distance from Sepphoris.[35]

Situated just a few miles from Jesus' home in Nazareth, Sepphoris was a cultural crossroads. Its positioning is crucial. Popular contemporary commentators speculate that Jesus of Nazareth can almost be called Jesus of Sepphoris, since he might have labored extensively in the town. Reza Aslan, for example, hypothesizes that Jesus "would have spent most of his life not in the tiny hamlet of Nazareth," but rather "in the cosmopolitan capital of Sepphoris," working from sunup to sundown "building palatial houses for the Jewish aristocracy."[36] Not necessarily rejecting such speculation, scholars need to explain the New Testament's utter silence about Sepphoris (the other Galilee city, Tiberias, gets passing mention in the New Testament, in the Book of John, but only as a way of referring to the Sea of Galilee[37]). Duke University scholar Eric Meyers accounts for this reticence by hypothesizing that Jesus would have avoided preaching at a locale like Sepphoris, since his messages would have been "uncongenial" to its upper class inhabitants, who were loyal to Antipas.[38]

Pushing for a view of Jesus coming of age in a relatively cosmopolitan culture, Strange argues that in a locale such as Sepphoris, Jews "participated more or less completely" in Roman "public space." Sepphoris was the hub of a "highly developed, local trade network in Galilee," and even small Galilee villages such as Kfar Hananiah and Nahaf were connected to this grid, producing pottery vessels for well-to-do, Romanized, inhabitants of Sepphoris. On the other hand, Strange acknowledges that excavations have identified evidence of a cohesive Jewish "private culture" in locales such as Sepphoris. Archaeological work has unearthed an array of Jewish ritualistic items, such as purification mikvot baths, on a scope sufficient to bar conjecture about how Jewish elites in Sepphoris who might have employed a carpenter from Nazareth would necessarily have been thoroughly assimilated Romans.[39]

The archaeological debate focuses on whether a likely site of Jesus' youthful daily labors, prior to the departure on his three-year ministry, had a Greco-Roman "urban overlay," or was primarily Jewish. This is a fascinating question, but it is not completely resolvable on the level of archaeological research. The problem with archaeology is that it only cracks the surface, literally and figuratively. Strange, who died in 2018 after investing great labor in Galilee archaeology, and who insisted that Jesus' home milieu had a conspicuous Roman veneer, made a telling admission, acknowledging that this "urban overlay" finding "does not tell us whether the local citizenry was glad or sad about Rome's presence."

Nonetheless, the emergence of two Roman-styled towns in rural Galilee under Antipas' rule has to have had great significance in the region's cultural and spiritual life, simply because this was a new development. Trying to measure the effects of these two enclaves of Galilee urbanization in the period of Jesus' life, Israeli archaeologist Mordechai Aviam looks backward. The question of whether Galilee was in social and cultural upheaval in Jesus' time can best be evaluated if we consider what happened socially and politically in the region prior to Antipas, he reasons.[40] Coarse ware found at the heart of Galilee, at a locale known as the "Beer Sheba of Galilee," hints that before Herod, in the late Hellenistic period, Galilee played host to Jewish demographic and cultural revival, Aviam believes. Early in the Second Temple period, Jewish patriots in Galilee resisted Herod's Romanization campaign. King Herod, in turn, "never forgot" this Galilean resistance, and in sharp contrast to his monumental building in other regions of the country, King Herod never sponsored major projects in Galilee. Possibly, Aviam believes, Herod deliberately antagonized the region's Jews—Aviam's excavations have uncovered suggestive evidence of nonkosher animal remains in Galilee, and of mikvot converted into garbage dumps, all dating from the Herodian period.

Antipas' reversed his father's course in the Galilee, embarking on signature, Roman construction projects in Sepphoris and Tiberias. Taken together, the gridded roads, aqueducts, an elaborate entry gate (on Tiberias' southern side), and a cardo (in Sepphoris, probably dating from the period of Jesus' life), and possibly theaters, can only mean that Jesus would have seen daily a prominent Roman landscape "overlay" when he worked in Sepphoris. On this point, the Israeli archaeologist Aviam concurs with conclusions reached by North American scholars who work mostly in New Testament studies. However, he too is limited by archaeology's fatal flaw, its inability to apply its physical findings in complicated cultural realms. As the chief excavator at Jotapata, the symbol (it will be recalled) of Jewish patriotism in Galilee during the anti-Roman revolt, Aviam is not sure whether a Romanized "overlay" means that residents of a Galilean settlement were assimilated accommodators of Rome. At Jotapata, Aviam's teams unearthed a mansion with Roman frescos on a wall—that is, even at Jotapata, the archetypal symbol of Jewish religious-national loyalty in Galilee, there is clear evidence of pro-Roman acculturation among Jewish elites. On the other hand, coins, mikvaot, pottery vessels, and other artefacts excavated at Jotapata and elsewhere point to strong patterns of Jewish cultural retention in Galilee during the successive late Hellenistic and early Roman periods, Aviam insists.[41]

The past generation of archaeological work in Galilee, pivoting around findings of Roman "overlay" in the Antipas period, has yielded speculation about how Jesus' presumptive encounter with this urbanized landscape propelled him in a morally rebellious direction—perhaps even a politically rebellious direction, as Reza Aslan's best-seller speculates. Writing as a scholar who is ever watchful of sources of sociopolitical rebelliousness in Galilee, Richard Horsley offers an assessment of the impact of this Roman "overlay" in Galilee which basically summarizes the passing research generation's conclusions regarding the broad issue of Galilee of the Gentiles—but there is really no reason to expect that future researchers will follow the same line of reasoning:

> In the first century, the urban culture of the [recently rebuilt] "royal" city of Sepphoris must have seemed like a foreign body set down upon a Galilean culture of the villages: as a provincial "urban overlay," a cultural mixture dominated by Roman political-cultural features. There is no question that both Sepphoris and Tiberias had an impact upon Galilean villagers. Given the political-economic structure, it seems likely reaction and resistance outweighed assimilation and acculturation.[42]

GALILEE AND MEDICAL HEALING IN MATTHEW AND THE OTHER GOSPELS

Of all the images and concepts associated with Galilee in the gospels, perhaps none has had greater resonance in commentary and popular consciousness than that of miraculous medical recovery. Compared to other parts of the New Testament, Matthew is less immersed in issues of healing, so in this short subsection we broaden our focus and relate to the other synoptic gospels as well.

The cornerstone of Galilee's reputation for medical wonder is Mark, 5:25–34, which relates healing stories. These events begin at a side of the lake, when a synagogue leader, Jairus, beseeches Jesus to cure his daughter; a woman who touches Jesus' cloak from behind is healed of a hemorrhage. Based on such events, "early followers of Jesus were quick to assert, as have subsequent generations of Christians to the present day, that Jesus was set apart from and superior to other healers of his day," writes Harold Remus, the author of a study of healing in the New Testament. One distinctive aspect of medical stories in the Gospels, he notes, derives from the fact that "most other healers of the time were not known as teachers, as Jesus was."[43]

Probably the least "medical" gospel,[44] Matthew is tersely reticent about Jesus' healing powers, as exemplified by the story of the healing of the leper (8:1–4), who is instructed not to tell anyone about his miraculous recovery. Healing tales relayed in Mark—the curing of the deaf and mute man (7:31), and a blind man at Bethsaida (8:22)—are nowhere to be found in Matthew. In Matthew, it bears mention, the list of sufferers cured by Jesus in Capernaum features persons (lepers, Roman soldiers) who are, in one way or another, distanced from Jewish society. Jesus' healing miracles therefore reinforce the inclusive character of Jesus' mission, as well as its determination to push past the borders of Jewish society.[45]

Mark is rife with healing stories—they are present in this gospel's first ten chapters (except for chapter 4), and outnumber other sorts of miracle tales in it. Jesus refers to himself, metaphorically, as a physician in Mark (2:17; see also Luke: 4:23), and the opening sections in Mark 2, culminating in the 2:17 declaration ("I have not come to call the righteous, but the sinners") are notable, Remus writes, because they elaborate on connections between "sin and sickness or death" in a manner that seems to draw upon Jewish tradition.[46] In some parts of Mark (1:41, 2:11, 10:52), Jesus heals through the power of words, though there are passages (as in the cloak incident) where his touch heals. This gospel also puts emphasis on demon possession and unclean spirits (1:32, 1:23, 3:11, 6:7); in fact, nineteenth-century commentators like David Friedrich Strauss emphasized how Mark seems to be saturated with belief in demonic possession. Though it also omits healing stories found in Mark, the gospel of Luke is rife with medical-related incidents. In fact, healing discourse is so prevalent in this gospel that Luke acquired a reputation as the patron saint of physicians: another nineteenth-century Biblical commentator, Adolf von Harnack, dedicated an entire volume to Luke the Physician.[47] In a few key cases, including the leper story (Luke 5:13) and the healed paralytic (Luke 5:24) this gospel gives a fuller medical report than what is presented in Mark (1:45; 2:12).

Scholars continue to wonder how these New Testament medical miracles ought to be interpreted, from an academic standpoint. One 2008 volume,[48] for instance, declares that there are four possibilities: Jesus treated actual physical diseases and performed miracle cures; he offered therapeutic comfort; he liberated sufferers from psychosomatic disorders; or the Gospels invented the healing stories so as to publicize Jesus as a messianic figure. Deploying what he calls an "anthropological-historical perspective," this author, Pieter Craffert, presents a "biopsychosocial" paradigm by which medical healing is viewed as a "complex cultural practice," and Jesus' medical work is compared to "shaman" practices in other cultures.[49] This reference to shamanism would distract or unsettle many; so authors of other books on "Jesus the Healer" rely on terms more familiar to the way secular-minded persons in the twenty-first century think of medical miracles. Stevan Davies, for instance, perceives Jesus as a faith healer. On his view, New Testament tales about curing of blindness, deafness, paralysis, and other disorders relate to psychosomatic illnesses, and Jesus more or less treated them the way they are described in the gospels.[50]

The relationship between Jesus' healing miracles and Galilee's landscape remains a hotly disputed topic, and it is probably irresoluble. Insisting that the crucial New Testament image of Jesus is that of a healer, Davies examines how miracles in this medical context essentially relate to two overlapping types of ailments, somatic disorders, and demonic exorcism. Reasonably enough, he concludes that Jesus' activities must be assessed in terms of how such phenomena were understood in their first-century Galilean context. Continuing, Davies adamantly rejects interpretations which draw direct connections between Galilee *politics* and these healing stories. This political interpretation, upheld by scholars such as Paul Hollenbach, John Dominic Crossan, and Richard Horsley, suggests that Galilean peasants attested to being possessed by demons because they had no other way of dealing with an exploitative sociopolitical order enforced by the Romans—according to Davies, this political interpretation is "preposterous."[51] Davies' analysis follows in the footsteps of religion scholars such as E. P. Sanders, who evaluate the miracle and healing stories in a Galilee devoid of Roman pressures, or even the presence of Roman power symbols, such as soldiers.[52] Demon possession was a widespread ailment in Galilee for reasons not related to oppressive Roman rule, Davies proclaims, suggesting that it was more of a family issue. "It is almost certain that the majority of the demon-possessed individuals whom Jesus exorcised found themselves to be in intolerable circumstances of social subordination *within their family groups* and it is likely that many and perhaps most of these were women," he writes.[53] New

Testament exorcisms, Davies explains, involved encounters between the positively spirit-possessed Jesus, and demon-possessed sufferers, such as Mary of Magdala. Thus, "the act of exorcism was a drama played by two alter-personae, each recognizing the alter-persona state of the other. The demons knew who Jesus was, the Son of the Most High, and the Son of the Most High knew who the demons were."[54]

By putting a feminist twist on an analysis of New Testament miracles, Davies is snared by the syndrome Schweitzer identified, a condition wherein scholars recast the historical Jesus in an image fashioned out of cardinal concerns in their own contemporary world (Davies, to be fair, is himself well aware of the hazards of this syndrome[55]). Each age re-communes with Jesus in tune with its own needs and concerns; so too does every age get the Galilee it deserves.

HOW AT HOME WAS JESUS IN GALILEE?

Complementing the issue of how much credence modern readers, Christian or not, can reasonably give to New Testament attestation of healing miracles, some nonmiraculous Galilee events in the Gospel of Matthew detract from its verisimilitude. Anachronisms or otherwise distortive interpolations, they are more polemic than documentation. Take for instance, Capernaum. This town, scholars note, is never mentioned in the Old Testament, and Matthew seems to fashion it as a largely gentile locale.[56] In Capernaum, Jesus is impressed by the submissive humility of the Roman centurion, and he cures the soldier's servant.[57] The problem is that there were no Roman legions stationed in Galilee in Jesus' day, and so Christian commentators have conceded that the centurion reference must be used "loosely" in this passage.[58] Implying that the Aramaic-speaking Jesus conversed in Greek or Latin with the Roman or Syrian soldier, the scene's linguistic status is also complicated, and its condonation of slavery is unusual in Matthew.[59]

The righteous faith of the Roman officer inspires another supersession prophecy: in view of the widespread faithlessness of the people of Israel, a new covenant will be forged with gentiles, persons "who will come from the east and west," and "will feast with Abraham, Isaac and Jacob in the kingdom of heaven."[60] The east-west phrasing deliberately recasts Old Testament prophecy, in accord with this gospel's supersession intent. Isaiah 43:5 uses the same phrase, but it heralds the gathering of Jewish exiles[61] ("I will bring your children from the east, and gather you from the west"). The subsequent verse makes this substitution explicit: Christianity's new converts will enter the kingdom, as its "subjects"—Jews, in contrast, are "thrown into the darkness" (this reference to hell is reinforced by Matthew's recurring metonym of "weeping and gnashing of teeth"[62]). At Peter's house, when Jesus cures his disciple's feverish mother-in-law, and exorcises demon-possessed sufferers who are brought to him, his activities are presented as further fulfillment of Isaiah (53:4), "he took up our infirmities and bore our diseases."[63]

Jesus crosses the lake and leaves Galilee ostensibly because a growing crowd of followers has become a distraction. His departure for a gentile region, the Gadarenes, in the Golan Heights (on the eastern side of the Sea of Galilee), implies that his prophetic work in Galilee has been completed—but, contrariwise, Matthew also conveys suggestions that this Galilee work has been frustratingly derailed. Language in the gospels precipitates speculation about how Jesus himself might have owned a home in Capernaum, but, in Matthew, he ends up inveighing about faithlessness in his relocated hometown in Galilee ("And you, Capernaum, will you be lifted to the heavens; no, you will go down to hell"[64]). While departing the town and setting out on what will become a turbulent, stormy sea, Jesus exclaims that Galilee can never really be home to him, because he has no home ("foxes have dens and birds have nests, but the Son of Man has no place to lay his head"[65]).

This sequence of events underscores Matthew's ongoing evasiveness on the question of fulfillment or supersession. On the one hand, Jesus has dwelled in Capernaum, worked curative miracles, and thus won crowds of followers who have come from all over the Holy Land, in fulfillment of Hebrew Bible prophecy in Isaiah. Equally true, it seems, his divinity has been unrecognized by the faithless in Capernaum, as well as in Bethsaida and Chorazin, and so he has become an unappreciated, vagabond prophet. There is fundamental ambiguity in Jesus' character: is he a Jewish prophet who has come to fulfill Jewish law, or is he the Christian savior whose experiences and preaching portend the establishment of a new faith? And there is fundamental ambiguity in Galilee's socioreligious landscape: is it Jewish or gentile, and is it inspired by Jesus, or antagonistic toward him? As in Josephus' "Jewish" narrative, the Galilee setting in the Gospel of Matthew is a projection of uncertainty about the hero's intentions or status, and the ambiguities of the regional setting, and of the protagonist's character and orientation are interconnected, and inseparable. This parallel avails, at least in some likely measure, because at the moment when Josephus' *The Jewish War*, and Matthew's book, were concurrently composed, Galilee's cultural-demographic character was itself in flux, as were the identities of the authors.

One way of reading Matthew's testimony is to conclude that Jesus' divine powers were well recognized in his home, Capernaum, particularly by Galilee gentiles like the Centurion. So having fulfilled the prophecies of the Hebrew Bible, Jesus proceeded onward, his sacrifice destined to atone for mankind's sinful state. With similar fidelity to the plain language of passages in this gospel, another way to interpret this Galilee sequence, culminating in Jesus' flight from the region and his subsequent outbursts about its faithlessness, is to assume that its Jews ridiculed Jesus' supernatural pretension. In light of such Jewish skepticism, articulated during Jesus' lifetime in Galilee venues such as Bethsaida and Capernaum, and then articulated decades later, following the Temple's destruction, in response to the proselytizing of Matthew's group (consisting of what would today be called Hebrew Christians, or, in Kampen's view, Jews of a particular sect), the gospel was written out of an ideological agenda of substituting a new religion for Judaism, in a period when Jerusalem's destruction by the Romans left a power vacuum wherein ambitious groups vied for social control.

Matthew enjoins the reader to reach a choice between these diametrically opposed, and all-encompassing, options. Jesus is either a Jewish prophet who is fulfilling his people's sacred scriptures and beliefs, or he is the divine representation of a new faith. On either interpretation, he personifies an eschatological expectation subversive of everyday routines and commitments, as Albert Schweitzer emphasized.[66] Either because it is such a placid reality conducive of rootedness in everyday, mundane life, or because its Jewish population has remained so surprisingly and intractably resistant to Jesus' miracle works and spiritual messages, Galilee cannot be home to Jesus or any of his followers, since they are all expectant of the imminent coming of the kingdom of heaven. Jesus drives home this point when he rejects the request of a disciple who wants to linger in Galilee to bury his father, saying: "follow me, and let the dead bury their own dead."[67]

How could Capernaum be both a productive earthly home for Jesus and also a hotbed of iniquity consigned to hell? Because there is no readily decipherable answer to this question, the town's complicated cultural demography has, over the decades, been imagined creatively to suit the purposes of commentators who purport to have deciphered the riddle of the "historical Jesus." In their recasting of Galilee's spiritual state and social character, links fasten between the search for the historical Jesus and the search for the historical Galilee—one cannot be discovered unless the other is unearthed. This topic will be explored in depth in this study's second volume, pertaining to Galilee in the modern era (we will argue that this parallel quest, for the historical Jesus and the historical Galilee, can be seen as symbol and cause of modernity-defining, secularization, processes). Here it suffices to give one example of how the refashioning of Capernaum is intertwined in an argument purporting to solve fundamental riddles of Jesus' identity.

In his popular 2013 volume, Reza Aslan insists that in a transformative Galilee period, under Roman rule enforced by the tetrarch Herod Antipas, "Capernaum was the ideal place for Jesus to launch his ministry."[68] Jesus, Aslan improbably hypothesizes, was a Jewish zealot committed to the anti-Roman rebellion. His insurrectionist messages had appeal to a social underclass in Capernaum, to its fishermen and farmers who had fallen behind socioeconomically, in a Galilee region where Antipas' investments benefited Jewish assimilating elites, or gentile notables, particularly in Sepphoris and Tiberias. On the whole, Galilee's economy might have been flourishing under Antipas, but the beneficiaries were a "new moneyed class in the Greek cities of Galilee." Jesus gathered around himself "a small group of like-minded Galileans, mostly culled from the ranks of the fishing village's disaffected youth." Aslan summarizes: "The majority of Capernaum's residents had been left behind by the new Galilean economy. It would be these people whom Jesus would specifically target—those who found themselves cast to the fringes of society, whose lives had been disrupted by the rapid social and economic shifts taking place throughout Galilee."[69]

Writing in a period of escalating economic polarization in America, in a post-Holocaust democratic political culture that boasts an unprecedented measure of amity and intimate interaction between Jews and Christians, Aslan projects a "really Jewish" image of Christianity's savior. Capernaum's economy and politics is cut in the cloth worn by this writer's "historical Jesus," and the coastal town appears as a cross between a Hasidic village and Lexington and Concord.

GALILEE'S SERMON ON THE MOUNT

Jesus' ascent to the mount in Matthew (5:1) thickens the gospel's creative ambiguity, functioning both as supersession of Moses' revelation of the law on Sinai, and also, as Jesus attests in the Sermon, as fulfillment of Jewish law ("do not think that I have come to abolish the law or the prophets; I have not come to abolish them but to fulfill them").[70] To whom is the sermon directed? On the whole, the Book of Matthew is a record of Jesus' interaction with his disciples, and also, indirectly but unmistakably, a record of a retrospective debate within Matthew's Jewish-Christian community as to whether its evangelical mission ought to remain limited to Jews, or to gentiles everywhere.

The most famous words of the New Testament are delivered at a deliberate remove from the Galileans, in the equivalent of an American football huddle. When the home team is on offense, everyone in the stadium is supportive of the play which will be called next, but the quarterback only shares this temporarily private knowledge with ten other initiates, who are huddled around him. The opening wording of the Sermon, inaugurating Galilee's historic role as a theater for the dissemination of private knowledge among disciples or kabbalists who have universal or cosmic aspirations, is telling. The Sermon on the Mount is both a private moral discussion and also semi-public council. Matthew records: "Now when Jesus saw the crowds, he went up on a mountainside and sat down. His disciples came to him, and he began to teach them."[71]

Significantly, Jesus is seated, and this posture is itself a statement in Matthew about the retention of Jewish communality in Jesus' lifetime, and about this gospel's writers' lack of resolve regarding the prospect of mass recruitment in the creation of a new religion comprised mainly of non-Jews. The seating of this sermon, it seems to me, reinforces claims made by commentators who view Matthew's group as a sectarian Jewish phenomenon, rather than a proselyting cadre determined to create a new religion. Had the sermon been delivered with a resolute intent of mass appeal and universal mission, the physicality of its presentation would have been different (it bears recalling that the sermon comes relatively early in the Book of Matthew, before Jesus' miracle healing working in the Galilee transforms him into a figure of presumed mass charismatic appeal). Still, as though to bear witness to Matthew's capacity for ambiguity, these presumptions seem not to have stood the test of time. Many centuries after its promulgation, religious leaders like Methodist founder John Wesley cited the Sermon on the Mount as inspiration for mass field preaching.[72]

Jesus and his group of devotees gather in what appears as an impromptu congregation, an educational session that draws both from Greco-Roman models of philosophical schools and teacher-disciples relations, and Jewish

Figure 2.2 View from possible site of the Sermon on the Mount—Mount of Beatitudes.
Source: Courtesy of Adi Lam.

synagogue worship (one scholar has called this New Testament sort of assembly an *ekklesia*).[73]

Formulaic constructions in the eight Beatitudes verses (5:3–10) convey this indefiniteness about the nature of the sermon's audience. Jesus' message calls upon his gathered disciples on the hilltop and also those who will follow them in the future, saying: blessed are those who abide by Jesus' words, as they will enter the kingdom of heaven which he proclaims. Who will enter, exactly? The third person phrasing in Matthew casts the Sermon as a kind of generic pronouncement referring to a non-bordered group of the blessed, whereas roughly comparable parts of the New Testament, most importantly Luke's Beatitudes, have more directly designated referents, addressed in the second person, "blessed are you."[74]

Generally, in Matthew, crowds loom as a "shifting, unorganized, but interested group, present with Jesus from the beginning of his public life to the end."[75] Jesus' disciples are organized and have a higher level of commitment to his teaching, but there is overlap between these two groups (presumably, members of the "crowds" subsequently became fully aligned with the disciples), and Jesus often seems to be addressing both groups simultaneously, "with varied success." Both groups, it will be recalled, abandon Jesus when he is arrested, though his disciples rejoin him after the Resurrection.[76]

Literally at the center of Matthew's transcription of the Sermon on the Mount (6: 9–13), the Lord's Prayer constitutes Galilee's most frequently recited, revered, and famous words. In the prologue to the Prayer, there is continuation of the Gospel's polemic against organized Jewish worship. Generally, by using phrases such as "their synagogues," Matthew's group consistently situates itself outside of sacred Jewish public space; here, in the Lord's Prayer prologue, Jesus chastises Jewish "hypocrites" who gather in synagogues just so that they can be seen as devout worshippers (the prologue also chides the verbosity of "gentile" prayers). The Prayer's first lines oblige the Jewish custom of not directly using the Lord's name. The "daily bread" reference at its midpoint makes, perhaps, glancing reference to provision of manna to the Israelites recorded in Exodus 16; such allusiveness is, at least, perceptible to those who regard the Sermon as a supersession event whereby Jesus ascends and descends from the Mount to promulgate a new moral code, replacing or transcending Moses' revelatory experience at Sinai.[77] By no means, however, are the Prayer's creative resonances circumscribed by the Gospel's basic tension about the future of Jewish law. The bedrock of Christian prayer, the Prayer's sonorous phrases soar beyond our pedestrian anxieties about contradiction and rational limits. For believers, it simultaneously furnishes unmitigated comfort and reassurance while also enjoining them to win God's favor by leading a moral life.

As such, within its own Christian context, the Prayer reflects and promotes another sort of creative tension in Matthew: is it promoting a theology of Grace, as advocated by Paul (who promoted this view in detachment from Matthew's Group), or, ultimately, is the Sermon, and Matthew as a whole, a call for good Christian works? Overall, scholars lean toward the second option, one which is supported, historically, by the fact that as centuries passed, Protestant thinkers who favored predestination and grace theologies preferred the Gospel of John to Matthew. "The important thing to note," writes one important scholar of Matthew's theology, "is that the Lord's Prayer is, to a high degree, the prayer of active men and women, a prayer that includes the actions of human beings and virtually makes those actions its contents." One reference, "as we also have forgiven our debtors," basically "incorporates human action" into the prayer, concludes Luz.[78]

In its intertextual setting, the prayer's admonition about debt forgiveness alludes to Matthew 18:23–35, a parable in which a king mercifully agrees to wipe out debts owed by an imploring servant. The unforgiving servant then proceeds remorselessly to prosecute a debt of a hundred silver coins owed to him by a fellow servant—once the king learns about this fickle behavior, about (to use our own vernacular) the servant's refusal to pay it forward, he sends the ingrate off to be tortured, so that he will pay off his own debts. Just as this parable's message is straightforward, so too has the anti-materialist exhortation in the Sermon, and elsewhere in Matthew, inspired idealism for ages. Equally true, the "easier said than done" quality of the altruism coached by the Lord's Prayer's advocacy of debt forgiveness shadows the Sermon, and Matthew in general. A few verses after the Prayer, Jesus issues a kind of summary proclamation against material accumulation: "Do not store up for yourselves treasures on earth, where moths and vermin destroy, and where thieves break in and steal."[79] This thought is quickly reinforced by the Sermon's abjuration of serving "two masters" ("you cannot serve both God and money"[80]). Outside of the Sermon, Matthew remonstrates against the association of material accumulation (or capitalist success, to use anachronistic formulation) and God's favor, most famously in 19:23–24 ("it is easier for a camel to go through the eye of a needle than for someone who is rich to enter the kingdom of God"). In Matthew, the brunt of Jesus' attacks on Pharisees or related Jewish spiritual leaders pivots on their alleged fixation with the superficial, external ("material" in a broad sense) side of rituals, rather than their inner, spiritual meaning, and in the Temple money-changer scene (21:12–13), Matthew's Jesus takes overt action against materialist corruption that is imputed to the Jews' most sacrosanct venues, castigating them as a "den of robbers."

For eschatological, organizational, and other reasons, Matthew's idealism about material comfort, debts, and other money matters does not appear to be viably consistent. Or stated perhaps more accurately, the gospel's outlook on issues of matter versus spirit could never have been, as centuries went by, readily applicable to the daily economies within which masses of believers became enmeshed, however much they were inspired by this gospel's idealism about earthly treasure.

Anointed in perfume at Bethany, Jesus informs incredulous disciples: "the poor you will always have with you, but you will not always have me."[81] The story of the "rich and the Kingdom of God"[82] reveals that it is not enough for a true follower to heed the commandments of the Decalogue: to be "perfect," and follow Jesus as a disciple would do, a person must sell his possessions and give to the poor. In church history, this passage gave rise to a "two-level" ethic which distinguished between Christians who uphold ordinary commandments, and those who aspire to perfection, and follow "evangelical counsels," and this passage's conception of perfection became deeply rooted in monastic movements.[83] A significant portion of Matthew's wrestling about material possessions reflects its composers' concerns about the formation of a non-corruptible leadership elite in its community (as it turned out, this community became the church). Finally, Matthew is not really opposed to capital formation, per se, so far as worldly treasures serve noble purpose. The parable of the Unprofitable Servant[84] in which a master bestows three servants with a different number of bags of gold, in accord with their abilities, and castigates the one who does not invest wisely and merely buries his bag in the ground, can be read on many different levels (some commentators suggested that the parable's heaviest investor, who accrues an additional five bags of gold on top of his original bequest of five bags, allegorizes how the richness of the Jews' Pentateuch will double after their conversion to Christianity). The parable's most palpable message is that newcomers in what became the church ought to apply their abilities diligently toward its strengthening, spiritual or material. Unlike anti-materialist passages in the Sermon and elsewhere in Matthew, the Unprofitable Servant pragmatically prognosticates about how economies of capital accumulation will serve Christianity's interests. The large sums of gold it describes "indicate that Matthew's community was familiar with finances and investments."[85]

For such reasons, the penultimate section in the Lord's Prayer, about debts, must be read in its plain sense, as prayerful supplication, rather than Christian praxis. Overall, as capitalism came to envelope Christianity, the ways whereby (in Ulrich Luz's words) human action became incorporated in the Lord's Prayer applied to exceptions and elites, to monks and saints, rather than to the regularities of religion and life.

Clarke aptly summarizes how the Sermon on the Mount inspires and confuses modern sensibilities: "Matthew tends to honor ideals and legislate goals that are, each in its own way, absolute—but that are ultimately irreconcilable in practice. Hence, marriage is indissoluble, but divorce is permitted; the dietary laws are valid, but may be modified; the Sabbath is holy, but may yield to emergencies; oaths are forbidden, but may be sworn under certain circumstances."[86]

Some scholars speculate that the Sermon's extreme, impractical moralism coheres with Schweitzer's eschatological theory holding that Jesus was teaching a group which believed that the end of time was imminent, or, indeed that this apocalyptic process was already underway.[87] Extreme idealism seems more cogent when it is upheld by persons who believe that the clock is winding down, and that there is no time to reap the benefits of moral temperance.

This eschatological reading of the Sermon has been modified or challenged by recent research, some of it utilizing the Qumran materials. Take for instance, Sermon passage 5:25, instructing followers to "settle matters quickly with your adversary who is taking you to court"—this dictate seems to reflect an apocalyptic moral focus, one not befitting people who believe in the continuity of earthly time and the concomitant need to attend to its trivial, ongoing affairs. However, newly processed Second Temple era documents, particularly the Dead Sea Scrolls, do not necessarily support this line of interpretation.

Looking at materials in the Qumran library ("4Q Sapiential Work A") which are not catalogued as though they belong exclusively to the Essene sect, one researcher identifies a series of instructions reflecting a "situation of ongoing poverty." The authors of these Dead Sea Scroll materials evince various concerns about dealing with creditors; this leads Jorge Frey to conclude that "debts, pledges and surety were thus a severe problem in first century Palestine." Q sayings in this regard, and their apparent inclusion in Matthew 5:25–26, emerged directly out of a particular socioeconomic reality. Possibly, they were intended more or less as practical advice, not as metaphorical statements or parables woven out of the expectant eschatological temperament Schweitzer attributed to the gospels.[88]

No less plausible than the eschatological interpretation of the Sermon's extremism, and its inconsistencies with other parts of Matthew, is a *compositional* explanation, one claiming that divergent opinion within the gospel's writers generated its ambiguities. Members of a group of mixed emotion regarding Judaism, and regarding the eventuality of a mission to the gentiles, this gospel's writers culled morally compelling statements from the Q document, in the absence of a single editorial viewpoint (and there is no obvious way of clarifying whether what struck subsequent readers of imperfectly translated versions of Matthew as moral inconsistency might have created the same sort of puzzlement among the original listeners/readers of the Sermon).

The final words of the Lord's Prayer, "deliver us from evil," are responsive to the Sermon's famous, and controversial, exhortation, "resist not evil."[89]

These words, including the injunction to "turn the other cheek," have inspired a long roster of history's most celebrated writers and moralists, including Leo Tolstoy, a Sermon on the Mount enthusiast who based his own idiosyncratic version of Christianity on it. Tolstoy attested that Jesus' instruction, "do not resist an evil person," caused "the veil to fall" from his eyes. As happened with other parts of the Sermon, church fathers who struggled with the injunction's practical implications found sophisticated ways to modify it. Among them was Augustine of Hippo, whose commentary was the first to identify Matthew's chapters 5–7 as the Sermon on the Mount. Writing for a rising but embattled Christian empire, Saint Augustine added a "just war" proviso to Matthew 5:39, arguing, in contradistinction to the unmitigated idealism of this and other key sermon passages, that rightfully constituted governments could use force under some circumstances.[90]

Arguably, the modification of such latter-day exegesis was unnecessary because the Book of Matthew itself added important provisos to the Sermon's unqualified counsel about turning the other cheek. In Matthew 10:34, Jesus presents himself not as a peacemaker, but rather as a fighter: "Do not suppose that I have come to bring peace on earth. I did not come to bring peace, but a sword." Some have hypothesized that this surprising and arresting passage is eschatological in reference, contradicting then-current Jewish beliefs about how the advent of messianic times would be peaceful,[91] but there is no dearth of commentators who stress the words' plain meaning, depicting Jesus as a political militant in earthly affairs (witness Aslan's recent book). Social activists who shunned guerilla warfare type tactics, it bears mention, have also drawn inspiration from Matthew 10:34—this includes liberal Protestants, as in America's Social Gospel movement.[92] The Lord's Prayer, at any event, eludes these dilemmas, modifications, and nuances. Its supplication removes the issue to another level, casting resistance to, and deliverance from, evil as the Lord's work.

There are a few final points to make about the Sermon on the Mount, connecting it to Matthew's sometimes blistering invective against Jewish religious elites and also to gender considerations. Awkward as it is to point to a specific issue as a kind of fatal flaw in a gospel that has been, and will remain, revered by millions, it has nonetheless become commonplace after the Holocaust to identify Matthew's polemic about the Pharisees and other Jewish groups as a moral anomaly and as a problem—not just in its own terms but also with regard to the compellingly majestic normative context set out by the Sermon on the Mount, and comparable passages in Matthew. "Blessed are the merciful," declares the fifth Beatitude.[93] In the parable of the unmerciful servant, where Peter indicates that he would be magnanimous to forgive a brother's sins seven times, Jesus corrects him, demanding forgiveness "not seven, but seventy-seven times."[94] In view of such prescriptions for mercy and forgiveness, as offshoots of Matthew's abiding, foremost commandment of love, the corrosive "seven woes" Matthew's Jesus accords to the Pharisees and Teachers of the Law,[95] and the ensuing imprecation ("You snakes! You brood of vipers!"[96]) are troublesome, but not really as augury of future anti-Semitism (Matthew's small group in 80 CE adhered to contemporary norms in a highly sectarian Jewish culture, where it was customary to vilify and demonize rival groups, and cannot logically be held accountable for what the Nazis did in the 1930s and 1940s[97]). That the anti-Pharisee philippic emanated out of social circumstances, from a power rivalry between Matthew's Christianizing group and Pharisees and other leaders of first-century CE formative Judaism is widely accepted, but the philippic is nonetheless problematic because it simply cannot be made to cohere, thematically, with Matthew's most memorable passages about love, mercy, and forgiveness. This point is made so routinely in scholarship that there is no reason to elaborate upon it.[98] It suffices to cite the conclusion reached by Howard Clarke, a scholar who has perceptively studied Matthew's reception over time: "Over the ages, the sentiments of the [Sermon on the Mount] have inspired, frustrated and puzzled its readers," he writes.[99]

The "mixture of moral idealism and religious realism" in the Sermon has "probably generated more comment" than any other part of the Gospels, writes Clarke.[100] Recommending toleration and restraint in politics, in his 1685–1686 Letter Concerning Toleration, philosopher John Locke cited the Sermon, Matthew 5:10, "blessed are those who are persecuted because of righteousness." Matthew 5:14's reference to a "town built on a hill" inspired John Winthrop's 1630 proclamation—"Consider that we shall be as a city on a hill; the eyes of all people are upon us"—which recirculated as a panegyric trope about America among Presidents of various persuasions (e.g., Kennedy and Reagan). The next verse, Matthew 5:15—Neither do people light a lamp and put it under a bowl—animated enlightened educational policies in a rich array of places and times. At the end of the eighth century, Charlemagne cited the passage, urging clergy to establish schools so that the young might learn to read. In the footsteps of Quaker founder George Fox, William Penn advocated educational enlightenment in North America's colonies, proclaiming "Let your light shine among the Indians, the Blacks and the Whites." Matthew 5:39, calling on believers to turn the other cheek, inspired the twentieth century's most compelling instances of political morality. Gandhi recalled his response to the verse: "I was simply overjoyed and found my opinion confirmed where I least expected it."

Such surveys of the Sermon's civilizational sweep are imposing, but it is interesting that powerful discussions, such as Clarke's analysis of the Book of Matthew's reception over the ages, chase this gospel's moral insights and influences on every spot of the globe, other than the place from where it came.

Since the history of Galilee, from the time of Jesus to Israel's 1948 birth, has never been written, few have been able to trace how this region has sponsored an intra-faith hilltop morality, a Jewish-Christian-Islamic view of the world that has interlocked elements, despite the obvious divergences of ritual and belief between the three great monotheistic faiths. For now, we can cite one example of this local morality, and we will elaborate upon it in this study's second volume, in its chapter on Jewish mysticism, Kabbalah, in sixteenth-century Safed. As it happens, I am sitting in my study on a hilltop in Safed, with the Sea of Galilee in direct view, looking at the presumed site of Jesus' Sermon on the Mount jutting up on a slope, off one of the lake's coasts. From this vantage point, it is hard not to wonder about what these hilltops have given to what is called, often naively, the "Judeo-Christian" tradition.

The Sermon on the Mount's centerpiece, the Lord's Prayer, has formulations which are usefully compared to what later won recognition as the Jews' most hallowed Galilee prayer. In its way, the Lord's Prayer coheres with patriarchal rules of power, directing itself to "Our Father who art in heaven," and, in this way, it befits a religion of rising power. Some 1,500 years later, after excruciating travails of exile, when some Jewish mystics returned to their ancestral homeland, establishing Safed as their center, one kabbalist, Shlomo Halevi Alkabetz, composed "Lekha Dodi," a liturgical song of mysterious, semi-erotic, allure which Jews have subsequently recited on Friday evening, to welcome the start of Shabbat.[101] As though to reflect the exilic experience of powerlessness, this beloved hymn (*piyyut*, as Jews call this genre), feminizes supplication, using images of a bride and a queen in reference to sacred experience, starting with God's day of rest. A communal evocation of female divinity, Lekha Dodi is an intriguing counterpart to the Lord's Prayer individualized evocation of "our Father," and it is Galilee' foremost Jewish prayer. The Lord's Prayer and Lekha Dodi are the highest soaring songbirds of prayer in Galilee's pluralistic spiritual tradition.

BANIAS: GALILEE'S VATICAN

Matthew uses space in Galilee to promote the gospel's supersession agenda. Galilee geography, in other words, cannot be separated from Matthew's religious politics. There are warps in this gospel wherein time, society, and space are bent so as to enhance the moral persuasiveness of Jesus' actions and preaching. Hence, no less than other expressions of disciplinary innovation in academia that are being applied to Bible Studies (for instance, literary criticism[102]), the development of "critical geography" seems to have promise. "Notions of space, boundary, and regionalism are entering the mainstream of scholarship pertaining to the ancient world, advocating a new, spatially-oriented look at even the most traditional sources in the process," writes John M. Vonder Bruegge, a "critical geographer" with a PhD from Yale, and the author of an interesting study on the use and abuse of Galilee's geography in Josephus, Luke, and John.[103]

One of the best-known warps in Matthew involves the presence of Pharisees in Galilee during Jesus' mission. They seem out of place, since in Jesus' day, with the Temple having been grandly refurbished by Herod, the Pharisees were probably a Jerusalem-based group—the likelihood that Pharisees operated in Galilee at the time of Matthew's composition, as the makers of formative Judaism after the Jerusalem Temple's destruction, some of them having settled and studied at Yavne for a stint, is much higher. Such instances of dislocation and anachronism are, however, necessary, not for the purpose of the gospel's facticity, but rather in terms of its moral and didactic agenda. The Pharisees need to shadow Jesus from the start of the mission in Galilee because they incarnate aspects of false spirituality (ritualistic rigidity, superficiality, etc.) against which the formation of Matthew's new communal theology, and through it, willfully or not, Christianity, can be justified. The miracles and healing wrought by Jesus in Galilee are partial revelations of his divinity, but, in themselves, they are not a warrant for a new theology. For that, as tokens of marred religiosity, Pharisees must come to Galilee. They are ubiquitous in Matthew, playing the role of anti-hero. Speaking of the moral needs of members of Matthew's group, Luz writes: "Their need for exhortation causes them to see things in black and white. Being antitypes, the Pharisees and the scribes *must* be denigrated."[104]

In Matthew, Jesus' disputation with the Pharisees in Galilee serves as prelude to one of the Gospel's most influential and controversial chapters, 16:13–20, in which Peter recognizes Jesus as "the Messiah, the son of the living God," and Jesus announces that "on this rock I will build my church." This passage, it seems to me, begs for a "critical geography" approach to Galilee's religious history. The purpose of such methodology is not to detract from the text's spiritual authority—in this case, at least, there is no need for that, since this passage, wherein Peter receives the keys of the kingdom of heaven, became embroiled historically in a labyrinth of authenticity accusations and counteraccusations between Catholics and Protestants, centered, of course, on the fact that this is the scriptural warrant for the Papacy.[105] Instead, a judiciously critical glimpse at this passage enriches our understanding of historical context and, more specifically, helps us grasp how Galilee became a hub of world monotheistic culture in the aftermath of the Temple's destruction in Jerusalem.

Jesus delivers to Peter the keys of the kingdom of heaven in Caesarea Philippi, a town in Upper Galilee's farthest northern reach with a long-standing pagan ethos. Matthew offers no particular reason as to why this event, one which is monumentally transformative in that it is the gospel's sole supersession reference to the Jesus movement building a "church" (*ekklesia*[106]), occurs in Caesarea Philippi. In contrast, though it contains a less-polished narrative, the Gospel of Mark provides, from a moral-didactic standpoint, a clearer geographic trajectory. In Mark, Jesus travels to Caesarea Philippi after he miraculously opens the eyes of a blind man at Bethsaida, thereby implying that Peter's recognition of the Messiah is responsive to an instance of divine intervention.

In fact, much in Matthew 16:13–20 reflects this Gospel's ongoing project of refining and elaborating upon Mark. Matthew amplifies Mark's record of Peter's words, "You are the Messiah," by adding "the Son of the Living God," and, memorably, confers to Peter the nickname, "rock."[107] The designated name reflects ratiocination, possibly with a playful twist, following Old Testament examples of name redesignation at a moment of reckoning (e.g., Abram/Abraham), this particular case featuring a pun, since Peter in Greek is *Petros*, and rock is *petram*.[108]

Given such evidence suggesting that Matthew deliberately tweaked and amplified details in this incident, why does this gospel not really account for its occurrence at Caesarea Philippi? Why would Matthew persist in this geography? The question has increased pertinence when we acknowledge that commentators who were not necessarily entangled by the controversy of the chapter's credibility as the basis for the papacy, nonetheless intimated skepticism about whether Jesus really used some its key terms, such as "church" at this Upper Galilee locale. Some suggested that these terms were introduced by Jesus at the Last Supper.[109]

Caesarea Philippi, the site of a spring from which flows a tributary of the Jordan River, is today in Israel a popular nature reserve known as Banias. Known in Hellenistic times as Paneas (for the Greek god of the wild, Pan), the site hosted cultic rites. Its history of cultural-political rivalry dates from at least 200 BC, and warfare between Syrians (who used elephants) and Egyptians described by Polybius.[110] Its reputation as Galilee's pagan northern edge was long-lasting.[111] In Palestine's Roman era, it was built up by Phillip the Tetrarch, one of Herod's sons, who ruled Iturea, Paneas, and other northern parts of what had been his father's kingdom, in a period roughly conterminous with Jesus' life; interestingly, much in the geography of the Gospel of Matthew overlaps with the lands of Phillip's rule.[112] In 14 CE, Phillip named the site Caesarea, in tribute to Emperor Augustus, and his own name was attached, not just as self-flattery but also to differentiate the site from the important Herodian city, Caesarea, located on the Mediterranean coast. About forty years later, the aforementioned Agrippa II, who has the undistinguished title of being the last Herodian ruler, held Caesarea Philippi as the capital of his slice and dice kingdom (Agrippa II was originally tetrarch of Chalcis, but

Figure 2.3 Archaeological Remains at Caesarea Philippi (Banias). *Source*: Courtesy of Adi Lam.

areas under his rather unpopular rule were periodically rearranged by Roman emperors, Claudius and Nero). Agrippa II became friendly with Josephus, and supplied information to the historian; Josephus mentions the Upper Galilee site in his writings.[113] Agrippa's charismatic sister, Berenice (28–81), held the title of queen and became possibly the most prominent woman in the Roman Empire in years before her death; since her power base was usually Caesarea Philippi, she would have been the most authoritative figure associated with this locale at the time of Matthew's composition.

A few associative factors relevant to Banias' appearance in Matthew can be adduced, though none of these carry conclusively determinative weight. In general, the area's connection with Pan-related fertility cults might have encouraged gospel writers to utilize it as a stage for the organizational birth of their religious outlook. Also, examining materials such as the apocalyptic Hebrew text, 1 Enoch, scholars have remarked that the Dan-Hermon-Banias area was known as a "place one went to for revelation."[114] Finally, some scholars have speculated that the Matthew group was actually located in the Banias area, meaning that the rock where Jesus' church was to be built might literally have been within its field of vision.

For our purposes, Josephus' most significant reference to Caesarea Philippi is found toward the end of his *Jewish War* (7: 23–24), in passages describing Roman celebrations subsequent to the crushing of the Jewish revolt in

Jerusalem. With Vespasian sailing triumphantly toward Greece, his son Titus decamps with his army from Caesarea on the coast, and heads for the other Caesarea, Caesarea Philippi, where he stays "for a long time," staging "a whole variety of spectacular shows" (possibly Titus' decision to stage these events at Caesarea Philippi was influenced by the fact that his father, at Agrippa's invitation, had enjoyed a pleasant, three week, stretch at the locale in summer 67). Jewish prisoners of war were executed by Titus at Caesarea Philippi, some by being "pitched to wild animals," others in equally lugubrious fashion, akin to the Hunger Games film series, being forced to combat one another.[115] Josephus, who (it will be recalled) exerts himself strenuously in *The Jewish War* to exonerate Vespasian and Titus of all responsibility for the Jews' lamentable fate, dryly documents this morbid circus celebration at Caesarea Philippi. Its veracity is supported indirectly by other passages in Josephus, including one which records Titus' general policies toward Jewish prisoners captured in the course of the rebellion (97,000 in number says Josephus, who is always a creative accountant): quite believably, Josephus writes that Titus "distributed large numbers" of Jewish POWs "around the provinces as free fodder for the amphitheaters, to meet their death in gladiatorial combat or savaging by wild animals."[116]

Titus' mass execution of Jews at Caesarea Philippi was protracted, gloating, sensationalized, and vindictive. Scholars have noted how the cruel punishments "certainly included a considerable component of *Schadenfreude*"[117] and have remarked upon the emotionally convoluted situation of some of its observers, such as the Jewish client king Agrippa II who was compelled to "rejoice as a Roman in the defeat of his people" (elements in Banias' local Jewish population, segmented as subgroups known, a little confusingly, as Itureans, Babylonians, and Caesareans, apparently did not rebel against Rome and were possibly spared[118]). The most "spectacular" (in Josephus' phrasing) celebration of the decimation of the Jewish rebellion to be staged in the country, this funereal circus at Caesarea Philippa constituted one of Galilee's most poignantly emphatic demonstrations of the Jews' loss of local sovereignty, of de facto communal self-rule—for Christians and Muslims, this Jewish humiliation in Galilee would be followed by the Crusaders' debacle at Hattin in 1187, and the Palestinians' Nakba in 1948. Jews were flayed, ravaged by animals and massacred at Caesarea Philippa *just one decade* before the Matthew group retroactively recorded Jesus and Peter establishing a new ekklesia assembly, a church, for their community at the same site (it bears mention that had this gospel been composed later, in the first decades of the second century, Caesarea Philippi would not have conjured the same sense of abject Jewish weakness[119]). Perhaps some members of Matthew's group had watched the blood of fellow Jews splatter in the teeth of beasts, and at the edge of gladiators' swords, at Titus' festivities at Caesarea Philippi.

More certainly, even if it was situated in Syria, outside of Galilee, when it composed Matthew, the group would by no means have regarded Caesarea Philippi as a blandly neutral venue in Galilee. Denial of this fact would be tantamount to imagining unrealistically that somebody in 2011 could have written a story about Manhattan's financial district without thinking about the toppled Twin Towers.

Caesarea Philippi's gentile atmosphere, as the former host of a Hellenistic temple cult, was useful, as a symbol of the target audience which would be proselytized by the new church of Peter and the other disciples, in its mission to all the nations. No less apposite, however, was Titus' cruel carnival at the site. Peter's rock, and the church, were planted at Caesarea Philippi by the logic of communal and spiritual rivalry, rather than the facts of geography. Matthew's cartography is determined by the Gospel's supersession agenda no less than by the hills and roads of Galilee. For the Matthew group, Caesarea Philippi symbolized the Jews' abject humiliation, essentially their return to slavery. Titus' festivities at the site commemorated not just the eradication of the rebellion and of the Jews' quasi-sovereignty in the Land of Israel but also the abolition of the promises of national freedom laden within the Moses Exodus narrative. Logically, the place where Moses' prophetic liberation of the Israelites was brought to an end was the rock upon which Matthew's community, in homage to its newly revealed, divine prophet, would build its church. Caesarea Philippi, in this layered way, is Galilee's supersession capital, its own Vatican.

GALILEE OF MERCY, JERUSALEM OF JUDGMENT

To be sure, much in the postmodernist spirit of twenty-first century "critical geography" recapitulates insights and approaches that have been incorporated in non-fundamentalist streams of Biblical study and criticism since the eighteenth-century Enlightenment. For hundreds of years, modern-minded commentators have observed ways in which the Gospels' impetus of revealing Jesus as the Messiah determined the map of where he journeyed, in and out of Galilee, in his preaching and healing. These critical approaches begin at the beginning, observing how details in the Bethlehem nativity were fashioned to conform with legends and prophecies of messianic descent from the House of David. Taken too far, such critical approaches yield dialogues of the deaf—no matter how liberal-minded they might be, believing Christians will eventually recoil from commentators who insist that way stations in the life of Jesus were marked out entirely by mundane hands, by mortal authors who were animated by power rivalries, who had axes to grind or sophistic theological points to make.

I am thinking, however, of an opposite operation wherein serious study of Galilee history enriches interfaith understanding. Much in postmodernist rhetoric is overblown and self-serving, but in this crucial sphere of religious studies, I think it accurately reflects an age which, while far less secularized than what was anticipated by modernists a century ago, is nonetheless salubriously accustomed to thinking of *aspects* of the Old Testament and the New Testament as stories not written from heaven above. In this "postmodern" context, the aforementioned brand of "critical geography" usefully reminds us that the real heroes in these stories are often not the *players*, but rather the *places*. In Galilee, geography is not a map, but rather symbols of diametric opposition on a spiritual compass, one end vanity, the other end forever. All within one or two days of walking, from the Sermon on the Mount to Banias, the Galilee geography of Matthew maps journeys between monotheism's loftiest moral aspirations, and the petty politics of religious rivalry.

Ultimately, the lasting opposition in Matthew is not between Jesus and transient players like the Pharisees. Largely due to the tantalizing lack of information provided by our main source of information on Second Temple sects, Josephus, efforts to establish what Matthew's "antitypes," the Pharisees, were "really" like, have proven elusive and frustrating. Understandably defensive about the negative portraiture conveyed by Matthew, modern Jewish commentators, such as the early Reform rabbi, Abraham Geiger, portrayed the Jerusalemite Pharisees as religious moderates and innovators, sometimes contrasting them with religiously ignorant Galilean Jews, *amei eretz* (Geiger went so far as to describe Jesus as a "Pharisean Jew," though one tainted with "Galilean coloring" and therefore not really an original thinker[120]). Jewish-Christian dynamics being what they were over the ages, it hardly comes as a surprise that when interpreting the gospels, one group's anti-heroes became the other group's heroes.

A more lasting contrast in Matthew is between places, particularly Galilee and Jerusalem. Galilee in the Book of Matthew features healing theology, whereas Jerusalem highlights hellfire. Galilee is about mercy, Jerusalem, judgment. In many ways, of course, these are facile oppositions, and innumerable exceptions to them are easy to find. Metonyms of hell, for example, "gnashing of teeth," are laced throughout the Gospel of Matthew, and not limited to Jerusalem, and hell even makes itself felt during the Sermon on the Mount, as in Jesus' admonition about anger ("But I tell you that anyone who is angry with a brother or sister will be subject to judgment"[121]). Nonetheless, Matthew's theology of final judgment unfolds in Jerusalem, not Galilee. The crux here is the "Judgment of the Nations" passage, featuring the parable of the separation of the sheep and the goats.[122] This complicated chapter has provoked considerable debate about whether heaven can be a reward for those who suffer and carry out good works, yet who do not have any known commitment to Jesus, and its evocation of hell has implicit precedent in Jesus' Jerusalem preaching, as in the parable of the wedding banquet,[123] which envisions spiritually recalcitrant guests, clearly Jews, being cast out of a marriage feast, the parable's symbol of the kingdom of heaven. The Sheep and the Goats parable, however, is where Jesus' Jerusalem theology of judgment becomes explicit, terrifyingly casting away the damned ("Depart from me, you who are cursed, into the eternal fire prepared for the devil and his angels"). "For the first time in this section of teaching, we are told what kind of life will be rewarded, and what kind of life will be punished," concludes one commentator.[124] "Matthew 25 has given the world much of what it knows, in fear and trembling, about the eternal fires of hell," writes another scholar.[125]

Not Matthew's Galilee, but rather its Jerusalem passages have inspired eschatological excitement at Christianity's most impassioned extremes. Significantly, the gospel's contribution to the Evangelical revival in our contemporary world is framed in Jerusalem. The key passages here are 24:29–31 and 24:36–40 which bequeathed to religious history the idea of "rapture," the sudden ascent of true followers of Jesus, with unbelievers left behind (the first passage refers to angels, a trumpet call, and the sudden gathering of the elect "from the four winds; two men will be in the field, one will be taken, and the other left," the second passage concludes). The rapture concept and imagery have powerfully captivated Evangelicals and other Christian groups, as evidenced by the best-selling "Left Behind" series, which since its inception in the 1990s has reached tens of millions of readers.[126]

In Israel today, it is not difficult to find Evangelical tourists in Galilee, just as it is not entirely correct to say that liberal Protestants from the mainline denominations currently exhibit a special attraction for Galilee (in fact, in past decades, many mainline Protestants have grown increasingly disaffected with Israel as a whole, owing to its right-wing settlement policies in the post-1967 territories). That is to say, the contrast sketched above, suggesting that Matthew's judgment sections draw one, Evangelical, sort of Christians to Jerusalem, whereas its Galilee descriptions have strong appeal to liberal sorts of theology and denominations, is overdrawn, and many readers will reject it—I think it is correct in its basic features, and devote a section in this study's second volume to it.[127] My point, however, is not to fasten, stereotypically and rigidly, any particular place in the gospels upon one group of believers. Instead, I am insisting that the Jerusalem-Galilee contrast in Matthew (and elsewhere in scripture) is far more lasting than this gospel's opposition between its mortal characters. When was the last time you heard someone (other than a theologian or a scholar) engaged in a serious debate about what the Pharisees were really like? In contrast, secular and religious tourists, political activists—all sorts of interlopers in the Holy Land of varying degrees of interest in its past and present—make choices all the time regarding where they want to visit, and these choices draw upon values and images culled, ultimately, from the Bible. More to the point, the surge of American Evangelical interest and support for Israel, a phenomenon of much geopolitical significance, is rooted in the 1967 Six Day War turning point, when Israel's triumph left Jerusalem fully under its control; before 1967, when Jerusalem was divided between Jordan and Israel, the Evangelicals were relatively apathetic toward Israel.[128] In contrast, as shown in a later chapter of our second volume, in the mid-nineteenth century, with religion presumably threatened by the rise of science and by middle-class secularity, Galilee exerted a special attraction upon liberal-minded American Protestants, who were searching for an enduring core of spirituality in the region where Jesus, and his vision, came of age. If you want to measure the temper of an era, watch how the people who lived in it read the map of the Holy Land, and whether, for whatever moral reasoning or eschatological computations, they were drawn to the Sermon on the Mount in Galilee, or to past and future images of the Temple in Jerusalem.

NOTES

1. Matthew 5:17.
2. Matthew 28:19.
3. As in the example of the recent forthrightly argued volume, John Kampen, *Matthew within Sectarian Judaism* (New Haven: Yale University Press, 2019).
4. The literature on Matthew's injunctions about the fulfillment of Jewish law is extensive. One example: Klyne Snodgrass, "Matthew and the Law," *SBL Seminar Papers 1988* (Atlanta: Atlanta Scholars, 1988), 536–54.
5. Ulrich Luz, *The Theology of the Gospel of Matthew* (Cambridge: Cambridge University Press, 2012), 126.
6. Matthew 13:11.
7. J.C. Fenton, *Saint Matthew* (London: Penguin Books, 1963), 217.
8. Luz, 185.
9. Anthony Saldarini, *Matthew's Jewish Community* (Chicago: University of Chicago Press, 1994), 1–2.
10. J. Andrew Overman, *Matthew's Gospel and Formative Judaism: The Social World of the Matthean Community* (Minneapolis: Fortress Press, 1990), 8–15.
11. Jacob Neusner, *From Politics to Piety: The Emergence of Pharisaic Judaism* (Englewood Cliffs: Prentice Hall, 1973).
12. Overman, 159; Kampen, 14.
13. Sean Freyne, *Galilee, Jesus and the Gospels: Literary Approaches and Historical Investigations* (Philadelphia: Fortress Press: 1988), 89.
14. Ibid, 54.

15. Susannah Heschel, *The Aryan Jesus: Christian Theologians and the Bible in Nazi Germany* (Princeton: Princeton University Press, 2008).

16. Luz, 8.

17. Matthew 4: 13–14.

18. Fenton, 66.

19. Mark Chancey, *The Myth of a Gentile Galilee* (New York: Cambridge University Press, 2002), 169–70.

20. Horsley, Hanson, *Bandits, Prophets*, 59.

21. Cited in Chancey, 13.

22. Ibid, 16.

23. Ibid.

24. "When Jesus entered Capernaum, a centurion came to him, asking for help."

25. Chancey, 61–2.

26. For example: "Jesus stepped into a boat, crossed over and came to his own town." Matthew 9:1.

27. "Then Jesus began to denounce the towns in which most of his miracles had been performed, because they did not repent." Matthew 11:20.

28. Chancey, 42.

29. Ibid.

30. Susannah Heschel, *Abraham Geiger and the Jewish Jesus* (Chicago: University of Chicago Press, 1998).

31. For an appraisal of this problematic term: Aharon Oppenheimer, *The Am Ha'aretz: A Study in the History of the Jewish People in the Hellenistic-Roman Period* (Leiden: E. J. Brill, 1977).

32. Abraham Geiger, *Judaism and its History in Two Parts* (New York: Bloch, 1911).

33. H. Graetz, *History of the Jews*, vol. II (from the Reign of Hyrcanus to the completion of the Babylonian Talmud) (Philadelphia: Jewish Publication Society of America, 1893), 148.

34. Jonathan Reed, "Instability in Jesus' Galilee: A Demographic Perspective," *Journal of Biblical Literature* 129, no. 2 (2010): 351.

35. James Strange, "First Century Galilee from Archaeology and From the Texts," in Douglas Edwards, C. Thomas McCollough (eds.), *Archaeology and the Galilee, Texts and Contexts in the Graeco-Roman and Byzantine Periods* (Atlanta: Scholars Press, 1997), 39–49.

36. Aslan, 44.

37. "Some time after this, Jesus crossed to the far shore of the Sea of Galilee (that is, the Sea of Tiberias)," John: 6:1.

38. Eric Meyers, "Jesus and his Galilean Context," in Edwards and McCollough, 64.

39. Strange, "First Century Galilee."

40. Mordechai Aviam, "First Century Jewish Galilee: An Archaeological Perspective," in Douglas Edwards (ed.), *Religion and Society in Roman Palestine* (New York: Routledge, 2004), 7–28.

41. Ibid.

42. Richard Horsley, *Archaeology, History and Society in Galilee: The Social Context of Jesus and the Rabbis* (Valley Forge: Trinity Press International, 1996), 60.

43. Harold Remus, *Jesus as Healer* (Cambridge: Cambridge University Press, 1997), 11.

44. Unless otherwise noted, this paragraph draws from Remus' research.

45. Gardner, 144.

46. Remus, 31.

47. Adolf Harnack, *Luke the Physician* (New York: G. P. Putnam's Sons, 1907).

48. Pieter F. Craffert, *The Life of a Galilean Shaman: Jesus of Nazareth in Anthropological-Historical Perspective* (Eugene, OR: Cascade Books, 2008).

49. Ibid, 258.

50. Stevan Davies, *Jesus the Healer: Possession, Trance and the Origins of Christianity* (New York, Bloomsbury, 1995).

51. Davies, 79.

52. E. P. Sanders, *Jesus and Judaism* (Fortress Press: Philadelphia, 1985), 157–73.

53. Davies, 85.

54. Ibid, 99.

55. Ibid, 8–9.

56. Howard Clarke, *The Gospel of Matthew and its Readers: A Historical Introduction to the First Gospel* (Bloomington: Indiana University Press, 2003), 55.

57. Matthew 8: 5–13.

58. Richard Gardner, *Matthew* (Scottdale, PA: Herald Press, 1991), 146.

59. Clarke, 99.

60. Matthew 8:11.

61. Clarke, 146.

62. Matthew 8:12.

63. Matthew 8:17.

64. Matthew 11:23.

65. Matthew 8:20.

66. Schweitzer, *The Quest*.

67. Matthew 8:22.

68. Aslan, 95.

69. Ibid.

70. Matthew 5:17. For an analysis measuring the extent to which Matthew's Sermon on the Mount is presented as fulfillment or supersession of Moses on Sinai: W. B. Davies, *The Setting of the Sermon on the Mount* (Atlanta: Scholars Press, 1989). Davies (99) concludes: "In the circumstances surrounding the actual delivery of the Sermon . . . there is little, if anything, to recall the giving of the Law on Mount Sinai."

71. Matthew 5:1–2.

72. Clarke, 62.

73. Saldarini, 101.

74. Gardner, 91.

75. Saldarini, 39–40.

76. Ibid.
77. These points about "Hallowed be thy name," and "daily bread," follow Fenton, 101.
78. Luz, 50.
79. Matthew 6:19.
80. Matthew 6:24.
81. Matthew 26:11.
82. Matthew 19:16–22.
83. Luz, 111.
84. Matthew 25: 14–30.
85. Clarke, 193.
86. Ibid, 63.
87. Schweitzer reached his view by drawing from claims and findings in: Johannes Weiss, *Jesus' Proclamation of the Kingdom of God* (Philadelphia: Fortress Press, 1892/1971).
88. Jorge Frey, "The Character and Background of Matt 5:25-26," in Hans-Jurgen Becker, Serge Ruzer (eds.), *The Sermon on the Mount and its Jewish Setting* (Paris: J. Gabalda et Cie Editeurs, 2005), 3–39.
89. Matthew 5:39.
90. Tolstoy and Augustine references follow Clarke, 74–6.
91. Fenton, 165.
92. Clarke, 111.
93. Matthew 5:7.
94. Matthew 18:21–22.
95. Matthew 23:32.
96. Matthew 23:33–38.
97. Overman, 16–19.
98. For instance, the editor of a well-annotated Penguin edition of the Gospel of Matthew (published in 1963) writes: "The reader may feel that Matthew has been severe and cold in his condemnation of the Jewish leaders; and we are told that in fact he has misrepresented them" Fenton, 365. Luz starts with a modification of Fenton's judgment, but then goes a bit farther, explicitly delivering his own criticism of Matthew on this point: "Today we know that the Pharisees were thoroughly capable of viewing themselves with a critical eye, and that there are points of agreement between Matthew's critique and Pharisaic self-criticism. Matthew's critique, however, is wholesale and therefore unjust." Luz, 123. "Readers have long noted that here [23: the Seven Woes] there is no talking of loving, blessing, caring and praying for one's enemies," observes Clarke. "The authority of Scripture, readily available and easily misapplied, and the terrible history of anti-Semitism within Christian societies have given these verses frightful repercussions," Clarke, 184.
99. Clarke, 111.
100. The following examples are taken from Clarke, 61–94.
101. The best one volume explication of this intricately layered, mystical, Jewish hymn is: Reuven Kimelman, *Lekhah dodi ve-ḳabalat Shabat : ha-mashma'ut ha-misṭit* (Jerusalem: Magnes Press, 2002).

102. Freyne, *Galilee Jesus*.

103. John M. Vonder Bruegge, *Mapping Galilee in Josephus, Luke and John: Critical Geography and the Construction of Ancient Space* (Leiden: Brill, 2016), 3.

104. Luz, 123.

105. Overviews about this debate over whether parts of Matthew 16:13–20 were inserted retroactively by the church, and also over the meaning of its key theological terms, can be found in: Fenton, 264–67; Clarke, 138–44.

106. This term, if truth be told, could also refer to a kind of alternative synagogue "assembly. Fenton, 266.

107. Fenton, 265.

108. Clarke, 139.

109. Fenton, 267.

110. John Francis Wilson, *Caesarea Philippi: Banias, the Lost City of Pan* (London: I. B. Taurus, 2004), 4–6.

111. Ibid, 75–6. Talmudic writers wondered whether Moses could possibly have exploited a loophole about crossing the Jordan and entering the Promised Land had he trekked on the northern side of the Banias springs.

112. Ibid, 83.

113. For example: Josephus, *The Jewish War*, 193, 343.

114. George Nickelsburg, "Enoch, Levi and Peter: Recipients of Revelation in Upper Galilee," *Journal of Biblical Literature* 100, no. 4 (Dec. 1981): 590.

115. Josephus, *The Jewish War*, 343.

116. Ibid, 339.

117. Aryeh Kasher, *Jews and Hellenistic Cities in Eretz-Israel* (Tubingen: J. C. B. Mohr, 1990), 305; cited in Wlison, 34.

118. Wilson, 71.

119. This is because after the Bar Kochba revolt, distinguished Tannaitic rabbis settled in the Banias area (and staged discussions about the pros and cons of accommodation with Rome). Wilson, 73–4.

120. Geiger, 131.

121. Matthew 5:22.

122. Matthew 25: 31–46.

123. Matthew 22: 1–10.

124. Fenton, 400.

125. Clarke, 194.

126. Ibid, 192.

127. In the study of what types of Christians tourists go where in Israel, a good place to start is Hillary Kaell, *Walking Where Jesus Walked: American Christians and the Holy Land Pilgrimage* (New York: NYU Press, 2014).

128. Caitlin Carenen, *The Fervent Embrace: Liberal Protestants, Evangelicals and Israel* (New York: NYU Press, 2012); Stephen Spector, *Evangelicals and Israel: The Story of American Christian Zionism* (Oxford: Oxford University Press, 2009).

Chapter 3

Mishnaic Galilee

WHERE MONOTHEISM MULTIPLIED: MAJOR THEMES OF GALILEAN ANTIQUITY

Galilee's history under Roman rule can be divided into two phases, each defined by a particular problem. The first period revolves around the issue of the obstreperous Galileans and is described from varying perspectives, elite Jewish and embryonic Christian, in parts of Josephus and the gospels. In social, economic, cultural, and religious terms, how well was Galilee's population adjusted to Roman control? Much in the portrayals of Josephus' command of the revolt in Galilee, and of Jesus' wandering mission in the region, can be seen as probing examination of this question. Neither Josephus, a political moderate from a Jerusalem priestly caste, nor Jesus, a religious reformer and, in the evolving Christian view, Son of God, was really supportive of dynamics of sociopolitical rebellion which had been manifest in Galilee from the period of Herod's debut as prince in the region. But just as neither (of course) would ever have resorted to Herod's brutal methods of anti-rebellion pacification, neither Josephus nor Jesus seemed happily resolved about a continuing future of Roman rule in the region. For ages, commentators have stumbled in efforts to sort out the precise attitudes in Josephus' relevant, internally contradictory, two texts, or in Jesus' "render unto Caesar" dictum such analyses focus on what these two figures, Josephus and Jesus, might "really" have thought about Rome, but the underlying common denominator in the commentary is the issue of the obstreperous Galileans.

Despite the obvious differences in their own self-perceptions, identities, and goals, Josephus' writings and the gospels evince tactical overlap in the protagonists' approaches to this regional population. Neither figure is a straight talker in dealings with the unruly Galileans. One relies on

Greco-Roman methods of rhetoric and wile, and the other on parables and ostensible miracles. Since the history of this period was never told broadly from an interfaith or multicultural, Galilean, viewpoint, few commentators have recognized how unlocking the riddle of monotheism's multiplication in this period of Roman rule largely depends upon clarifying the disposition (in religious and political, if not genetic-racial, terms) of the Galileans themselves. For Jews fascinated and demoralized by the course of the anti-Roman rebellion, the brunt of attention has attached to whether Josephus ought to be regarded a Jewish hero or Jewish traitor, whereas Christian commentary (as well as discussions contributed by non-Christians) has typically been dominated by the search for the historical Jesus. We are witnessing in this volume how long-standing questions germane to the evolving, pluralistic history of monotheism need to be addressed from a Galilean vantage point, one centered on the issues of what the region's population groups were really like, and what they really wanted.

These are all complicated questions. Did Josephus patriotically serve the cause of the Jewish rebellion, both as military commander in the region, and, retrospectively, as a historian writing under Roman patronage? Was Jesus really at home in Galilee, where he grew up? If so, or, if not so, how is the mission to the gentiles evoked at the end of the Gospel of Matthew to be grasped? Would Christianity have departed from Judaism as a separate faith had Jesus been more (or less) at home in Galilee? However, one reflects upon such questions, it becomes apparent not just that their intelligible analysis depends upon evaluation of the disposition of these figures' Galilean constituencies. More than that, in our time, the most promising way to decipher riddles of Galilean sociopolitical, and religious, disposition, is to utilize newly honed methodologies in fields we encountered in the previous chapters—archaeology, literary criticism, critical geography, and more. Over past decades, scholars, particularly in the field of New Testament criticism, have been deploying such innovative research techniques, but their inquiries lack the sort of clarity which comes when topics of socioreligious fracture are viewed in their proper regional dimension. Galilee's history remains the Greatest Story Never Told. Few have seen how the search for the historical Jesus is, to a large extent, the search for the historical Galilee, just as the search for Josephus' identity and soul is, in great measure, the search for the historical Galilee.

The second phase of Galilean history in antiquity is post-*hurban*, that is, subsequent to the decimation of the Second Temple and the elimination of Judaism's core in Jerusalem and in the Temple cult. If truth be told, this phase can be divided into subperiods, since the challenges Jews faced after the calamitous failure of another rebellion against Rome, the Bar Kochba revolt (132–135 CE) overlapped, but were not identical to, problems and dilemmas they encountered after the failure of the first revolt and the destruction of the Temple in 70 CE. Some nuances differentiating responses to these two tragically failed revolts will be elucidated in this chapter, but for the purposes of broadly understanding themes in Galilee's history, it suffices to think of this relatively late period in Antiquity as a post-hurban phase wherein Jews, some of them refugees from the Jerusalem Temple catastrophe (or their descendants) were compelled to chart out a spiritual future and new national religious identities, in the frightening limbo which yawned after the Jerusalem cult's demise.

In chapter 2, we observed how groups of Jesus' followers, one of which presumably composed the Gospel of Matthew, responded not only to the hurban with some ambivalence but also with manifest mounting resolve to depart from Judaism. Eventually, the Christian faith they constructed related to the Temple's destruction as irrefutable proof of Judaism's irreversible loss of God's favor. Writing, it seems, concurrently with the embryonic Christians in Matthew's group, Josephus shared its apocalyptic view of the hurban as a symbol of Judaism's forfeiture of its divinely special ("chosen") status, but he viewed this as an ephemeral setback particular to one, fallen, generation. How would Judaism reinvent itself now that its foundation in the Jerusalem Temple cult was lost, either in the interim, or forever? By consolidating rabbinical Judaism as an effective surrogate for Temple observances, Jews in the Mishnaic period provided their own answer of Jewish renewal, at least implicitly as a rebuttal to the developing Christian project of full schism.

In chapter 2, we observed how the Matthew group's sometimes inchoate push toward the establishment of a new religion, as symbolized by its gospel's evocation of a mission to the gentiles, is, on multiple levels, a story that belongs to Galilee. In this chapter, devoted to the origins of Talmudic Judaism, we will see how the same thing can be said about Jews who mobilized in the name of their religion's renewal—in unmistakable ways, the Mishnah is a story that belongs to Galilee. Historically, no other region played host to this dual dynamic of religious fracture and revitalization. Galilee is where monotheism multiplied.

EXILE DEFERRED

After the disastrous Bar Kochba revolt (132–135 CE), Jewish life recovered in Galilee. The conventional understanding of Jewish history as roughly two millennia of exile following the destruction of the Second Temple, and the failure of the Bar Kochba rebellion sixty-five years later, is plainly wrong, since Jews developed a lively new culture in Galilee through the third century, and even after it. In Galilee, the Tannaim (religious teachers) set about consolidating the Jews' oral law and completed the first phase of this project by finishing the Mishnah around 220 CE, almost a century after the Bar Kochba insurrection was brutally stifled (literally, "Mishnah" means to study by repetition). The completion date of the Mishnah is more or less contemporaneous with the death of Rabbi Judah HaNasi (also known as Judah the Prince), who redacted and edited this bedrock early work of rabbinical Judaism.

The nature of the relationship between Tannaitic Mishnah compilers, and masses of Jews who remained in the country after 135 CE, remains in dispute. Some scholars view these early compilers of Judaism's oral law as a small, perhaps estranged, scholarly elite whose interpretations were not necessarily representative of the way other literate Jews viewed religious law in a period when it could not be known whether the Jerusalem Temple would be rebuilt, and when the status of the vast complex of rules regarding worship at the temple was therefore questionable. Mishnah compilers were not really congregational leaders. With Jewish society divided between illiterate masses of dubious piety, *amme ha'aretz,* and a religiously solid elite of "members" (*haverim*), these early progenitors of rabbinic Judaism remained aloof in small circles, located in segregated *bet midrash* academies. The Tannaim never developed "any sort of outreach program" to strengthen religious culture on a popular level.[1]

The synagogue in this Mishnah period served communal functions of a mixed, religious and mundane, character. Rabbis who devoted themselves to scholarly compilation of the law did not maintain a well-defined relationship with these early synagogues. "For Jews throughout Palestine, the synagogue was first and foremost an institution of the local community," and, at most, the rabbis "were but one of a number of elements in Jewish society of late antiquity which had a hand" in developing the early synagogues.[2]

Whatever their communal status in their own contemporary world of second-century Galilee, these Tannaitic rabbis left an indelible mark in the region's history due to their work in the consolidation of the Mishnah. This initial generation of Galilee Tannaim, migratory overachievers, had formerly been based in Judea. They moved into Galilee[3] in flight from persecutory measures (*gezerot,* or *shemad*) of some level of severity[4] which were enforced in Judea by Emperor Hadrian. Galilee served as the focal point of Jewish resettlement, and as the early springboard for Judaism's momentous transformation from a Temple cult to a rabbinical creed, because it had remained relatively placid during the 132–135 CE Bar Kochba insurrection,[5] and the Roman crackdown therefore did not reach into the region.

Because it implies that Judeans had a more highly developed, or militant, national religious culture a few decades into the second century CE, scholars have debated this claim about the non-involvement of Jewish Galileans during the Bar Kochba revolt.[6] One scholar conjectures that compared to Judeans, Galileans were not necessarily more deferential toward Roman rulers in this period, but their nationalist energy had been exhausted prior to the 132–135 CE rebellion, since Jews in Galilee had been involved in prior acts of insubordination, including the 115–117 CE Kitos War.[7]

Among scholars, there is lively debate about the reliability of documentary accounts of Jewish life in the region in this Tanniatic period. The most contentious part of this debate features the problem of using Talmudic commentary as source material for historical accounts of Jewish life in Galilee in the era of Judah HaNasi, but there are also various methodological concerns about the incorporation of written materials left by early Christian, or Roman, writers, and also of physical materials uncovered in archaeological excavations.[8]

The most serious impediment to a realistic understanding of Jewish readaptation to Roman rule, following the Bar Kochba failure, is the tight grip, if not chokehold, exercised by an apocalyptic view of mass Jewish extermination, and exodus, in years after 135 CE. The incorrect image of Jewish life being extinguished throughout the country after the Bar Kochba failure is perpetuated by political agendas which consolidated in modern times, picking up steam in late decades of the twentieth century. For instance, in the early 1980s, Yehoshafat Harkabi, a former Israeli army intelligence officer, produced a polemical book which cast the anti-Roman Bar Kochba rebels as fanatical precursors of post-1967 Jewish settlers on the West Bank and the Gaza Strip.[9] The tenor of this book suggested that almost nothing was left of Jewish life in Eretz Israel after 135 CE. Transparently, Harkabi's apocalyptic view about the near extermination of Jewish life around 135 CE served as a Cassandra warning about possible bleak consequences of Israel's contemporary settlement movement.

Yet more significantly, the story of Jewish revitalization in Galilee in Tannaitic times has been ignored, again and again, because Christian polemics about the curse of Jewish life in late antiquity became canon in western culture.[10] On this interpretation, the destruction of the Temple, and Jewish exile after the failed rebellions against Rome, came as punishment for Jewish rejection of Jesus' divinity. Needless to say, searching for their own explanations to account for the traumatic destruction of the Temple, Jewish scholars in late antiquity and the Middle Ages did not consciously accept this specific argument about the consequences of Jesus' rejection. Nonetheless, the power exercised by this image of mass Jewish exile engendered immediately at the end of the Second Temple period could never have become so extraordinarily potent had not a time frame suited to Christian theology been sublimated and condoned by Jews, for one reason or another.

Take as an example Israel's national anthem, *Hatikvah*. On Israel's political left, the anthem is sometimes challenged because its references (e.g.,

"Jewish soul") are not suited to the country's Arab minority, about 20 percent of the country's population. But any serious historian would identify another problem with the anthem, namely, its chronology. To say, as the anthem more or less does, that Jews were exiled from their land for 2,000 years is to undervalue a wealth of evidence about the achievements of the Tannaitic era, based in Galilee. Tannaitic Galilee is a story of exile deferred.

TANNAITIC GALILEE: DEMOGRAPHIC AND SOCIOECONOMIC SURVEY

The Galilee region's second-century population is rated as being "large" but is not quantified in the sources. Its two cities were Tiberias, Herod Antipas' creation, and Sepphoris. Also, over fifty villages have been identified in Galilee in this era—but this estimate is not overly helpful, since the demographic dimensions of a "village" (*kfar*) are unclear (as we have seen, sources make hyperbolic references to a village as having "no less than 15,000 inhabitants").[11] Perhaps seven Jewish villages in Galilee disappeared during the tumult of the Bar Kochba rebellion.[12] Oxford University scholar Martin Goodman estimates that in 135 CE, around when the Sanhedrin rabbinic court was moved from Yavne in Judea, to Usha in the north, Galilee's population was about 300,000 persons.[13] Jews constituted about three-quarters of the population in Galilee[14] (by some accounts, the pagan minority in the region was substantial[15]). The total population of Palestine, on both sides of the Jordan, was about two and a half million.

One indication of Jewish population movement from Judea to Galilee is rosters of priestly duties for the Temple. Up to the Bar Kochba revolt, decades after the Temple's destruction, twenty-four priests shared various ritual duties for the Temple, the obligation being apportioned on a weekly shift basis during which time the designated priest abstained from drinking wine. These twenty-four holy men were apparently chosen from different regions of the country, though most were based in Judea. From the mid-second century, however, following the Bar Kochba debacle, the priestly shift-holders were increasingly based in Galilee.[16] A mix of archaeological and literary evidence, featuring liturgical song (*piyyutim*), and stone tablets that have turned up in Israel and as far away as Yemen, attests to how Jews in Palestine and well beyond its borders would keep track of this rotation roster, originally in the hope that a new Temple would "speedily be built." As centuries went by, and hopes for a speedy Temple restoration vanished, a new routine arose whereby diaspora Jews would pray for the restoration of esteemed priestly shift-holders in Galilee, as though the sacred priestly rotation's origins at the Jerusalem Temple had been forgotten. Documents in the

Cairo Genizah show that Jewish communities would read aloud these weekly priest schedules through the eleventh century.[17]

As we will see, the Mishnah relays scattered, sporadic detail about relations between Jews and gentiles in specific Galilee locales, particularly Tiberias and Sepphoris. These Mishnah snippets are supplemented in other Tannaitic materials, including rulings and discussions on matters such as selling animals to gentiles and the supervision of non-Jewish workers in wine production. The materials suffice, Goodman argues, for the sketching of a rough composite portrait of interaction between Jewish and gentile populations.[18] He assumes that most such socioeconomic interaction transpired not within the Galilee region itself, but in areas that bordered on Galilee, such as the plain of Megiddo,[19] and Aharon Oppenheimer, a prominent Israeli scholar on this Mishnaic period, adds some interesting detail about Galilean Jews' dealings with pagan culture in Acre, and also with Phoenicia, further north on the Mediterranean coast, in today's Lebanon.[20] Some discussions in Jewish sources indirectly reflect close degrees of friendship or intimacy between Jews and gentiles; rabbis worried about intermarriage, particularly in coastal cities proximate to Galilee.[21] Pagan worship in public venues was mostly negligible in Galilee; at most, such practices could be found at the region's edges, as in the case of the Paneas cult center at Caesarea Philippi,[22] and also in Acre (for the purposes of Jewish administration, Acre was not in this period included within Galilee's borders, precisely because of its pagan shrines and foreign majority[23]). Sympathetic gentiles evinced a pick-and-choose attitude toward the Jews' monotheistic religion, sometimes conveyed by funding ambiguous inscription dedications in synagogues which did not necessarily express support for the Jews' "chosen people" conceptions.[24] The number of gentile conversions to Judaism was large enough to irritate Roman officials—the circumcision of male converts sometimes created health problems, and this practice was actually banned after Hadrian. Many circumcisions appear to have been administered by non-rabbinic Jews.[25]

Second-century Galilee possessed a farm economy primarily dependent upon olive production and export. Olive production became especially important after the Bar Kochba revolt, when the region hosted an influx of immigrants from Judea. When these newcomers reached Galilee, the region's valleys were already extensively farmed and so not accessible to the newcomers. Putting down roots in the region's sloping landscape, the Judea emigres found it hard to cultivate grain. Such factors explain the focus on olives, a product valued in this era as a fuel and soap source, as well as a culinary item. In terms of livestock, sheep and goats were the most profitable, but some farmers found it more feasible to engage small-scale cattle breeding (Talmudic writings indicate that bans were sometimes attempted on small cattle grazing owing to land acquisition considerations[26]). Fisherman worked in the Mediterranean, the Jordan River, and the Sea of Galilee.[27] A strong indication of the agricultural foundations of Galilee's economy is the way the Mishnah relates to the Jewish Sabbath and the suspension of work routines: about half of the occupations it lists are in farming and food-processing spheres (garment production accounts for a third).[28]

Commerce was traded in open village markets in a monetary economy. The use of metal coins connected Galilee to other regions throughout the Roman empire, and coin use penetrated a diversified network of transactions, including divorce payments. Moneychangers operated according to well-defined norms, and, in contrast to gospel records of the Second Temple period, purveyors of this service were generally men of high moral stature about whom complaints are scarce in the sources. Scribes wandered to and fro in marketplaces, reading aloud to clients various sale, rental, or marital documents. Shops clustered around the open markets, and customers established relations with their favorite proprietors, sometimes making their purchases on credit. Jewish craftsman in Tannaitic Galilee were of many types, including blacksmiths, tanners, potters, and weavers (most wool weaving, as the Mishnah makes clear, was done by women). Wealthy Galileans imported high-quality goods, with gold, glass, and ointments heading this import list.[29] Some overviews of Galilee's economy in this period are noticeably bullish, stressing that the region, in normal years, was mostly "independent of food imports from abroad," that it boasted "socially healthy" economic arrangements pivoting around "a multitude of small peasant owners," and that its economic realities and potential were "formidable."[30]

In terms of culture, Aramaic was, more or less, the lingua franca in the Middle East. From the time of Jesus, this language was in use in Galilee; yet in all likelihood Hebrew was also "spoken in most parts of Galilee in this period."[31] Greek was not widely spoken in Galilee, perhaps not at all in its upper parts, whereas rabbinic scholars had some general knowledge of Greek (and some attained a high degree of fluency).[32] As the Tannaitic period progressed through the second century, the rabbis evinced an increasingly lax attitude toward the biblical ban against visual images. The Tosefta, an oral law compilation supplemental to the Mishnah, "permits a picture of a possible pagan divine figure to appear on everyday things such as boilers, kettles, pans, basins," but not on precious items such as jewelry.[33] After the Bar Kochba revolt, a "dramatic and rapid" change in Galilee art and architecture is manifest, with Greek influences becoming increasingly important[34]—we will see that this trend in art parallels a sociopolitical trend of accommodation with Roman administration which was personified and promoted by Judah HaNasi.

Not all Jews in Galilee were literate, and rabbinical students "formed a separate group within the population,"[35] an elite. Roman institutions and methods constituted structural models in this rabbinical education sphere. Jewish students learned in academies whose structure was similar to Roman institutions that catered to young gentile sophists.[36] Jewish students were unlike their young Roman counterparts: their conspicuous use of *tefilin* phylacteries was one of many things that set them apart. These Jewish students congregated in close-knit groups, and they were subordinate to teachers who possessed quasi-parental authority. Formal lessons featured teachers orating articles of *halakha* (Jewish law), which students were expected to learn by repetition.[37]

USHA FOUNDING

Between the two Jewish anti-Rome rebellions, in the period known for the initial development of rabbinical Judaism under Yohanan ben Zakkai's leadership in a Judea town, Yavne, Galilee had clear links with the first generation of Tannaitic sages. Following the death of his teacher, Hillel the Elder, Yohanan, whose birth details are unknown, spent about two decades in Galilee, in Arav (near Sepphoris) perhaps between the years 20–40 CE. He did not stand out in this period as a rabbi of stature; in fact, he is known to have adjudicated just two religious disputes in Galilee.

Intriguingly, the noncanonical Gospel of Thomas alludes to a meeting between Jesus and a Galilean schoolteacher named Zaccheus, apparently Yohanan ben Zakkai. On this account, the elderly Zaccheus offers to teach Jesus good manners (*derech eretz*), but ends up being humiliated by the more discerning, sagacious younger man. In all probability, Christianity's messiah and the patron of rabbinical Judaism lived for some time within a few miles of one another in Galilee, but nobody knows whether the encounter recorded by Thomas occurred.[38]

Writing in the third century, an Amoraic sage named Ulla claimed that Yohanan ben Zakkai ended this pre-Yavne term in frustration, exclaiming: "Oh Galilee, Galilee! You hate the Torah! Your end will be to be besieged."[39] This prominent Tanna indeed seems to have been unhappy in Galilee, but scholars have suggested that Yohanan's exasperation stemmed from specific complaints about mystical variants of Judaism circulating around Arav, largely at the behest of his own student, Rabbi Hanina ben Dosa, rather than from a general critique about levels of Jewish observance and knowledge in Galilee.[40]

During the Yavne period, Galilee hosted Torah scholars and *batei midrash* places of study, such as one supervised at Sikhnin by Rabbi Hanina ben Teradion. Other Tannaim located in this period in Galilee are Rabbi (Abba) Halafta, from Sepphoris, and Rabbi Yohannan ben Nuri, from Beit She'arim.[41] Evidence of Tiberias hosting flourishing pockets of rabbinical sages before the Bar Kochba revolt can be gleaned from writings appended to the Mishnah's Avot tractate, referring to Rabbi Jose ben Kisma; this rabbi affirms that he would not budge from his great Galilee city of sages for all the money in the world.[42]

Around 80 CE, following Yohannan ben Zakkai's, death, Rabbi Gamaliel II became head of the religious court at Yavne and received the honorific title "Nasi," the prince. Between 96–115 CE, Gamaliel II (his grandfather was Gamaliel I) made grand tours around Eretz Israel, apparently mimicking the practice of Roman imperial officials who visited areas under their dominion. Gamaliel maintained properly deferential relations with the Romans, but these tours implicitly asserted the Jews' renewed desire for partial sovereignty, certainly over their own religious matters. In fact, modifying the way Roman rulers would roam around conquered lands, dictating answers to political-legal questions that arose in them, Gamaliel II reportedly addressed questions of *halacha*, Jewish religious law, in Galilee venues such as Achziv, and also in Tiberias (where he ordered locals to stop using a certain kind of lock to close shut their synagogue on Shabbat). Also, as we will see, in Acre, on the coastal edge of Galilee, Gamaliel II articulated his views on how Judaism might, and might not, interact with pagan culture. All told, in this period stretching between the two anti-Rome revolts, Gamaliel II's extensive presence in Galilee suggests that Jews in the region remained willing to submit to the authority of rabbinical leadership institutions in Judea, despite the loss of the Temple.[43] For his part, Gamaliel toyed with innovations which symbolized or even accelerated Judaism's transition from the Temple cult to a new, rabbinical form. Such initiatives deemphasized the role played by the priestly Kohanim at holidays such as Passover and Yom Kippur, and instead put a focus on family or community forms of worship.[44]

Following the failed Bar Kochba revolt, the Jews' religious leadership relocated from Yavne to a small lower Galilee town, Usha. The small village, located north of Shfaram, was apparently selected in 138 CE out of a desire to escape Roman notice, in a period when Hadrian's persecutory *shemad* decrees were enforced.[45] The textual record of the gathering appears in Shir Hashirim Rabba (2:5), the Talmudic midrash on the Song of Songs. Responding to these shemad decrees, says this passage: "Our rabbis assembled at Usha. They were Rabbi Judah and Rabbi Nehemia, Rabbi Meir and Rabbi Jose and Rabbi Simeon Bar Yochai and Rabbi Eliezer, the son of Rabbi Jose the Galilean and Rabbi Eliezer ben Jacob. They reached out to the elders of Galilee, saying: 'whoever has studied, let him come and teach, and whoever has not studied, let him come and learn.'"[46]

The first Usha rabbi mentioned, Rabbi Judah bar Ilai, was a native of the town, and known, in Tannaitic circles, as having an accommodating attitude toward Rome[47] (he is not to be confused with the Mishnah's redactor, Rabbi

Judah HaNasi, who belonged to, and dominated, the next generation of Tannaitic rabbis; to avoid confusion, and since this second Judah was also a political figure, we refer to the latter as Judah HaNasi). The Babylonian Talmud, in fact, ascribes an outright pro-Roman position to Rabbi Judah, citing a passage in one of his sermons: "how pleasant are the Romans deeds, since they have built and restored markets, bridges and bathhouses."[48] As we will see, in Jewish legend this pro-Roman assimilatory enthusiasm figures as a trigger in the process which drove the anti-Roman Tannaitic hero, Rabbi Shimon Bar Yochai, to hide in a Galilee cave.[49]

Horrified that any Tanna would have evinced such a laudatory view of the Jews' mortal enemies, some scholars vehemently dispute this attribution to Rabbi Judah. Whatever its documentary verisimilitude, the quote's focus on practical results such as road improvement and bridge building accords broadly with Rabbi Judah's character.[50] Associated with the House of Shammai, Rabbi Judah's religious rulings were relatively moderate, but they tended to concentrate strictly on the actual results of actions, rather than their perpetrators' intentions, as exemplified in a Talmudic passage wherein Judah holds that food accidentally prepared on Shabbat cannot be eaten, not even after the day of rest.

In the Mishnah, Rabbi Judah often appears to be looking for ways to ease the burdens of impious Jewish commoners, the *amei haaretz*, presumably out of sympathy for the tax burdens and lean seasons they faced in agriculture. For instance, in one section dealing with violators of the seventh, fallow year, farming requirement (*shmita*), Rabbi Judah suggests that the time period when a farmer is barred from fertilizing his fields with manure ought to be shortened (he bases his calculations on seasons when grounds become moist).[51] Unlike other Tannaim who viewed themselves as a religious elite and who emphasized their own detachment from amei haaretz who shirked tithing and purity regulations, Rabbi Judah maintained an inclusive attitude toward Jewish groups, and his accommodating personality, commentators believe, suited this early stage of Judaism's reconsolidation in Galilee.

Not as spiritually creative as others who belonged to Rabbi Akiva's small circle of favored students, particularly Rabbi Meir, Rabbi Judah is in some sources dubbed "a wise sage when he wanted to be," an epithet which, to some critics, sounds like detraction by faint praise.[52] These skeptics point to a section in the Babylonian Talmud where Rabbi Judah loses his temper after his students allow a devotee of Rabbi Meir to enter their study group. Striking an anti-intellectual chord, Rabbi Judah complains about Meir's "querulous" pupils who frequently try to "overwhelm" him with arcane musings about Jewish laws (the implicit contrast is between Judah's exegetical focus on evaluating the plain results of actions, as opposed to Meir's mystical penchant for seeking inner meanings of scripture and religious law).[53]

Overall, however, Jewish tradition honored Rabbi Judah, going so far as to using his name as a kind of shorthand symbol for the Tannaitic generation of the Usha assembly—"The generation of Rabbi Judah, son of Rabbi Ilai, who lived after the decrees of Hadrian, when the people were impoverished and oppressed."[54]

Talmudic legend depicts the revival of core functions in Judaism, including the ordination of rabbis,[55] as being a result of this Usha assembly. One well-known account refers to a Tanna, Rabbi Judah ben Bava (sometimes called the "Hasid"), who escaped the clutches of the Romans, and managed to ordain a small circle of rabbis in a desolate Galilee stretch, between two hilltops and two towns, Usha and Shfaram. The Talmud describes this as a bold act of defiance against "the wicked kingdom of Rome," whose acts of religious persecution had the aim of abolishing the rabbis' ordination privileges, and hence Tannaitic authority as a whole. This Talmudic account portrays Judah ben Bava as a martyr—when cruel Roman soldiers approach his study circle, the frail rabbi sacrifices himself, turning his body into a sieve for three hundred iron spears, so that his young Tannaitic disciples can flee.[56]

Scholars doubt the authenticity of this record, pointing to its inaccurate landscape references, and also evidence suggestive of disease as being the real cause of Rabbi Judah ben Bava's death.[57] Still, this retrospective Talmudic legend about Judaism's resurrection at Usha underscores how Tannaitic culture, and the world of rabbinic Judaism which emerged from it, is rooted in trauma. After two catastrophic rebellions, it was impossible for later generations of sages to imagine an origins story which was not apocalyptic. Three hundred gory iron spears impaling the body of an old Galilean sage became Romulus and Remus in the civilization of rabbinic Judaism. The Talmud cannot imagine that its brand of Judaism might have replanted itself in Galilee, from Yavne, in any state other than perpetual danger.

The ascendance of Galilee in the aftermath of the Bar Kochba tragedy was challenged by the growing diasporic Jewish community in Babylonia. The battleground in this challenge was the calculation of the Jewish calendar year (*ibur hashanah*, literally to "impregnate the year"), one of the few aspects of Jewish religious practice where "rabbinic authority was essential."[58] This Babylonian challenge was adamantly stifled by the Usha council.[59]

This calendar intercalation struggle between Galilee and Babylonia merits mention because it loosely foreshadows power dynamics in subsequent periods of Jewish history, including our own contemporary situation where there are essentially two Jewish centers in the world, a large diaspora community in the United States whose members hold differing attitudes about their Jewish identity, and a more Jewishly assertive entity in Eretz Israel, the state of Israel which, following 1948, is a "new" player. Somewhat analogously, in the final decades of the second century, the evolving, rabbi-based, Jewish patriarchate in Galilee expressed a new collective Jewish identity, and it competed with well-rooted Babylonian Jewish communities. Based on Talmudic materials which were compiled in subsequent decades and centuries, and which are steeped in mythology, the documentation we have of the brief intercalation power struggle is problematic. It is nonetheless suggestive of enduring creative tensions in Jewish culture on this diaspora-Eretz Israel axis.

The star of this drama is a Tanna, Rabbi Hanania ben ahi R. Joshua (he has a lengthy name because he is named after his uncle, necessitating the construction "ben ahi," meaning the "son of the brother of . . ."). Rabbi Hanania migrated to Babylonia after the Bar Kochba revolt. Some, sensible-sounding, midrash materials suggest that he fled the Romans, but there is also one intriguing legend, in the aggadic commentary Kohelet Rabba, which suggests that this Tanna was exiled after an illicit encounter with Christians in Capernaum. Rabbi Hanania's uncle rubs a partially effective oil balm to mitigate these sinful contacts with Christians and associated, doubtful, forms of behavior (e.g., riding a donkey on Shabbat), but he informs his nephew that his still-poisoned body can no longer dwell in the Holy Land.[60]

Whatever its impetus, Rabbi Hanania's relocation in Babylonia cast a spotlight on a thorny question of ritual law: with the Temple long gone, where could the calendar year be designated, based on lunar calculations? Such intercalation was no trivial matter: it crucially affected holiday and ritual schedules for Jewish communities all over the world. In fact, a Tannaitic precedent could be found for the justification of calendar intercalation being done outside of Eretz Israel: one Mishnah passage relays that Rabbi Akiva "went down to Nehardea," a center of Babylonian Jewry, "to intercalate the year."[61]

Supplementing this Tannaitic example, the Jerusalem Talmud refers to a few ancient examples of such overseas intercalation (Jeremiah, Ezekiel, Baruch ben Neriah). It then tells a long story about Rabbi Hanania's intercalation challenge. Denying that rabbis who left Yavne had exclusive authority to designate the calendar from a new center in Galilee, Rabbi Hanania throws down the gauntlet. Hanania argues with messengers who come from Galilee bearing three consecutive messages (one of these message bearers, Rabbi Nathan, comes with his own illustrious Babylonian pedigree). Rabbi Hanania points out that Akiva intercalated in Babylonia, but the messengers mock this precedent. The messengers insist that Hanania is no Akiva, and they claim that the "young goats" which Hanania left behind in Eretz Israel have turned into "horned bucks," meaning that the rabbis in Galilee have become authoritative. In fact, as the messengers see it, Galilee-based Tannaim are even empowered to excommunicate the renegade Hanania—referring to Judges: 9, and the curse of Yotam, the messengers threaten that Hanania will be cast to the brambles [*atad*] lest he accept the calendar sovereignty of Galilee rabbis.

Subsequent dialogue lampoons Hanania's pretensions (in willful Freudian slips, the messengers imply that Hanania would blasphemously rename sacred dates after himself).[62]

Hanania remained a figure of notoriety among suspicious sages in Eretz Israel, but in Babylonia, his influence on Jewish life was positively regarded. Hence, compared to the Jerusalem Talmudic passage we have summarized, the Babylonian Talmud puts a different sort of twist on this intercalation drama, mitigating Hanania's rebellion.

The gist of this episode is not to be found in mythologized details of any Talmudic account. Instead, the calendar designation struggle should be seen broadly, as an exemplification of how the Tannaim struggled to accumulate authority in Galilee, hoping to prove that religious sovereignty in world Jewish affairs remained in Eretz Israel, albeit not in Jerusalem.[63]

ESTABLISHING THE TANNAITIC PATRIARCHATE: SHIMON BEN GAMALIEL II

The Tanna responsible for planting the patriarchate in Galilee, and for renewing the princely role of *nasi*, was Shimon ben Gamaliel II. The son of Gamaliel II and father of Judah HaNasi, Shimon's name does not appear in records of the Usha council's founding, presumably because he was at the time on the run, hiding from Roman authorities.[64]

In his childhood, Shimon received instruction in Greek culture, owing to his father's close connections with Roman officials. Tosefta materials and other reports refer to articles of pro-Roman assimilatory leanings in Shimon's childhood milieu, including mimicry of the *komi* Roman hairstyle.[65] According to Talmudic writings, Shimon's most conspicuous contribution to the establishment of the patriarchate in Galilee was essentially formal, featuring status arrangements in the Sanhedrin (called the "council building," *beit va'ad*, in sources). The council leadership was comprised of triumvirs. These three were the *nasi*, who was responsible for relations with Roman authorities and also, at least nominally, for administering affairs of Jewish communities throughout the empire; the *av beit hadin* (court president), who was responsible for judicial matters; and a designated sage (*hakham*) who presumably had authority over religious learning, though this is a more amorphous position whose entitlements and traits are not uniformly described in Babylonian and Jerusalem Talmudic writings.[66]

As happened in the case of Usha assembly founder Rabbi Judah, Shimon faced challenges posed by Rabbi Meir. In these cases, Rabbi Meir, and followers in his camp, seem to have been unnerved by the fact that leadership in Galilee's embryonic patriarchate devolved on Meir's peers/rivals because of their pedigree, administrative talent or strong relations with the Romans, that is, for reasons other than religious learning and acuity. Acutely sensitive about leadership qualifications, Rabbi Meir seems to have been chagrined by the advantage enjoyed by Shimon, who was, literally, a prince, being Gamaliel II's son. Quite unlike other Tannaim, Meir had no pedigree at all—since nothing was known about his patrimony, rivals and skeptics who related retrospectively to Meir's distinguished, but controversial, career, indulged innuendo about how he might have descended from goyim, from relations of the notorious Emperor Nero![67]

Meir's conflict with Shimon erupted when the new nasi altered ceremonial protocol in the Sanhedrin, to the detriment of Meir, who held the hakham position. When the three entitled officials, nasi, av beit hadin, and hakham, entered the council, its members observed elaborate obeisance rituals, setting up a special row, maintaining specified distances from the triumvirs, sitting, and standing, and so on.[68] Meir's feathers were ruffled when Shimon changed procedures regarding the welcome afforded to the hakham, not requiring all Sanhedrin members to stand.[69] According to the Babylonian Talmud, Rabbi Meir basically challenged the nasi, Shimon ben Gamaliel II, to a duel—but under Tannaitic circumstances, dueling was a nonviolent contest of wits and learning about scripture.

Meir prepared for Shimon an intellectual test, a *bohan uktzin* (בוחן עוקצין), a term that conventionally refers to an entry quiz given to young pupils in a beit midrash, prior to their enrollment in advanced classes. This Tannaitic scene seems similar to an incident in the Scroll of Esther, when the heroine's wise cousin Mordecai overhears conspiratorial plotters—here, one relatively obscure Tanna, Rabbi Ya'akov ben Karshi, catches scent of Meir's plan. Rabbi Ya'akov coaches Shimon, who passes this surprise religious quiz and then quietly admits, "had I not prepped and studied, they would have humiliated me."[70]

Hence, in order to establish Galilee as Judaism's new capital, following the Bar Kochba revolt, Shimon ben Gamaliel II overcame two threats, one in foreign policy and one in domestic policy, each involving status. One threat involved the intricacies of calendar intercalation, while the other featured the learning minutiae of a bohan uktzin.

Under Rabbi Shimon in this formative Usha period, the patriarchate issued a number of regulations, *takanot usha*, based on administrative precedents dating from the time of Joshua's conquest of Canaan. The level of the regulations' enforceability is questionable, and many of them simply layered atop ongoing social norms. For instance, according to the Babylonian Talmud,[71] parents are required to provide for their children and otherwise treat them well, and similar regulatory truisms refer to the obligations of grown children toward the elderly parents.[72] Some regulations, however, point to the complexity of rabbinic Judaism's early development vis-à-vis competing trends in second-century Christian groups. For instance, the same Talmudic passage (Ketubot 50a) relays that "in Usha the sages instituted that anyone who donates to charity should not dispense more than one-fifth" of his total income. The Talmud's explanation for this stipulation refers to social problems created by overly zealous alms givers. The unstated, likely, subtext is that these rabbis were influenced by monastic trends and social idealism among early Christians, who acted in concert with messages delivered in the Sermon on the Mount, as in Matthew 5:42 ("give to the one who asks you, and do not turn away from the one who wants to borrow from you"). In second-century Galilee, the Mishnaic compilers who established rabbinic Judaism, and the early groups of the Jesus cult that became Christianity, maneuvered to regulate earthly idealism, but not stifle it. The Usha one-fifth rule was apparently necessitated by the hyper-charitability of a Tanna, Rabbi Eleazer ben Judah of Bartota, who, knowingly or not, enacted Matthew 5:42 as his modus operandi.

One day, records the Talmud,[73] Eleazer went to market "to purchase what he needed for his daughter's dowry." Cognizant of the Tanna's unhealthy penchant for self-abnegation, charity collectors on the street tried to hide from him, but Eleazer tracked them down, clarified that they were raising money for an orphaned boy and girl, and declared piously "I swear by the Temple" that these charity cases "take precedence over my daughter." He emptied his purse of all but one dinar, which he then used to buy some wheat for his granary. Miraculously, the next day, when his daughter opened the granary door, she nearly drowned in wheat, as though the almighty had rewarded Eleazer's munificence by supplementing farm products that would now be used for a hefty and alluring dowry. The daughter was naturally delighted by this wondrous turn of events, but her stern father proclaimed that he would set aside for his child no more than a small portion of wheat, one scaled as though to "befit one of the poor Jews."

Set next to such amusing but disturbing examples, Usha regulations such as the 20 percent charity rule can be viewed as elements in the Tannaitic project which became the Mishnah, a monumental effort to regulate religious behavior in line with Sinaitic revelation and also normal communal needs. In this case, in indirect battle with inspirational but problematic behaviors of early Christianity, the nasi, Shimon ben Gamliel II, along with his Usha associates, promulgated regulations to protect a young woman of regular social aspiration from the idealistic asceticism of her father.

MEIR AND BERURIA

We return to Rabbi Meir, the loser in the Sanhedrin status struggle against the nasi, Shimon ben Gamaliel II. As it turns out, following this setback, Meir's socially tempestuous career was far from over. Meir is well remembered not only for the challenge he posed to the patriarchate but also for the way he probed existential limits and possibilities in other spheres of Judaism's new, growing, rabbinical culture, including gender.

Meir's challenges to Rabbis Judah and Shimon had a cogent foundation. By and large, power in Tannaitic culture was a function of religious learning. That culture was also deeply patriarchal. These two points being indisputable, Rabbi Meir entered into the most challenging marriage of Talmudic times, to Beruria. In effect, he ended up administering to her a sexual *bohan uktzin*. Both failed the test miserably, one going into exile, the other committing suicide.

An accomplished Torah scholar, Beruria possessed compelling, attractive traits, sometimes displaying feisty assertiveness, and other times genuine sensitivity. The incongruous combination of her exemplary character and accomplished learning, on the one hand, and her tragically unfair fate, on the other hand, has made her an alluring character for commentators. In recent decades, in fact, Beruria's status in Galilee's Tannaitic culture has become a kind of weathervane, with postmodernist critics using her story as leverage to field various critical hypotheses about patriarchy in Talmudic culture,[74] and also for Orthodox commentators tasked with explaining why her career should or should not be seen as an illustration of rabbinical Judaism's punitive attitude toward the diffusion of religious knowledge, and of a learning ethos, among women.[75]

Insightful studies have also been published questioning aspects of authenticity in Beruria's story, suggesting that her name is affixed to different, not really cohesive and uniform, situations and characters, in ways which reflect editorial confusion and shifting sociopolitical agendas.[76] This angle of criticism, it bears mention, really applies to *all* Tannaitic characters, since legends about their lives were invariably distorted or embellished by subsequent Talmudic commentators, who wrote in different times and places. Indeed, among many other disparities and hermeneutic challenges, the careers of prominent Tannaim typically have a "Jerusalem" version and a "Babylonian" version in Talmudic recording.[77] Arguably, though, Beruria is exceptional in this context since, despite the typical loose ends and inconsistencies (among them, occasional lack of clarity about whether allusions to "Beruria" really reference Meir's wife), the Jewishly mea culpa documentation of her life seems unusually discomfiting. Owing to the way its finger of blame points back to the misogynist men who wrote the Talmud, the record of Beruria's fate seems almost foreign and Sophoclean.

This outcome of self-blame seems so unusual that Jewish folklore experts, who wrote in the 1970s, just before tides of deconstructionist exegesis crested powerfully, baldly ignored its peculiar aspects. Not dealing with crucial items in the story, particularly Meir's unhappy banishment from Eretz Israel, these critics argued that Beruria's tale is didactically unidimensional, its point being that women who engage in the teaching and refinement of the oral law are committing a capital crime.[78] To a large extent, this monochromatic view of patriarchy in the Talmud applies to the Beruria story, but, paying attention to ambivalent tensions in records of her life, subsequent, radical-spirited, critics like Daniel Boyarin have pointed to a more complicated, nuanced interpretation. Boyarin's analysis also pivots on the premise that Talmudic writers in second-century Galilee might have held views about women and religious learning that were not identical to those held by scholars who, outside of Eretz Israel, compiled the Babylonian Talmud a few centuries later.

Unlike the case of her husband Meir, Beruria's heritage is well known, and it has illustrious and martyrological dimensions. Her father was the aforementioned sage, Rabbi Hanina ben Teradion, from Sikhnin (Sakhnin, today a large Arab town in Galilee; the industrial zone of the adjacent Jewish council, Misgav, is named after this rabbi). This Tanna, Rabbi Hanina, was reportedly killed with nine other sages as a result of Roman pacification policy (the death of these Ten Martyrs is commemorated annually in a poem, *Eleh Ezkereh*, chanted on the Day of Atonement, Yom Kippur). As legend has it, Hanina and his wife were murdered, and one of his daughters was consigned to prostitution, per standard Roman policy in the punishment of rebellious peoples—Beruria, some scholars speculate, was exempted from these truculent sanctions since she was at the time already married to Meir, and thus legally outside the orbit of the family punished for the deeds of Rabbi Hanina, who taught Torah in violation of Roman dictates.

In one of the Beruria legends, she tells Meir that she is haunted by her sister's fate, and urges him to rescue her. Meir takes a *tarqeva* of coins and vows that if the sister has not sinned, a miracle will save her—he eventually saves the guiltless sister, thanks to the coins, a culpable Roman guard, and a miraculous incantation ("God of Meir, answer me!"—*eloka dmeir aneini*).[79]

Beruria is a learned, merciful character. The Babylonian Talmud makes reference to her learning three hundred ritual laws one day from three hundred rabbis, and it relays a provocative anecdote suggestive of her moral and intellectual superiority relative to Meir. Beruria is a compassionate woman who has a subtle understanding of the psalms (104:36, in this case). The anecdote describes two neighborhood "hooligans" who trouble Rabbi Meir, "who would pray for them to die." Beruria queries her husband, asking "what is your view?" Is Meir basing his vindictive prayer on Psalms 104:36, "Let the wicked be terminated from the earth?" Beruria then provides her superior interpretation of psalms: "Does it say 'wicked people'? 'Wicked deeds' is written! Moreover, interpret it according to the end of the verse, 'And there are no more evildoers.' Now if the first half means that the wicked are dead, why do I have to pray that there will be no more evildoers? Rather it means that since wicked deeds will exist no more, there will be no more evildoers."[80] Taking his cue from Beruria's exegesis, Meir then prays for these two hooligans, and they repent.

Another incident points to an assertive, almost perky, side to Beruria's learnedness. She comes across a Tanna, Yosi the Galilean, on a road, and he asks, in lengthy formulation, "by which road should we go to Lod (באיזה דרך נלך ללוד?)" Her answer seems rather insolent: "Galilean fool! Did not the sages say, 'do not talk too much with a woman.' You should have said, 'by which way to Lod (באיזה ללוד)?'" The story's didactic aim is not entirely clear, but some commentators view it not as an expression of female hubris unpalatable to Talmudic writers, but rather as an expression of Beruria's commendable self-confidence.[81]

The tables turn in the disturbing "Beruria incident." The only extant account of the affair was recorded by the premier medieval Talmudic interpreter, Rashi (Rabbi Shlomo Yitzhaki), who was buried in Troyes in 1205—the incident appears in Rashi's commentary on the tractate, b'avodah zarah (that the earliest known appearance of this Rashi commentary is in a manuscript dated 200 years after his death is of one of many issues which engage scholars who try examine this incident's authenticity and details, and how it came to be recorded[82]). The Rashi commentary discloses the following: "One time she [Beruria] mocked the sages' saying, 'women are lightheaded.' [Rabbi Meir] said to her: 'By your life, you will eventually affirm their words.'" Meir then instructed one of his followers to seduce Beruria. This disciple "urged her for many days until she consented. When the matter became known to her, she strangled herself, and Rabbi Meir fled out of disgrace."[83]

Beruria kills herself and Meir banishes himself in exile—this is truly an incident which invites speculative commentary.

Writing in the critical-spirited *Tikkun* journal in 1988, Rachel Adler argued that this gruesome tale projects the radical ambivalence of patriarchal Talmudic writers. On the one hand, the Beruria legends of a learned and powerful woman who mocked less-studious and less-intelligent Tannaim threatened these writers, but, on the other hand, they were positively beguiled by the imaginary prospect of being befriended and loved by such a woman. Beruria, for them, became a kind of thought experiment—the male Talmudists wondered, *"what if there were a woman who was just like us?"* In the end, they concluded, the feminine sexuality of such a scholar would invariably be "a source of havoc."[84]

Boyarin follows much of this analysis, but he stresses the shifting cultural contexts out of which the Beruria legends emanated. As he sees it, there was nothing really anomalous in the identity of a female Tanna in second-century Galilee ("there is no hint of censure" regarding her Torah learnedness in this setting, he points out). In contrast, centuries later in Babylonia, in the late Amoraic context or Gaonic period "it was unthinkable and perhaps terrifying that a woman might study Torah."[85] That Goodblatt, the scholar who opened the door for such critical reevaluation of the Beruria legends, viewed these cultural contexts in a diametrically opposed manner, holding that a learned female Tanna could never have existed in second-century Galilee, shows how difficult it is to generalize about these settings.[86]

More persuasively, Boyarin points to "dark double" similarities between the Beruria incident and the aforementioned rescue of the sister from the brothel: the learned Beruria sinfully allows herself to be seduced, whereas her ignorant, sexually enslaved, sister avoids sin when there is a choice (in the sister rescue story, Meir dresses himself as a Roman soldier, and tries to seduce his sister-in-law; she deflects him, claiming that she is menstruating[87]). Thanks to Boyarin's ingenious pairing of mirror image tales, the Talmud's didactic message is well elucidated: ill-advised Torah study leads Jewish women into sin.

We have elaborated on interpretations of Beruria's career because it is tailor-made for postmodernist interest in what male power elites omit from canonical texts, such as the Mishnah. It is as though her career is about everything the Mishnah ordinarily would not have said about second-century Galilee. As Adler puts it, Beruria's story raises the issue of how Galilee's Tannaitic culture treated capable Jewish women. It raises the issue of what would have happened (or perhaps in some way *did happen*) had a woman identified herself as a Tanna. I think, though, this "gender studies" approach to Beruria's life can be placed within a larger cultural context, one that hinges on the issue of how rabbinic Judaism set limits of what it was about, of what it could, and could not, be. In this connection, Meir, not his precocious female partner, actually embodies the Tannaitic thought experiment.

We have seen how tales of Meir's career probed the nature of political authority in the new Galilee patriarchate. These tales ask: would this patriarchate be based on learned prowess alone, or would non-studious considerations such as heritage descent (in the Gamaliel II-Shimon line) also count? Throughout his career, Meir also probed the nature of sin and human culpability—"the dark double" incidents with the sisters, their nadir being his horrendous treatment of Beruria, is part of this examination; but the "dark double" couplet is far from the entirety of this examination. Consider, for instance, a chilling Talmudic anecdote about Meir's encounter, on two sides of a river, with Satan, who is disguised as a woman. For all his male studiousness and intelligence, Rabbi Meir succumbs to this temptation (he ropes his way half across the river, before the devil loses interest).[88] Here Meir's behavior is analogous to that of his astute, studious female partner in the separate, Rashi-recorded, "Beruria incident," meaning, somewhat in contradistinction to Boyarin's interpretation, that religious learning proffers no immunity from sin for either gender.

Moreover, in view of the highly patriarchal character of Tannaitic culture, it is not surprising that some "Beruria" legends are essentially projections of Meir's needs and character. This fact applies to another funereal incident in the life of the challenged couple, wherein Meir is at Shabbat prayer, and Beruria discovers that their two sons are dead. Temporarily hiding the children's bodies from their father in tune with ritualistic considerations, her behavior is religiously meticulous but mechanical. Her comportment poses a contrast to Meir's more spontaneously expressed sorrow, emotion that is not connected to the moment's religious requirements.[89]

Essentially, this lugubrious tale of the dead children is an examination of how raw emotion is supposed to fit in the scrupulously regulated regime of religious devotion which the Tannaim were incorporating into the Mishnah. Meir's good heart and empathetic bearing might possibly lead him beyond newly defined borders of Talmudic Judaism—this possibility is tacit in many phases of his career, but it becomes explosively viable in his friendship with his mentor, Elisha ben Abuyah, the most haunting relationship forged in second-century Galilee. As we will see, the way Jews have, over the centuries, responded to the Meir-Elisha relationship reflects, as a kind of referendum, the way they feel about the Mishnaic project as a whole.

JUDAH HANASI

In its several versions, the death of the Tanna, Rabbi Akiva, symbolizes the crushing end of the Bar Kochba revolt. On Jewish tradition, Judah HaNasi was born on the day when Akiva was martyred. This Talmudic chronology seems more or less correct—dates and basic facts of Judah's life are clouded by uncertainty,[90] but he seems to have been born around 138, and, as the adage implies, his emergence symbolizes Galilee's rise, following the Roman crackdown in other areas of the country, including Akiva's hometown, Lod.

Judah grew up in Usha and, probably to his benefit, he was educated by lower pedigree Jewish sages—his father, Rabbi Simeon Ben Gamliel II, was too busy evading Roman prosecutors to attend to his son's education. His career as a Jewish leader in the Mishnah period (Judah died around 220) pivoted on Judaism's transition from Temple-based worship to rabbinical authority.

Titled as "prince" (the Hebrew term is "nasi," which in modern usage came to mean "president"), the years of Judah's leadership, 175–220 CE, are considered the acme of Jewish politics and culture in Eretz Israel in the period stretching between the Temple's destruction and the Muslim conquest in 640

CE.[91] The "nasi" title had earlier been conferred to Simon Bar Kochba, the demiurge of the 132–135 CE revolt, and, as will be recalled, it had also been awarded to Judah's father, Simeon Ben Gamliel. The royal-sounding title is suggestive of its holder's august lineage (Judah was regarded as a descendant of the House of David). The "nasi" title underscored Judah's preeminent role as the Jewish population's liaison with Roman rulers, and also his supreme religious authority as the head of the Sanhedrin-in-the-making, and as redactor of the Mishnah, the oral law compilation project initiated a generation earlier by Rabbi Akiva.

Judah HaNasi's scholarly aptitude, his strong connections with Roman officials, his ample wealth, and his reform policies on land ownership and other issues, contributed to his rise as an admired, Galilee-based, Jewish leader. The extraordinary reverence he inspired is exemplified by the fact that his presumed burial place in the Galilee town Beit She'arim (close to the contemporary suburb Kiryat Tivon) fostered a cult. Beit She'arim came to host a burial-cave filled necropolis; the town became a favored spot for burying dead in Eretz Israel in a period when Roman repression impeded access to Jerusalem's Mount of Olives.

Conscious of playing a part in a major Jewish revival in Galilee, Judah HaNasi at one point issued a remarkable recommendation, urging that the Tisha b'Av fast commemorating the destruction of the Temple be annulled, even though a Third Temple remained to be built atop the Jerusalem rubble.

Figure 3.1 Necropolis at Beit She'arim. *Source*: Courtesy of Adi Lam.

His recommendation was not accepted, but its promotion serves as a noteworthy indication of how Galilean Jews in this era lacked a crippling sense of living in exile subsequent to the catastrophic destruction of the Temple in Jerusalem.

Judah HaNasi's activities combined secular and religious leadership roles. Scholarly criteria requisite for leadership of the rabbinical council, retrospectively referred to in the Babylonian Talmud as the "Sanhedrin," were far from identical to aptitudes necessary for administrative success in Jewish communal affairs and in dealing with Roman officials. Judah's character uniquely possessed these different skill sets in strong measure, whereas subsequent generations entrusted two or more individuals with leadership roles in these different, religious and administrative, spheres.

One of Judah HaNasi's important reforms was to ease the process for the purchase of lands earlier expropriated from Jews by the Romans.[92] Hoping to alleviate hardship faced by struggling Jewish farmers, Rabbi Judah tried to annul the *shmita* seventh sabbatical year, under which farm fields are supposed to remain fallow (religious elites eventually forced Judah to abandon this reform). Aiming to boost economic and cultural activity, he updated and revised *takanot* (regulations)—among other takanot changes, he authorized the payment of interest on loans. Personally supervising the emergence of a new rabbinical elite in Galilee, Judah HaNasi exerted hegemonic control over the conferral of *hasmacha* accreditation for new rabbis—such consolidation of religious authority in one man's hands was unusual.

Talmudic sources provide tellingly hyperbolic accounts of Judah HaNasi's extensive network of connections with Roman officials. Rife with suggestive tension about sexuality, personal enrichment in mundane affairs, the power and limits of religious learning, and other subjects, these Talmudic Judah HaNasi legends are revealing, and warrant mention. No doubt, as retrospective historical documentation, these legends attest honorifically to Judah's affairs and achievements, but they also reflect ambivalent accommodations in post-hurban Jewish society made by the rabbinical commentators themselves, generations after Judah's career. These are post-trauma reflections expressive of Jewish sages' psychic need for revenge and empowerment in an era when objective conditions of Jewish life had been crushingly weakened by the Bar Kochba failure, and when exilic diaspora consciousness was consolidating.

In fact, in an era of post-Bar Kochba dispersion, the Judah HaNasi legends served emotive needs in a fashion comparable to the way the Kabbalah alleviated the traumatized consciousness of mystics in Safed, in their post-1492 era of dispersion from the Iberian Peninsula. In one such Judah legend, the Rome-based emperor and the Galilee-based nasi confer by flitting effortlessly through a transcontinental tunnel which connects their two residences (the emperor has a greater need to burrow in this diplomatic back channel tunnel).[93] Judah's allegorical function here is akin to that of the sixteenth-century mystic's esoteric knowledge of Kabbalistic truths—though everyone else might have imagined the Jews to be a ruined people after the humiliation of the Bar Kochba debacle, and then, 1,300 years later, after the banishment from Spain, Judah's magical power, and then that of the Kabbalah, soothed and psychologically reversed the Jewish situation in the minds of Jewish commentators, allowing them to imagine that the Jews actually ruled the intimidating, hostile, empire, Rome or Spain.[94] In both these cases, Galilee functioned as an imaginative playing field for folkloristic, hyperbolic images of Jewish empowerment in a period of national trauma.

The Judah HaNasi legends are emblematic of Galilee culture in this period, when Jews confronted realities of trauma and dispersion, but their scholarly investigation has proven to be somewhat frustrating. As noted by Aharon Oppenheimer, basic parameters of these legends remain to be sorted out. Among other issues, the confusion stems from contradictory identifications of Judah HaNasi's main political interlocutor and supposed partner, a Roman emperor confusingly identified in the Talmudic commentaries as "Antonius," or "Antoninus" (one contender would be Elagabalus, Roman emperor from 218 to 222 CE, but Oppenheimer and Avi-Yonah suggest that the commentators had in mind Caracalla, originally known as Marcus Aurelius Severus Antonius Augustus, who reigned during the main period of Rabbi Judah's tenure, 198–217 CE).[95]

These Talmudic legends include an anecdote wherein the Roman emperor Antoninus consults with Judah HaNasi, explaining that in view of the upgrading of Tiberias' municipal status, he is unsure about appointing his son Asverus to govern the city. Judah responds with an allegory about a dove, implying that the Roman emperor should take the burden of ruling the new colony off his own shoulders; taking the tip, Antoninus prepares to inform the senate of his desire to delegate responsibilities for Tiberias to his son.[96] In another anecdote, the Emperor complains to Judah HaNasi about how various prominent Romans had been challenging his authority—Judah takes the Roman ruler into the garden and proceeds to pick some radishes, one by one. "Said [Antoninus to himself] his advice to me is: do away with them one at a time, but do not attack all of them at once."[97] Another anecdote rates Judah HaNasi's fortune as being comparable to that of the Roman emperor's—since both men had control or access to large swaths of land, "neither lettuce, nor radish nor cucumber was ever absent" from Antoninus' table or from Judah's table, neither in summer nor in winter.[98] Also, the Mekhilta (*Mekhilta of Rabbi Ishmael*), a midrash commentary on the Book of Exodus, includes episodes in which Emperor Antoninus turns to Judah HaNasi for advice on vexing existential questions about the soul's relation to the physical world.[99]

All told, in these Jewish commentaries, Judah HaNasi looms as the Roman emperor's equal, or superior, in crucial matters of political power, material wealth, and spiritual understanding.

The Talmudic legends, of course, exaggerate, but Judah HaNasi was undoubtedly a well-connected figure who possessed a fortune from land dealings. As it turns out, not all of Judah's real estate fortune resulted from Roman concessions, and his holdings were apparently not limited to Galilee.[100] Due to his lofty status, the Romans awarded Judah a land-holding concession at Beit Shea'rim, which became the home of the rabbinical council (Sanhedrin), following its location at Usha and then, for a stint, Shfaram. A unifying figure, Judah's strong connections with the Romans apparently attracted the interest of assimilated Jewish figures (sometimes known as "takifim") in Galilee population centers, particularly in Sephhoris, who had previously remained detached from Jewish affairs.

During the last seventeen years of his term as nasi, Judah's rabbinical council relocated in Sepphoris. Jewish sources attribute this relocation to Judah's aged infirmity, but this explanation lacks merit (Sepphoris, today's Zippori, and Beit She'arim are similar, inland, locales). The shift to Sepphoris appears to have been socioeconomic in character, and it bears witness testimony to Judah's ability to bridge between Hellenized and Jewish nationalist elements in Galilee's population.[101]

During the reign of Emperor Septimius Severus (193–211 CE), adjustments in urban administration changed and enhanced the role of Jews in city councils, both in Sepphoris and also Tiberias (where the Sanhedrin would relocate, after Judah's death). High official and councils (known as *boule* and *strategoi*) quarreled over allotments of crown taxes, and there is Talmudic evidence of such functionaries appealing to Judah HaNasi, asking him to establish equitable divisions of this tax burden.[102] In short, the Severan administration delegated to the Jewish patriarch, Judah, considerable authority in this cardinal area of tax administration. Much of Judah's activity was class biased in that he reasoned, strategically, that his power base depended upon forging new or strengthened relations with Jewish elites, particularly in Tiberias and Sepphoris.[103] As a civil patriarch whose own pro-Roman leanings matched those of these Galilee elites, Judah met challenges that had frustrated Josephus, when the latter served as military commander in the region a century and a half earlier.

Exercising his powers in this area of urban administration, Judah HaNasi took steps to ensure that some cities outside of Galilee (Ashkelon, Caesarea, Beit Sha'an) which had mixed populations would remain conceptually within the boundaries of Eretz Israel. Judah prevented the cities' detachment from the land by resisting initiatives to declare them as being impure, or by exempting their Jewish residents from various religious commandments performed in Eretz Israel.¹⁰⁴ Oppenheimer explains that this exemption from Eretz Israel ritualistic commandments was basically tax relief, and its aim was to augment Jewish settlement in these mixed cities¹⁰⁵—in modern times, the state of Israel follows a similar logic when it encourages Jewish citizens to settle in peripheral areas in Galilee and elsewhere by providing them with tax breaks. Such steps taken by Judah HaNasi to augment Jewish settlement in Galilee and elsewhere in the country illustrate how his leadership as nasi had a nationalist component.

TANNAIM AND AMEI HA'ARETZ

What sort of society evolved in the eras of these Tannaitic patriarchs, Shimon ben Gamaliel II and Judah HaNasi? How did the evolving class of rabbis position itself, vis-à-vis the "ordinary" Jews of Galilee?

Religious rules in the Mishnah sanction social hierarchies and inequalities in Jewish society. The underclasses in Jewish society are the religiously unobservant, the *am haaretz* (literally, people of the land). This category of ignorant, impious Jews applied perhaps mostly to the country's socioeconomic underclass—the specific definition of *am haaretz* is a Jew who neglects tithing obligations, and it is logical to assume that a prime reason why someone would have shirked this commandment to set aside a portion of his produce for the temple priests, or for their rabbinical successors, is impoverishment. But there were clearly also Jews with disposable income who did not feel religiously motivated to pay such tithing tribute to the priests.

The Mishnah relates to amei ha'aretz as belonging to a stratum just above what would be called, in other cultures, untouchables. Thus, in one Mishnah passage, some Tannaim rule that a Jew cannot be regarded as a reliable ("trustworthy") member of the community if he comingles with an am haaretz. Rabbi Judah, who is often given something close to the final word in such discussions, finds this overly harsh and rules that "one who accepts the hospitality of an am haaretz is trustworthy."¹⁰⁶ In the Mishnah, the exclusion of amei haaretz extends to key economic spheres. Because the amei haaretz did not pay tithing tribute to the priests, and their rabbi successors, they are punished harshly, at least in theory, as evidenced by a rule holding that a landowner of a field whose produce are ripe for tithing cannot sell it to an am haaretz.¹⁰⁷

A noticeably sober and pungent assessment of social stratification in Tannaitic Galilee was produced early in the twentieth century by Adolf Buchler, an Austro-Hungarian rabbi who at the time was serving as the principal of London's rabbinical seminary, Jews' College.¹⁰⁸ Writing about politics and society in Sepphoris in the second and third centuries, Buchler managed to research and think about the amei haaretz issue outside of the "Galilee of the Gentiles" polemic in which the claim holding that the rise of Christianity can be attributed to the relatively un-Jewish character of Galilee was, and still is, volleyed back and forth between Jewish and Christian scholars and commentators.[109] Quite unapologetically, Buchler assumed that up to the end of the Bar Kochba revolt, "the Galilean Jews knew little about rabbinical law" due to a lack of scholars and schools in the region.[110]

These uneducated Jews in Sepphoris held Tannaim in outright disdain. When the town was stricken by pestilence, drought, or other afflictions, amei haaretz commoners were outraged by the inefficacy of the town's prestigious scholars, who seemed solely concerned about protecting themselves. Amei haaretz did not turn up at the scholars' funerals, and sometimes contemptuously bid Tannaim good riddance; such phenomena are apparent in various recorded rabbinical complaints.[111] Striking back, scholars at the Usha assembly passed a rule that would have slapped fines as penalties for particularly offensive acts committed by amei ha'aretz. That writ was surely not enforceable, so the Tannaim kept grumbling. One second-century Baraitha (oral law traditions that were not incorporated in the Mishnah) confides that animosity harbored by amei haaretz toward Tannaim exceeds malice shown by gentiles toward Jews.

In fact, Talmudic writings convey expressions of rabbinical contempt for the amei ha'aretz of such an extreme nature that they have left readers scratching their heads for centuries. For instance, one Amoraic rabbi, Eleazar ben Pedat, went on the record with praise for anyone who would dispose of amei ha'aretz, even on the holiest day of a seven-year cycle—"an am ha'aretz may be stabbed on a [Yom Kippur] Day of Atonement which falls on a Shabbat." On other Talmudic reports, rabbis swear that there is no place in heaven for amei ha'aretz. In Sepphoris, Judah HaNasi, added to the screed, announcing that "God's punishment falls on the world only on account of amei ha'aretz."[112]

"All of this," writes one historian, referring to the rhetorically violent incitement against Jewish commoners in the days of rabbinical Judaism's consolidation, "has caused surprise and led to difficulties from Gaonic to contemporary times."[113] Geonim, authorities active in Babylonian Talmudic academies from 600 to 1000, sometimes invented apologetic arguments, hoping to extenuate their rabbinical predecessors' violent incitement against Jewish commoners. One, Sherira Gaon, tried to defuse the aforementioned explosive comment warranting the liquidation of amei ha'aretz on the holiest of days by referring to a bygone Day of Atonement on a Shabbat, when an amei ha'aretz supposedly went berserk. This self-defense argument strained credulity.

The truth is that the rabbinical invective about Jewish commoners in Galilee has never been swept under the rug. One Israeli study of the Tannaim, published in 1977 under education ministry auspices and formatted as a textbook, records these comments at length. Its author, Yehezkel Cohen, states flatly that hatred between Tannaim and amei ha'aretz in Galilee was deep, strong, and mutual.[114] In contrast, in his expose of social stratification in Tannaitic Sephoris, Buchler advised against taking the rabbis' most explosively bitter statements at face value, calling them "burlesque exaggerations."[115] In his work on amei ha'aretz, Oppenheimer tries to clarify successive historical contexts relevant to the sages' outbursts. In the Yavne period, he suggests, the sages were highly sensitive about their own status in view of general trends of Jewish egalitarianism and removal of the old (Pharisee-Sadducee-Essene) Second Temple era sectarian divisions. Trying to substitute Torah study for Temple cults, they took umbrage when amei ha'aretz displayed irreverence about scripture. Then, in the Usha period, the rabbis were surely furious when recalcitrant amei ha'aretz reinforced Galilee's reputation for impudence and ignorance, relative to Judea; more importantly, on Oppenheimer's interpretation, the Usha assembly generation of Tannaim had to deal with socioeconomic woes which gripped the country after the Bar Kochba debacle, and so their vitriol and bitterness about amei ha'aretz impiety reflected the challenging complexity of prioritizing spiritual, rather than material, pursuits at a time of economic distress.[116]

During the anti-Roman revolts, the Jews' inability to resolve issues of internal solidarity had left them excruciatingly vulnerable. Provocative evidence, such as Buchler's portrait of Sepphoris, suggests that internal Jewish tensions may not have abated when Judaism regrouped at Yavne and Usha, though the tension's terms and frames were certainly changing. Josephus' sectarian categories (Pharisees, Saducees, Essenes) are not the ones we find in Tannaitic culture, where we meet categories like haverim, and amei ha'aretz; also changing are social status scope finders in the telescopes through which we view stratification issues in Second Temple era Galilee, as opposed to second-century Tannaitic Galilee.

Josephus, our window to the first era, looked down at Jewish society as a whole, having belonged to Jerusalem's priestly class. Mostly, Josephus looked out at Jews in Galilee as an undifferentiated rabble; feeling no need for precision, he tossed around the confusing term, "Galileans." In contrast, venomous commentary about amei ha'aretz in Tannaitic and Amoraic writings betokens a more complicated situation. The evidence in Buchler's book does not fully support his own suggestion that this philippic was "insincere," but his and subsequent research studies show that the Tannaim needed to forge connections in lower strata of Jewish society with an urgency not displayed in Josephus' writing about his military stint in Galilee, a term during which Josephus was in a duck and deflect mode, and biding time.

Some Tannaim appear to have come from well-to-do homes, but many did not. By and large, they did not get along with wealthy Jewish elites in a locale like Sepphoris. In Sepphoris, Tannaim remonstrated against affluent Jews in the town who wrested plum appointments as judges by coddling Romans—these judges were bribe-takers who shafted the Jewish underclasses, preached the Tannaim.

For their part, these wealthy Jews in Sepphoris faced onerous tax burdens, being classified as boule and strategia by the Romans. Trying to shift their tax onus to the amei ha'aretz, these elites could be cutthroat and exploitative: one Baraitha accuses these elites of withholding wages owed to workers, and for being uncharitable, and references in some Talmudic writings to violent thugs and robbers (החמסנין הגוזלין) apparently apply to these Jewish notables.[117]

While Josephus ultimately discards Jewish society in the late Jewish Temple period, regarding the generation as a mass of infidelity that lost God's patronage, the Tannaitic view of Jewish society is more dynamic and even, potentially, inclusive, despite the corrosive venting about impious and ignorant amei ha'aretz. Because they needed allies, the rabbis set themselves out as champions of the Jewish poor; the ranting about amei ha'aretz evinces disappointment over how this reaching out did not pay off for the rabbis, at least not throughout the first decades which passed after the Usha assembly.[118] For the Tannaim, and the Mishnaic culture they created, Jewish social solidarity might have been a distant goal, but it remained an aim, whereas it becomes a lost cause in Josephus' record of the revolt against Rome. And, in fact, there is evidence that the Amoraim, successors to the Tannaim, "modified their attitude" toward the amei ha'aretz, "even to the extent of vindicating [them] despite their want of knowledge of the Torah."[119]

Josephus, on many levels, is a detached writer, whereas the Tannaim belong, at least in part, to classes they are attacking. Prominent Tannaim descended from the amei ha'aretz.[120] The best-known example in this connection is Rabbi Akiva, whose reported, self-abasing, confession says much about social dynamics in Tannaitic times: "When I was an am-haaretz, I [would] say: 'would that I had a sage [talmid hakham] before me, I would bite him like an ass'" (Akiva's amused pupils then proceed to debate whether it is preferable for impious Jews be attacked by dogs or donkeys).[121]

In Sepphoris, socially aspirant Tannaim sometimes indulged aspects of Greco-Roman culture which might have been prominently on display in the lifestyle of the town's nonscholarly Jewish elites. One provocative example is Tannaitic sexual adventurism, a phenomenon underscored by rabbinical rulings implying that students need not be expelled from batei midrash if they are seen with prostitutes.[122] That the Tannaim in Galilee were sometimes caught between the Scylla of Greco-Roman acculturation, and the Charybdis of ammei ha'aretz impiety and ignorance is reflected in a Baraitha (i.e., a non-Mishnaic teaching) which identifies various ways a scholar might disgrace himself: woe be the Tanna who goes out in public wearing scents, who roams a town alone at night or speaks to a woman on a street, or who eats a meal with an am ha'aretz.[123]

RASHBI'S GALILEE, THEN AND NOW

The Mishnah's composition reflects the most massive religious-national reconstruction effort in Jewish history, certainly up to the Holocaust. The Mishnah, writes Jacob Neusner, was "a vast systematic" response to the *hurban*, the poignantly resonant Hebrew term for the catastrophic destruction of the Jerusalem Temples. Viewing the Mishnah as a post-trauma endeavor to reaffirm Jewish collective identity, Neusner compares it to revival efforts the Jews have been making since the Holocaust (the lapse of time between the ruinous defeat of the second Jewish rebellion against Rome, the Bar Kochba revolt, in 135 CE and the compilation of the Mishnah is roughly equivalent to the span of time between the Holocaust and our contemporary reality).[124]

Other apt comparisons highlight Galilee's crucial role in Jewish reinvention and revitalization. In their collective memory, Jews imagine that they were cast into exile after the successive anti-Rome rebellions calamitously failed (as this chapter illustrates, this well-known narrative is a myth because Jews sustained a lively presence in Galilee and elsewhere in Eretz Israel for some three centuries, at least, after the first, main 66–70 CE rebellion and the destruction of the Second Temple). On this narrative, the most promising "Golden Age" attempt made by Jews to live among gentiles in Exile occurred in Spain, but this era was decimated by the Inquisition and the expulsion of Jews from the Iberian Peninsula at the end of the fifteenth century, an event which Jews understandably view as the traumatic nadir of two millennia of Exile, up to the twentieth-century Holocaust. In the sixteenth century, following the expulsion from Spain, the most creatively inspired act of Jewish revitalization was centered in Galilee, in Safed, where charismatic Jewish sages developed a full-blown mystical order, based on Kabbalah.

As we will see, it is a little misleading to present the Mishnah as a "rational" counterpart to mystical Kabbalah, since the Mishnah, the inaugural compilation of Jewish oral law in an ongoing, centuries-long, transnational effort that came to be known as "Talmud," is rife with eccentric sophistry, and its legalistic approach pivots on faith in precepts divinely revealed to one chosen people (and subsequently embedded in Torah). As such, Talmud differs substantively from the way "rationalism" and law was conceptualized after the eighteenth-century enlightenment, as the application of universally valid rules inherent in nature that are not divinely revealed, but rather discovered by empirical study. Still, the Mishnah has what might be called, a little oxymoronically, a rationalistic ethos in that it attempts to regulate the minutiae of everyday life and, significantly, assumes that this quasi-totalitarian control of behavior is entirely *explicable*. Rabbis, whose authority stems not from control of the Temple cult, or of means of violence, but rather from their argumentative skill, effectuate the Mishnah, and in this sense, Jewish revitalization in Galilee after the Temple hurban and the Bar Kochba fiasco, centered on a code of learning and knowledge, and was thus a "rational" response to trauma.

In contrast, what happened in the same place, Galilee, 1,400 years later, following the expulsion from Spain, was a mystical reaction to trauma. As we will see in the opening chapter of our second volume, in sixteenth-century Safed rabbis delved in a trove of esoteric knowledge and espoused various unusual practices and rites to enact a new mystical, Kabbalist order. Whereas the Mishnah fastidiously insists on regulating "ordinary" religious behavior, the Kabbalah seeks to transcend everyday normality; and it relies on charismatic insight as a source of authority, rather than the sagacious learnedness of the Mishnah's rabbinic compilers. Two Jewish tragedies, the Temple destruction and the expulsion from Spain. Two different responses, rationalism and mysticism, Mishnah and Kabbalah. Same place, Galilee.

Jews have a lachrymose way of viewing their own history, but if we liberate ourselves from this fixation with suffering and victimhood, another comparison to the Mishnah comes into view. Its arena is also Galilee.

The challenge posed to the Tannaim who authored the Mishnah was not exclusively overcoming "trauma." If truth be told, we have little verifiable information about the early lives of these several dozen figures. Insofar as many of them were not refugees from Judea, where the Bar Kochba revolt mainly flared, and were rather born and bred in Galilee, where this second rebellion may not have been acutely felt, it may be, at least in some cases, a misnomer to think of them as trauma "victims." The puzzlement most faced was not political but existential. It featured the retention of sacred aura following the destruction of the Temple, the presumptive acme of Jewish sanctity.

The Temple had served as a matrix of lavishly intricate purity and tithing rules. Once it was gone, the rabbis could only have lived in dread and anxiety about the prospect of reconstructing a religious society, one devoid of the priestly devotions (tithes), sacrifices and other aura-conjuring practices, in which a sense of the sacred might still endure, and be shared.

One way they faced this challenge was through wishful thinking and cognitive dissonance. The Mishnah, as we will see, is full of suggestions hinting that many of the rabbis believed in the Temple's imminent reconstitution—interestingly, the incident which probably obliterated this hope once and for all (the ill-conceived attempt, in 363 CE, of a Christianity-hating Roman

Emperor, Julian, to build a Third Temple) is roughly coterminous with the end of a viable Jewish majority in Galilee, almost as though Jews remained in their country so long as they retained hope for the rebirth of its capital.

More realistically, the Mishnah rabbis refashioned Jewish law as a substitute for the Temple. This formative document of Jewish oral law, the Mishnah, inculcates the sacred in daily life by explaining, in prodigiously overwhelming detail, how seemingly mundane rites and practices are actually rooted in Torah and divine revelation. In Galilee, in the Mishnah era, the Tannaim insisted that Judaism would survive as a *religion* because its aspirations for sacred eternity could be radically recalibrated. By necessity, they could be taken from the Temple cult and relocated in the authorized regulation of every possible facet of daily life and religious practice.

Here, the counterpart to the Mishnah is what developed in Galilee in the pioneering communes that took root in the first Zionist immigration waves (each one called "Aliyah," a resonant Hebrew term referring to ascent in a number of contexts) in years leading up to World War I and the 1917 Balfour Declaration. These self-styled Jewish pioneers (in Hebrew, "halutz," singular; halutzim, plural) promoted an agenda which stood the Tannaitic rabbis' project on its head: in the late nineteenth and early twentieth centuries, a newly secularized age, they were trying to reinvent Judaism as a national, rather than religious, concept.

They too can be thought of as victims. The bulk of these Zionist *halutz* pioneers came from the Russian empire and attested to having suffered in successive waves of anti-Semitic persecution (1881–1882, 1903–1905), known in the Jewish vernacular as "pogroms." Historians, however, have questioned whether the pogroms should be thought of as the main animus of Jewish emigration from the Russian empire (not just to Ottoman Palestine), and so these immigrants are probably viewed more cogently as existential pioneers tasked with an agenda that inverted the Mishnah project of the Tannaim.

On their newly established farm communes, branded (in the 1920s and 1930s) "kibbutzim" and "moshavim," the halutzim argued incessantly about the meaning and limits of communitarianism, and about how their pioneering lifestyle would contribute to the refashioning of Judaism as a national concept. To be sure, Zionists established pioneering colonies in several regions of Ottoman, and then British, Palestine, but the most impactful kibbutzim, and pioneer leaders, took root in Galilee, as we will see in volume two. Their exhausting pontification about their *halutz* pioneering style and its *hagshama* (fulfillment), layered within fastidious bickering in kibbutz dining hall debates about what had to be shared ("tea kettle" arguments, *vikuhei kumkum*, as they became known), constituted essentially a secular Mishnah, an analogue to the punctilious concordance of religious behaviors recorded by the Tannaim.

In 200 CE, or thereabouts, the Tannaim reinvented Jewish religion in Galilee. In 1910, or thereabouts, the Zionist halutzim invented secular Jewish nationalism in Galilee. Two rather different Judaisms. The same Galilee.

There is one Tannaitic figure whose career and mythologized reputation threads together these associations and comparisons.

After the Bar Kochba catastrophe, one Tanna described its geographic and cultural implications in clear, emphatic terms. Galilee was now Jerusalem. "When a man is banished from Judea to Galilee . . . this cannot really be called exile,"[125] proclaimed Rabbi Shimon Bar Yochai, who is known by his name's Hebrew acronym, Rashbi.

As though to reward Rashbi for consecrating the relocation of Judaism in Galilee, Rashbi is the most commemorated Tanna in Galilee today. In fact, in contemporary Israel, no rabbi or any other sort of figure in Jewish history receives as much annual veneration as Rashbi. In late spring, on the Lag B'Omar holiday, the pilgrimage to Bar Yochai's assumed burial cave, in Meron (near Safed), is Israel's largest annual public event, drawing tens of thousands of religious celebrants. During Israel's most important secular-national holiday, *Yom Atzmaut* (Independence Day, celebrated earlier in the spring), no spot in the country gathers a crowd comparable to what happens during the annual *hillula* for Rashbi in Meron.

Among other feats, this mythic character, Rashbi, is celebrated for having dwelled in a Galilee cave, with his son, for thirteen years (with one brief hiatus), where he escaped from Roman persecution associated with the defeat of the Bar Kochba rebellion. The cave offered a number of advantages (on one Talmudic version, the patriarchal writers mention that had Rashbi stayed, as a wanted fugitive, in his own home, his loquacious wife would have compromised him), but mostly it enabled this pious Tanna to study. Of all the Tannaim, Rashbi was the most outspoken advocate of religious study, as a gateway to God, going so far as putting on the Talmudic record his view that working for a living was a waste of time.

For this studious zeal, Bar Yochai can, of course, be linked with fellow Tannaim who, in a display of prodigious learnedness, compiled the Mishnah.[126] In a yin-yang way, or as Jacob to their Essau, Bar Yochai is the ancestral antithesis to the Zionist halutzim, who rejected learnedness in Torah and Talmud as the anchor of Jewish identity, going so far as turning kibbutz labor into a new secular religion (they are known in Israeli historiography as "Labor Zionists").

And to connect one final thread: Rashbi's learnedness by no means applied solely to the legalistic rigor and sophistry of the Mishnah. Rashbi was a mystic, and according to a factually untrue, but widely held, legend, he authored the Zohar, the Kabbalah's bedrock text.

Not so much Rashbi's own life, whatever really happed in it, but rather the myths it generated, are at the cutting edge of all the semi-stereotypical, essentialist, questions which Jews can't seem to stop asking about themselves, and which have long left their friends and enemies wondering. Are they a practical people, or are they other-worldly? Are they mystics or are they rationalists? Embodying such queries and quandaries, Rashbi is an intriguingly prominent figure in Galilee history. We will see (in volume two) how, in mystical belief, his soul was reclaimed in early modern times, by Isaac Luria and by Rabbi Nahman of Breslov, just as we will follow how the cult of his grave became intertwined, symbolically and causally, with Safed's mystical renaissance in the sixteenth century, a major cultural event in Jewish history. Rashbi's life and legend is thus an indelible part of Galilee history.

RASHBI'S LIFE

Little is known of Rashbi's birth and boyhood—the extant Talmudic materials stress the young man's constant proximity to his mentor, Rabbi Akiva, and also his unmitigated zeal for Torah study.[127] In his guise as the leading Tannaitic lobbyist for unalloyed religious study, Rashbi enters Jewish history during one well-known Talmudic debate. The authority of Rabbi Akiva, Rashbi's mentor who was also a zealot for Torah study, is challenged by Rabbi Yishmael ben Elisha, a native of Upper Galilee. In a dispute about the meaning of Joshua 1:8, Yishmael insists that its pro-study exhortation ("keep this Book of the law always on your lips") is not a prescription for idle learning. "Set aside time not only for study, but also for work," declares Yishmael.

Incredulous, Rashbi rejoins: should a man sow and plow and harvest in successive seasons of the agricultural year, "what will become of Torah?" Advocating a vision that is similar to the way ultra-Orthodox view their place in Israel today, Rashbi announces that Tannaim should commit themselves entirely to Torah study, and let others attend to the laborious practicalities of the everyday world. "One must dedicate entirely to Torah, and set aside other endeavors," Rashbi proclaims. "When Israel performs God's work, its [daily] work is carried out by others."[128] As scholars recognize, in the debate with Yishmael, Rashbi's message is really "Torato emunato,"[129] a Tanna's profession is Torah study and nothing else (Torato emunato is the motto that ultra-Orthodox Jews utilize or exploit in Israel today, to justify the military service exemptions they receive from the government).

In its immediate context of second-century Tannaitic culture in Galilee, was Rashbi's "Torah study only" position realistic, and representative? Benny Lau, an Orthodox rabbi in Israel known for forging dialogue with left-leaning secular groups, views Rashbi as an oddball, in this connection.

Among scholars in the Talmudic era, he concludes, Rashbi's "Torah only" view was "unusual," since most of the sages busily worked in everyday roles. Similarly, in his impressive survey of Galilee's socioeconomic circumstances in the second century, Goodman assumes that the Tannaitic culture had firm working roots—in Judea, up to the Bar Kochba revolt, these rabbis were generally artisans, he claims. However, less than two decades after his 1983 study, Goodman backtracked somewhat on this point.[130] In fact, from a common sense view, it is hard to view the Mishnah as being compiled by anyone other than religious scholars for whom Torah study had prerogative.

Not just on this religious study issue, Rashbi's words and deeds, despite (or because of) their mythologized cast, are emblematic of lasting strands in Jewish culture. Rabbi Judah, the Tanna who is most readily identified with the relocation of rabbinical learning from Judea to Usha, in Galilee, sometimes sounded dejected about this work-study issue. Before the Hadrianic persecutions, he quipped, his peers made study their priority and relegated commerce and work as a secondary endeavor; they ended up succeeding in both domains. In contrast, the first generation of Usha Tannaim were failing in both spheres, worried Rabbi Judah. He leaned strongly toward Rashbi's position, opining that a sage who made Torah study his main task, and subordinated daily work, would ascend to high rank in the world to come.[131]

In Jerusalem and Babylonian Talmudic writings, there are many variations in accounts of Rashbi's thirteen years in the cave (with his son Eleazer), and his subsequent activity, including his reported purification of Tiberias. Because the accounts are segmented in different units (before, during and after the cave episode), each with its own levels of supernatural occurrence vis-à-vis plain reportage of regular events, it is difficult to judge which of these two broad sets of materials, Palestine or Babylonian, seems preferably "authentic." Lee Levine, an American-born Hebrew University of Jerusalem archaeologist and historian of Jews in antiquity, believes that the Babylonian version of Rashbi's doings in Tiberias have a relatively high level of historicity, whereas its cave description is "a full-blown legendary account with a plethora of folkloristic accretions."[132] Since appreciation of Rashbi's lasting impact in Jewish consciousness must give ample weight to the mythologized parts of his life, this judgment hardly disqualifies the Babylonian materials. Indeed, for our purposes, this Babylonian version seems preferably apposite, partly because its opening, a debate about the pros and cons of Roman rule, reinforces one theme we will follow in our survey of the Mishnah: regarding sociopolitical matters, some of a life-and-death character, Tannaitic culture was argumentative and pluralistic. In this sociopolitical context, Rashbi was one personality type, but there were contrasting Tannaitic approaches. We summarize the Babylonian cave story here—extended English translations are cited in the footnotes.[133]

In a discussion featuring Rabbi Judah and Rashbi, the former extols Roman rule, commending the markets, bridges and bathhouses it has brought. Recoiling, Rashbi counters that Roman accomplishments simply serve Roman interests—the Romans build bridges in order to collect tolls; they establish markets to place prostitutes in them; and so on. An eavesdropper reports this conversation to Roman authorities, who decide to reward Rabbi Judah, and to execute Rashbi. With his son Eleazar, Rashbi hides in a beit midrash, where he wife brings bread and water each day. As Roman searchers circle near the area, Rashbi worries that his wife, being "easy-minded" like other women, might spill the beans. So the father and son hide in a cave, where a carob tree miraculously sprouts to provide them food, and a spring slakes their thirst. Their bodies covered by sand, the two cave-dwellers study day after day, for twelve years.

Elijah comes to the cave and announces that Rashbi (and son) can leave it, since Rome's emperor has died and the man-hunt orders against him have been annulled. After leaving the cave, Rashbi is distraught because he sees Jews engaged in farm work—they forsake study and busy themselves with pedestrian labor, he bitterly exclaims. Meantime, everything he and his son gaze upon burns-up; and so the pair returns to the cave after hearing a heavenly voice warn that their fire-producing eyes will destroy the world. After another year, the two finally quit the cave for good; Rashbi heals whatever is injured by Eleazer's gaze.

Subsequently, Rashbi's cave-scarred body is soothed in a bath-house by his son-in-law. Having been delivered from persecution, Rashbi resolves to carry out a repair (tikkun) as repayment for his good fortune. Obliging this resolution, Rashbi purifies Tiberias. Closure in this story happens when Rashbi meets the informant (Yehuda b. Gerim) whose treachery had set the Romans against him, and turns him into a heap of bones.

Some of the Palestinian versions of the cave story provide imprecise information about its locale (in "Beka" or "Peka"), along with details about the carob tree and the Tiberias purification episode, that are different or missing in the Babylonian version. Replacing the Yehuda b. Gerim closure-revenge ending in the Babylonian version, Palestinian materials substitute a very different tale located in the Beit Netofa valley, whereby Rashbi, in an exchange about technicalities of the *shmita* fallow years, turns an insolently clever farmer into a heap of bones. The departure from the cave, in these non-Babylonian sources, is quite different, not being prompted by the prophet Elijah: as he leaves the cave, Rashbi observes a vignette where birds are freed from, or caught by, hunters, thanks to heavenly intervention, or despite the heavenly voice (*bat kol*), and this causes him to ruminate about human destiny and free will.[134]

Why, of all the Tannaim, did Rashbi's life and legends acquire such a magical allure, a spell visibly apparent today in Israel, in the annual *hillula* celebration at Meron? We can say, straight-forwardly, that this magnetism does not really result from Rashbi's special powers, per se (among other special abilities, Talmudic writings attribute eye-blazing power to many sages); instead, his charisma draws from two spectacular biographical events, the years-long cave experience and the purification of Tiberias. These are nowhere to be found in the lives of other Tannaim (more precisely, the events have precedents and analogues in other Jewish and gentile lives—the patriarch Abraham, for instance, escapes from Nimrod in a cave—but in the Tannaitic setting they are affixed uniquely to Rashbi). Yet this answer only pushes the question down the road: once we assume that at least some aspects in Rashbi's career are folkloric in character, rather than authentic biographical documentation, the question becomes, how did Rashbi become remembered as a singularly magical and empowered Tanna in this second-century Galilee landscape? As we will see in volume two, the source of Rashbi's mystical allure to Kabbalists and Hassidim is his mythical authorship of the *Zohar*—but this point also merely kicks the can down the road, since there remains the question as to why Rashbi remained singularly interesting to Moses de Leon, the *Zohar*'s actual author, and to his circle of late thirteenth-century Jewish mystics in Castile.

No historian has produced a thorough reckoning with such questions comparable to the excellent biographical work done on Isaac Luria Ashkenazi (the Ari), Rashbi's mystical successor in the Kabbalah setting of sixteenth-century Safed whose life story is also awash in supernatural rumor and legend.[135] Yet detailed scholarly assessments of exceptional occurrences in Rashbi's life point loosely to a general explanation.

The Rashbi legends lasted because, as invariably happens, they have some roots in reality and because retrospective mythologizing of Rashbi's life suited various purposes important to later generations. Also, compared to other Tannaim, Rashbi was an identifiable and likely retrospective target for myth-makers because (as we have seen) he stood out by articulating outspoken positions on key social, religious, and political issues, including the imperative of Torah study and the depredatory character of Roman rule in Eretz Israel. Rashbi's fame also owes much to posthumous luck, to the fact that his grave was in the right place at the right time.

Solid reasons can be found to discredit the Tiberias purification story.[136] Our knowledge of the purity issue in Tiberias stems from a few lines in Josephus's *Antiquities*, referring to Herod's knowledge of the religious illegality of Tiberias' establishment on "the site of tombs that had been obliterated."[137] Yet, as we have seen, as military commander in Galilee, Josephus's stature had been chewed up in the mouths of rival power groups in Tiberias, and so he may have been a frustrated and unreliable chronicler of the city's past. We have also noted how the Mishnah records that Tannaim flourished in Tiberias even before the Bar Kochba revolt, as exemplified by Jose ben Kisma's enthused testimony. Still, as Lee Levine argues, while grave contamination issues in Tiberias were clearly overcome by many Jews, there might well have been lingering concerns about priests and purity in the city, and Rashbi's positions, rather moderate in character, on priestly purity issues were well-known. Also, explains Levine, all the Talmudic accounts of Rashbi's purification work in Tiberias make reference to a religious council voting to enact purification work—such details lend authenticity to the story of Rashbi's contribution to the renewed purification work in the city.[138] There is, in fact, no reason to doubt the Babylonian Talmud's documentation of this purification episode because its references to cutting down and removing lupines from tithed portions (*terumah*) do not imply that there was anything supernatural about the contamination removal.

How, and why, did Rashbi's enactment of a purification rite in Tiberias take on larger-than-life proportions? The scholar Lee Levine offers some fascinating hypotheses.[139] His answer features needs and circumstances which arose in decades and centuries after Rashbi's short stint in Tiberias, or after his reported, lengthy, stint in the cave. In the mid-third century, Tiberias hosted the patriarchate and could be seen as a Jewish capital. Its status likely irked resentment among rival groups, possibly in Sepphoris, where, on St. Epiphanius' account, Christianizing work undertaken in the fourth century by a Jewish apostate, Joseph, was making headway (we will hear more about Joseph in the next chapter). Digging in their heels, Jewish elites in Sepphoris possibly had incentive to cast aspersions about impurity in Tiberias, long regarded as a rival town. Whatever the precise dynamic, it is not hard to see why Jewish spokesman in the third and fourth centuries might have utilized and embellished the reputation of an esteemed second-century Tanna, Rashbi, in an argument defending the sanctity of the patriarchate's home, Tiberias.

After the early fourth century, there was no stopping the momentum of Christianity's rise, everywhere, following Constantine's sponsorship of it in the Roman empire. For Jewish spokesmen, there was growing incentive for the embellishment of Rashbi's biography. At issue now was not an apologetic about the purity of the country's Jewish capital—instead, pressure mounted in favor of exploiting legendary icons in an apologetic for Judaism as a whole. Christians were busily foisting supernatural abilities upon their own martyrs and saints-in-the-making. So what did the Jews have to say about their own heroes?

Sensing this void, a fourth century rabbi in Tiberias, Jeremiah, accorded to Rashbi supernatural status and ability. Rabbi Jeremiah solemnly wrote that Rashbi brought treasure to a valley simply by calling out that it should be filled with gold dinars. No rainbow had appeared in Rashbi's lifetime, added Jeremiah, since the Tanna's preternaturally salubrious comportment eliminated the need for symbolic reaffirmation of God's covenant with his people.

If truth be told, the extent to which Jewish commentators who mythologized Rashbi were inspired by a rivalry with Christian hagiographers remains open to question. Undoubtedly, a portion of the Rashbi legends was drawn from gentile, non-Christian sources. In this connection, Levine mentions a pre-Socratic philosopher named Epimenides: in the second century, a number of writers stressed experiences, tendencies, and abilities in Epimenides' biography, including the purification of cities, cave-dwelling, and mysticism, which might have encouraged embellishment in Jewish writing about Rashbi.

From one source or another, an eighth-century apocalyptic work about Rashbi, called *The Secrets of Rabbi Simeon ben Yohai*, made the crucial link between this revered Tanna, and mysticism (nothing in rabbinical writing up to this point had associated Rashbi with mystical philosophy). The road on which Rashbi would be credited with authorship of the core Kabbalist text, the *Zohar*, which was actually composed in the thirteenth century, was now being paved.

This factually untrue, but emotionally mesmerizing, attribution of *Zohar* authorship helps explain the popularity of the annual celebrations in Meron. Contemporary Jews of mystical inclination flock to the presumed grave of the Tannaitic figure who is thought of as the procreator of Kabbalah. Still, without disparaging the spiritual intensity of the *hillula* event, it is indisputably what historians call an "invented tradition."[140]

The hillula at Meron does not really date from the heyday of Kabbalist culture, in sixteenth-century Safed. Neither the Ari, who communed intensely with Rashbi's memory, to the point where he considered himself the *gigul* incarnation of this Tanna's soul, nor other prominent Safed mystics (*mekubalim*) in this period, had anything to do with commemorations at Rashbi's grave on Lag B'Omer. To be sure, they visited Rashbi's grave with reverence—grave prostration rites were a staple in Safed's Kabbalah culture—but they did so on other dates of the year. How, then, did the Rashbi *hillula* develop? Without question, as a result of all the attainments and legends (the cave, Rashbi's zeal for study, Tiberias purification, among others) we have mentioned here; but also from happenstance.

Up to the end of the sixteenth century, annual events had been held at Meron, but they were connected to caves associated with Hillel and Shamai and to unexpected rises of spring water in them.[141] Characteristics of the

Rashbi *hillula*—lighting bonfires which can be seen from afar, first-ever haircuts for three-year-old boys—became apparent in Meron at this time, but not thanks to the Kabbalists of Safed. These hillula features were brought to the Galilee hilltop, and to Rashbi's grave, mainly by groups of Mustarabim, Jews of North African and Middle East descent.

For centuries, dating from the Crusader period, these Jews had paid annual homage to the prophet Samuel, at his reported grave on a Jerusalem hilltop, fittingly called Nebe Samuel. Delving deeply into reports filed by travelers and local commentators through the sixteenth century, the scholar Abraham Ya'ari shows that haircuts for young boys, grave-site candle vigils, and various other rituals are rooted originally in these Nebe Samuel observances, which were held on the twenty-eighth of Iyar, the day known traditionally for Samuel's death, which is just ten days before Lag BaOmer. As a result of the rise of Mamluk and then Ottoman rule in the country, Jews lost access to Nebe Samuel in the Jerusalem area. Relocating the festival, to Galilee and the Meron Hilltop, they revamped the *hillula* as homage to Rashbi, in lieu of Samuel.

ELISHA BEN ABUYA, AHER

Evaluative judgments about the Mishnaic world which the Tannaim built can be overly broad and trite, but there is one, acutely precise, measure of how Jews over the centuries have regarded this post-hurban, second-century Galilee culture. A telling standard of judgment is how they have assessed the career of the Tanna heretic, the "other" (*aher*) who chose the evil pathway (*yatza le'tarubt ha'ra'a*), Elisha ben Abuya.

Because Elisha becomes an anti-hero in the Talmud, one whose activities challenge the Tannaitic prerogative given to Torah study, conflicting attitudes displayed toward Aher's career by commentators over the centuries, leading up to our own time, are tantamount to a referendum on the Mishnah. To put it simply: Jews who condemn Elisha, ratify the Talmud, whereas Jews who applaud his rebelliousness reject the Talmud.

The Israeli scholar Nurit Be'eri usefully brings this scorecard into modern times, cataloguing relatively recent responses to the Elisha stories.[142] As it turns out, in the late nineteenth century, Jewish modernizers who consciously sought to lower the status of the oral law, and of rabbinical authority, valorized Elisha. Following the principle, "the enemy of my enemy is my friend," these iconoclasts, some of them cultural heroes of the embryonic Zionist movement (Moshe Leib Lilienblum, Mica Josef Berdichevsky), embraced the Tannaitic anti-hero, viewing him as sound precedent for their own rebellion against Talmudic culture.

Elisha's timeline can be adduced in relation to Rabbi Meir's life, since he is projected in Jerusalem Talmudic writings as Meir's mentor. On all accounts, Elisha is said to have died before Meir, meaning that insofar he was a palpable being, and not entirely an imaginary figment conjured in the Talmud to embody immorality, he lived through the middle part of the second century.[143] Elisha receives one honorific mention in the Mishnaic tractate *Avot*, meaning that there probably was a respected rabbi in Tannaitic times named Rabbi Elisha.[144] His debut as an allegorical representation of a sinner sage occurs in the Mishnah supplement, the Tosefta, in the enigmatic, and widely debated, tale of "four who entered an orchard (*pardes*)," and thereafter Elisha appears as the heretic gadfly of Tannaitic culture in the Jerusalem (Yerushalmi) and Babylonian (Bavli) versions of the Talmud. These Talmudic versions vary somewhat, with the former, the Yerushalmi, allowing a bit more biographical detail (Elisha is known by the sobriquet "Other," not by his own name in the Babylonian Talmud, and the Galilean landscape can only be inferred by references in these Bavli materials, whereas the Yerushalmi specifically puts him in locales like Tiberias).[145]

Elisha is a moral marionette whose strings are pulled by the sages as a test of fundamental principles. Since even apostates are considered Jews, can a transgressing "other" become entirely excluded from the Jewish community? What moral responsibilities are assumed in teacher-student relationships? Can a religious student lose his place in the world to come due to his association with a reprobate mentor? What guarantees heavenly reward: irreproachable behavior, or deep Torah study? The Babylonian materials put this last question in sharp focus, and ultimately cast Torah knowledge and Torah commitment as being powerfully, perhaps infinitely, redemptive.

The "four went into the orchard" tale tells of four rabbis in the *pardes*: "one gazed and perished, one gazed and was smitten, one gazed and cut the shoots, and one went up whole and came down whole." Elisha is the rabbi who "cuts the shoots" (קיצץ בנטיעות), and Rabbi Akiva is the survivor. Some scholars have viewed the orchard as a metaphor for mystical experience, going so far (in Gershom Scholem's case) as to suggest that there was a pre-Kabbalist strain of Jewish mysticism running through Tannaitic culture.[146] Other modern commentators pare down this mysticism angle, suggesting that, at most, the pardes metaphor applies to one specific mystical context (i.e., *merkava* divine chariot stories based on the first chapter of Ezekiel), and some scholars completely extract mysticism from this orchard, viewing the story as, among other things, one variant in a lasting template of four Jewish types (a la the four children in the Passover haggadah). With complicated twists and turns, the sin attributed to Elisha in this orchard tale, "cutting the shoots," widens in the Talmud as willful transgression on "evil courses" (*tarbut ha'ra'ah*), and as the sinning individual's exclusion from Jewish communal life, as an "other" (*aher*).

As with many other Talmudic issues, efforts to sort out exactly when and how Elisha stories were composed can be vexing; and so it is a little misleading to view these legends as a consecutive moral narrative. Still, Elisha basically descends down a slippery slope. Sometimes his "sin" refers to acculturation in second-century Palestine's Greco-Roman settings that is not necessarily transgressive. Here is one example:

> What is Aher?
> Greek song did not cease from his home.
> It is told of Aher that when he would leave the beit midrash, many heretical books used to fall from his lap.[147]

Writing in the mid-twentieth century, in a setting where Jewish adaptation in America was picking up steam, one commentator, Milton Steinberg, focused on this sort of Elisha legend. A Conservative rabbi, Steinberg viewed Elisha's heresy as a problem of Jewish assimilation in enticing gentile settings, and he wrote an engaging historical novel about "Aher," which was translated into Hebrew.[148]

Some offenses attributed to Elisha belong to the moderately severe category of *shevut* (prohibitions not specifically listed in the Torah). These include riding a horse on Shabbat. In other cases, Elisha appears on the scene of a transgression, but his participation in the offense seems ambiguous, and the focus of the Talmudic writers is not the "actual" Elisha. Instead, as in the example of a scene featuring Aher and a prostitute wherein the Tanna sinner gives her a radish, in a kind of semiotic vignette pertaining to metonymic signs of "otherness," and of "cutting the roots," the writers seem fixated on spinning around words, and also existential possibilities. Here Elisha can be seen as a symbol, not necessarily as a human life.[149]

Then come stories where Elisha is violently deranged and flamboyantly heretical. In one episode, touring with Rabbi Meir, Elisha chops a child into thirteen pieces, and sends them to the town's thirteen schoolhouses (this number evokes Tiberias, since the town reportedly had thirteen synagogues in this period).[150] In another incident, Elisha mocks the Torah-only zeal articulated by Tannaim like Rashbi: entering a beit midrash, he scatters its young Torah prodigies, sending out one to be a mason, another to be a carpenter, a third youngster to be a hunter, and a fourth, a tailor. The same passage shows Aher maliciously conniving with Roman authorities so as to foil attempts undertaken by Jews to uphold Sabbath rules.[151]

From the standpoint of our portrait of Tannaitic culture in second-century Galilee, the most significant Elisha legend opens with dramatic flourish. Rabbi Meir interrupts his teaching in a Tiberias synagogue on a Shabbat (a highly unusual and problematic act), in order to engage his mentor, Elisha, in a lengthy and learned theological discussion. This riveting opening should be quoted: "Rabbi Meir was sitting teaching in the beit midrash in Tiberias. Elisha, his master, passed by, riding on a horse on the Sabbath day. They came and said to him, 'look your master is outside.' He stopped his teaching and went out to him.'"[152] The legend, recorded in the Jerusalem Talmud, is long and filled with scriptural references, but its gist is readily apprehensible: Meir is desperate to reserve a place in the world to come for his mentor, Elisha, despite Aher's innumerable religious infractions.

At one stage, Meir exclaims that his mentor's inclusion in heaven takes precedence over that of his own father. In the next world, he declaims, "I will visit my master first, and, after that, my father." The sequence and declamation of events illustrate the creative dynamism of Meir's relationship with Elisha (particularly in Babylonian materials, Aher is not really identified as Meir's teacher). The tale also pivots around the Tannaitic image of the teacher as morality's ultimate guide, a force which supplants parental authority. Finally, a suggestion entertained in one study—speculating that the real "star" in these Aher stories is not its nominal protagonist, Elisha, but rather Rabbi Meir[153]– is reinforced in this intriguing story.

Scrambling for authority in a void created by the Temple's destruction, the Tannaim had to provide incentive for young scholars, who were expected to apply themselves in batei midrash. Their key selling point was that Tannaitic teaching provided a place in the world to come for industrious, pious students. Meir flips this teaching ethos on its head in this well-known legend about Elisha on a horse on a Shabbat in Tiberias. He becomes a student who saves a place in heaven for his sinful teacher. This teacher-student turnabout, I think, symbolizes Meir's unique place in Tannaitic culture, as the figure most richly associated with its aspiration to establish new precedents, and also to set behavioral limits, in evolving projects, the patriarchate and the Mishnah.

As we have seen, owing to subsequent agendas and experiences, many of which unfolded long after the Tannaitic and Amoraic periods, Jewish commentators and ritual practitioners found cause to elevate Rashbi's reputation, sometimes to celestial heights. Yet, I believe, in the inner world of Talmudic compilation, Meir was thought of as the representation of ultimate cultural limits and principles. In fact, had the Talmud evolved with a greater degree of geographic and compositional continuity, his life story would have been presented with genuine acuity as a kind of Jewish Pilgrim's Progress in Galilee, after the hurban.

Informative and insightful as Talmudic scholarship has become on North American campuses, its focus on hermeneutic and halakhic complexities in stories about figures such as Elisha and Meir and Beruria can be problematic. This scholarship invariably promotes the same basic conclusion about these differing figures, holding that they are "unreal" exegetical composites. In a broad cultural sense, this conclusion is questionable.

We will illustrate this critique with an example: one insightful interpretation of the Elisha-Meir relationship cites an encounter in which Meir asks Aher, "Rabbi, what is the punishment for adultery in the coming future?"[154] The study in hand views this query in a rather abstract exegetical context, and does not mention that, as decades and centuries went by, many readers who came across it must have put it in an emotionally poignant biographical context. Why would Meir not be thinking of the worst transgression of his own life, in his treatment of Beruria, when he posed this question to his sinful teacher, Elisha? Would not Meir have been worried that the horrendous seduction trick he pulled on his wife might have blocked her, or his own, access to the world to come? Indeed, once we recognize that Talmudic legends of Tannaim are a form of biography, hagiography but nonetheless biography, much in their inchoate anomalousness dissipates.

Think back to the "Beruria incident," and to the way deconstructionist-spirited commentators who view Meir's wife as an abstract projection of Talmudic misogyny find unstated meanings in the gruesome episode precisely because, to them, "it doesn't make sense." Yet when we view Talmudic legends on a biographical level, elements of anomalousness that might be laden within the Beruria incident appear to stem from character inconsistency, rather than textual ellipses. And when we piece together biographical fragments that are scattered throughout Talmudic writing, even this impression of inconsistency can be challenged, since, when his Humpty-Dumpty parts are glued back together, Meir comes across as a large-hearted character with a healthy capacity for contrition. On such a biographical reading, the Beruria incident resembles a deliberately plotted tragedy and need not be seen as a curiosity wrought by the unstable psychological state of the writers and their consequent compositional erraticism. The coherence of Meir's biography might be questioned by postmodernist critics, but it is appreciated annually by streams of observers of yahrtzeit memorials, on Pesach Sheni, at his assumed Tiberias grave site.

Talmudic writers, and readers, certainly had "real" life stories in mind whenever they cited or encountered names like Meir and Beruria. If we want to understand how biographies of these beguiling figures from Tannaitic times have become enshrined in Galilee's landscape, contemporary, postmodern scholarship needs to be read in conjunction with commentary of Israeli Orthodox scholars like Lau, who write for audiences which hold Rashbi, Meir and other Tannaim in iconic reverence, affirming, credulously or not, many wondrous items on their biographical record. Their point of view belongs to Galilee's history, just as do parts of the gospels, and of Josephus, that are similarly elided by modern critics who find them disagreeable.

THE MISHNAH

"History as an account of a meaningful pattern of events, making sense of the past and giving guidance about the future, begins with the necessary conviction that events matter, one after another. The Mishnah's framers, however, present us with no elaborate theory of events," writes Neusner.[155] In contrast to the Pentateuch, he explains, there is nothing "prophetic" about the Mishnah's perception of events. Single events, including the Temple's destruction, are not seen as having monumental effect, and there is no teleological interconnectedness in the events' narration; that is, Mishnah narration does not point to some future consummation, an apocalypse or messianic utopia. The Mishnah is thus an ahistorical document, its purpose being to create an all-encompassing system by which Jews can live and sanctify some mundane affairs.

The codifiers' concern was the creation of the system itself. They were engaged, in Neusner's words, in a "vast labor of classification, an immense construction of the order and rules governing the hierarchization of everything on earth and in heaven."[156] For this purpose of classification, the actual present, and its relation to past realities and future possibilities, were virtually irrelevant—the Mishnah relates to "actual" events, past and present, only inasmuch as they are illustrative of problems and potentialities in the system of religious law it hoped to establish. In fact, the concluding two divisions in the Mishnah's six divisions ("Holy Things" and "Purities") relate to an entirely nonreal subject, stipulating sacred purity procedures for the Temple, in blatant disregard of the fact that this religious structure no longer existed.

This ahistorical approach can be maddening, sometimes causing study of the Mishnah to feel like a scholastic video game. On the other hand, the ahistorical approach proved lasting, redounding to the credit of the Tannaim. Who else codified a set of religious laws that kept together, for millennia, a people which was in the thrall of defeat, dispossession, and exile? Is there a better way to teach a group to prepare for the long term than to encourage it not to fuss over events in its ephemeral present, or to fight over interpretations about how its past led to its present?

No less important than any other way of looking at this formative, Talmudic, text, the Mishnah can be seen as a record of how Judaism refashioned itself in Galilee. As in the case of Kabbalistic mysticism in sixteenth-century Safed, the Tannaitic Mishnah's contents and religious outlook are creatively intertwined with the Galilee landscape. The Mishnah, in this sense, is one of Galilee's great contribution's to Jewish culture and history, and so this section analyzes connections between the Mishnah and Galilee, and describes features of second-century Galilee religious culture that are reflected in this cornerstone Talmudic document. When we ask "who were the Tannaim," we are basically asking "what was Galilee" during this transformative period.

The context of the Mishnah's classification work is largely rural and agricultural, befitting Galilee. Its first division is itself called "agriculture," and a tractate such as "Kilayim" (literally "mixture") exemplifies the Mishnaic mania for classifying everything under the sun. At issue in this tractate is what sort of seeds, or animals, can be mixed together in ways that do not trespass various religious prohibitions. The following section, a kind of taxonomic talent show, displays Tannaim acting as experts in religion and veterinary sciences:

> A wild ox is considered a kind of domesticated animal/And Rabbi Yose says, "It is considered a kind of wild animal."/A dog is considered a kind of wild animal. Rabbi Meir says, "it is considered a kind of domesticated animal."/A swine is considered a kind of domesticated animal./An Arabian onager is considered a kind of wild animal./An elephant and a monkey are considered kinds of wild animals./And a man is permitted to be joined with all of them [with either a wild or domesticated animal] to pull a wagon, plough, or to be led.[157]

Mishnah classifications can confusingly mix hypothetical items, Pentateuch references and parts of the contemporary second century landscape—this animal safari discussion is a case in point. Particularly prominent in animal references are deer,[158] and their Talmudic presence, recapitulating Old Testament imagery, remained on the minds of secular Zionists who were prone to use deer as symbols of the land of Israel, even if few were to be found in it when they arrived at the end of the nineteenth century.

Religion and society intermingle in the Mishnah, and it often becomes impossible to distinguish one sphere from the other. As noted, the extent to which, in third-century Galilee and elsewhere, this commentary was mostly moot and theoretical, or practically effectual, remains open to debate in scholarship—Goodman, for instance, opines that the Mishnah's influence extended mostly to Jewish consciences, but may not have really changed what residents did after they woke up, and went to the fields.[159] At least in aspiration, the Mishnah is a theocratic constitution deeply engaged in telling communal members what they can, and cannot, do in society, and at work.

In the agricultural division, for instance, passages on the biblically mandated seventh fallow year meticulously tell farmers what counts as prohibited work, or sanctioned activity, during this shmita period. The passages relate to how manure is to be handled during shmita, whether stones may be removed from fields and whether fences and terraces may be restored or built.[160] The two rabbinic groups, houses of Hillel and Shamai, quarrel over specific points of shmita, one saying that a farmer can prune an olive tree during this year of rest, the other arguing that an agriculturalist can uproot such a tree. As often happens in the Mishnah, such quibbling disputation about arcane shmita details pushes the sages toward conclusions that relate to rather more consequential matters. Thus, while ruminating about whether rue, goosefoot, eruca, and wild coriander are purchasable during shmita, the Mishnah codifiers suddenly map the borders of Galilee, a cartographic exercise fraught with juridical-social implications weightier than the esoteric details of the fallow year (Kfar Hananiah, they rule, is the dividing point between the Upper and Lower Galilee).[161]

The Mishnah's geography is centered in Galilee. Of course, other regions, including ones outside of Eretz Israel, receive attention, but Galilee roots of Talmudic Judaism are lucidly perceptible on page after page in the Mishnah, just as the origins of Christian morality cannot be extracted from the Galilee hilltop where Jesus delivered his epochal sermon.

The Mishnah sometimes deploys a trial and error kind of approach toward the practice of Judaism in Galilee. This is because Galilee is the first place where the rabbis contemplated how Judaism might be reinvented and survive in some form of exile, after the decimation of the Jerusalem cult. Not for the last time, they grappled with the question of Jewish continuity in a world where mundane improvement is generated by foreign, untrusted sources.

In second-century Galilee, the goyish threat was posed by Roman engineering, and a major venue for such early Talmudic disputation about modernization and its limits was Tiberias. The reasoning here about hydraulics, Tiberias and Shabbat (the Jewish Sabbath), would subsequently be applied to countless technological contrivances:

> The people of Tiberias brought a pipe of cold water through a spring of hot water. Sages said to them, if this was done on the Sabbath, the water has the status of hot water which has been heated on Shabbat. It is prohibited for use in washing and drinking. If this was done on the festival day, the water has the status of hot water which has been heated on the festival day. It is prohibited for use in washing, but permitted for use in drinking.[162]

When the Tannaitic writers mused about how Tanakh precedents ought to be incorporated in their recommendations and rulings relating to state, society, and economy in late second-century Palestine, they sometimes looked out to trends of wealth accumulation and absorption of Greco-Roman material culture in Galilee. Hence, in the course of a densely detailed discussion about rental properties, the rabbis refer to leisure elites in Sepphoris: "In Sepphoris, a person hired a bathhouse from his fellow for twelve golden [denars] per year . . ."[163]

This Tannaitic confrontation with Greco-Roman culture and affluence continued also on the edge of Galilee's borders. As mentioned, in the Jews' own cartography during the Tannaitic period, the important seaport town, Acre, was not in included as part of Galilee, because its majority was not Jewish and because it was filled with pagan shrines. In a well-known episode, documented in the Mishnah, the aforementioned Yavne nasi, Gamaliel II, indulgently washed himself in a gentile bathhouse in Acre, not perturbed by its devotions to Aphrodite. Challenged about his visit to this venue, Gamaliel produces a learnedly recondite justification[164]—the important point is that, in view of evolving social networks and acculturation processes in Palestine's northern regions, the episode was not intolerably scandalous, and so the Mishnah's compilers did not exclude it.

Innumerable Mishnah discussions convey an impression of second-century Jewish gentrification in rural Galilee. One example is the discussion of home-owners renovating their property by adding an upper level and new rooms, and by replacing windows.[165] Social annoyances in Galilee's landscape, such as tax farmers or bandits, stroll through the Mishnah.[166] Mishnah passages which impose, theoretically or practically, regulatory systems in various socioeconomic spheres, feature Galilee items. One example is its classification of various types of interest lending in the economy—here, the Mishnah highlights exchanges of coin and wheat, and its ensuing discussion refers to livestock, a vat of olives, and kiln pottery.[167] The Mishnah's fascinating fifth division, "The Order of Damages," is seemingly one of its more "modern" parts since its legal reasoning can be connected, in various ways, to subsequent principles and procedures in tort law. Galilee's landscape is no less present in this division than in other parts of the Mishnah. The examples of damages adjudication are taken largely from Galilee farm holdings, as in the case of a dog or goat which jumps from the top of a roof and damages implements, or eats a neighbor's grain.[168] Oxen, who are superstars of second-century Jewish torts law, engage the Tannaim in lengthy discussions. What happens when one such farm beast knocks out the tooth of a slave, sets fire to grain on Shabbat, or gores four or five other oxen, or even human neighbors?[169] When must an ox be stoned to death: when it kills an Israelite? When it kills a gentile? Read the Mishnah.

In just a few cases, the Mishnah concedes that regional and cultural differentiation prevent the uniform enforcement of its religious laws across the country. For instance, in the tractate on oath-taking, Rabbi Judah allows that a Galilean who makes a promise about tithe delivery is not bound by it. "A statement referring . . . to heave offering made in Judea is binding, but in Galilee it is not binding. For the men of Galilee are not familiar with heave offering," nor, Rabbi Judah adds, are they "familiar with things devoted to the priests."[170] This appears to be over-statement, and it casts an untowardly long shadow of am ha'aretz ignorance over Galilee. The remark is not consistent with many other images and statements in the Mishnah; but it undeniably recognizes differences in Judaism observance in regions of the country. The important point is that affirmations of such differentiation are hard to find in the Mishnah,[171] meaning that scholars who have insisted that there was never anything like a separate "Galilean halakha" are probably correct.[172]

Beyond the controversial issue of amei ha'aretz, the Mishnah meticulously details who counts as being inside the tent of Jewish religious law, and who is left outside. This "who is a Jew" sort of classification is particularly pronounced in tractates which cover tithing obligations, wherein the rabbis announce who owes them perks and who does not. Throughout the Mishnah, the roster of who remains outside the tent is fairly constant, featuring the deaf and dumb, the unintelligent (or imbecile, שוטה), minors and, in most contexts, gentiles. Minors are described with physiological precision, mostly as pre-adolescent boys who do not have at least two pubic hairs.[173] Conversely, the Mishnah stipulates conditions about remaining in the tent, sometimes deliberating about odd contingencies such as a situation wherein the wife of a priest is dining on some food tithed to her, and suddenly discovers that her husband has died.[174]

Logically enough, slaves have some prominence in Mishnah discussions. Scholars doubt that slaves were used on a large-scale in agriculture, by Jews or others, in the Near East region in this period, but their deployment on a "smaller domestic scale" was commonplace; and while there is scarce discussion of the religious-national origins of the enslaved, Goodman judges that "it is too often asserted that by this [Tannaitic] date *no* slaves kept by Jews were themselves Jews."[175] His claim finds support in one Mishnah passage, referring to damage compensation, which draws an explicit contrast between a Jewish ("Hebrew") slave and a gentile ("Canaanite") slave.[176] In some places, the Mishnah treats slavery as a partial and somewhat negotiable condition, quite in contradistinction to subsequent understandings of it as an absolute loss of human freedom. The House of Hillel applies its characteristic judicious leniency to the subject, opining: "He who is half-slave and half-free works for his master one day and for himself one day."[177] The Mishnah is systematic in its discussion of which religious obligations apply to slaves. For instance, the tractate on *Sukkot*, the autumnal Feast of the Tabernacles, is quite specific about the issue of whether traditional requirements of sleeping and dwelling in the *sukkah* booth apply to slaves.[178]

In these, and many other, Mishnah passages, the slave's derogatory status has rough equivalence to that of Jewish women. In the divorce tractate (Gittin), for instance, lengthy discussions impose equivalence between the status of the two groups ("He who says, 'Give this writ of divorce to my wife, and this writ of emancipation to my slave,' if he wanted to retract in either case, he may retract . . ."[179])

The most formidable presence "outside the tent" belongs to pagans, and the Mishnah devotes one full tractate, *Avodah Zarah*, to relations between Jews and gentiles. Owing to Christianity's consolidation in this period, and its subsequent rise, this tractate became perhaps the mostly closely scrutinized Tannaitic document. Indeed, since it generally relates to gentiles with suspicion, and, specifically, distinguishes between ways Jews should act among themselves in socioeconomic affairs, on the one hand, and ways they should relate to gentiles in these same settings, on the other hand, the tractate became controversial. There is, however, no strong evidence to suggest that the rabbis were thinking about Christians in this tractate's references to gentiles. On the contrary: key sections refer to gentile paganism, not monotheism. One masterfully formulated passage, which manages to call gentiles "idiots," while also grudgingly recognizing that foreigners are less intolerable when they are being piously worshipful of *anything*, is obviously not about Christians: "They asked sages in Rome, 'If God is not in favor of idolatry, why does he not wipe it away?' They said to them, 'if people worshipped something of which the world had no need, he certainly would wipe it away.' 'But, lo, people worship the sun, moon, stars, and planets.' 'Now do you think he is going to wipe out his world because of idiots.'"[180]

Undeniably, many passages in this tractate evince outright disdain and contempt for gentiles. One section advises Jews not to leave their cattle with gentile innkeepers, because goyim partake bestiality. Jewish women should not be left along with gentiles, because they are fornicators. A Jewish man best not mix with a group of gentiles, because they are bloodthirsty killers, and so on.[181]

Sex, in the Mishnah, is evaluated largely in terms of its utility in the Tannaitic national reclamation project. Much as in the case of Israel's governmental policy today, the Tannaim were enamored with *Genesis*' prescription to the Jews, to be fruitful and multiply. When one rabbi muses that this rule might apply to Jewish males, but not females, he is immediately corrected by Rabbi Yohanan b. Beroqah—both sexes are commanded to procreate, this rabbi insists. The sages keep parsing the "fruitful and multiply" rule. They wonder: when, in bed, can a weary husband turn away from his wife, once and for all? Only after they have had two boys, says the House of Shammai. A boy and a girl will do, rejoins the House of Hillel.[182] In tune with its predilection for classification and regulation, the Mishnah sets forth a sex schedule for husbands, at least prior to the reaching of this goal of two children. Claiming *Exodus* 21:10 as proof text, it writes: "The sexual duty of which the Torah speaks: (1) Those of independent means, every day; (2) workers—twice a week; 3) ass drivers—once a week; (4) camel drivers—once in thirty days; (5) sailors—once in six months."[183]

The required labor of a married women, according to the Mishnah, includes bread baking, meal preparation, laundry, child care and clothes-making ("wool work"). Here, the Mishnah's penchant for associating women's fate and slave labor redounds to the benefit of married women. If she has one slave girl, the wife is exempt from laundry, flour grinding and bread duties. With two slaves, she need not feed her children. With three slaves, the woman does not need to make her bed for her husband. And with four, quip the redactors, "she sits on a throne."[184]

The rabbis are manifestly anxious about how the mass of marital requirements they have classified is liable to promote a mundane life. With noticeably little enthusiasm, they end up discussing what sort of trade they, or their sons, should take up, to sustain married life. Lacing through these sober discussions is the idea that nothing but Torah study really matters. This thought is subversive to the Mishnah's project of classifying the voluminous practices of daily life: why bother to talk about them, if all you're going to do is study Torah?

An important, concluding, section of the Qiddushin tractate opens with telling ruminations attributed to Rabbi Simon b. Eleazar. Their images, tone and conclusions overlap with the fatalism of faith projected by Jesus' preaching about the birds in the sky, in Matthew 6:26: "Rabbi Simeon b. Eleazar says, 'Have you ever seen a wild beast or a bird who has a trade? Yet they get along without difficulty." The Tannaim then discuss various job options for their sons, stigmatizing some of them as the devil's work: "Rabbi Judah says: 'Most ass drivers are evil, most camel drivers are decent, most sailors are saintly, the best among physicians is going to hell [Gehenna], and even the best butchers are partners of Amalek." Rabbi Nehorai seems to have the final, pious word in this discussion: "I should lay aside every trade in the world and teach my son only Torah."[185]

The clearest Tannaitic term of approbation for someone inside the tent, that is a Jew who obliges tithing and purity codes, is *haver* (member). A haver is the opposite of an impious am haaretz. The Mishnah half-heartedly acknowledges some subdivision stratification among these upstanding haverim, members of the community, implying that they formed their own associations, each keeping its distance from the other. This association subdivision was problematic, since the Mishnah's carefully delineated purity, tithing and other religious laws should not have been subject to interpretation, with one group applying them one way, and another group pursuing a different route; generally, coming from Yavne, the Galilee patriarchate inherited a post-hurban distaste for the sort of sectarianism that had characterized Second Temple Judaism.[186] Here we have the sort of ambiguity for which the Mishnah devised its trademark mechanism of religious relativism: in some contexts, the Mishnah acknowledges that God's mysterious will and ways are seen one way by the House of Hillel, and another way by the House of Shammai.

Hence, in the tractate devoted to the *eruv*, a Shabbat enclosure within which observers are allowed to perform acts that would otherwise be prohibited, the rabbis ponder a case where five haverim associations of Sabbath observers partake a meal in a common dining hall. The House of Shammai dictates that five eruvim would be required to serve each such association separately, whereas the House of Hillel judges that one eruv could serve them all.[187]

Codifying and compiling, hard at work on the Mishnah, the Tannaim were committed to two somewhat contradictory goals. On the one hand, in the aftermath of the Temple hurban, they realized that if Judaism were to survive, it would have to spread well beyond Jerusalem and accommodate itself to the vernacular of communities who lived outside of their Galilee enclaves, beyond Eretz Israel. At the same time, as a religious elite, they insisted upon scriptural and ritual control in ways that hedged against Judaism's continuing refashioning in its assimilation by the masses. A concise example of these cross-currents is the Megillah tractate which, in addition to detailing observances relating to the Megillah reading during the Purim holiday, stipulates practices for public reading of the Torah and associated rites in Judaism's early, evolving synagogue culture. One passage implicitly recognizes the advantages of presenting scripture in public in Aramaic translation or some other language, but insists that any such reading does not meet ritual requirements. The Mishnah writers are relating to a relatively complex, polyglot Jewish reality, and are formulating their words in a mixed vein of communal pragmatism and religious punctiliousness: "But they do read the Megillah to those who speak a foreign language, in a foreign language. Still, one who speaks a foreign language who has heard it in Assyrian [Hebrew] has fulfilled his obligation."[188]

Were the Tannaim codifying rules with genuine expectations of the restoration of Temple-based Jewish sovereignty in Eretz Israel? The Mishnah's final two divisions relate to purity and related symbolic matters, but their referencing of the Temple can be hypothetical; so I propose probing this question by examining the Mishnah's first divisions, which stipulate rules relevant to the daily lives of Jews at the time. Telling farmers what to do with figs they picked from their trees, the rabbis were trying to exert authority over socioeconomic matters; and this presumptive arrogation of power for governance raises a series of questions: Were the Tannaim pragmatists about sociopolitical realities in late second century Palestine? Or were they implicitly messianic, demanding that Jews sacrifice portions of their daily labors in tribute to a Temple-based conception of Judaism that they could not have rationally expected to arise anew in the near future?

The answer, I believe, features a delicate balance between these two extremes. Had the rabbis pulled too hard in the first, pragmatic, direction, "Judaism" would have downsized, and become equivalent to the contemporary needs of Jews in the land, which is to say that it would not have transcended beyond the Tannaitic era and continued to evolve for centuries. On the other hand, had the Tannaim been too messianic and un-pragmatic, they would never have been able to accumulate authority in this, and ensuing eras, and so the 1,500 or so years of Jewish exile would never have been known as the period of "rabbinic Judaism" (the first post-Tannaitic era is called the "Amoraic" period, the name referring to rabbis "who say"—some Amoraim remained in Palestine, but others personified the process of exile dispersion, relocating in Babylon; the Amoraic period lasted from 200 to 500, or thereabouts).

The Mishnah maintains this complicated equilibrium between pragmatism and messianism in several passages. For instance, referring to one of the Jerusalem tithing rules (*maaser sheni*), it discusses a case where a pious pilgrim to the holy city purchases some fruit to oblige the requirement—the Mishnah relays that "if the Temple does not exist," the man should "let the pieces of fruit rot."[189] In the case of this and similar rulings, Rabbi Judah has something like the final word, and he generally implies that their practical implications are suspended because the Temple is not standing.

Rabbi Judah, in the Mishnah, does not really have veto or other special legislative powers, but his voice appears at the end of disputations, as though he is the meeting chairman. So it is significant that he tends to talk about recondite tithing matters in the past tense, as in this maaser sheni example, where he refers to tithing rules of yore in Jerusalem during select Passover years: "At first they would send [word] to the householders in the provinces, 'hurry and remove [tithe tributes] from your produce, before the time arrives . . .'"[190]

Another, blood curdling, example can be found in the Mishnah's adultery (Sotah) tractate, in a passage which vividly records how, in the Temple's vicinity, at Nicanor's Gate, high court officials would enforce the Penateuch's "bitter water ordeal" (Numbers: 5:11–31) wherein a woman accused of infidelity is coerced into drinking a potion. Responding to a description of how a priest would tear the woman's hair and clothes, Rabbi Judah issues some qualifications ("If she had pretty breasts, he did not let them show. And if she had pretty hair, he did not pull it apart").[191] Once again, owing to the tenor of recollection, doubt is cast over the applicability of an Old Testament ritual, bitter water, in second century Galilee, and also about the normative or practical viability of hopes for Temple restoration.

Were Tannaitic composers of the Mishnah writing in the expectation of full national restoration, in plain senses of military power and political sovereignty? Surely they were not soothsayers capable of anticipating the images and circumstances we associate with subsequent centuries of rabbinical Judaism (exile, statelessness, alienation from military roles, among others), but does this mean that they expected a more "conventional" relationship to power in the Jewish future? Here, relevant internal evidence in the Mishnah is quite indefinite, but it is probably significant that there is no discrete, relatively extended conversation about power and arms in the tome. When such topics come up, they have a hypothetical feel, and are awkwardly contextualized. One example is the Sanhedrin tractate, in which the commentators mention that war-making powers reside with this Jerusalem judicial tribune of seventy-one elders—such specification seems moot, since it refers to a Jerusalem Sanhedrin council that was no longer in existence.[192]

In this connection, the most significant snippet is to be found, in all sections, on the tractate on adultery. The question at issue is not whether Jews, after two catastrophically failed rebellions against the Romans, ought to somehow upgrade, or jettison, their use of arms; instead, the issue is whether various bedroom requirements, and complicated property adjustments, attendant to marriage are to be frozen in a military emergency. Rabbi Judah seems to treat the subject as moot sophistry: "In the case of an obligatory war, everyone goes forth to battle—even a bridegroom from his chamber, and a bride from her marriage canopy.'"[193]

On a psychological level, perhaps, the Tannaim found cause to bring up weighty issues of war in a tractate on adultery owing to lingering confusion about whether the imprudent rebellions against Rome were acts of punishable infidelity. Such speculation finds some support in the intriguingly elegiac ending of this adultery (Sotah) tractate. Unlike anything else in the Mishnah, these several hundred words have an apocalyptic edge, ending in a chilling forecast attributed to Rabbi Eliezer the Great: "From the day on which the Temple was destroyed, sages began to be like scribes, and scribes like ministers, and ministers like ordinary folk. And the ordinary folk have become feeble. . . . And the government turns to heresy. . . . And Galilee will be laid waste."[194]

This dystopian pessimism is preceded by hyperbolic evaluations of the meaning of the passing of prominent sages: "When Rabbi Yohanan Ben Zakkai died, the splendor of wisdom came to an end. When Rabbi Gamaliel the Elder died, the glory of the Torah came to an end." A glancing reference to the Bar Kochba rebellion, located at the start of this passage, proves unmistakably that its gloomy, apocalyptic meandering stems, in one way or another, from the horrific failure of that revolt. More to the point, just as Rabbi Judah had done a few passages earlier, this section draws connections between, on the one hand, the politics of personal relationships and marriage, and, on the other hand, political loyalty and war. Its opening words recall: "In the last war [Bar Kochba revolt], they [the Romans, presumably] decreed that a bride should not go out in a palanquin inside the town. But our rabbis permitted the bride to go out in a palanquin inside the town."[195]

By defining "history" in a prophetic sense, whereby particular events are vested with teleological significance in the unfolding of time toward some utopian, or apocalyptically dystopian, conclusion, Jacob Neusner is undoubtedly correct in identifying the Mishnah as an ahistorical corpus. On the other hand, the Mishnah is immersed in historical description, particularly of Temple life, written largely in a nostalgic key. The effect is ambiguous, mixing sentimental sorrow about the probable loss of the cherished Temple cults with a kind of Pascal's wager wherein the Mishnah writers reasoned that they ought to describe how the Jews sanctified the Temple in view of the not-outlandish prospect that its third iteration might someday arise.

Consider, for instance, an extended passage on "first fruit" ("bikkurim") sacrificial offerings brought to the Temple during the early summer Pentecost (shavuout) holiday: "How did they bring the first fruits up to the Temple? . . . Those who come from nearby bring figs and grapes, but those who come from afar bring figs and raisins. And an ox walks before them, its horns overlaid with gold. A flutist plays before them, until they reach the Temple Mount."[196]

This idyllic, nostalgically sentimentalized portrait, acknowledges that sharp class distinctions persisted in the Second Temple period, but argues that they were defused or suspended in the atmosphere of reverence inculcated by Temple rites, such as the first-fruit sacrifices: "The rich bring their first fruits to the Temple in baskets of silver and gold. But the poor bring them in baskets made of peeled willow branches. And both the baskets and the first fruits are given to the priests."[197]

Another tractate, devoted to the half-shekel tax paid annually by Jews for the upkeep of the Jerusalem temple, is meticulous in its documentation, to the point of citing by name the various functionaries whose activity was supported by the impost (the roster is lengthy, starting with "Yohanan b. Pinhas is in charge of the seals, Ahiah is in charge of the drink offerings"[198]). Today, this would be called a strategy of "transparency" designed to support the rationale of a possibly unpopular tax payment. In fact, the passage reads almost like a quarterly corporate disclosure. Yet the ensuing sections in this tractate suggest that the main animus is outright historical documentation. The Tannaitic teachers are concerned to tell students what the Temple was really like: "Two chambers were in the Temple, one, the chamber of secret gifts, the other, the chamber of utensils. . . . Thirteen tables were in the sanctuary, eight of marble. . . . Thirteen shofar chests were in the sanctuary . . ."[199] Other tractates similarly record the Temple's labyrinthine purity and sanctity procedures; these include graphic, detailed descriptions of the high priest's preparation for his annual entry in the Temple's holiest chamber, on the Yom Kippur Day of Atonement. One such description even comes with price tags:

"At dawn he [the high priest] would put on a garment of Pelusium linen worth twelve manehs, and, at dusk, he wore Indian linen worth eight hundred zuz.²⁰⁰

The Mishnah baldly reflects Judaism's chaotic and confused state in the aftermath of the Temple hurban. When the Tannaim set out to refashion the religion, there was no real consensus regarding the hierarchy of holidays. Accordingly, the Mishnah documents quibbling on the subject: "Rabbi Eliezer says, 'after the Temple was destroyed, Pentecost [Shavuout] is deemed equivalent to the Sabbath.' Rabbi Gamaliel says: New Year [Rosh Hashanah] and the Day of Atonement [Yom Kippur] are deemed equivalent to festivals' [e.g., Sukkot, Shavuout]."²⁰¹

In its moral discussions, the Mishnah imposes an elaborate web of sanctions and punishments in response to deviant behavior, almost always based on Tanakh precedents and proof texts. Significantly, though, these disquisitions sometimes refer to a second, nonmortal, level of punishment—in this early Talmudic project, the rabbis manifestly aspire to systematic control or regulation of every conceivable profane or religious deed done by man, but they are not hermetically separated from a second system of heavenly rewards and punishments that was powerfully influencing evolving Christian theology at the time. Here is one example from the Mishnah's impressive legal tractate on damage restitution: "He who causes a fire to break out through the action of a deaf-mute, idiot or minor, is exempt under the laws of man, but liable to punishment under the laws of heaven."²⁰² In a more broadly formulated passage, the rabbis reflect, optimistically, that "all Israelites have a share in the world to come." They then backtrack and, in an apparent display of lingering sectarianism from the Second Temple period, churlishly deny access to heaven to Sadducees, or at least their second-century ideological successors (those "who say the resurrection of the dead is a teaching which does not derive from the Torah"). Rabbi Akiva chimes in, barring from heaven "he who reads heretical books."²⁰³ This discussion is so impromptu and, by Mishnah standards, disorganized, that the redactors, perhaps anxious about the rise of Christian communities, found it necessary to append a short section that explicitly announces "townsfolk of an apostate town have no portion in the world to come."²⁰⁴ Now and then, some Mishnah rabbis lean heavily into after-life theology, as in the example of Rabbi Jacob in *Avot*, a tractate famed for its practical and worldly moral sayings, who proclaims, "This world is like an antechamber before the world to come. Get ready in the antechamber, so you can get into the great hall."²⁰⁵

The Mishnah tractate which deals exclusively with moral matters is called *Avot*, and the fact that it circulated over centuries as a discretely printed treatise, translated in many languages, reflects its extraordinary status. Instead of classifying and promulgating religious laws (halachot), *Avot* issues a series of moral precepts, mostly in detachment from Torah proof texts. Many of the moral adages are inspiring, and circulate widely today, but they are often elusive to contextualization in this Tannaitic setting and are not always internally consistent.

One dictum attributed to Hillel widely circulates in our contemporary culture, being particular popular among political speechwriters whenever their gentile bosses speak out on Jewish issues. Hillel queries: "If I am not for myself, who is for me? And when I am for myself, what am I? And if not now, when?"

Cynics will regard Hillel's motto as being fit for Chinese fortune cookies, whereas many others, Jews and non-Jews, are deeply engaged by it. Much like the case of the Gospel of Matthew and its Sermon on the Mount, where an outsider looking in might observe that issues of consistency challenge the most eloquent precepts preached by Jesus, astute critics of Hillel and other sages cited in *Avot* might point to similar sorts of "are they practicing what they preached" sorts of issues.

The first line of Hillel's famous dictum—"If I am not for myself, who is for me?"—has special resonance among assimilated Jews who are a minority group, as in the case of the United States, and who struggle to find strength to assert themselves, as Jews. For such Jews, Hillel's adage is heard as a rallying cry for constructive ethnocentrism.[206] It summons them, challenging them to fortify their individual ethno-religious identities by fighting for positive, collective, Jewish issues; and it tells them to act right now ("if not now, when?").

Hillel's *adage* certainly seems to be telling his distant descendants to do all that, but I am not sure that the Mishnaic Hillel abides by this own message. Hillel taught humility, not positive ethnocentricity; and he was disdainful about ignorant Jews, doubting that they could remake themselves. On the pages of *Avot*, not long after the famed motto, Hillel spins out these discordant messages: "Do not have confidence in yourself until the day you die," and "an am ha'aretz will never be pious." He adds, ascetically, "lots of property, lots of worries" and concludes, in patriarchal disdain, "lots of women, lots of witchcraft."[207]

It is not easy to adduce a Tannaitic moral viewpoint from *Avot*. Judah HaNasi's son, Gamaliel, illustrates this issue. His father was deeply engaged in Jewish governance in this period and so Gamaliel's pronouncements on government are apparently immersed in generation gap tension, insofar as they apply to Jewish political leaders; insofar as they apply to Roman governance, they perhaps also implicitly criticize his father, Judah, who was renowned for forging productive relationships with the Romans. Gamaliel announces: "Be wary of the government, for [its officials] get friendly with a person only for their own convenience. They look like friends when it is to their benefit, but they do not stand by a person when he is in need." Gamaliel's sensible call for balance between work and Torah study (putting the two, work and Torah, together preempts sin, he announces) is not a consensual Tannaitic statement, since some of the rabbis projected themselves as Torah zealots. In fact, Gamaliel in this Mishnah tractate seems to go out of his way to critique the stance taken by Rashbi, saying, "All learning of Torah which is not joined with labor is destined to be null and cause sin."[208] Rabbi Meir, for one, does not seem to have been persuaded by Gamaliel's moderation. Leaning toward Torah zeal, he pronounces in Avot, "Keep your business to a minimum, and make your business Torah."[209]

Many rabbinical statements recorded in *Avot* brim with accumulated wisdom and sudden insight, and proffer sound counsel. "Tradition is a fence for Torah," declares Akiva. "On three things does the world stand," opines Simeon ben Gamaliel, "justice, truth and peace." Simon the Righteous espouses a different triad: "Torah, Temple service and deeds of loving kindness." Eleazar ben Azariah recites a hypnotic dialectic, "if there is no wisdom, there is no reverence; if there is no reverence, there is no wisdom; if there is no understanding, there is no knowledge; if there is no knowledge, there is no understanding." Returning to the Mishnah's modus operandi, classification, Avot's final passages identify various moral types in human society. The diagnosis is quite astute: "There are four sorts of people: He who says, 'What's mine is mine, and what's yours is yours—this is the average sort.' 'What's mine is yours and what's yours is mine'—this is a boor. 'What's mine is yours and what's yours is yours'—this is a truly pious man. 'What's mine is mine and what's yours is mine'—this is a truly wicked man."[210]

Mishnah morality lacks recognition of "equality before the law" as an absolute precept. Instead, it juggles its deference for class status (class as a religious status group, not less than as a socioeconomic one) with an inchoate notion of innate human rights. This balancing act is on display in its torts tractate, wherein Rabbi Judah accords special weight to status and class considerations, but his quite hierarchical view of dispute adjudication and compensation settlement is challenged by other rabbis. Regarding slaves, Rabbi Judah rules, not surprisingly, that they "are not subject to compensation for indignity." Continuing, he refers to an over-arching "governing principle," associating justice with class status: "Everything is in accord with one's station." Rabbi Akiva, a former am ha'aretz, seems to qualify this position by stressing the rights of the Jewish underclass: "Even the most impoverished Israelites should be seen as free men who have lost their fortunes."[211]

As often happens in our own contemporary discussions, the Mishnah's ruminations and rulings on moral issues reaches its apex with an emotional, and unresolved, debate about capital punishment. In supposed order of severity, the Mishnah lists four methods of execution, stoning, burning, decapitation, and strangulation (in fact, the rabbis keep quibbling about which method is the most terrifying[212]). It classifies crimes that warrant a particular method (burning for incest transgressors, among others), and this discussion is gruesomely detailed. To a significant extent, it is theoretical, an exegetical exercise in the classification of the Pentateuch's handling of serious crime.

If the Torah was their constitution, the Tannaim had loose and strict constructionists, meaning that there was no clear consensus among them as to how the Torah's more extreme rules were applicable in their own world, and in Jewish worlds to come. This divergence of opinion could never amplified in "on point" discussion of the issue at hand, since elaborating on the practical inapplicability of Torah in the mundane administration of the Jews' second-century society in Galilee and elsewhere would have been tantamount to blasphemy. So the Mishnah adopts a slide and defer exegetical strategy, wherein the weightiest moral aspect of an issue under discussion is never identified at the time. If it is addressed at all, it slides into another tractate.

In the case at hand, we learn about the largely moot character of the Sanhedrin tractate's extended, grisly discussion of stoning, burning, decapitation, and strangulation in a later tractate, where it suddenly emerges that the Tannaim were not of one mind about capital punishment. The debate between them bears strong resemblance to disagreements on the subject in our own world. Revelation of this Tannaitic debate is disarmingly pungent and pithy: "Rabbi Tarfon and Rabbi Akiva say, 'if we were on a Sanhedrin, no one would ever be put to death.' Rabbi Simeon ben Gamaliel says, 'So they would multiply the number of murderers in Israel.'"[213]

So, who, or what, were the Tannaim? A presumptive religious government of the Jews whose members struggled, sometimes not successfully, to maintain cabinet discipline on the most vexing current issues of state, society, and economics? A rabbinical debating society, and not much more than that? How did the Tannaim themselves relate to such questions?

In the Mishnah, revelations of Tannaitic collective self-image are hard to find, but one telling instance of the rabbis' understanding of their group identity and purpose occurs at the start of a protracted presentation of divergent opinions between the houses of Shammai and Hillel. The opinions apply to a morass of matters, some esoteric, others urgent, and it becomes dizzyingly hard to identify "loose" or "strict" interpretive consistency in either house. The Mishnah writers themselves are indisputably aware that, at some stage, punctilious documentation of differences between these schools becomes a scholastic exercise. Why, then, record how back-and-forth argumentation is a rabbinical method?

Answering this question, the Tannaim issue what should be seen as a mission statement of Galilee's Mishnaic project as a whole. The statement opens with a third person pronoun, but it should be read as though it comes from a Tannaitic "we":

And why do they record the opinion of Shammai and Hillel to no purpose? To teach the generations to come that a person should not be stubborn about his opinion; for, lo, the patriarchs of the world were not stubborn about their opinion.[214]

First and foremost, the Tannaim were teachers. They, and their rabbinical descendants, led by virtue of their intense attachment to Torah, and not necessarily due to the rectitude of their pronouncements about its meanings. Besides being an excellent teaching tool, the argumentative method they developed was, they believed, homage to their religious descent ("the patriarchs were not stubborn about their opinion") and, more importantly, an affirmation of their own imperfect mortality.

They argued. To have done otherwise, to pretend that one's interpretation of scripture was flawless, would have been egotistical blasphemy.

This much seems clear. More speculatively, I think that the interpretive intensity of the Mishnah, and its argumentative character, should be seen not as the depoliticized taming of Jewish rebelliousness, but rather as its relocation in a new medium. It is impossible to ignore the fact that the Tannaim emerged in Galilee as a religious leadership after Jewish political leaders in Judea had produced two astonishingly devastating debacles, two failed rebellions against Rome. While the patriarchate under Judah HaNasi gained genuine sociopolitical status, Tannaitic society nonetheless remained mired in an authority crisis. This crisis is interpolated in the Mishnah, a corpus which issues pronouncements for hundreds of pages, often on matters of inconceivable triviality, without managing to make a single one of them definitive. As decades went by, Judah HaNasi's achievement as the Mishnah's redactor was widely admired, but his spiritual authority was severely challenged—one commentator describes this ongoing authority crisis as "tragic."[215]

To be sure, external influences, such as the Greco-Roman penchant for establishing philosophical schools, help explain why some Tannaim divided into contrasting houses like Shammai and Hillel, as well as some other Mishnah traits. But I think that the best way of thinking about the Galilee Tannaitic quest to compile an authoritative, official code for Judaism is to recognize that the Mishnah's authors were operating in an isolated Galilean enclave, and were deeply anxious about authority, about how to assert it. Jews made their own choices after the Temple was destroyed, and after the ruinous Bar Kochba experience showed that a third one would not be built anytime soon.

The Jews' restless and rebellious culture had not changed. It was just that now brains, and not bodies, were doing its work.

NOTES

1. Shaye J. D. Cohen, "The Place of the Rabbi in Jewish Society," in Lee Levine (ed.), *The Galilee in Late Antiquity* (Cambridge, MA: Harvard University Press, 1992), 167.

2. Lee Levine, "The Sages and the Synagogue of Late Antiquity: The Evidence of the Galilee," in Levine, *The Galilee*, 222.

3. Martin Goodman, *State and Society in Roman Galilee, A.D. 132–212* (London: Valentine Mitchell, 1983/2000), 137.

4. The severity and expanse of these anti-Jewish, punitive *shemad* decrees has been questioned by past generations of scholars. For instance, it had traditionally been understand that the Romans, in retribution for the Bar Kochba insurrection, expropriated all Jewish-owned land in the country, but this interpretation was apparently based on a faulty translation, and has been proven to be erroneous. Aharon Oppenheimer, *Yehuda Ha-nasi* (Jerusalem: Shazar Center 2007), 84–85.

5. Ibid.

6. For a bibliographic roster of scholarly arguments in this debate, see: Aharon Oppenheimer, *Ha-galil be'tekufat ha-Mishnah* (Jerusalem: Shazar Center, 1991), 30 n.1.

7. The Kitos War transpired in the period of Lucius Cossonius' governorship in Phoenicia and has been branded or conceptualized as the diaspora rebellion. Oppenheimer believes that a number of its rebellious acts actually occurred in Galilee: owing to the Roman crackdown in the Galilee following the War of Kitos, there remained in the region relatively little energy or opportunity for participation in the Bar Kochba rebellion two decades later, he claims. Oppenheimer, *Hagalil*, 32. See also: D. Rokeah, "The War of Kitos: Towards the Clarification of a Philological-Historical Problem," *Scripta Hierosolymitana* XXIII (1972): 79–84.

Oppenheimer also espouses a complementary theory holding that Romans were relatively well disposed to accommodating Rabbi Judah, and Jewish rebirth in the Galilee, because the Jews "chose the right horse" in the Roman political power struggle of 193–194 CE between Septimius Severus and Pescennius Niger. The Samaritans supported the loser, Niger, much to the detriment; Jews in Galilee and elsewhere were rewarded for having collaborated with the victor, Oppenheimer claims. *Yehuda ha-Nasi*, 41–42.

8. In his path-breaking 1983 volume, Goodman (5) asserted an aim to "combine all the evidence—rabbinic, epigraphic, classical, patristic and archaeological—without affording primacy to any and bearing in mind the inherent bias of each." He admitted, however, to giving precedence to the Talmudic materials "simply because they are so extensive." Subsequently a 2001 volume, published by Jewish Theological Seminary scholar Seth Schwartz, argued that the Talmud ought not to be used straightforwardly as a cohesively unified source in historical reconstruction of past eras—this book associated untowardly distortive, used of Talmudic sources with Zionist historiography. Seth Schwartz, *Imperialism*. Countering this argument, Israeli scholars, led by Oppenheimer, argue that judicious use of extensive Talmudic

references can and should serve as the primary source for historians' accounts of Jewish life in Galilee in the Tannaitic era—Oppenheimer, *Yehuda ha-Nasi,* 12–13. My own view, reflected in this chapter, is that identifying modes of posterior reinterpretation, as compared to more or less reliable historical documentation, in Talmudic materials is not an insuperable problem, and Schwartz's concerns about Zionist-inflected research on the Tannaitic period, and other eras, is a shrewd assessment of much extant scholarly literature, but not a determinative methodological critique.

9. Yehoshafat Harkabi, *The Bar Kochba Syndrome: Risk and Realism in International Politics* (Chappaqua, NY: Rossel Books, 1983).

10. Oppenheimer, *Yehuda Ha-Nasi,* 25–30.

11. Ibid, 28, 193.

12. M. Avi-Yonah, *The Jews of Palestine: A Political History from the Bar Kokhba War to the Arab Conquest* (Oxford: Basil Blackwell, 1976), 18; Oded Avissar, *Sefer Tiveria* (Jerusalem: Keter, 1973), 81.

13. Goodman, *State,* 32. Goodman's study is extraordinarily rich in socioeconomic detail and thus much in the following paragraphs rely on it. Information contributed by other scholars is specifically footnoted.

14. Avi-Yonah, 19.

15. Joan Taylor, *Christians and the Holy Places: The Myth of Jewish-Christian Origins* (Oxford: Clarendon Press, 1993), 69–85.

16. For critical discussion of when priestly rotation rosters might have been moved from Judea to Galilee: Stuart Miller, "New Perspectives on the History of Sepphoris," in Myers, *Galilee through the Centuries,* 152; Dalia Trifon, "Did the Priestly Courses Moves from Judea to Galilee after the Bar Kokhba Revolt?," [Heb.] *Tarbiz* 59 (1990): 77–93.

17. Oppenheimer, *Ha-galil,* 53–57.

18. Goodman, *State,* 42.

19. Ibid, 43.

20. Oppenheimer, *Ha-galil,* 134–158.

21. Goodman, 44.

22. Ibid, 46.

23. Oppenheimer, *Ha-galil,* 134–145.

24. Goodman, *State,* 51–52.

25. Ibid, 52–53.

26. The Mishnah, for instance, states: "They [Israelites] do not rear small cattle in the Land of Israel." [Baba Qamma: 7:7]. See Yehezkel Cohen, *Prekim b'toldot ha'tekufah ha'tana'im,* (Jerusalem: Ministry of Education and Culture, 1977), 99–105; also, Avi-Yonah, 22, 28.

27. Cohen, *Prekim* 22–24.

28. Avi-Yonah, 20.

29. Goodman, 54–63.

30. Avi-Yonah, 21–25.

31. Goodman, 66.

32. Ibid, 67.

33. Ibid, 69.

34. Ibid, 70.
35. Ibid, 77.
36. Ibid, 80–81. This line of interpretation is pursued, often brilliantly, in Schwarz's scholarship, which relates to how Jewish political-religious culture morphed under Roman influence over a prolonged period, from the Second Temple period through 640 CE.
37. Goodman, 77–79.
38. Jacob Neusner, *A Life of Yohannan ben Zakkai* (Leiden: Brill, 1962), 56–57.
39. Ibid, 50–51.
40. Oppenheimer, *Ha-galil*, 21; see also Neusner, *A Life*, 51–53.
41. Oppenheimer, *Ha-galil*, 18; Shmuel Safrai, "The Jewish Cultural Nature of Galilee in the First Century," *Immanuel* 24/25 (1990): 153–155.
42. Safrai, 160. For a list of rabbis who stayed in Tiberias during the Bar Kochba revolt: Avissar, 82.
43. Oppenheimer, *Ha-galil*, 23–28; Aharon Oppenheimer, "Rabban Gamaliel of Yavneh and his Circuits of Eretz Israel," in Oppenheimer, *Between Rome and Babylon* (Tubingen: Mohr Siebrook, 2005), 145–156.
44. Oppenheimer, *Yehuda Ha-nasi*, 27.
45. Oppenheimer, *Ha-galil*, 45–46.
46. As translated in: Aharon Oppenheimer, *The Am-Haaretz, A Study in the Social History of the Jewish People in the Hellenistic-Roman Period* (Leiden: Brill, 1977), 185. Passage from: Shir Hashirim Rabbi (2:5).
47. Oppenheimer, *Ha-galil*, 46.
48. Bavli: Shabbat, 33.
49. This Talmudic passage reflects contrasting, moderate and oppositional, attitudes toward Roman rule in Tannaitic political culture, Avi-Yonah, 65.
50. Binyamin Lau, *Hakhamim: tekufat Ha-galil* (Tel Aviv: Yedioth Aharonoth Books, 2008), 74–75
51. Mishnah: Shebiit, 3:1.
52. Lau, 75–77.
53. Bavli: Kiddushin, 52b–14–15.
54. Lau, 77 (Bavli: Sanhedrin: 20a).
55. For a discussion of the substantive impact of ordination rights in this period: Avi-Yonah, 55.
56. Bavli: Sanhendrin 14a.
57. Oppenheimer, *Ha-galil*, 47.
58. Goodman, *State*, 108.
59. Oppenheimer, *Hagalil*, 49–51.
60. Lau, 265–266.
61. Yebamot: 16:7.
62. Lau, 267–273.
63. Ibid, 272.
64. Oppenheimer, *Hagalil*, 49.
65. Lau, 253; Bava Kamma 83a.
66. For a detailed discussion of this division of powers: Avi-Yonah, 54–60.

67. Lau, 168.
68. See: Yehushalmi: Horayot 13:b.
69. Lau, 256–257.
70. Ibid, 259–260.
71. Ketubot, 50a.
72. Lau, 286–291.
73. Bavli: Taanit 24a.
74. Daniel Boyarin, *Carnal Israel: Reading Sex in Talmudic Culture* (Berkeley: University of California Press, 1993), 181–196; Rachel Adler, "The Virgin in the Brothel and Other Anomalies: Character and Context in the Legend of Beruriah," *Tikkun* 3 (Nov. 1988).
75. Iris Brown Holzman, "Forgotten and Revived: The Bruria Incident in Contemporary Orthodox Discourse," [Heb.] *Daat: A Journal of Jewish Philosophy and Kabbalah* 83 (2017): 407–442.
76. The ground-breaking article was: David Goodblatt, "The Beruriah Traditions," *Journal of Jewish Studies* 26 (1975): 68–85. See also: Tal Ilan, "The Search for the Historical Beruriah, Rachel and Imma Shalom," *Association of Jewish Studies Review* 22, no. 1 (1997): 1–17; Itamar Drori, "The Beruriah Incident: Tradition of Exclusion as a Presence of Ethical Principles," https://www.researchgate.net/publication/2935 81537_The_Beruriah_Incident_Tradition_of_Exclusion_as_a_Presence_of_Ethical_Principles.
77. Rashbi's life is a salient case in point, as exemplified in: Lee Levine, "R. Simeon b. Yohai and the Purification of Tiberias: History and Tradition," *Hebrew Union College Annual* 49 (1978): 143–185.
78. Aliza Shenhar, "Le-Ammiyutah shel agudat beruria eshet rabbi meir," [Heb.] in *Mehkari hamerkaz le-heker ha-folkore* (Jerusalem: Magnes Press, 1973) 3 (1973): 223–227.
79. Bavli: Avodah Zarah, 18a; Lau, 214–215; Boyarin, *Carnal,* 190.
80. Berakhot 10a, Boyarin's translation, 184. For the identity of the hooligans, possibly as Christians, and other translation issues: Lau, 210.
81. Lau 209; Ilan, 6.
82. Drori, 101.
83. Ilan's translation, 4.
84. Adler, 29–32.
85. Boyarin, *Carnal,* 192, 195.
86. This point is insightfully made by Ilan, 8.
87. Avodah Zarah 18a.
88. Ilan, 5.
89. Lau, 212–215.
90. This biographical survey relies on Oppenheimer, *Yehuda ha-Nasi.*
91. Ibid, 28.
92. An overview of these land policies, and some other reforms, can be found in: Cohen, *Prekim,* 25–38.
93. Oppenheimer, *Yehuda ha-Nasi,* 46.

94. In the case of the Kabbalists, such revenge power fantasies are found (for instance) in Haim Vital's dream diary, *Sefer Ha-Hezyonot*, as discussed in book two of this study.

95. Oppenheimer, *Ha-galil*, 64; Oppenheimer, *Yehuda ha-Nasi*, 47; Avi-Yonah, 39–42.

96. Bavli: Abodah Zarah: 10a.

97. Ibid.

98. Ibid, folio 11a.

99. Oppenheimer, *Yehuda ha-Nasi*, 45–46.

100. Oppenheimer, *Ha-galil*, 70.

101. Ibid, 68–69.

102. Aharon Oppenheimer, "Roman Rule and the Cities in Talmudic Literature," in Levine, *The Galilee*, 115–125.

103. Oppenheimer, *Yehuda ha-Nasi*, 90–92.

104. Oppenheimer, "Roman Rule and the Cities in Talmudic Literature," 121.

105. Oppenheimer, *Yehuda ha-Nasi*, 69.

106. Demai: 2:2.

107. Maaser Sheni: 5:3.

108. Adolf Buchler, *The Political and Social Leader of the Jewish Community of Sepphoris in the Second and Third Centuries* (London: Jews College, 1909).

Buchler's work on Sepphoris has been critiqued by Stuart Miller—Miller suggests that Buchler projected various challenges he faced in the early twentieth-century Anglo-Jewish community onto Sepphoris' Tannaitic landscape, that Buchler read too much into rabbinical sources, and that social tensions he traced in Sepphoris "could have been found in any of the larger towns of Galilee and the Roman Near East." Stuart Miller, "New Perspectives," 146–148 (see, 148, for the bibliographic references).

109. Due to divergent, though usually unstated, views about the abiding or mutating character of Jewish nationhood, and of Jewish interaction with gentile cultures, the same Maginot line can be found in internal discussions among Jewish scholars who wrote and researched in different modern settings, such as early twentieth-century Europe and early twenty-first century Israel. For instance, Oppenheimer flatly rejects Buchler's characterization of Judaism in Galilee through the Bar Kochba revolt (*The Am-Haaretz*, 185 and passim).

110. Buchler, 31.

111. Ibid, 55: "Those who show neglect at the mourning of a scholar do not live long;" "whoever speaks evil behind the back of a scholar will fall into hell."

112. Ibid, 58. Judah HaNasi also warned sages "not to teach pupils in the market place"—Oppenheimer, *The Am-Haaretz*, 186.

113. Oppenheimer, *The Am-Haaretz*, 178.

114. Cohen, *Prekim*, 91–94.

115. Buchler, 58.

116. Oppenheimer, *The Am-Haaretz*, 178–186.

117. Ibid, 38, 43.

118. Buchler puts a different twist to Galilee dynamics, suggesting that the Tannaim hated the amei haaretz "in return for the hatred exhibited by the wealthy against them," 61.

119. Oppenheimer, *The Am-Haaretz*, 188.

120. Implications of this fact are discussed in Cohen, *Prekim*, 93–94.

121. Oppenheimer, *The Am-Haaretz*, 176–177.

122. Buchler, 51 ("When you see a scholar committing a sin at night, do not think badly of him the next day, as he may have repented in the meantime").

123. Buchler, 52; Oppenheimer, *The Am-Haaretz*, 174.

124. Jacob Neusner, *In the Aftermath of Catastrophe: Founding Judaism, 70 to 640* (Montreal: McGill-Queen's University Press, 2009).

125. Oppenheimer, *Ha-galil*, 53.

126. Rashbi's name makes just one quick appearance in the Mishnah, in a discussion on Temple offerings (Hagigah, 1:7), but elsewhere in Talmudic literature, he is a prolific contributor of halakhot (Jewish laws).

127. Lau, 119.

128. Bavli, Berakhot 35b.

129. Lau, 120.

130. Goodman, *State* xi (Preface to the Second Edition).

131. Buchler, 68.

132. Levine, "R. Simeon b. Yohai," 167.

133. Levine, "R. Simeon b. Yohai," 164–166; also, the abridged translation: "Shimon Bar Yochai's Cave" at http://www.bronfman.org/sites/default/files/content/users/71/Shimon%20Bar%20Yochai%20and%20Platos%20Cave%20-%20BYFI.pdf.

134. Levine, "R. Simeon b. Yohai," 145–157.

135. Lawrence Fine, *Physician of the Soul, Healer of the Cosmos: Isaac Luria and His Kabbalistic Fellowship* (Palo Alto: Stanford University Press, 2003).

136. The following analysis is drawn from Levine's article, "R. Simeon b. Yohai," 167–184.

137. Ibid, 167.

138. Ibid, 172.

139. Ibid.

140. Eric Hobsbawn, Terence Ranger (eds.), *The Invention of Tradition* (Cambridge: Cambridge University Press, 1992).

141. This account is taken from: Abraham Ya'ari, "History of the Pilgrimage to Meron," [Heb.] *Tarbiz* 31 (1961): 72–101.

142. Nurit Be'eri, *Yatsa le-tarbut ra'ah: Elisha ben Avuyah, 'Aher,'* (Tel Aviv: Yedioth Aharonoth Books, 2007), 17–20.

143. A sample of analyses of Elisha's career: Jeffrey Rubinstein, "Elisha ben Abuya: Torah and the Sinful Sage," *The Journal of Jewish Thought and Philosophy* 7 (1998): 139–225; Alon Goshen-Gottstein, *The Sinner and the Amnesiac: The Rabbinic Invention of Elisha ben Abuya and Eleazar ben Arach* (Stanford: Stanford University Press, 2000); Be'eri, *Yatsa*.

144. Goshen-Gottstein, 40–42.

145. For a clear and persuasive account of how Elisha legends differ in these two Talmudic corpuses, see Goshen-Gottstein's study.
146. Be'eri, 12–13; Goshen-Gottstein, 48.
147. Goshen-Gottstein, 78.
148. Milton Steinberg, *As a Driven Leaf* (New York: Behrman House, 1939).
149. Goshen-Gottstein, 111–119.
150. Ibid, 142–145.
151. Ibid, 81.
152. Ibid, 165.
153. Ibid, 125–162.
154. Ibid, 182.
155. Jacob Neusner, *The Mishnah: A New Translation* (New Haven: Yale University Press, 1988), 28.
156. Ibid, 27.
157. Kilayim: 8:6. Throughout this summary of the Mishnah, I rely on the Neusner translation. In a few cases, I supplement connecting phrases so as to clarify meanings, or simplify punctuation.
158. E.g. maser sheni: 3:11.
159. Goodman, *State*, 101.
160. Shebiit: 3:5–10.
161. Shebiit: 9:2.
162. Shabbat: 3:4.
163. Bab Mesia: 8:8.
164. Avodah Zarah: 3:4.
165. Baba Batra 3:7.
166. Baba Qamma: 10:1–10:5
167. Baba Mesia: 5:1.
168. Baba Qamma: 2:3.
169. Baba Qamma: 3:7–4:5.
170. Nedarim: 2:4.
171. Some passages refer to various technical-juridical differences between Galilee and other regions in Palestine, but do not really imply that Judaism is practiced differently in them. See, for example, the discussion of usucaption, Baba Batra: 3:2.
172. Lawrence Schiffman, "Was there a Galilean Halakah," in Lee Levine (ed.), *The Galilee*, 143–156.
173. Terumot 1:1–3.
174. Terumot: 8:1.
175. Goodman, *State*, 37–38.
176. Baba Qamma: 8:3.
177. Gittin: 4:5.
178. Sukkah: 2:1, 2:8.
179. Gittin: 1:6.
180. Avodah Zarah, 4:7.
181. Avodah Zarah 2:1.

182. Yebamot: 6:6.
183. Ketubot: 5:6.
184. Ketubot: 5:5.
185. Qiddushin: 4:14.
186. Oppenheimer, *The Am-Haaretz*, 178–186.
187. Erubin: 6:6.
188. Megillah: 2:1.
189. Maaser sheni, 1:5].
190. Ma'aser Sheni, 5:7.
191. Sotah: 1:5.
192. Sanhedrin: 1:5.
193. Sotah: 8:7. For passing reference to the sedan-chair symbol; Avi-Yonah, 70.
194. Sotah: 9:14.
195. Ibid.
196. Bikkurim: 3:3–4.
197. Bikkurim: 3:8.
198. Sheqalim: 5:1.
199. Sheqalim: 6:1–5.
200. Yoma: 3:6.
201. Moed Qatan: 3:6.
202. Baba Qamma: 6:4.
203. Sanhedrin: 10:1.
204. Sanhedrin: 10:4.
205. Avot: 4: 17.
206. Scholars chime in, using the adage in precisely this sense. Ruth Wisse, *If I am Not for Myself: the Liberal Betrayal of the Jews* (New York: Free Press, 1992).
207. Avot 2:4–6.
208. Avot: 2:2–3.
209. Ibid.
210. Avot 2:10–5:10.
211. Baba Qamma: 8:6.
212. Sanhedrin: 7:1, 9:3.
213. Makkot 1:10. Whether, in its heyday, the patriarchate aspired to win from the Romans the privilege of enforcing the death penalty is not clear. Avi-Yonah, 49.
214. Eduyyot, 1:4.
215. David Weiss Halivni, "The Reception Accorded to Rabbi Judah's Mishnah," in E. P. Sanders (ed.), *Jewish and Christian Self-Definition: Aspects of Judaism in the Graeco-Roman Period*, vol. 2 (London: SCM Press, 1981), 212.

Chapter 4

Byzantine Galilee

INTRODUCTION

Consider this roster of questions about Galilee's history in late Antiquity, in the period when Christianity's early consolidation and Judaism's revitalization in the rabbinic-Talmudic mold were, more or less, accomplished facts, when monotheism had now multiplied as two religions:

Had Emperor Constantine not converted to Christianity in the early fourth century, would Jewish civilization in its new Talmudic guise have continued to flourish in Galilee, thereby forestalling the familiar mode of Judaism as an exilic religion? Without Constantine, would Christianity have essentially dissipated in the region, Galilee, where Jesus first preached its underlying principles on hilltops and lakeside towns, due either to Roman hostility or to some other sort of socio-political process vis-à-vis other cultures?

In Jesus' home region, would Judaism and Christianity have developed in interactive antagonism, had not the latter been greatly empowered by Constantine's conversion? Following the political-religious revolution wrought by Constantine in the early fourth century, why did Byzantine Christianity not become irreversibly entrenched on its own home turf, where Jesus had come of age? Perhaps the encroachment, and conquest, of Islam in Galilee in the seventh century can be considered, on some level, a non-inevitable contingency—that is, what sort of strategic decisions and military deployments were reached at this crucial, seventh century, moment by Byzantine rulers, and how ought they be evaluated, in view of the arrival and triumph of yet a third monotheistic faith, Islam, in Galilee, and elsewhere in Palestine?

Other than Rome, what sort of influence was exerted by nonmonotheistic powers as political-culture control in Galilee shifted through Roman, Jewish,

Christian and Muslim frames? How, for instance, can the brief interval of Sassanid (Neo-Persian) imperial control in Palestine be related to the Jews' belated propulsion into exilic dispersion, half a millennium after the failed Bar Kochba revolt (which is conventionally marked as the starting line of the Jews' diaspora)?

Generally, in view of the wealth of evidence marshalled in the last, Mishnaic, chapter, for how long after the Tannaim did Judaism persist as a major religious culture in Galilee, alongside Rome's political dominance?

For how long, after Constantine, was Christianity, in its Byzantine mold, really the dominant force in Galilee? How, and when, did Christian sites in Galilee become pilgrimage magnets? Was a tradition of sacral Christian pilgrimage in Galilee firmly rooted in it by the time Byzantine power became upended by Islam? If so, does that mean that the Christian campaign for restoration, the Crusades, in the region, and in Jerusalem, can be seen virtually as an historic inevitability, even though Islamic rule prevailed in Galilee and elsewhere for several centuries, before Crusaders donned armor and clutched swords?

This chapter on Byzantine Galilee tries to provide persuasive, or at least partially satisfactory, answers to such questions, but its primary argument can be separated from any specific interpretive response to any such, particular, problem. Our main claim is that extant scholarship provides a series of non-integrated, often counter-intuitive, replies to these, and related, questions, essentially for two reasons, First, because Galilee's history has never been surveyed as a whole, as a coherently consecutive story of monotheism's pluralistic multiplication and development, it has been relatively easy for specialists to proffer disjointed, and probably exaggerated, hypotheses about particular phases in the region's history. Surely, it is easier for a person to twist out of shape one part of a puzzle when he or she is not obligated to connect it to its other parts. Second, because there has never been an intellectually engaged, ideologically diverse, local university framework in Galilee, scholars have found perilous comfort when they consider their own hypotheses and findings in narrowly constructed contexts, in the absence of cross-cultural comparison, and interdisciplinary monitoring and discussion. In this chapter, as we review responses in extant scholarly literature to the series of questions we just asked about Byzantine Galilee, we will suggest ways in which they might have been more richly rounded off, had their proponents not labored in Galilee's higher education vacuum, and had they instead been able to benefit from resources, local expertise, and collegial interaction made available by a serious regional university.

JEWS IN LATE ROMAN GALILEE

From its peak under Judah HaNasi, Galilee's Jewish population declined through the fourth century. Population estimates in antiquity are invariably problematic, but the trend of Jewish population erosion in the region is widely acknowledged.[1] Avi-Yonah maintains that there were one hundred Jewish settlements in the region in 135 CE, at the end of the Bar Kochba revolt, whereas just nineteen remained in 640 CE, when Islamic rule consolidated in Galilee.[2] In the early period, the time of the Usha assembly, he counts some 225,000 Jews in Galilee; in the early seventh century he estimates that 150,000–200,000 Jews remained in the country as a whole, implying that perhaps 55,000 Jews lived in Galilee.[3] Archeologists and historians who specialize in Byzantine Palestine estimate that at the height of this period, through the sixth century, several million persons inhabited the country, with Christians constituting the "overwhelming majority." At this time, Jews were still a "sizable" minority, perhaps 10 to 15 percent of the population, concentrated mostly in Galilee.[4]

During the century which elapsed between the end of Judah HaNasi's term in the patriarchate and Emperor Constantine's conversion to Christianity in 312 CE, the fortunes of Jews in Galilee were tied closely to general sociopolitical circumstances in the Roman empire. Between the reigns of Commodus (180–192 CE) and Diocletian (284–305 CE), the empire became mired in a crisis which essentially marked the end of antiquity. Culturally, the transformation can be seen, of course, in the transition from the empire's Greco-Roman foundations to a new basis in Christianity after Constantine. Politically, the empire was unstable at the top, with its ruler lasting an average term of four years during this century. Plots and assassinations were rampant, and some emperors fell in battle. The empire's frontier borderlands were frequently under attack and relations between Rome and the provinces were strained. Causes of such stresses in the imperial system may not have been apprehensible to Jews and others in Galilee, but the onerous effects of the crisis, in military, labor and tax spheres, became increasingly difficult to avoid.[5]

Straggling or drifting into Galilee from Judea after two brutally stifled rebellions, the Jews could not have maintained carefree relations with Roman soldiers. Still, the Talmud conveys evidence of good relations between these soldiers and Galilee Jews in the early third century. One anecdote relates how a Jew is ill-treated by a butcher in Sepphoris; a soldier arrives on the scene and purchases some meat for the hapless customer (the incident was apparently brought to Judah HaNasi's attention). The Talmud also describes a fire on Shabbat around the house of Joseph ben Simai of Sikhnin; a Roman, from the garrison in Sepphoris, comes to extinguish the blaze, but the

Shabbat-scrupulous sage disallows it (the rabbi nonetheless later conveyed a payment of gratitude to Roman soldiers).[6] Such displays of goodwill notwithstanding, Jews remained suspicious, and their culture kept itself shielded—the Mishnah stipulates that if Roman patrols enter a town during peacetime, any open wine bottles in Jewish homes have to be discarded. A few Talmudic references relay suggestions of rape crimes perpetrated by Romans. More frequent are complaints about Roman *burgi* tower-forts which lined the coast from Tyre to Acre, via Achziv.[7]

In years before the Bar Kochba rebellion, the Romans had one legion (Legio X Fretensis) stationed in Palestine. Later they added another, Legio VI Ferrata, near Megiddo, and Hadrian supervised the construction of a road from its base straight into the heart of Galilee, at Sepphoris.[8] Third-century dissatisfaction in Galilee with the Romans did not stem from army service. Very few Jews served in the Roman army; one Talmudic reference about a fourth-century rabbi in Sepphoris who allows Jews to sell their houses to purchase exemptions from *numerus* conscription orders is unusual.[9] Instead, Galilee Jews were aggrieved by what the Talmud calls *angaria*, meaning compulsory labor stints in support of the Roman soldiers; this angaria burden affected Jewish farmers, merchants, and religious scholars alike. Soldier billeting also weighed on third-century Galilee; apparently, observance of the seventh, sabbatical, fallow farm year was sometimes suspended in order to meet burdens imposed by billeting. Tax burdens worsened as Rome's socioeconomic crisis dragged on, up to Diocletian's reign. Already during Judah HaNasi's patriarchate, Jews (and others) faced a new imperial tax, the *annona* (called *arnona* in the Talmud). Originally a special impost requiring residents in the provinces to supply provisions to Roman troops on the march, this tax became a permanent aggravation because the Roman soldiers were always on the move. Another ingenious Roman innovation designed to shift financial burdens to the provinces was a crown-tax (*mas ha-kelila*, in the Jews' idiom), a "voluntary" offering of a gold crown provided by towns anytime a Roman general turned up.

Among other problems, these new, special taxes were not regularly scheduled obligations, and so Galileans and other provincials struggled to find improvisational ways of effectively collecting revenue to discharge the duties. As time passed, responsibility for tax collection devolved mostly upon middle-class residents in cities, who served on *boule* municipal councils—ostensibly an honor, ever-increasing numbers of respectable Jews in Galilee found ways to shirk boule service. Those who were unable to wriggle out of it naturally became embroiled in tax assessment arguments (there is record of a dispute between council heads, the *strategoi*, and others which had to be adjudicated by Judah HaNasi).[10]

After the Tannaitic period, life for established Jews in Sepphoris and Tiberias worsened. In the second generation of the Amoraic period (260–290 CE), so many boule members simply fled to Egypt, leaving their property behind in Galilee, that a term (*anachoresis*) had to be invented for the phenomenon. One second-generation Amora, Rabbi Yose ben Hanina, flatly confided that "it is difficult to live in cities."[11] In the Tannaitic period, it will be recalled, a rather complicated and fragile social equilibrium had been maintained. Jews were divided internally between scholarly rabbis and putatively ignorant amei ha'aretz, and, as exemplified by the anecdotal discussion between the anti-Roman Shimon bar Yochai, and the accommodating Rabbi Judah bar Ilai, as to whether Roman rule ought to be appreciated owing to the bridges, roads, and bathhouses it yielded, attitudes held by Jews toward Roman overlords divided between assimilationist and zealot extremes. As the third century advanced, and as Jewish life in Galilee limped from billeting hassles to boule burdens, the tide shifted somewhat in favor of the disaffected elements. Patriarchs who succeeded Judah HaNasi experimented with measures aimed at easing socioeconomic distress in Galilee (for instance, his grandson, Judah II, allowed Jews to use olive oil produced by gentiles), but these were sporadic reforms of doubtful overall effect.[12] Unable to stem trends of impoverishment and flight to other lands, the patriarchs, themselves large landowners, lost status, and respect. Judah HaNasi's stewardship of the Mishnah proved to be exceptional; his successors in what became, inauspiciously, a line of hereditary descent, were not scholars, and they referred decisions on halachic matters to rabbis. By the end of the third century, the patriarchate had not degenerated as an entirely ceremonial institution, but rabbis were openly challenging its authority. Conscious of this trend, Roman officials sometimes dealt with rabbis, not the patriarch, as though they represented the Jewish collective—when this happened in the case of Rabbi Abbahu, who resided in Caesarea, Tiberias' status as the effective Jewish capital was tarnished.[13]

Just as doubt was cast upon Galilee's primacy in Eretz Israel, trends among third to fifth generation Amoraim reflected the surge in status of Babylonia (now the Neo-Persian, or Sassanid, Empire) relative to Jews in Roman Palestine. So many scholars were migrating for study in the Sassanid Empire that a long-standing rule banning the emigration of a *haver* from Eretz Israel had to be overturned. Halakhic rulings reached by sages in Eretz Israel were met by skepticism among Babylonian colleagues. The rise of Babylonian scholars in Judaism's evolving rabbinical culture in this Amoraic period could be seen within Galilee. Among third-generation Amoraim, the foremost scholars lived in Tiberias, but had Mesopotamian origins.[14]

Since Galilean communities were largely dependent on Roman patronage, and since the theme of decline in the Roman empire in decades before Constantine's conversion pervades scholarship, induces anachronism, and nudges nuance aside, this narrative arc about erosion of the patriarchate seems both inevitable, and also somewhat overdrawn. For example, the fact that patriarchs after Judah HaNasi lost authority does not really attest to Jewish communal weakening in Galilee. Tannaitic culture, it will be recalled, was inherently argumentative, and so the consolidation of political and even religious power in Judah HaNasi's hands was unusual. Arguably, when rabbis in renowned academies in Tiberias and Caesarea challenged his successors, their behavior reflected Judaism's vitality. This trend perhaps also reflected a survival instinct, a penchant for decentralization in post-hurban Judaism which lasted up to the advent of Zionism in the late nineteenth century, at least. True, the drift of rabbis and others from Galilee to historic Babylonia is suggestive of exhaustion generated by aforementioned socioeconomic realities in areas under Rome's dominion, and perhaps also of resentment which lingered on for decades after the crushing failure of two major rebellions—Jews who migrated to the Sassanid Empire were "voting with their feet" in rejection of the Roman empire, casting their ballot for life in a different, Persian, imperial network. But evidence in this connection is not conclusive. For seventy years, between 220 and 290, up to a generation before Constantine, about thirty-five notable Jewish scholars voted with their feet in the opposite direction, immigrating to Roman Palestine from the Neo-Persian Empire.[15]

Was there in Galilee an accumulated culture of religious-political opposition to Rome that would have inhibited the flourishing of rabbinic Judaism in Palestine, had Byzantine Christianity not taken hold of the empire in the fourth century? Perhaps not. Some suggestive details connected to this question, and related issues, indicate that the familiar path of Jewish history, that is, almost two millennia of exilic dispersion from the ancestral homeland, might have followed a different byway, had not Constantine triggered fateful processes in the fourth century. The fate of the family of Galilee's most militantly anti-Roman Tanna, Rashbi, merits mention here, for instance. Rashbi's son, Eleazar ben Shimon, reputedly a large man of intimidating presence, ended up working as a kind of public order commissar for the Romans. Some older rabbis bitterly noted that Eleazar's work capturing Jewish zealots on behalf of his Roman employers reversed the logic of his famed, years-long, experience hiding in a cave with his father, but Rabbi Eleazer seems to have adjusted to Roman stewardship in Palestine, affirming that opportunities abounded in Galilee.[16]

In theory, questions related to this vexing issue about the character and depth of Jewish readjustment to Roman rule in Galilee, during the approximately two centuries which elapsed between the Bar Kochba revolt and Christianity's ascension in the Byzantine era, should be best clarified by an examination of developments in the region's two cities, Tiberias and Sepphoris. That is because complicated cultural and political attitudes are most identifiably evident in writings composed in, and about, such urban locales, and also in physical representations and remains that can be excavated from them. Tiberias has special interest because it became Judaism's capital, at least in Eretz Israel, for centuries, up to the seventh-century Islamic conquest, and probably even long after it. Also, in addition to the continuing controversy about the implications of the city's proximity to the youthful Jesus, Sepphoris generates considerable excitement among scholars because archaeological excavation points to a high level of Jewish assimilation of Hellenistic physical culture, whereas there is no strong literary or archeological evidence of deep Jewish "spiritual" identification with Roman ways or Christian ways. In a dynamic whereby physical accommodation is contrasted with mental outlooks or spiritual identification, and which, I suspect, reminds these scholars of Jewish life in twentieth century and twenty-first century America, they are suggesting that this well-known Galilee enclave, Sepphoris, represented a viable "acculturation" alternative for Jews, one where out-and-out "assimilation" was effectively resisted.[17] On this theory, in Sepphoris (and elsewhere), Jews might have, for centuries, acted like Romans or Byzantines, but nonetheless persisted in mentality, in private observance, and in other substantive realms, as "Jews," had not the successive encroachments of Persian, Christian, and Islamic rule utterly changed the rules of life in Galilee and the rest of Palestine, and propelled Jews into exilic dispersion.

The problem, as University of Connecticut scholar Stuart Miller points out, is that Jewish writers in the early Talmudic period do not display anything like the "interest in urban matters taken by their Greco-Roman contemporaries or later by Christians and Muslims." Following other scholars, he notes that "the internalization of the Halakah may have provided the Jew with a sense of *politea* that transcended the physical parameters and idea of the city."[18] In terms of city life, where social interaction is most fluid and intense, the Jewish sources are parsimonious and inconclusive about what happened in Galilee *after* monotheism multiplied. Could Jews, pagans and early Christians have found some way to live in the same one region and country?

In 235 CE, about five years into Judah II's tenure, the patriarchate moved from Sepphoris to Tiberias. The city continued to host the patriarchate up to its nullification in 415 CE, and Tiberias thereafter retained its lofty status for centuries, thanks to its Sanhedrin and groups of scholars. Its premier status in Jewish affairs was erased gradually, in a centuries-long process that began when Jews gained provisional entry rights to Jerusalem following the Islamic conquest of the country. Thus, for some five hundred years, Tiberias functioned "as Judaism's center, and as the capital for Jews in Eretz Israel and beyond its borders," claims a semi-official history of the city, produced in Israel in the 1970s. The Amoraim who produced the Palestine Talmud called it the "Jerusalem Talmud" due to reasons of prestige in rivalry with Babylonian colleagues who were producing their own version of the oral law, but, in essence, this was the Tiberias Talmud, claims this history. The various yeshivot where Amoraim labored in the country, in Lod, Yavne, Usha, Sepphoris, Beit Sha'arim, and Caesarea, were "satellites" orbiting around the Tiberias center, where this Talmud was produced, it claims.[19]

The Tiberias Yeshiva was headed by Rabbi Yohanan bar Nafha, and his students included luminaries such as Rabbi Shimon ben Lakish (Resh Lakish), Rabbi Eleazer ben Pedat, and Rabbi Hiyya bar Abba. Rabbi Yohanan studied for a period under Judah HaNasi's tutelage, and some Talmudic sources describe him as an active supporter of Judah II. These sources cast him as a lenient, somewhat effeminate scholar (he could never grow a beard); Galilee women are said to have wished for their children to look like him. Allowing students to study Greek, Rabbi Yohanan reversed a key policy in the yeshiva. He had slaves (whom he reportedly treated well) and ten children.[20]

Rabbi Yohanan's brother-in-law, Resh Lakish is one of the most colorful characters in this Amoraic period. He grew up, according to Babylonian Talmudic accounts, as a gladiator and as a bandit. The record of his first meeting with Rabbi Yohanan is beguilingly suggestive of polarized, homoerotic, and rapacious, instincts in Resh Lakish's ruffian character. A hulking figure, Resh Lakish splashed his way across a stretch of the Jordan, where Yohanan was bathing—he was drawn by what he thought was a beautiful woman. "You are powerful but also built for study," uttered Yohanan. "Your beauty is fit for a woman," replied Resh Lakish. Yohanan took the bandit under his wing, teaching him Torah and arranging the marriage with his sister ("who is yet more handsome than I am," Yohanan promised, during this initial Jordan River encounter). The story's obvious contrast is between the violently rapacious Romanized world of Resh Lakish's upbringing as a bandit, and the mental challenges and piety of yeshiva study; but recent commentary on this incident stresses its implicit criticism not just of the troubling misogyny by which Yohanan deflects a rapist by offering him his sister, but also of Yohanan's domineering status in the yeshiva hierarchy. Eroticism in this story is not nullified, as it would be in a Christian parable about a violently abusive man's transformation as a monk, claims Admiel Kosman; instead, he argues, Resh Lakish is an Amoraic prototype of how sexual energy persists in a redefined way in the yeshiva, and is poured out in Talmudic debate.[21] A creative, liberal-minded student, Resh Lakish scandalized fellow students by suggesting that the book of Job was a poem whose main character and descriptions should not be taken literally. Worse, he caused an uproar in Tiberias' Jewish circles when he insisted that should a patriarch sin, he too could be bastinadoed. Judah II threatened to arrest Resh Lakish for insubordination, but Rabbi Yohanan protected his impolitic brother-in-law. Tense relations between the patriarch and Resh Lakish continued to simmer. Once, Judah II complained to Resh Lakish about onerous tax burden imposed on him by the Romans. "Don't take anything and nothing will be taken from you," commented the irrepressible Resh Lakish.²²

As to the other prominent Amoraim in the Tiberias yeshiva: Eleazer ben Pedat was one of the Babylonian scholars who found his way to Galilee; and Rabbi Hiyya bar Abba is known to have left Galilee for a stint due to its conditions of socioeconomic hardship and to have raised funds as an Eretz Israel emissary outside of the country.

As a foil to these exemplars of Amoraic Talmudic achievement in Tiberias, the city's symbolic personification of crisis, as Roman Palestine became Byzantine Palestine in the fourth century, is the aforementioned Count Joseph the Apostate. Information about his colorful career comes from Epiphanius, a fourth-century bishop in Cyprus whose tome, *Panarion,* copiously details eighty cases of heresy; Epiphanius met Joseph in Beit Sha'an (then Scythopolis) in 353 CE, in a tumultuous period of natural disaster and political upheaval.²³ Born in Tiberias in 288, Joseph claimed to have had close relations with the patriarchate. He became a member of the Sanhedrin and was assigned by the aging, frail patriarch Gamaliel III to tutor his young son (Judah HaNasi's grandson), Judah II. Joseph attested to having tried, in vain, to countermand the young Judah's illicit ways—cavorting in Roman bathhouses at Hamat Gader's hot springs, courting gentile women, and so on. In this period, Joseph admitted to perusing Hebrew translations of Christian scripture, solely (he claimed) for the purpose of honing his defense of Jewish beliefs in polemics with Christians. In 310 CE, sometime after Judah II became patriarch, he rewarded his former tutor by sending Joseph on a prestigious and lucrative fund-raising errand to Cilicia; subsequently, Joseph's fate was sealed when he was caught perusing Christian materials. Brought to a Jewish court, Joseph was whipped and tortured. He converted to Christianity around 325 CE, and his case came to Constantine's attention. The emperor conferred to Joseph the *komes* title of respect, basically as a count, and outfitted him with power and resources to build churches and convert souls around the country.²⁴ Many aspects of Count Joseph's story, including his claim to have heard the deathbed conversion of patriarch Judah III, are doubted by scholar Stephen Gorannson, who wrote a dissertation on Joseph.²⁵ Joseph was discharged to build churches in Sepphoris, Tiberias, Capernaum and Nazareth—as far as the chronicler of these Joseph events, Epiphanius, was concerned, these locales lacked "real" churches (however, Gorannson explains, they might have held religious institutions where Jewish-Christian groups, or splinter factions, such as Ebionites or Nazarenes, worshipped).²⁶ Tiberias' semi-official history claims that Joseph got nowhere in the town. Joseph originally tried to build his church in the south part of Tiberias, in the decaying, unused Hadrianeum, but local Jews heckled and chased him away. Joseph eventually managed to erect a St. Peter's church in Tiberias, but it did not attract Jewish apostates, and the discouraged, excoriated Count Joseph spent his final days in Beit Sha'an, not his own native town, concludes this Tiberias history.[27]

Not all archeologists and historians accept this interpretation, which downplays Joseph's career, and its impact on Galilee's cultural landscape. In fact, one interesting account of excavations on the western side of Capernaum (controlled by the Franciscans, and today a site of considerable international tourist activity), speculates that its "House of Peter," located, intriguingly, next to an ancient synagogue, dates from a fourth-century campaign to designate various holy sites in Palestine, exactly what historians call "the invention of tradition,"[28] sponsored by Constantine. This author, Joan Taylor, Professor of Christian Origins at Kings College, London, declares, "it seems very likely that Joseph constructed the house-church in Capernaum."[29]

SUPERSESSION, THE SEQUEL

Between Jesus and Constantine, Christianity had an uncertain history in Galilee. Our review of the Book of Matthew uncovered powerful impressionistic evidence about the presence of nascent Christian groups in Galilee, decades after the Anastasis. Some scholars believe that Matthew's group was Jewish-Christian, beholden to Jewish law in some measure and also to Jesus' divinity, and positioned in a locale like Sepphoris, but there is considerable dispute about this "Jewish-Christian" categorization, and other locales for this particular group, such as Antioch, have been suggested. If, from the presumed composition of the Gospel of Matthew, we jump ahead some 250 years, to the authoritative Christological assembly of Nicea convened by Constantine in 325 CE, Galilee is not really "on the map" when Christianity consolidated its creeds. No bishops from Galilee attended the Nicea Council, whereas other regions in Palestine sent bishop delegates. The presence of Christian communities in this third-century Constantine era has been confirmed on the outer, western and northern, edges of Galilee, for instance, at Acre (then Ptolemais) and Banias (Paneas), but, by and large, these communities belonged to other regions, including the southern coast (Ascalon/Ashkelon, Gaza), the Bashan (then Aere Bataneae), and Jerusalem (then Aelia Capitolina). Also, an important indicator of Christian communities in third-century and early fourth-century Palestine, *Martyrs of Palestine* (authored by a bishop/Christian historian from Caesarea, Eusebius), points to significant Christian concentrations in Gaza and Caesarea, but not Galilee.[30]

Such findings, it bears mention, rub against implications of the "Galilee of Gentiles" theory. On this theory, Galilee had a substantive population of relatively unrooted Jews, relatively recent descendants of converts to Judaism, and also Jewishly ignorant *amei ha'aretz* who gravitated naturally to a new faith compounded out of Jesus' mission in the region. If this is the case, why is it hard to identify Christian, or hybrid Jewish-Christian groups, in Galilee, decades or centuries after the reported Resurrection?

Compounding this mystery is the issue of the Jews' anecdotal or ritualistic consciousness of Christian heretics, "minim," in Galilee and elsewhere, not long after the catastrophic Temple *hurban*, and more or less coterminous with the compilation of the gospels. An exclusionary prayer, *birkat ha-minim*, included in the eighteen benedictions (*Amidah*) and recited three times daily, apart from Shabbat and holidays, is thought to have been devised, at least in part, in antipathy to Christians; on this conventional understanding, the prayer took shape quite early in the rise of Christianity, possibly at the supposed founding conference of rabbinical Judaism, Jamnia (Yavne), held against the backdrop of the hurban. Also, the Talmud retrospectively refers to minim, presumably Christians, in key Galilee locales such as Sepphoris in the Tannaitic period. All this being the case, why, then, are archaeologists and historians not finding substantive literary and physical evidence of Christians in Galilee before the Byzantine period?

Here, again, we face the consequences of how knowledge about Galilee has been organized over the centuries, to the advantage of stakeholders in exclusionary visions of monotheism, those who are not really thinking of the "Holy Land" as a multicultural entity cherished by peoples of different orientations and faiths. At present, in a post-Holocaust environment wedged fortuitously in a way that ought to leverage meaningful Christian-Jewish dialogue, the situation is particularly anomalous. Christian scholars are turning somersaults in support of what are, from their standpoint, problematic precepts, foremost among them the idea of "Jesus, the Jew," but this theological latitudinarianism and good will cannot yield genuine insight about the circumstances, consequences and meanings of monotheism's fracture in first century Galilee.

Part of the problem is that Israel is unwilling to pitch a big tent, to facilitate learning about Galilee in one systematic university framework. This is because Israeli decision-makers are too ambivalent about Christian interests in Galilee—tourist revenue, from this official standpoint, is terrific, but too much talk about Jesus and his native grounds makes them, and most other Israelis, uncomfortable. They are also hamstrung by their suspicions about the educational empowerment of Galilee's non-Jewish populations, which are, or almost are, a majority in the region. As much as anything, because they are so over-invested in the neocolonialist project of establishing a disputed university for Jewish settlers, Ariel, on the occupied West Bank, their hands are tied, and unable to sponsor democratic, pluralistic university development in Galilee.

Nowhere is the unimaginative, disjointed character of scholarly research on the cardinal question of monotheism's multiplication in Galilee more frustratingly on display than in Sepphoris, today called Ziporri.[31] Because Israel has never provided a high-level academic forum for creative interaction on deep cultural-religious questions embedded in Galilee's soil and history, scholarship on Sepphoris in the past two or three academic generations turned into an unremittingly disappointing affair. Scholars were brought together nominally by overseas institutions, often from the U.S. Bible Belt, which command relatively large budgets, and have no driving interest in research work in Galilee other than to exploit the fund-raising attractiveness of work done in the Holy Land, provide their own scholars a profound-looking platform, and guard against overly provocative conclusions that might alienate funders, sometimes of an Evangelical Christian stamp, sometimes of Jewishly defensive bent about Israel and anti-Semitism. Often, Israel-born or American-born Hebrew University of Jerusalem scholars on Talmud or Second Temple era history supervised these projects, nominally as codirector (in tandem with the "Talmud guy," or the "Christian-Jewish origins guy" from the sponsoring U.S. institution); the real supervision in these sort of projects features behind-the-scenes ideological gatekeeping. It is impossible not to suspect that the glossy photographs of genuinely interesting archeological findings are pasted liberally on the pages of these half-scholarly, half-popular volumes to camouflage how intellectually stifled and methodologically dogmatic they really are. Their three manifest failings are (1) no serious effort is ever made to integrate archaeological work and written text analysis; (2) no supervisory voice is ever there to remind scholars that when their own rigidly monochromatic use of their own one single methodology does not point to alternative possibilities, this does not mean that the particular ideological angle they have been recapitulating throughout their careers is entirely correct; (3) the looking-at-Galilee as through a fishbowl orientation of scholars from overseas, or central cities in Israel, who have no genuine life experience in the region. How these failings would be mitigated, at least in some measure, if scholars of different backgrounds and ideological-religious orientations found themselves in the same humanities faculty, one in its archeology department the other in its history of religions unit (and both periodically in the same research seminar), always a short drive, or a long walk, from Zippori or Capernaum, requires no elaboration.

In a 2006 archaeology specialist volume on Sepphoris,[32] coauthored by James Strange, Thomas R.W. Longstaff and Dennis Groh, the writers devote half a paragraph in the preface to the motivation, from a Christian standpoint, of archaeological work at Sepphoris. Without calling it by its "Galilee of the Gentiles" name, the authors cite their research rationale: "A new stage in the investigation of Sepphoris emerged with the 'new' biography of Jesus written by the American scholar Shirley Jackson Case of the University of Chicago in 1924. Case argued that the universal message of Jesus was most reasonably affected by the universalism that Jesus encountered in the urban environment of Sepphoris, not in his rural environs at Nazareth."[33] Has their archaeological work done anything to strengthen this supposition that a "universal" atmosphere at Sepphoris might have inspired Jesus, and thereby contributed to the fracture between the presumably parochial monotheism of Judaism, and the new universalist monotheism of Christianity? Readers of this volume will find no answer. It includes an informative chapter on past scholarship and excavation work at Sepphoris,[34] but evades any sort of conclusion analytically tied to the problem which caused researchers to put shovels to the ground at this Galilee site in the first place. In a specialist publication of this sort, the multivolume framework creates distractions, playing the role of the glossy photographs in popular-oriented publications—since we are reminded that this technical publication, "volume one," is part of a work in progress, we are encouraged not to expect tight analytical cohesion.

That such cohesion may never come, because specialists are talking right past one another, is illustrated by a handsome 1996 publication, *Sepphoris in Galilee*, produced by the North Carolina Museum of Art.[35] The concept of this book is to keep a popular feel in an anthology of articles written by specialists. None of them budge toward a methodologically integrative, intellectually stimulating, discussion of how the Romanized veneer (as illustrated on the volume cover, a mosaic of a spear-holding soldier) of a town located close to where Jesus spent his short life might have contributed to monotheism's fracture. Take, as an example, University of Connecticut scholar Stuart Miller propounding his familiar view of Sepphoris as a staunchly Jewish Tannaitic and Amoraic venue, where there was little input of heretical *minim* (whom cannot necessarily be classified as early Christians, in his view), and minimal social tension between rabbis and Jewish laymen. "Sepphoris was largely [*sic*] regarded as a Jewish city," declares Miller.[36] But if this is the case, why all the fuss about Sepphoris?

If Miller is right, what is the reader supposed to do with all the glossy photographs of statuettes of Prometheus and Pan, of a synagogue zodiac mosaic, of a Roman-looking market cardo, among others, which fill this book? This is a serious question, and if it is answered in a negative key, the rationale of the book's production, and much of the archaeological work it aims to summarize and popularize, is presumably negated—but, for Miller, it suffices to provide a disparaging half sentence about the insignificance of Sepphoris' "Hellenistic veneer" and of "the periodic presence of Roman troops" in it.[37]

What about the after-effects of Jesus' mission in Sepphoris? If, on the Galilee of the Gentiles theory, universalism became imprinted in his messages partly due to the inspiring cosmopolitanism of Sepphoris, might it follow that early Christians were drawn, almost magnetically, to the town? In an earlier chapter, we encountered a hypothesis speculating that the Book of Matthew might have been composed in Sepphoris—has archaeological work done anything to strengthen such a supposition? Sean Freyne is dispatched in this *Sepphoris in Galilee* volume to address this question, but he balks. He discusses how Christian sites and communities consolidated under Byzantine rule in other Galilean towns, including Nazareth, but then confesses, "thus far it has not yet been possible to trace fully a similar trajectory for Christians at Sepphoris."[38] This is yet another deflating let-down statement which grates against the volume's copious visual evidence of powerful gentile cultural influence in Sepphoris.

E.P. Sanders, an erudite New Testament scholar and author of the widely acclaimed volume *Jesus and Judaism*,[39] contributed a short article in this anthology on "Jesus' Relation to Sepphoris." The article is short because Sanders, in contradistinction to a long roster of commentators, dismisses the issue: "Sepphoris is not mentioned in the New Testament, which contains the only direct information about Jesus. . . . The discussion might end at this point."[40] In fact, for Sanders, it does. Given that we know nothing about thirty years of Jesus' life, other than its basis in Nazareth (and the "Disputation" scene in Luke, chapter 2), why is it less reasonable to assume that he was influenced by a major urbanization project undertaken within easy walking distance from his home, than it is to proclaim, as Sanders does, that there was no influence because the New Testament is silent about Sepphoris? If the New Testament conveyed a fair amount of detail about Jesus' youthful years, but failed to mention Sepphoris, Sanders' position would have obviously validity, but as things stand, he is howling dogmatically about the nonexistence of the dark side of the moon.

No better, Sanders exploits the anthology's confusingly self-contradictory message—that is, Sepphoris was a much more Jewish town than all these glossy Hellenistic mosaic and zodiac photos make it look—to promote a debatable psychological model about Jesus and Christianity's origins. Just for the sake of argument, Sanders allows a brief discussion about Sepphoris' cultural character, and insists that it was much less cosmopolitan than other scholars have assumed: Antipas's urban development program, for instance, encouraged the use of Jewish laborers, the town's administrators were Jewish, and its famous theater might not have been built "until at least fifty years after his death."[41] So what? Is the psychological model here that it would have taken "a lot of universalism" to shake Jesus and his followers away from the parochial self-involvement of their Jewish upbringings? Why is it self-evident that a modest "veneer" of Hellenism in Sepphoris, rather than a hefty amount of it in the town, undermines the argument about how the Galilee environment of Jesus' upbringing subsequently impacted on the spirit and content of his preaching? In fact, a standard motif in conventional biographical writing about history's "great" personalities is that a brief but intense exposure to some passing reality which challenges their value system can be a turning point in their career—has there ever been a rule about "how much" exposure is necessary?

One scholar in this anthology who follows the logic of its visual presentations, and rejects the contrarian thesis of many of its written contributions, is Isaiah Gafni, an American-born Second Temple scholar, then of the Hebrew University, subsequently President of Shalem College, also in Jerusalem. Gafni suggests that Hellenistic culture infusion in Sepphoris probably triggered important subconscious processes among Jews, affecting their perceptions of status, worth, and even of time and space. He concludes his article with a discussion of how Jews in the town, including rabbis, appear to have acclimated their sensibilities of private space, and of home living, to salient norms in "the surrounding Hellenistic-Roman environment of Palestine." Whether his judgment is on target or not, its analytic depth and quality stands out in the lackluster scholarly literature on Sepphoris produced after 1948, in the Israeli era. To find anything comparably stimulating about Sepphoris, one has to examine pre-1948 writings, such as the aforementioned brilliantly provocative booklet written by Adolf Buchler. Gafni notes that "the very terms that the rabbis used to describe various portions of the house," such as *kiton* (bedroom) and *traklin* (entertaining room), suggest that spiritual leaders of the Jewish Galilean community were, in fact, "part of their cultural surroundings and so employed the same Greek terms used by their neighbors." Hence, he concludes, "although Jews, Christians and pagans all embraced particular religious beliefs and tenets, daily life linked every element of Galilean society and thereby rendered the various lifestyles therein far more similar to one another than the individual groups may have realized."[42]

On this view, Jews in this part of Galilee were involved, consciously or not, in an acculturation process, one that undeniably refashioned the character of their Judaism, as has happened to innumerable Jewish communities in many places and times. The problem with Gafni's contribution is not that he chooses not to apply this finding to the issue of Christianity's emergence from Judaism—that is a large issue for any scholar, and, of course, he or she can choose the right time, if ever, to address it. The problem is that Gafni is oblivious to the high-profile, well-invested, multidisciplinary character of the Sepphoris project as a whole. His conclusion has *everything* to do with this volume's glossy photographs of zodiac mosaics in synagogues, but Gafni does nothing to show it. He opens his article by declaring that "our knowledge of the daily life in Galilee in the first five centuries of the Common Era derives primarily from literary sources," which is a reasonable statement once we omit, in his case, the word "primarily." His knowledge is exclusively literary—were it not, how could he have omitted reference to the volume's expensively produced visual materials, given the nature of his conclusion? That, too, is fine—many professionally trained scholars are most securely in a comfort zone when working with written materials. The problem with this volume, and similar ones, is that it invites distinguished scholars like Gafni to make a false show of interdisciplinary methodology, as though they are involved in a common research project with archeologists, when they are not. In the middle of Gafni's article (p. 52) appears a 160-word paragraph, under a caption titled "The Archaeological Evidence." That is false advertising: not a single word in Gafni's paragraph applies to archaeological evidence.

Sepphoris is much more interesting than anything that has been written about it in the last two generations, despite extensive field work undertaken in that period. The only thing which might possibly compel scholars from different disciplines, history and archaeology, comparative religion and philosophy, to take one another seriously on such a Galilee topic is an on-site, sustained, academic framework. A university where Muslims, Christians, and Jews—academics not just of different faiths, but from different academic fields—might freely talk about a region whose history is the Greatest Story Never Told.

In decades after the Anastasis, Jews in Galilee encountered Jesus followers. The frequency of such contacts (like any other social phenomenon in antiquity) cannot be determined, but it suffices to note that Talmudic commentators did not ignore them.[43] Two Tannaitic sources record rabbinical encounters with followers of Jesus, who is called Jesus ben Pantera. Scholars identify the locales in these incidents as two Galilee villages north of Nazareth, Kefar Semai, and Sakhnin.[44] The first incident, in which Rabbi Eliezer ben Hyrcanus is arrested by the Romans on suspicion of Christian heresy (*minut*), has been closely scrutinized by scholars due to its unusually explicit reference to a Jesus follower.[45] Eliezer is acquitted but remains disconsolate because of the shadow of suspicion that has been cast over his faithfulness to Judaism. Rabbi Akiva comes to console him.

Akiva's approach to Eliezer is quite revealing, since it implies that Tannaim were not plugging their ears completely to Jesus' teaching, and also attests to a steady measure of contacts between the Tannaim and the nascent Christian *minim*. "Perhaps one of the minim told you a word of minut, and it pleased you," Akiva queries, jogging Eliezer's memory. "By heaven you have reminded me!" exclaims Eliezer. "Once I was walking along a street of Sepphoris, and chanced upon Jacob of Kfar Sichnin, and he spoke to me a word of minut in the name of Jesus ben Pantiri, and it pleased me."[46] As far as the Talmudic writers were concerned, decades after Jesus' mission, boundaries between Jewish rabbis and Christian heretics in Sepphoris were so porous that a Roman officer might not have been able to distinguish between the two groups. As some scholars point out, a Babylonian Talmudic version of this incident might have anachronistically transposed realities of Jewish-Christian interaction in Mesopotamia upon this Tannaitic landscape, but the same scholars state that the description of the arrest and trial of Rabbi Eliezer accords reasonably with the way the Romans policed late-first-century Galilee.[47] From their standpoint, a conspicuous Jew like Rabbi Eliezer and an early Christian might have been, physically, indistinguishable. More importantly, as Reuven Kimelman points out, the incident illustrates that "there was nothing exceptional" about a rabbi stumbling upon a Jesus follower, a *min*, from a nearby Galilee village.[48]

In a second incident, an early second-century Tanna, Rabbi Eliezer ben Dama, is bit by a snake. A *min*, Jacob from Kefar Semai, offers a presumed antidote, in the name of Jesus (again, called Jesus ben Pantera), but another rabbi, Ishmael, intervenes, and prevents his associate, or nephew, Eliezer, from being treated by heretics. Interestingly, Eliezer pleads, insisting that the Jesus followers have healing powers ("I will bring you a proof that he may heal me"). From the standpoint of rabbinic Judaism, the episode ends in an appropriate, moralizing, key—Eliezer dies, and Ishmael righteously proclaims, "Happy are you, ben Dama, for you have departed in peace, and have not broken the ordinances of the wise."[49] As Kimelman observes, this incident practically begs to be "read against its rhetoric" (in fact, some commentators believe that the incident can be read in a way which incriminates Ishmael[50]). In second-century Galilee, "borders between Christianity and Judaism were far more porous than desired by authorities on either side," Kimmelman explains.[51] Just as early church fathers remonstrated against Christians who blithely attended Jewish synagogue services, so too did Tannaitic authorities such as Rabbi Ishmael preach to Jews about how they had nothing to gain from contacts with the minim, who quite plausibly were not "Christians," but rather Jewish Christians in some fluid, not easy to define, sense (Kimelman speculates that the presumed snakebite healer in this episode was one such Jewish Christian[52]). It is facile and misleading to suppose that there were two identifiable groups of nascent Christians in this Galilee setting, one belonging to a Matthew stream, and Jewish-Christian in its adhesion to Jesus' stricture about the fulfillment of Jewish law (Matthew 5:17), and the other Christian, belonging to a Pauline stream, Kimelman maintains. The reality, he says, was "polythetic," meaning that several characteristics might be attributed to a *min* in this setting, not the least of them being devotion of some substantive sort to Jesus, but not a single trait was necessarily definitive. Minim and Jews might have had a pick and choose attitude on religion, being drawn to attractive aspects, such as therapeutic power in this case of the Rabbi ben Dama snakebite temptation incident, attributed to one religious way of life. In a telling analogy, Kimelman writes: "The situation is comparable to people whose primary allegiance is to modern medicine but will try out alternative medicine when needed. These people frequently decline to inform their physician."[53]

This final twist in Kimelman's analysis, serving Jewish-Christian relations in first century and second-century Galilee on a consumerist platter, might be symptomatic of the aforementioned ailment Albert Schweitzer diagnosed, in his groundbreaking work on Jesus' scholarship (which we will discuss at length in volume two). Just as nineteenth-century scholars engaged in the "search for the historical Jesus" invariably planted on his face a comforting vision of reality known to them from their own modern worlds, so too might contemporary scholars be guilty of the same anachronism in their descriptions of what came after Jesus in Galilee. Kimelman's description of Jewish-Christian interaction in second-century Galilee bears a strong resemblance to non-ascriptive, pick and choose what you need, religious phenomena in twentieth-century America described by scholars as "Sheilaism."[54] The Tannaim, as we have stressed, were mired in an authority crisis, but this does not mean that Jews in Galilee (and elsewhere) lacked sanctions, mental habits, and social norms inhibitive of heresy. Jews, as a group, had endured unbearable realities in the defense of their own religious-national boundaries in two major struggles against Rome, and there thus might be something awry in a suggestion holding that they emerged from those rebellions with a relatively carefree, consumerist, orientation toward their own religion.

In fact, generations of scholars have assumed that by the end of the first century, Jewish attitudes, by and large, toward nascent Christianity, in Galilee and elsewhere, were disdainful, not carefree. The basis for this view is, of course, *Birkat Ha-Minim*, which, in a version uncovered in the Cairo Genizah, contemptuously wishes for the instantaneous destruction of Christians (*nosrim*), as well as the "speedy" uprooting of the "arrogant government" (Rome).[55] There is some wriggle room away from a plain reading of this prayer, based on suppositions about the possible forged interpolation of the word, *nosrim*, its construction next to the frustratingly elusive term *minim*, and so on. Kimelman exploits these openings, and weds them to other types of non-textual, social evidence, particularly the fact that patristic sources, such as John Chyrsostom's harangues, suggest how many Jewish sectarians (i.e., Christians-in-the-making) were attending synagogue observances. This might have happened, but if there was such mixed synagogue attendance in Galilee, who can say whether the phenomenon was voluntary, or more like a shotgun wedding? How could it be possible, Kimelman basically asks, that "Christians were welcome" in the Jews' synagogues while the Jews were praying for their obliteration? His anti-empirical conclusion is that there was no such prayer (or at least no "unambiguous evidence" of it). Revising a view held by a long roster of distinguished scholars, pointing to the prayer as proof of how an irreparable breach between the religions took hold around the year 100, he claims that "there never was a single edict which caused the so-called irreparable separation.... The separation was rather the result of a long process dependent upon local situations."[56]

This last point is correct, but facile. Generally, a proclamation ("a single edict") is not a causal factor in history, but in this *birkat ha-minim* case (and many others) it reflects genuine emotional and cultural realities. The design of Kimelman's methodologically confused argument is to downplay these cultural realities. The supposed contradiction between Jewish sectarians (minim) attending synagogue occasions, and the recitation of birkat ha'minim, is a false opposition. Christianity came from Galilee, and Christians came, originally, from Jews; so, *of course*, there was a period when Jewish Christians and Jews were sitting uncomfortably in the same synagogues. A wide array of reasons might have brought the sectarians there, but none of them preclude the recitation of this prayer, and the likely fact that Jewish loyalists were hoping fervently that the evolving new creed of the minum would just go away. Kimelman alludes to one dynamic—the prayer was included in services out of consciousness that minim were sometimes in attendance in synagogues, and so birkat ha-minim prevented a heretic from acting as a reader in a holy place ("a *min* would not want to curse himself").[57] But there were probably many other factors at play—still-standing friendship and kinship ties, economic relations and interests, even, paradoxically, sheer cordiality—and none of these would necessarily have debarred Jews from stating, in prayer, their true feelings about Rome and about what we know as Christianity.

Kimelman's analyses, as we have seen, are cognizant of the probable intensity and frequency of contacts between Jews and nascent Christians in Galilee in this period, but the tendency to jettison plain readings of texts and to reach evasive and relativistic conclusions about the indeterminacy of historical processes ("the 'so-called' irreparable separation between Judaism and Christianity [was] the result of a long process dependent upon local situations") strikes me as troublesome. It is not just saying that "what we plainly see about the past in Galilee might not have happened"; this approach adds, as a kind of anti-positivist orthodoxy, that "what we plainly see about the past in Galilee probably did not happen."

Not indefinite or arbitrary "local conditions," but rather identifiable and steady ideological rivalry, and contrasting belief systems, dictated the course of Jewish-Christian relations in Galilee past the Tannaitic period, up to the Byzantine era. Its imprint in the landscape is readily perceptible. Almost certainly during the early phase, in which sectarians ("Jewish Christians") represented the not-yet-consolidated new faith, physical proximity prevailed between the two groups in Galilee, but, thereafter, the dominant physical, and presumably emotional, trend was separation. The two groups had reasons not to live near one another, and not to like one another. This trend of separation can be backpedaled, meaning that the situation in the mid- and late-Amoraic eras, ahead of the Persian occupation, when Jews were an outright majority in Galilee, can be inferred retroactively from circumstances in the Byzantine period, when Christians became an empowered majority, and the Jews were an attenuated minority.

Mordechai Aviam, the preeminent Israeli archaeologist of Galilee in the passing generation who worked extensively on Byzantine sites in his graduate work and thereafter for Israel's Antiquities Authority, uncovered this indelible rule of separation. In Western Galilee, excavations revealed that only a few Jewish families lived scattered in what became an overwhelmingly Christian locale.[58] As evidenced by well-ornamented churches, Christian communities thrived along the Galilee coast (Evron, Shavei Tzion, Nahariya), and monasteries buffeted the Christian villages in the interior; in one zone of Upper-Western Galilee, a Christian site was found in each square kilometer. Living apart from Christians, Jewish settlements could be found east in the region, and particularly in Lower Galilee, including the two cities, Tiberias and Sepphoris. From time to time, archaeologists publish counterclaims, speculating about interfaith proximity and daily contacts in this Byzantine period at Galilee locales such as Shlomi, but Aviam resolutely rejects the evidence which grounds them.[59] No archaeological evidence attests to interaction or proximity between Jews and Christians in late stages of the Roman era, and in the Byzantine period, and so there is no physical evidence to doubt the cogency of a text expressive of late-first-century rupture between the two religions, such as birkat ha-minim.

Archaeological or literary evidence of noninteraction and distance between the two groups does not necessarily mean that one of them did not exist in the late Roman period, however. As we have seen, in the literary source realm of the Talmud, evidence of Jesus followers mounting a conspicuous presence in Galilee decades after the Resurrection is not copious, but nonetheless rather clear and non-impeachable. However, due to imprecision in uses of the term "minim" and the lack of verifiable archaeological findings about second-century Christianity in Galilee, some scholars push the envelope with a counter-intuitive, and counter-empirical, claim, announcing that virtually nothing remained of the Jesus movement in the place where it started, until the advent of Byzantium (roughly a 350 year stretch of time). An example is Stuart Miller's article which challenges the common sense assumption that Talmudic references to "minim" in Tannaitic Sepphoris refer to Christians, or to Jewish Christians in the making—this article proposes that some such references applied to Jewish Gnostics, or nonconformists in Sepphoris who resisted the rabbis' evolving Mishnaic program.[60] Critics of Miller's approach complain that "he has worked minimalism on *minim*." They suggest that he has narrowed his search field with undue rigidity and extrapolated manipulatively about the nonpresence of nascent Christians in a key Galilee locale ("If we wanted to know about, for example American colonial Jews in Providence, Rhode Island, would we limit ourselves and our research only to the texts that explicitly include the words 'Jews' and 'Providence," asks one critic).[61]

A variation on Miller's thesis is Joan Taylor's study, subtitled *The Myth of Jewish-Christian Origins*. Seemingly in contradistinction to Miller, she concedes that perhaps a substantive number of *minim*, understood as Jewish Christians, dwelled in Galilee and elsewhere through the mid-second century, but thereafter, she writes, "nothing indicates" that they are anywhere to be found in Roman Palestine.[62] Between 135 and 324 CE, she argues, Galilee was populated by Jews; Samaritans lived in the Mount Gerizim strip; Christians resided in a few southern villages and a "few cosmopolitan cities" such as Caesarea, and the country hosted a large pagan population (pagans lived in the Negev, east of the Jordan River, the Hauran and Hermon areas, and their presence was felt around northern stretches of Galilee).[63] On her theory, what happened in fourth-century Palestine is part of a larger story of a rupture in history caused by Constantine's conversion and subsequent Christianization program. She cites approvingly commentators who branded Constantine's policy of religious change "one of history's great surprises," and "the most audacious act ever committed by an autocrat in disregard of the vast majority of his subjects."[64] Taylor doubts that in the empire as a whole even 5 percent of the subjects were Christian at the time of this Constantinian rupture—and the aim of her detailed work on Roman Palestine is to prove that the same ultra-slim minority of Christians dwelled in the country, their marginal character, compared to other reaches of the empire, not affected by the fact that their religion came from where they lived. In implication, her contentions, like Miller's, represent a kind of reversal of Christian supersession theory. Whereas, according to traditional Christian theology, due to Jewish rejection of Jesus' divinity, the Jews' covenant in the Holy Land was annulled, and their special relationship with God has been superseded, this new research theory denies that Christianity has any special, ongoing relationship with the region where it started, Galilee. Any Jesus followers, embryonic Christians or Jewish Christians, who might have been left in the area after what they beheld as the Resurrection were quickly superseded, in a palpable sense, by Jews, and pagans.

Unlike other scholars in this supersession of supersessionism school, Taylor is relatively candid about why she is so invested in disproving that significant numbers of Christians dwelled in Galilee, and elsewhere in Palestine, in the late Roman period. She objects to a thesis propounded, mostly after the 1960s, by Franciscan archaeologists and scholars, Bellarmino Bagatti and Emmanuele Testa, holding that Christian presence and attachments to sacred sites in the Holy Land date back to the first century. As exemplified by her claim about Count Joseph of Tiberias and the House of Peter at Capernaum, Taylor contends that holy site veneration is a post-Constantine phenomenon, and was catalyzed by "invention of tradition" sort of processes in the fourth century and thereafter. Whatever Taylor's own innermost motivations, a dispute of this sort, featuring conflicting claims about the pedigree of holy sites, has, of course, a litany of possible ramifications in areas of religious diplomacy, tourism, theology, and more.

What motivates others in this school is harder to ascertain. There are glancing references in scholarly articles to intellectual gatherings, such as a certain McMaster Symposium, which highlighted "the lack of evidence for any formative impact of Christianity on any major element of Tannaitic Judaism."[65] As formulated, this proposition sounds plausible, in light of our detailed review of the insularity of Tannaitic culture; but, it will be recalled, while there is not an abundance of material about Jesus and Christians in this early rabbinical Judaism context of the Mishnah, the few relevant documents are qualitatively suggestive.

All told, the theory of Christian irrelevance in Galilee for *three centuries* after Jesus is peculiar. Ultimately, it can only be explained by the way the monotheistic faiths developed—because each one had its own propaganda machinery, and became heavily invested in testimony of the exclusive righteousness of its successive conquest of the Holy Land, an "other" religion's origins story in Galilee or Jerusalem became instantly controversial, and everlastingly contested. An interesting parallel to this school's negation of Christian roots in Galilee is afforded by the history of Zionism. In light of Rome's attitude toward early Christianity, the apparent disappearance of *minim* from Galilee after the middle of the second century can be thought of as exilic dispersion, comparable in some ways to the attenuation and then marginality of Palestine's Jewish population for 1,500 years between the late Roman and late Ottoman eras. In Zionist historiography, some notable scholars, most famously Ben Zion Dinur (who became an education minister in Israel's early years), insisted that the few Jews who remained in four holy cities of the Yishuv (Jerusalem, Hebron, Tiberias, and Safed) had important stories to tell, despite the numerical marginality of their communities. Dinur's approach has been criticized, even ridiculed, by his own successors in Israeli academia, and in overseas academic settings, for reasons that go beyond the exposure of his obvious political motivation of establishing that the Zionist movement had historic roots in the land where it was determined to establish a state. Joan Taylor writes about what she calls the "Bagatti-Testa Hypothesis" in a vein of sophisticated, and quite detailed, polemic that is comparable to the sort of polished hyperbole laden within critiques of the hypothesis of Dinur's "Jerusalem School" about continuous Jewish settlement in Eretz

THE RISE OF CHRISTIAN RULE IN GALILEE

Jews militantly opposed the advent and consolidation of Christian rule in Galilee and the country. A few decades after the Byzantine take-over of the Holy Land, they initiated a short-lived but significant revolt, really a successor rebellion to the two great prior uprisings against Rome. This third insurrection generated out of Galilee. Toward the end of the Byzantine period, Jews sided with the Christians' enemy, the Persians, massacred Christians in Jerusalem during the ephemeral period of Persian occupation of the country, and exploited the power vacuum caused by the Persian-Byzantium rivalry in an intense, but unsuccessful, military effort to liberate brethren up the coast, north of Galilee, in Tyre. From the Jewish standpoint, this period was marred by calamitous political miscalculation, particularly with regard to the alliance with the Persians, who proved unreliable. By the end of the Byzantine period in the country, the Jews were an attenuated and marginalized element, and so, even though the Jews' preference for the country's new Umayyad rulers, relative to the Christians, was undeniable, they proffered relatively little support to the Muslim newcomers.

All told, this Jewish phase in Galilee history, highlighted by Judaism's revitalization in the Tannaitic period, was extinguished due to the animosity which raged between Jews and Christians. The Jews would not earn a restored, prominent place in Galilee history for another thousand years. This return, in the Kabbalist era, would also be precipitated by the violence of their relations with Christianity—in the late medieval period, Christian inquisitorial persecution on the Iberian Peninsula drove Jews back to Galilee.

As Rome's Christian emperor,[67] Constantine did not dramatically change its laws regarding Jews. He reinforced existing laws banning Jews from proselytizing and extended legal protection to Jews who converted to Christianity. In 335 CE, he granted liberty to slaves who had been circumcised by Jewish owners (this issue of Jewish slave-owning would be regarded as an irritant by Byzantine law for a protracted period). At Constantine's direction, the municipal territory of Aelia, the area of Jerusalem from which Jews were banned, was extended. Concurrently, Constantine instituted a new tradition, allowing Jews to mourn on the ruins of the Temple once a year, on Tisha b'Av (this ritual continued four or five generations into the Amoraic period). In Constantine's own time, such changes in Roman law toward the Jews were not overly onerous, but the Christian emperor introduced a newly

Israel.[66] Because they penetrate so deeply in realms of personal identity, existential authenticity, and religious narrative, origins claims, in the Holy Land context, are automatically targets of intense contestation.

contemptuous discourse about this group, referring to Jews as defiled perjurers in his correspondence.[68]

As hinted earlier, Constantine's revolution did not instantaneously alter demographic realities in Palestine, but his rule triggered a major transformation in the perception of the land's holy places. With his mother Helena, he embarked on a church construction campaign in Jerusalem and Bethlehem; and Constantine extended patronage to Count Joseph, the convert from Tiberias, who sponsored Christian construction projects in Galilee, with mixed success. Palestine was becoming a Holy Land pilgrimage magnet for Christians from overseas.

Scholars have identified early pilgrims. The first, an anonymous traveler identified simply as the "Bordeaux Pilgrim" who toured the country in 333 CE, made it within a day of Galilee, but did not think to visit Nazareth or Capernaum, and his itinerary suggests that when Constantine changed religious realities in the empire, holy shrines were not instantly designated in the region of Jesus' childhood and mission. This had changed a half century later, during the pilgrimage of a woman named Egeria. In Nazareth, she believed that she visited a garden where Jesus played as a child; and, near Capernaum, she visited the reported site of Matthew's tollbooth, and she was thrilled to find that the "original walls" of Peter's house "are still standing."[69]

As rivalry over sacred space in the country began to take shape, there were signs of restiveness among Jews. In 387 CE, John Chrysostom, a malicious detractor of Jews who would become patriarch in Constantinople a decade later, claimed that in Constantine's time, Jews tried to rebuild the Temple but were quickly thwarted (they had their ears clopped off, he claimed). A few other non-Jewish sources, from early medieval and mid-medieval times, allude to the incident; modern historians suspect that a zealot Jewish group attempted a desperate "coup-de-main in order to keep Jerusalem from becoming a Christian city."[70] Whatever happened in this Jerusalem incident, it symbolizes how the imposition of Christian power in the Roman empire instigated new trends of rebelliousness among Jews, and phenomena which had not been seen since the Bar Kochba revolt.

Jewish objections emanated out of legal and economic spheres. Constantine did not fundamentally alter Roman law toward Jews, but his successor, his son Constantius II, was innovatively oppressive in this area, using the law to bar intermarriage between Jews and Christians, and banning Jews from owning gentile slaves. The slave ban, argues Israeli historian M. Avi-Yonah, hampered Jewish artisans and manufacturers in their competition with gentile producers. The prohibition thus might have factored as a prime precipitant in the 351 CE revolt against Gallus Caesar,[71] the third such Jewish rebellion against Roman rule in the Common Era—much smaller in scale, and far less devastating in its consequences to Jews, this was nonetheless a significant event, and it was mostly a Galilee occurrence.

Gallus, a nephew of Constantius, became in 351 CE vice-emperor, and nominal ruler, of the eastern part of Rome's empire. But his authority was quickly challenged by army officials, and also by Persia's king (Shapur II), who held ambitions to reconquer northern Mesopotamia. Probably sensing Gallus' vulnerability, Jews, led by a rebel known to us only by his name, Patricius, began the uprising in June 351 CE, in Sepphoris (known then as Diocaesarea), where they seized an armory. Jewish rebels spread throughout Galilee (Tiberias quickly took part in the revolt), and then worked their way down the coast, and reached Lydda, where they managed to block-off an important road. One source refers to the temporary establishment of a "kind of kingdom" of the Jews; none of the sources allude to an attempt to attack Jerusalem, nor to assaults on noncombatant Christians.

Fighting back, the Romans used Ptolemais (Acre) as a launching pad, just as Vespasian had done in Rome's campaign against Galilee in 67 CE. The rebellion did not last long, and since there is no hint of a siege on a Jewish-held city, historians reason that Romans settled the issue on plain-lands around Acre. Sepphoris was reportedly destroyed by the Romans (within decades it revived as a Jewish city), and Jewish populations in three towns and fifteen villages were apparently destroyed as a result of the revolt. Sources refer to several thousand Jewish casualties, including women and children. Rabbi Huna, a native of Mesopotamia who was in Galilee at the time, recalled hiding with fellow Jews in a cave near Tiberias; and Roman soldiers reportedly burned a Torah scroll in a village south of that city.[72]

If *birkat ha'minim* can be regarded as an early swivel in the turnstile deterioration of Jewish-Christian relations, its arms were now swinging fast in Byzantine Palestine. Jewish leaders in the patriarchate may not, at the time, have seen this descent as irreversible. They seem to have hoped that the modus-vivendi which Judah HaNasi and his successors had forged with pre-Constantine Rome could be renewed in the new Byzantine era, but this hope proved illusory.

An eighteen-month interregnum (November 361 CE–June 363 CE) in Byzantine pressure against the Jews occurred during Julian's brief, colorful reign. Julian set about to de-Christianize the empire for an array of reasons unrelated to the fate of Jerusalem, but his intentions to support the Jews and their rebuilding of the Temple were serious. In summer 362 CE, when he unveiled his plans to Jews at an Antioch conference, no Tiberias representatives from the patriarchate were on hand, as these Galilee leaders "were feeling the need for caution."[73] On theological grounds, some Amoraim argued that only a descendant of the House of David could bring about Temple restoration in messianic time, but other, more historical-minded, rabbis pointed to the past example of a gentile ruler, King Cyrus, sponsoring Temple restoration. Hillel II, patriarch at the time, could have felt excluded by Julian's plan, since the patriarchate's line of descent in the House of Hillel rendered him ineligible for a role as high priest in the Temple. No less plausibly, the patriarchate's hesitation might have stemmed from practical doubts about Julian's prospects. If this was the case, Hillel II was prudent. The Temple construction was thrown up in flames, either by deliberate arson or by a devastating earthquake which coincidentally convulsed the country in this period (Julian's Christian detractors naturally viewed this blaze in the designated Temple's southeast corner as a miraculous symbol). Julian was slain in June 363 CE, and replaced by a Christian, Jovian.

A new round of anti-Jewish legislation was initiated in the last decade of the fourth century by Emperor Theodosius I. After his death (395 CE), the oppressively, anti-Jewish, character of these laws was periodically lessened or harshened, but by 415 CE Jewish rights and powers in the sphere of communal authority had shriveled or disappeared. Key issues involved participation on municipal councils, the power of rabbinical courts, and rights to build synagogues. While laws detrimental to Jewish interests in Palestine were being written into the books, attacks on synagogues erupted in other parts of the evolving Byzantine empire. During these first decades of the fifth century, Christians quite possibly became a majority in Palestine.[74]

In a nominal sense, Galilee's status as the Jews' capital district was overturned in this period by the Byzantines. Language in a Byzantine law from 429 CE refers to the demise of the patriarchs (*excessus patriarcharum*). Apparently, the emperor simply refused to appoint a successor after the death of patriarch Gamaliel VI.[75] In a divide and conquer sort of strategy, the Byzantines tried to instigate rivalry between Jewish communal leaders in Caesarea and those in Tiberias. This aim is laden within the emperor's administrative redesignation of Palestine in 429 CE, whereby *Palaestina prima* included the coastal plain and Judea and Samaria, whereas *Palaestina secunda* was comprised of Galilee and the former Decapolis areas, east of the Jordan. For some time thereafter, Jews in Palestine regarded Tiberias as their socioreligious center, despite this Byzantine maneuver.[76]

In this mid-fifth century period, Christianity took steps to stem theological disputation and to consolidate its creed. Church delegates met in Chalcedon in 451 and confirmed that Christ had two distinct natures. Scholars believe that the majority of Christians in Palestine accepted this formulation, and can be classified as Chalcedonians. Splinter groups, however, maintained a presence in the country. For instance, Monophysites, who insisted that Jesus' nature remained fully divine despite his adoption of a mortal body, had an ecclesiastical hierarchy in Jerusalem, and could also be found in Galilee. The Ghassanids, for instance, members of a Christian Arab tribe which fought in alliance with the Byzantines on the country's northern frontier, were Monophysites.⁷⁷

By the sixth century, Christians constituted a strong majority in Palestine. Most members of this majority group were ethnically Semitic, and spoke Arabic, or Syro-Palestinian Aramaic. Greek was the language used for writing inscriptions and documents.⁷⁸ Jews were now a relatively small minority in the country, constituting perhaps 10 percent or 15 percent of its population, but they remained as a significant concentration in Galilee.

Archeologists over the past generation uncovered interesting evidence of a concerted Byzantine effort to dominate Galilee's landscape, at the expense of its Jewish population, in decades preceding the turmoil of Persian and Muslim conquests which ended Christian rule in the country by the mid-seventh century. Justinian I, Eastern Roman Emperor from 527 to 565 CE, brought this rivalry into the Jews' capital, Tiberias: he seems to have been behind the construction of a wall whose remains have been found around Hammat Tiberias on the city's south side, and on its slopes on its western border. Atop the most dramatic peak in this walled off area, Mount Berenice, Justinian built a breathtaking church whose gold cross and tiled roof could be seen widely around the area, as a statement of Byzantine power in Galilee. An Israeli excavation team, led by Yizhar Hirschfeld, began work at the site in 1990,⁷⁹ falsely expecting to find a palace mentioned by Josephus which belonged to Tiberias' founder, Herod Antipas (a contemporary of Jesus). Instead of this fabled palace, the team stumbled upon remains of this splendid Byzantine church. Much about it, including the fact that it was maintained by a group of olive oil producing monks, conforms with Byzantine customs and standards, but there are indications of a conscious attempt to rise above, literally and figuratively, Tiberias' Jewish institutions and leadership on the other side of the wall. The Hirschfeld team's finding is called the "Anchor Church," owing to a huge, 478 kilogram, basalt stone located at its apse. This cultic stone is one of Galilee's intriguing objects—its use for ritual probably dates to the Early Bronze age, and its cult meaning was redefined by the Byzantines as an anchor symbolizing Jesus' mission on the Sea of Galilee.⁸⁰

The aforementioned building work at Capernaum exemplifies how after several decades of Byzantine rule, a surge of interest in pilgrimage travel, and the increase in Christian residents in the country, propelled church construction work in Galilee, and beyond it. A large basilica with striking mosaic floors was constructed at Taghba, and excavators have identified a cathedral at Susita-Hippos, as well as a monastery at Kursi. Western Galilee, in later phases of the Byzantine period, was deluged by church construction—Aviam and others excavated 140 Byzantine sites in this area, and found evidence for churches at fifty-one of them.⁸¹ This archaeological work bears witness to a major transformation in Galilee's landscape in the stretch running between the Tannaitic era and the Islamic conquest. Up to the fourth century, archeological evidence of Christianity in Galilee is (as mentioned) lacking—excavation work proves that over the next 350 years, it turned into a Christian region.

WORLDS COLLIDE: THE ROAD TO YARMUK, 636

Christianity and Islam were set on a collision course from year one of Islamic civilization, or 622 CE according to the West's calendar. In less than a generation, in 636 CE, these two religious forces crashed in one of history's most decisive battles, fought just east of the Sea of Galilee, in an area around the Yarmuk River which is, today, a disputed zone between Galilee, the Golan Heights and Syria, and is monitored by the United Nations.

Three times Muslim armies fought in Galilee, or on its edge, in battles of formidable import wherein a different outcome would have changed the religious, political, and cultural character of Galilee, Palestine as whole, and the region we know as the Middle East. Worlds collided in these battles. All three outcomes ushered in, or ratified, Muslim control of the region. In all three clashes, the victory of Muslim armies can, ultimately, be explained only by reference to the inspirational power of faith in the Prophet Muhammad and in Islam, but there was a plethora of battlefield calculations and maneuvers that have absolutely nothing to do with conventional or stereotypical explanations about nomadic ferocity, the use of stirrups, and so on. Each battle—Yarmuk 636 CE, Hattin 1187 CE, Ayn Jalut 1260 CE—could quite easily have yielded different results, meaning that Christian Crusaders, Mongols, or some amalgamated configuration featuring one of these elements, could have been in charge of Galilee, and the Middle East (or a significant part thereof), when Zionist farm pioneers returned to the region at the end of the nineteenth century, to reestablish Jewish presence in it, in a campaign for the restoration of statehood sovereignty after a lapse of 1,900 years, since Josephus cringed in the cave at Jotapata and looked out for number one.

Of course, Islam's sacred devotions apply preeminently to Mecca. But had the religion remained confined predominately to the Hejaz, Islam would have come to be thought of as a monotheistic oddity, as a religious curiosity consigned to the sort of quizzical acceptance American Protestants eventually accorded to Mormonism, or that which American Jews assign to Reconstructionism. As its caliphs, theologians and publicists grasped after the mid-seventh century, Islamic presence or control in the Holy Land made the religion a major force in monotheism (more precisely, from their perspective, the religion's splendid building works on Haram esh-Sharif, the Temple Mount, validated and symbolized its status as the perfected version of the significant but flawed monotheistic prophecies of Judaism and Christianity). From a historical perspective, the Galilee area is where Islam fought for, and won, this status as monotheism's third great factor. Had its sword failed at Yarmuk, at the Horns of Hattin, or at Ma'ayan Harod, Byzantine Christians, Crusader Christians, or Mongol warriors might have consigned Islam to a different fate, perhaps as a second-class schism capable of thriving only on the Arabian Peninsula. Reinforcing its status as the region where monotheism multiplied, these three battles constitute another incalculably momentous aspect of Galilee history.

In 622 CE, after months of dealing with worrisome sociopolitical circumstances, Muhammad sent his followers to Yathrib, an oasis town 250 miles north of Mecca, where some locals had been won over to his prophetic message. This *hijra* to Yathrib (renamed Medina, the prophet's city) transformed his small, oppressed group into an "autonomous religio-political community of believers that dominated the oasis of Medina." The year 622 CE thus marks "the beginning of Islam's long life as a political force, a fact symbolized by the selection of that year to serve as the first year of the Islamic era."[82]

The same year, Byzantine's emperor Heraclius launched his grand campaign to reconquer the Middle East. Born about five years after the Islamic prophet,[83] Heraclius was Armenian in descent, and the son of a Byzantine general who had considerable experience fighting the Christian empire's many enemies, including the Persians. Around 600 CE, the father, Heraclius the Elder, became a Byzantine governor-general ("exarch") in North Africa, based in Carthage. The son, who, as an adult, gained a reputation as a learned monarch, grew up bilingual, speaking Armenian and Greek (he never knew Latin), and apparently benefited from the instruction of learned tutors in Armenia; but the formative period in his life was the decade in Africa, when Heraclius was between the ages of twenty-five to thirty-five, and spent his time hunting lions and boar, and soaking up military knowledge from his father. The Byzantines had dotted the North African coast with churches, and they were engaged in relatively prosperous cultivation and trade of olives and grain. Up to this point, 610 CE, Heraclius had no known encounters with Jews.

The turning point in his young life occurred in this period, after his father declared open rebellion against Byzantine emperor Phokas, who was unpopular and considered a usurper. This was a high-stakes showdown since its loser, or losers, would endure incredibly excruciating torture and mutilation. As became one of trademarks, Heraclius the Younger forged secret agreements which undermined his enemy's seemingly advantageous position—in this episode, he made alliances with ranking Byzantines in Egypt (ironically, later in his career, Heraclius chronically neglected the Egyptian flank in his maneuvering, and this was costly to him). After sailing from

Carthage to Constantinople (his precise route remains unknown), Heraclius overcame Phokas, and ordered that his rival be skinned and mutilated, with various impaled parts put on public display. The father was not a factor in this overthrow sequence, and so at age thirty-five, Heraclius became Byzantine emperor. He quickly won a strong following, partly because he wisely adjudicated various social disputes in Constantinople; but he also embarked on an unhappy course in family affairs (his first wife, Eudokia, died young, of epilepsy; Heraclius later, probably in the fateful year 622 CE, became involved in a controversial marriage to a niece, Martina, and incest-related illness then plagued his family).

From the start, the emperor's main challenge was posed by the Persians. Perhaps sensing that the palace overthrow had weakened the Byzantines, Sassanian armies, loyal to the ruler Khusrau II, crossed the Euphrates in 610 CE, and marauded on the Anatolian Plateau. The Persians also spread disinformation about the capture of various Byzantine notables. Relying on his key general, Shahrbaraz, King Khusrau II launched an invasion in Syria. Mobilizing against this Persian threat, Heraclius solidified his dynastic status (in 613 CE, he had his son, Heraclius Constantine, crowned with imperial designation), and, still more significantly, decided to become a fighting emperor.

This was a major, courageous innovation. Heraclius was the first Byzantine ruler, in generations, to lead personally his armies on the battlefield.[84] Quite clearly, points of reference in this adopted role as a fighting monarch were Hebraic—this is illustrated in the richly ornate, silver "David Plates," found in Lampousa, Cyprus, which, in depiction of key phases of the struggle against the Persians, dress-up Heraclius as David overcoming Goliath, and also depict his Byzantine soldiers as Israelite warriors.[85] As it turned out, Heraclius' initial preparations for the struggle against the Sassanid menace were for naught. In spring 613 CE, Heraclius and his cousin Niketas were devastatingly defeated by the Persians, and the Byzantines lost Antioch, the cradle of Christianity's early growth. Heraclius' empire was effectively severed in half, with communications blocked between Constantinople and Byzantine Anatolia, on the one hand, and Byzantine reaches of Syria, Palestine, and Egypt, on the other hand.[86]

The Persian attack on Jerusalem was launched from Damascus, and the Sassanid armies probably moved through Tiberias and Sepphoris, before moving southward from Caesarea. Scholars assume that the Galilean Jews, alienated and embittered by Byzantine rule, welcomed the Persians, or at most, offered token resistance to them.[87] Going father than this interpretation, Avi-Yonah suggests that the Persian assault on Byzantium raised messianic hopes among Jews.[88] Jews, he reasons, generally preferred Persian imperial power because, in contrast to the Byzantine situation, it was not based on religious ideology, and they also certainly remembered how the first Israelite return to Zion had been sponsored by Persia's first kings, Cyrus and Darius I.[89] A tenth-century Christian historian, Eutychius, the Melkite patriarch of Alexandria who wrote in Arabic, claims that Jews of Tiberias, Nazareth, and other Galilean areas teamed up with the Persian forces.[90]

As to what happened when Shahrbazaz's troops reached Jerusalem, in spring 614 CE, there are a number of reports—these were composed by an Armenian historian, Sebaeus, by Eutychius, and by a monk called Strategius, who was an eyewitness to the events. The siege lasted twenty days, its breakthrough occurring when the Persians dug a hole under a wall in the city's northeast area, today's Herod's Gate. The Persians first destroyed churches outside the city's walls, and then, for three days at the end of this attack, they killed and plundered inside the city. Eutychius insists that Jews joined in the savagery: when they reached Jerusalem, he writes, Galilean Jews gave "a hand to the Persians by destroying churches and killing Christians."[91] Avi-Yonah assumes that this atrocity occurred, writing about it in a defensively apologetic vein: "No man or nation should be condemned because they were unable to rise above the common morality of [the seventh century]."[92] In his dissertation, Schick carefully compared Eutychius' account to others Christian chroniclers' reports about Jerusalem's capture by the Persians, and concluded these "Christian literary sources are hardly free from polemical distortions."[93] The leader of Jewish activities in Jerusalem in ensuing months is known only by a symbolic name, Nehemiah, and the assumption is that Jews briefly resumed Temple sacrifices in the city, for the third time, the prior efforts transpiring during the Bar Kochba rebellion and during Julian's brief de-Christianizing tenure.[94]

For our purposes, it bears mention that the upheaval in the country caused by the Persian invasion and by the Byzantine setbacks stirred ephemeral yet revealing Jewish activities in the Galilee area. Since the Persians were strong cavalrymen but weak seamen, they assigned to Jews the task of seizing harbors along the Phoenician coast. Jewish fighters were successful in Acre (then Ptolemais), wresting control of the city with the help of some of its own Jewish residents. A more protracted, and ultimately unsuccessful, Jewish assault was launched further north, in today's Lebanon, against Tyre. Eutychius' report of what happened in Tyre could hardly be more dramatic. The harbor town's four thousand Jews, he relays, sent incendiary letters to brethren in Tiberias and other locales in Galilee, along with Jerusalem, Cyprus, and Damascus, begging them to come to Tyre at Easter, and exterminate its Christians. Twenty thousand Jews answered this call. Meantime, the city's gentiles had intelligence of this development, and so they imprisoned the Jews, locking them in chains. On Easter night, the invading Jews "demolished every church located outside the walls of Tyre," but Tyre inhabitants beheaded one hundred Jewish prisoners for each decimated church (all told, this resulted in twenty destroyed churches and two thousand decapitated Tyrean Jews). In the end, the invading Jews were worn out, and tried to flee; many were chased down and slaughtered by Tyre's gentiles.[95] This Tyre siege apparently occurred in summer 617 CE—designating this date is important, because it allows us to measure the period, around three years, when Jews controlled Jerusalem, before the Persians backtracked and reneged their alliance with them.[96] Pertaining to this period, there is suggestive, but not altogether conclusive, archeological evidence of ruined churches on the coast hugging Galilee, from Acre up to Tyre.[97]

In 614 CE, the time of Byzantine Jerusalem's fall and its Sassanid capture, Muhammad had been publicly preaching in Mecca for just several months. What was to become Islam had at the time only a following of "many people of lower stature in Mecca—clients, freed slaves and individuals of lesser clans of Quraysh."[98] Heraclius, for his part, was utterly despondent. Years later, he would open the most outstanding chapter of his uneven career, but this could not have been foreseen in a survey of his responses at the moment. Compounding the loss of Jerusalem, a crushing spiritual blow for Byzantium, the empire had lost a huge portion of its population, and a concomitant, large measure of tax revenue.[99] Shahrbaraz, the driving force behind the Persian conquest in Palestine, proceeded quickly and vanquished Egypt; this quashed Byzantine hopes of salvaging holy relics which had been whisked out of Jerusalem, and the humiliating loss of these sacred items rankled. Heraclius, it appears, just wanted to go home—which, for him, meant North Africa. His plan was to rule what was left of the empire from there, but it never actualized because a ship bearing loads of his treasures sank at sea, before reaching Africa, and because the Patriarch of Constantinople, Sergios, pressured him not to leave the city.[100] Heraclius tried a few economic reforms, such as devaluing currency by printing a new coin, but mostly he was paralyzed by uncertainty and depression. The seven-year period, 614–621 CE, was the only one in his long reign when he went nowhere, not finding cause to crusade for his empire and the Cross.[101] The Byzantine Balkan frontier was in upheaval, and Avars joined Heraclius' long roster of antagonists. Plague ravaged his empire in this period, and subjects kept complaining about nightmarish apparitions floating from Carthage to Constantinople.

In 622 CE, when, at last, Heraclius headed eastward, apparently toward Pontos, in a campaign for restitution against Shahrbaraz, he invoked King David in motivational speeches to his troops. Their Persian enemies, the Byzantine emperor told them, were direct descendants "of the ones about whom David divinely spoke out, saying 'blessed is he who strikes down the sons of Persia and smashes them against the rocks.'"[102] Early in this campaign, the Byzantine troops crushed some small parties of Arabs who were allied with the Persians—this displayed sound reconnaissance work and also the fact that the Byzantines were making productive strategic alliances on the ground.

In this connection, Ghassanid Arabs make their debut in the chronicle of how civilizational worlds collided on the edge of Galilee, a few decades into the seventh century. Of Arab groups with roots in Galilee and the Golan Heights, the Banu Ghassan (a federation of clans) is distinctive due to the longevity and import of its alliance with the Byzantines, as a bulwark against encroachment of Persians and then, more fatefully, Muslim soldiers, and also for its uncompromising resistance to Islam.[103] Though Ghassanids were Christians, the Byzantines never really overcame their prejudicial view of them as "wild, untamed beasts," and as the "Old Testament 'hosts of Midian.'"[104] Yet, at key junctures, they relied on their military alliance with the Ghassanids. While their clans spread around northern Palestine, the Ghassanids kept their effective capital at Jabiya, a town on the Golan Plateau accessed by a Roman road whose hilltop view of outlying areas is so penetrating that the site, in our era, has served as a key observation post for the Syrian army. Their tribal leader, Jabala b. al-Ayham, was called condescendingly *Strategos Parembolon* (commander of nomadic auxiliaries) by the Byzantines, but he retained a king-like aura in Galilee and elsewhere. He was destined to fight with the Byzantines against the Persians and the Muslims for a quarter century.[105]

In summer 626 CE, the Byzantines managed to withstand a Persian assault on Constantinople, led by Shahrbaraz, who was, for the last time, loyally following orders from Khusrau II. Constantinople's successful resistance against the Persians, who were assisted by Avars and Slavs, was a turning point, in many respects. Heraclius, who in phases of the struggle against the Persians spent years in the field, away from the Byzantine capital, forged strategic alliances with disaffected groups and leaders, starting with Kok Turks. "Heraclius was winning victories through diplomacy more than sheer military might," remarks his biographer. "Or, as his contemporaries may have put it, he was winning through cunning."[106] The diplomatic tipping point was offered by the disaffected Persian general, Shahrbaraz. The failure of the siege on Constantinople had driven a wedge between Khusrau and Shahrbaraz, and the Byzantines exploited it. The exact details in the sequence which enabled Heraclius to neutralize Persian forces commanded by Shahrbaraz have never been uncovered, but a key link in the chain seems to have been a letter intercepted by the Byzantines, perhaps in Galatia, and craftily shown to the beleaguered Persian general—his king reportedly outlined Shahrbaraz's ouster in this message.[107] Whatever caused the disarming of key units in his enemy's army, between 624 and 627 CE, Heraclius had now set the stage for his epochal conquest of Persia. He had the Kok Turks with him, excellent intelligence regarding roads and circumstances in the Sassanid Empire, and an alliance, of sorts, with Shahrbaraz.[108]

In Palestine, the annulment of Persian conquests, and the subsequent replacement of Sassanid power by Heraclius' Byzantine soldiers, administrators, and clerics had sweeping effect. From the Jewish standpoint, it is hard to underestimate the ramifications of Persia's unreliability as an ally. That the Roman emperor Julian would be able to effect Jewish restoration in Jerusalem for no longer than a few months appears (it will be recalled) to have been anticipated by Jewish leaders in Tiberias, and elsewhere. Nobody, however, seems to have expected the mighty Persian empire to withdraw its patronage of Jews in Jerusalem and the country after a fleeting period of time, just a year longer than Julian's quixotic effort. The Persians betrayed the Jews even before Heraclius' soldiers reconquered Jerusalem, and this prompted a potpourri of speculation. Why did Khusrau decide to expel Jews from Jerusalem and let it be rebuilt it as a Christian city? Some commentators guessed that Jews had promised to fetch for the Persians secret treasures which Christians kept buried under the church of the Holy Sepulchre—when they came up empty-handed, the Persians decided to break with the Jews.[109]

Whatever caused the fracture, the Persian betrayal left the Jews utterly vulnerable in their ancestral homeland. Nobody knew it at the time, but the Persian-Byzantine rivalry we have reviewed utterly exhausted *both* empires, leaving them vulnerable to Islamic forces which, within a decade, rose up, with sufficient intent and power to conquer many lands in the Middle East, Palestine included. Islam accorded Jews status as People of the Book, but innumerable political, social, and religious reasons, not the least of them being the Prophet Muhammad's confrontations with many of Medina's Jews,[110] precluded the potential of a real power alliance in Palestine between these two groups. The Persians were gone, and the inimical antagonism between Jews and Byzantine power has been amply demonstrated here. The Jews, in short, had no friends left within Palestine's field of vision, and they constituted no more than 15 percent of the population of the country. It was *this* sequence of events, and categorically not the squashing of the Bar Kochba revolt half a millennium earlier, which propelled Jews into exile. As the foremost scholar of this 500 year stretch in Jewish history put it, not thinking of the events of 1948, many years into the future: "The deception which the Jews suffered in their alliance with the Persians, marks the end of the political history of Judaism in Palestine."[111] At the start of this half millennium, Galilee served as refuge sanctuary for the Jews' sociopolitical revival, and for the Tannaitic reformatting of Judaism, from a Temple cult to a rabbinical religion. Now Galilee was where Christianity lost its political foothold in the Middle East for 350 years, until the Crusades. And now Galilee was the gateway through which Islam began its non-interrupted status as monotheism's paramount power in the region as a whole. Such is the meaning of Yarmuk.

Events proceeded at a rapid clip. In 627–628 CE, Heraclius reached the walls of Ctesiphon, Persia's capital, capping a remarkable comeback conquest. From there, in spring 629 CE, he headed, in triumph, for Palestine. For the Jews, it was not completely delusional to hope for a measure of clemency from the Byzantine emperor. Virtually contemporaneous with this Byzantine reconquest of the Holy Land, the Persians evacuated Edessa. Heraclius' brother Theodor entered the city and his men promptly took up the plunder and murder of Jews. One escaped, found Heraclius in Upper Mesopotamia, and convinced the emperor to spare Edessa's surviving Jews.[112] With this encouraging precedent in mind, Jews in Galilee begged for an audience with Heraclius. The emperor graciously received them in Tiberias, and, thrillingly, issued pardons to the Jews for past offenses against Byzantium, even taking an imperial oath to vouchsafe this promise of mercy. That Jews at this moment were being swept out of their wits, by fear and elation, is illustrated by the exploits of the wealthy Tiberias Jew, Benjamin, who hosted this hope-stirring meeting. Benjamin accompanied Heraclius on the journey to Jerusalem, and decided, en route, to convert to Christianity. His baptism apparently demoralized the country's Jews.[113] In Jerusalem, the Jews were double-crossed by Christians, not excluding Heraclius. Priests and monks in the city explained to the emperor that Jews, more than Persians, had been responsible for the murders of their colleagues. Heraclius did not disbelieve them, but he felt bound by the oath he had taken in Tiberias. To assuage his guilt, the priests arranged a special penitential fast.[114] This salved the emperor's conscience. Heraclius expelled Jews from Jerusalem, ordering them to keep three miles from the city. Christians put Jews on trial and executed them on charges of murder and destruction of churches in Jerusalem and Galilee; other Jews fled. Some who remained under Byzantine jurisdiction circumvented Heraclius' ban on public worship by singing their prayers in the form of *piyyutim* hymns. Heraclius' hardening, in fact, is what gave birth to this distinctive form of Jewish liturgical poetry.[115] Meantime, what the Byzantines regarded as the authentic Cross was delivered to Heraclius in a sealed container, so he became credited as its restorer in Jerusalem. Modestos, then or later the Patriarch of Jerusalem, verified that it had not been desecrated by the Persians.[116]

What happened in the heart and mind of this remarkable Byzantine emperor? Some scholars speculate that Heraclius' unpredictable behavior in the last phase of his career, when he unexpectedly faced a mortal challenge from Islam, can be attributed to psychological disorder. "He may have suffered from Post-Traumatic Stress Syndrome due to his protracted exposure to military combat and related strains," writes Walter Kaegi, in all earnestness.[117] A poignant example of Heraclius' late erratic tendencies, the order he issued in 632 CE for the forcible baptism of Byzantine Jews, can be explained in more pedestrian, and perhaps more persuasive, terms. The 630 CE triumphant visit to Jerusalem changed Heraclius. The episode with Benjamin, among other events, could have convinced the emperor about the feasibility of mass conversion of Jews. If this is the case, then, at the start and at the finish of Palestine's Byzantine era, two Jewish apostates from Tiberias, Joseph and Benjamin, exerted influence on the crucial issue of Christianity's relations with Jews, one helping to enact Constantine's vision of a Holy Land studded with shrines and pilgrimage sites, the other inadvertently prodding Heraclius' ill-fated conversion order, the Byzantine empire's contribution to a roster of Christian schemes for the annihilation of Judaism and Jews. Heraclius' "harsh and unrealistic and ineffective" conversion order also betokens confusion stirred in this period by Islam's militant advance—when Arab raiding gained notice among Byzantine elites, various theories linked Jews to this new, unknown menacing Arab phenomenon.[118] Whatever the reason for breakdowns in his judgment, the aging Heraclius was evidently not at his fittest precisely when his empire faced its most dire challenge, posed by Muhammad's followers.

Meantime Islamic rule was consolidating on the Arabian Peninsula, and Muslim soldiers were poised to explode out of it. Muhammad died in 632 CE, plunging his followers in a crisis over the nature of succession, one whose ripples continue to be felt today. At the time, his followers forged a solution by selecting Muhammad's father-in-law, Abu Bakr, as supreme representative, *caliph*, of the faith. The new caliph had staunch supporters in Mecca, Medina, and Taif, and among nomadic groups which roamed between these towns, but Arabia was filled with groups which challenged Muhammad's succession in the new caliphate on various levels, such as tax revolts, or by sponsoring local prophets. This challenge is known as *Ridda*, the apostasy, and Abu Bakr's soldiers needed two years to stifle it and control the peninsula. In 634 CE, Islam was ready to move onward.[119]

In the early years of his prophetic activity, Muhammad had not thought of Christians as enemies. The two religions became antagonists in 629 CE, when the prophet's followers clashed at Mu'ta (in today's Jordan) with Arab tribesmen who were loyal to the Byzantines. Several months later, the Muslims forged a peace agreement with Jordanian tribes at Aila (Akaba, today). Heraclius, who was at this time basking in triumph in Jerusalem, could not really have known about this Islamic encroachment. The Byzantine empire's defense lines ran along the Gaza Strip and the Dead Sea, and left areas in the south outside of its jurisdiction. Heraclius concentrated his military forces in northern Syria, to deter his traditional nemesis, the Persians.[120] His tools of imperial power were not in the right place at the right time, and he was distracted by wondrous results of the triumph over the Persians, such as the restoration of the Cross.

Many explanations have been proffered in analyses of how and why Islam so rapidly became a formidable military force, much to the detriment of Byzantine Christianity, and many facets of this long-standing conundrum need not occupy us here.[121] On a technological level, it suffices to mention that the mobility and dexterity of armed forces were not, in this period, boosted by the stirrup. Instead, in the steppes and the desert, the key innovation was the placement of a North Arabian type of saddle atop a camel's hump—the older (South Arabian) type of saddle left the camel useless in warfare.[122] On a leadership level, the astounding wave of Islamic conquests outside of Arabia occurred during the term of the second caliph, Umar ibn al-Khattab (634–644 CE).[123] A respected, albeit not beloved, leader, Umar kept his autocratic character wrapped under an outward veneer of austere humility. He organized Islam's army with a regular *Diwan* roster of soldiers and payments, and established a number of military base locales (some of which became major cities).[124]

The second caliph was bolstered by a capable cadre of officers, some of whom were newcomers to Islam after having originally opposed Muhammad. Foremost among them was Khalid ibn al-Walid, one of the more remarkable characters who gathered for the fight at Yarmuk, who is known by his nom de guerre, the Sword of God. A brutal fighter, Khalid cut an effectively pragmatic figure off the battlefield—he seems to have been an innovator who allowed vanquished enemies to surrender and endure by paying the *jizyah* tax, and then used the revenue to pay his own soldiers (the policy proved controversial, as we will see). Khalid had an ingenious knack for solving logistics and supply problems, such as water conveyance. On his legendary march in the desert from Iraq to Syria, his men filled their camels to the gills with water, and later slaughtered one of them so as to lap out the water from its belly.[125]

Information in the sources allows us to picture the sort of weaponry which these two armies, Christian and Muslim, brought to Yarmuk. Byzantine cavalrymen were armed with a long sword, called a *spathion*, modeled after Avar or Persian weaponry. They used a wooden lance (*kontarion*) and kept forty arrows in a quiver attached to a saddle, or a belt. Infantry troops carried small shields, bows on their backs and quivers slung over shoulders, and sometimes also a device (*solenarion*) used to shoot short darts. For weaponry, Muslim armies tapped armories and resource sources that had been active in pre-Islamic days, in Syria, Armenia, Yemen, and Iraq (armor came from Iraq, whereas Yemen supplied leather products). Muslim soldiers wore egg-shaped (*baidah*) helmets which were not dissimilar to ones worn by Byzantine foes. As body armor, Muslim fighters wore a *dir*, a hauberk comprised of small metal rings. They used well-oiled leather shields and hurled spears that were two and a half meters long. Their most valued weapon was the sword—some Arab warriors carried two.[126]

The first war between Christianity and Islam began on Easter, 634 CE, when Khalid ibn al-Walid's force defeated a local force in the Ghassanid federation in the Damascus area. Khalid's force, comprised only of some 600–700 men, had marched through the desert and managed to enter Syria behind Heraclius' Byzantine line of defense; these infantry camel-riders won renown in Islamic history. In summer 634 CE, the two armies engaged a major battle, known as Ajnadayn, west of the Ella Valley's Beit Natif—the Byzantines were routed, though most of their soldiers managed to flee to walled-off cities. Islamic soldiers pressed on, capturing nearby Bethlehem, prompting the Patriarch of Jerusalem, Sophronius, to bewail about "the sword of Saracens . . . beastly and barbarous, and filled with every diabolic savagery." According to legends which circulated about this battle, the Byzantines were spooked from the start, when the Muslims sent out the star warrior in their commando elite ("champions"), Zarrar ibn al Azwar, to fend off a preliminary volley of Byzantine stones and arrows—normally, Zarrar fought unarmored (his nom de guerre was "the Naked Warrior"), but in this case he came out with a helmet, and wielded an elephant-hide shield stripped from a slain Byzantine soldier. Hollering about how he was the scourge of white Romans, Zarrar reportedly killed several counterpart Byzantine commando champions, including the governor of Tiberias.[127]

In truth, not the ferocious Zarrar, but rather Byzantine overconfidence and faulty tactics settled outcomes at Ajnadayn, the specific problem being Byzantine incompetence in open field warfare, compared to the more dexterous Muslim raiders. Victorious Islamic officers ostentatiously claimed spoils. Amr ibn al As, who, with Khalid, commanded Islam's army, took hold of a large estate at nearby Beit Gibrin. Heraclius, in Jerusalem, was apprised of the setback, and showed some anger by relieving his brother, Theodore, of command, and sending him, in disgrace, to Constantinople. Yet, in this late, heady phase of his career, the emperor was slow to grasp the strategic implications of what happened just fifteen miles southwest of the holy city. Heraclius was at the time focused on sponsoring the rebuilding of Christian buildings and communities, after Persian depredation.[128]

The emperor's wake-up call happened in following months, as Islamic forces, often led by the Muslim convert Shurahbil ibn Hasana, throttled Byzantine antagonists on a march northward in Palestine, claiming Beit Sha'an (then Scythopolis) in the "Battle of the Mud," fought in January 635 CE, and then conquering Tiberias. After a skirmish on the "Golden Meadow" (Marj al Suffar), west of the Ghassanid base at Jabiya, Khalid, Zarrar, Shurahbil, and their men proceeded on to Damascus, capturing the city, after a six-month siege, in September 635 CE.[129] This, of course, left Heraclius no choice. In August 636 CE, the Byzantines mobilized for a massive attack on Islam's army.

What would have happened in the Galilean frontier in summer 636 CE had Heraclius been a decade younger, had he not been worn out by the traumatic stress of warfare against the Persians, and had he not been lulled into a false cocoon of invincibility by pious admirers and church sycophants? Would the Crusades have happened 350 years later? If not, how, in this counter-history universe, would the tenacious durability of Byzantine power have affected how we today view power balances (e.g., in Samuel Huntington's ominous-sounding division between the "west and the rest")? How would it have affected the development of military power, through the modern period? And how would it have affected the course of relations between the monotheistic faiths, specifically the futures of anti-Arab "Orientalism" and of anti-Semitism?

Moving beyond this realm of counterfactual speculation, we rub against the classic riddle of personality versus culture in history. Heraclius' weakening impacted the outcome at Yarmuk, of course, but a more forceful emperor who deployed Heraclius' proven, winning tactic of "cunning," of diplomatic maneuvering prior to an entry onto a battlefield, might well *not* have tipped the balance in this fateful stretch of the Galilee-Golan Heights, in 636 CE. Though they shared the same point of origins in monotheism, Islamic culture and Byzantine Christian culture were, at this moment, worlds apart. In contrast, and despite the manifest contrast between Sassanid Zoroastrianism and Christianity, lines of communication between the Persians and the Byzantines had been readily exploited by Heraclius, as in the example of his alliance with Shahrbaraz (whose son Niketas fought for the Byzantines at Yarmuk). From the Christian standpoint, in a frustrating matrix of events in this battle at Yarmuk, perhaps the most poignant development was the inability of the Byzantine generals to negotiate any sort of arrangement before or during the fighting with the Muslims, particularly on the fifth day when troops subordinate to the main Byzantine commander, Vahan (an Armenian), were pinned between the Ruqqad and Yarmuk gorges.[130] Malice and mistrust between the two armies neutralized the Byzantines' strongest weapon. Diplomatic talent, precisely what Heraclius' biographer identifies as his strongest asset—"Heraclius was winning victories through diplomacy more than sheer military might"—applied to an old Middle East, where the Greco-Roman fascination with the power of persuasion was subsumed within models of masculinity and military power. Witness the way Josephus, at least on a personal level, talked his way out of the Jewish catastrophe at Jotapata. In this new Galilee of war between the monotheistic faiths, the sword parried away anyone's smooth-talking. No Christian, not even Heraclius, could talk his way out of the catastrophe at Yarmuk.

The Byzantines mobilized a force *four* times larger than their Muslim antagonists at Yarmuk. The army commanded by Vahan had perhaps 20,000 troops. Because of the rugged, hilly terrain in the Yarmuk gorge, Wadi Ruqqad and beyond, the Byzantine line of attack stretched out, and the six-day battle often had the appearance of "a series of almost separate battles between divisions."[131] The Byzantine force was a conglomerate which included Christianized tribes, such as the Ghassan federation (which remained staunchly loyal), and other clans (Lakham, Judham, Bal-Qayn, Bali, and Amila) of wavering fidelity, and there is evidence that indiscipline among these groups, compounded by the fact that the vastly outnumbered Muslim enemy was being reinforced by Yemeni recruits, is what finally prompted Vahan to attack, in mid-August, after three months of watchful waiting in Galilee and the Golan.[132]

The Byzantines had selected a superb base of operations, at Yaqusah, a day and a half's march from Damascus, nestled within the Yarmuk and Ruqqad valleys to the southeast, and shielded by the slopes of the Golan Heights in the northwest (today, this Quenitra area, east of the Sea of Galilee, belongs to the buffer zone, patrolled by the United Nations, as designated by negotiations subsequent to Israel's 1967 and 1973 wars; three hundred years before the Yarmuk battle, Paul's conversion on the Road to Damascus occurred in the vicinity). The Byzantine fighters had good access to the main Golan Plateau via a four kilometer wide isthmus.

After one day of dueling between "champions" from the two sides, the Byzantines attacked, as a coordinated mass, at dawn of the second day, catching the Muslim enemies during their morning prayers. From their position, perhaps in a stretch between Saham al Jawlan and Tal al Jabiya, many Muslim cavalrymen and infantry tried to pull away. According to legend, and more or less verified by modern scholarship on the battle, stalwart Muslim women came out of tents, and stopped their husbands and comrades from retreating. The most colorful such incident, transpiring on the second day or perhaps fourth day of the fighting, featured a tough, corpulent fifty-year-old woman named Hind bint Utba, who shamed her elderly husband, Abu Sufyan (a former opponent of Muhammad, and an experienced warrior horseman), and his fellow Muslims, out of retreat. "If you attack, we will embrace you; and if you retreat, we will forsake you," sang the woman, prodding her seventy-three-year-old husband back into battle, with a tent pole; these, incidentally, were the parents of the founder and first caliph of the Umayyad dynasty, Mu'awiyah, about whom we will soon have more to say.[133] The Byzantines remained on the attack on the third day; at least apocryphally, some Muslim fighters were pinned between the Byzantine enemy, and their own ferocious women. "It is easier to fight the Rumi [the Christians] than our wives," exclaimed one of them, returning to the battlefield.

Military scholars agree that tides turned in this near week-long, epochal, struggle because of a flanking ambush pulled off by Khalid ibn al-Walid, though there is disagreement whether this occurred on the fourth or final day of the fighting.[134] Whatever the day, this ambush succeeded largely because the Byzantine units were spread too far apart, always at the risk of detachment, as Khalid seems to have noticed. His maneuver forced Byzantine cavalry, largely comprised of Christian Arabs auxiliaries from the Lakham and Judham clans, to flee north.

This is when Zarrar and other commandos swooped in, chasing the Byzantines on their flight to Ayn Dakhar. The key strategic point in this area is a bridge over Wadi Ruqqad—Zarrar easily captured it.[135] Byzantine soldiers in the field were thus trapped, cut off from their army's base at Yaqusah. With just a few variations of detail, the gruesome horror which now awaited these eastern Christians would be recapitulated in the travail suffered by their western counterparts, the Crusaders, at Hattin, in 1187.

Zarrar seems to have stormed out to Yaqusah, 18 kilometers away, right after he captured the bridge. It is doubtful that the Byzantine defense of this main base lasted very long. On the final day of Yarmuk, the entire Muslim army went on the offensive, aiming mostly at enemy soldiers who remained around the bridge. Helpless on a spur between the Ruqqad and Yarmuk, the Christian soldiers were slaughtered. Some tumbled to their death on slopes and cliffs, as a grisly symbol of how Byzantine rule in Palestine ended, on this gateway to Galilee, where Christianity began.[136]

Byzantine losses over the week at Yarmuk were costly, whereas relatively few Muslims perished. As to the Byzantine commanders: Vahan was either killed or became a monk in Sinai; Niketas fled to Emesa, and tried to convert to Islam, but was rejected; the Ghassanid leader, Jabala, escaped, entered into negotiations with the Muslim victors but remained loyal to his Christian identity, eventually resettling with his comrades in central Anatolia (at the start of the ninth century, one of his heirs, Nicephorus, became a Byzantine emperor).[137] In an ironic twist, the Muslim hero of Yarmuk, Khalid ibn al-Walid, was stripped of his army rank by the Caliph Umar, right after the historic Islamic triumph. Punctilious about how the spoils of war were to be divided in his Caliphate, Umar mistrusted Khalid.[138] For his part, Heraclius sounded sadly reconciled, and philosophical. He is said to have reflected: "Peace be with you, Syria: what a beautiful land you will be for the enemy."[139] Three hundred years earlier, at Jotapata, at the conclusion of another decisive Galilee battle, Josephus had more or less said the same thing, speaking from the Jewish vantage point.

"Here, on the Yarmuk, was fought the great battle between the Muslims and the Greeks in the Caliph Abu Bakr's days," wrote Yaqut al-Hawami, a prominent Islamic medieval geographer renowned for his encyclopedic *Mu'jam ul-Buldan*. Writing some 600 years after the battle, Yaqut's depiction reflects how Yarmuk was remembered in Islamic culture: "The field of battle was a wadi called *Al Wakusah* [the place of breaking-up].... The Muslims lay encamped on the Yarmuk and then marched to make their raid against the Greeks. They fell on the idolaters and Khalid [ibn al-Walid] hastened on the people to the slaughter," Yaqut recorded. The enemy was pursued until it came to a high place, over a ravine, he explained. The Greeks fell off the cliff, not having seen it, either because the day was misty, or perhaps because night had already fallen. "By estimate, 80,000 Greeks perished. This ravine has been called Al Wakusah from that day until now, because the Greek army was 'broken-up' there," wrote Yaqut.[140]

NOTES

1. See the bibliographic discussion in: Andrew Jacobs "Visible Ghosts and Invisible Demons," in Eric Meyers, *Galilee through the Centuries* (Winona Lake: Eisenbrauns, 1999), 361.
2. M. Avi-Yonah, *The Jews of Palestine: A Political History from the Bar Kokhba War to the Arab Conquest* (Oxford: Basil Blackwell, 1976), 20.
3. Ibid, 241.
4. Robert Schick, *The Christian Communities of Palestine from Byzantine to Islamic Rule* (Princeton: Darwin Press, 1995), 12–13.
5. Avi-Yonah, 90–102.
6. S. Safrai, "The Relations between the Roman Army and the Jews of Eretz Yisrael after the Destruction of the Second Temple," in Tel Aviv University, *Roman Frontier Studies 1967* (Tel Aviv, 1971), 224–230.
7. Ibid.
8. Avi-Yonah, 36.
9. Ibid, 93.
10. Ibid, 98–101.
11. Ibid, 101.
12. Ibid, 109. This point, and several similar details about challenges faced by the patriarchate in this period of socioeconomic hardship, can be found in Avissar's volume on Tiberias, 81–86.
13. Ibid, 122.
14. Ibid, 124.
15. Ibid.
16. Ibid, 24, 71. A Galilee stalwart, Eleazar declared "it is easier for a man to rear a legion on the olives of Galilee than one infant in the rest of the Land of Israel."
17. The two-dimensional and linear development connotations of this distinction between "acculturation" and "assimilation" are debatable, but they have inspired a wealth of scholarship, and have utility in Jewish history research. The distinction

was originally drawn in: Milton Gordon, *Assimilation in American Life* (New York: Oxford University Press, 1964).

18. Stuart Miller, "New Perspectives on the History of Sepphoris," in Myers, *Galilee through the Centuries*, 145–146.

19. Oded Avissar, *Sefer Tiveria* (Jerusalem: Keter, 1973), 84.

20. D. A. Friedman, *Rabbis of Ancient Times: Biographical Sketches of the Talmudic Period* (Indianapolis: Hollenbeck Press, 1921), 74–76.

21. Admiel Kosman, *Masekhet gevarim: Rav ve-hakatsav ve-od sipurim al gavriyut ahave ve-otentiyut be-sipur ha-agadah uva sipur ha-hasid* (Jerusalem: Keter, 2002), 34–51.

22. Ibid, 129–132.

23. Stephen Goranson, "Josephus of Tiberias Revisited," in Myers, *Galilee through the Centuries*, 336.

24. Avissar, 85–86.

25. Goranson, 336–338.

26. Ibid, 338.

27. Avissar, 86.

28. Eric Hobsbawn, Terence Ranger (eds.), *The Invention of Tradition* (Cambridge: Cambridge University Press, 1992).

29. Joan Taylor, *Christians and the Holy Places: The Myth of Jewish-Christian Origins* (Oxford: Clarendon Press, 1993), 288.

30. Information here taken from Taylor, 56–63.

31. The site's name, and its origins, are complicated, and there is no clear rule as to how it ought to be designated in scholarship. Mostly, we use "Sepphoris" in this book when the ancient city is in reference. See James Strange, Thomas R.W. Longstaff, Dennis Groh, *Excavations at Sepphoris*, vol. 1 (Leiden: Brill, 2006), 9–10.

32. Strange, *Excavations*.

33. Ibid, xv (preface).

34. Ibid, 9–35.

35. Rebecca Martin Nagy, Carol Meyers, Eric Meyers, Zeev Weiss (eds), *Sepphoris in Galilee* (Winona Lake: North Carolina Museum of Art, 1996).

36. Stuart Miller, "Hellenistic and Roman Sepphoris," in Nagy, 24.

37. Ibid.

38. Sean Freyne, "Christianity in Sepphoris and in Galilee," in Nagy, 71.

39. E.P. Sanders, *Jesus and Judaism* (Philadelphia: Fortress Press, 1985).

40. E.P. Sanders, "Jesus' Relation to Sepphoris," in Nagy, 75.

41. Ibid, 76.

42. Isaiah Gafni, "Daily Life in Galilee and Sepphoris," in Nagy, 56.

43. Peter Schafer's 2007 volume on the subject of Jesus and the Talmud commendably surveys a rather larger amount of earlier work on the topic. Though some of his argumentation is interpretatively speculative, Schafer's volume persuasively shows that Talmudic writers were quite engaged with, and often polemically scathing about, Jesus and Christianity. This author usually does not try to determine when Talmudic writers might have been talking about the "historical Jesus," or about his "real" followers, as opposed to when they might have reinvented these figures as

symbols, in line with third century, or later, realities in the Neo-Persian Empire; but in some cases, as noted below, he assumes, logically, that Tannaitic or Amoraic rabbis had encounters with Christian "minim" roughly similar to what was subsequently documented in the Talmud. Peter Schafer, *Jesus in the Talmud* (Princeton: Princeton University Press, 2007).

44. Reuven Kimelman, "*Birkat Ha-Minim* and the Lack of Evidence for an Anti-Christian Jewish Prayer in Late Antiquity," in Sanders, *Jewish and Christian*, 232.

45. See the bibliographic reference (footnote 4) in: Joshua Schwartz, Peter Tomson, "When Rabbi Eliezer was Arrested for Heresy," *Jewish Studies Internet Journal* 10 (2012): 147.

46. This follows the translation in: Reuven Kimelman, "Identifying Jews and Christians in Roman Syria-Palestine," in Myers, "Galilee through," 324. Language and details differ in various Talmudic descriptions of this incident, as described by Schwartz, Tomson, "When Rabbi."

47. Schwartz, Tomson, 180.

48. Kimelman, "Identifying," 324.

49. Ibid, 325.

50. See, for instance, the interesting interpretation in Schafer, 52–58. The author believes that the incident quite possibly "reflects some kind of historical reality."

51. Kimelman, "Identifying," 303.

52. Kimelman, "*Birkat*," 232.

53. Kimelman, "Identifying," 323.

54. Robert Bellah et al., *Habits of the Heart: Individualism and Commitment in American Life* (Berkeley: University of California Press, 1995).

55. "For the apostates let there be no hope./And let the arrogant government be speedily uprooted in our days./Let the nosrim and the minim be destroyed in a moment."

56. Kimelman, "Birkat," 244.

57. Ibid, 227.

58. Mordechai Aviam, "Christian Galilee in the Byzantine Period," in Myers, *Galilee*, 285–294.

59. Ibid, 298.

60. Stuart Miller, "The *Minnim* of Sepphoris Reconsidered," *Harvard Theological Review* 86, no. 4 (October 1993): 377–402.

61. Goranson, 340.

62. Taylor, 334.

63. Ibid, 335.

64. Ibid, 298.

65. Kimelman, "Birkat," 233.

66. David Myers, *Re-Inventing the Jewish Past: European Jewish Intellectuals and the Zionist Return to History* (New York: Oxford University Press, 1995).

67. Controversially, Constantine put off baptism until his deathbed.

68. Avi-Yonah, 164–165.

69. Blake Leyerle, "Pilgrims to the Land: "Early Christian Perceptions of the Galilee," in Myers, *Galilee through the Centuries*, 346–353.

70. Avi-Yonah, 174.

71. Ibid, 175. The three Jewish centers of the revolt, Tiberias, Sepphoris and Lydda, all had active textile manufacturers who were presumably hamstrung by the slavery ban.

72. Ibid, 179–181.

73. Ibid, 197.

74. Ibid, 220–221.

75. Ibid, 228.

76. Ibid.

77. Schick, 11.

78. Ibid.

79. Yizhar Hirschfeld, "The Anchor Church at the Summit of Mount Berenice Neat Tiberias" [Heb.], *Qadmoniot: A Journal for the Antiquities of Eretz Israel*, no. 3–4 (1993): 120–127.

80. Aviam, "Christian Galilee," 296.

81. Ibid, 288.

82. Fred Donner, "Muhammad and the Caliphate," in John Esposito, *The Oxford History of Islam* (New York: Oxford University Press, 1999), 9.

83. The biographical information in this section relies on: Walter Kaegi, *Heraclius: Emperor of Byzantium* (Cambridge: Cambridge University Press, 2003).

84. David Nicole, *Yarmuk 636 AD: The Muslim Conquest of Syria* (London: Osprey Military, 1994), 17.

85. Ibid, 19.

86. Kaegi, 77.

87. Schick, 21.

88. Salvation midrashim, prophesizing messianic events, evinced avid anticipation of a Byzantine defeat, but they seem to have been written a few years before the Persian invasion. Avi-Yonah, 261.

89. Avi-Yonah, 262.

90. Chapter 17 of the *Annals of Eutychius* of Alexandria, as translated and posted by Roger Pearse: https://www.roger-pearse.com/weblog/2016/03/17/the-annals-of-eutychius-of-alexandria-10th-c-ad-chapter-17-part-9-and-end/ Avi-Yonah (263) concurs with this report.

91. Annals, chapter 17.

92. Avi-Yonah, 266.

93. Schick, 26.

94. Avi-Yonah, 266.

95. Annals, chapter 17.

96. Avi-Yonah, 268.

97. Schick.

98. Donner, 8.

99. Kaegi, 87.

100. Ibid, 88.

101. Ibid, 100.

102. Ibid, 114.

103. Moshe Gil, *A History of Palestine, 634-1099* (New York: Cambridge University Press, 1992), 19.
104. Nicolle, 12.
105. Ibid, 18–19.
106. Kaegi, 145.
107. Ibid, 150.
108. Ibid, 155.
109. Avi-Yonah, 268.
110. Donner, 9–10.
111. Avi-Yonah, 270.
112. Kaegi, 203.
113. Avi-Yonah, 271.
114. Ibid. For centuries thereafter, Copts in Egypt held a special "Heraclius Fast."
115. Avi-Yonah, 272.
116. Kaegi, 205.
117. Ibid, 238.
118. Ibid, 216–217.
119. Donner 11.
120. Nicolle, 14.
121. For a typical explanation in the *Oxford History of Islam* (Esposito, ed.), see: Jane Smith, "Islam and Christendom," 312.
122. Nicolle, 11–12.
123. Donner, 12.
124. Nicolle, 20.
125. Ibid, 20, 50–51.
126. Ibid, 30, 40–43.
127. Ibid, 46–49.
128. Kaegi, 218–219.
129. Nicolle, 54–59.
130. Ibid, 77.
131. Ibid, 65.
132. Ibid.
133. Ibid, 70–72.
134. Ibid, 72–73.
135. Ibid, 64.
136. Ibid, 77–81.
137. Ibid, 19, 81; See Gil, 118, for various accounts of Jabala's fidelity to the Byzantines.
138. Gil, 48.
139. Nicolle, 85.
140. Guy Le Strange, *Palestine Under the Moslems: A Description of Syria and the Holy Land from A.D. 650 to 1500* (Beirut: Khayats, 1965), 54.

Chapter 5

Early Islamic Galilee

THE RISE OF ISLAMIC RULE IN GALILEE

After the Islamic conquest, "Palestine" disappeared from the map, in semantic and juridical senses. By and large, the conquerors referred to the country as *al-Sham* (the Arabic refers to the "left" and the "north," and evokes how Palestine could be seen from the Arabian peninsula; in some usages, the term, *al-Sham*, seems to have reference to two geographical units, Syria and Palestine). The Arabic for Palestine, *Filastin*, referred to just one of three administrative units in the country.

In this administrative breakdown, the Arabs basically followed the precedent set by the Byzantines, when they divided the country into *Palestina prima/Palestina secunda/Palestina tertia*. Now, under Islam, the first two units were called *Jund Filastin, Jund Urdunn* (for the Jordan River), and the third (southern) sector ended up being divided up, part of it allocated to *Jund Filastin*, the other to *Jund Dimashq*. Jund Urdunn, the sector of importance to us, featured Galilee and included outlying areas of the Sea of Galilee, as well as Galilee's coastal edge, particularly Acre, up to Tyre in today's Lebanon; it was also comprised of the Jordan Valley (or an elongated version, from Beit Sha'an to Eilat), and northern Samaria. During this early phase of the Muslim conquest, under the Umayyad Caliphate (which under Mu'awiya became based in Damascus and which maintained closer contacts with Palestine than subsequent caliphates), Jund Urdunn was divided into the following subdistricts: Tiberias, Samira (part of Samaria), Beit Sha'an, Bayt Ra's, Gader, Avel, Susita (Susiya), Sepphoris, Acre, Qedesh, Naphtali, and Tyre.[1]

Though overlap can be identified between forms of the bygone Byzantine administration and the new Islamic bureaucracy, it bears mention that sociopolitical points of emphasis in the country changed significantly during this

Umayyad period (661–750 CE), despite the fact that Muslims were, in all likelihood, not yet a majority. This is the period when Islam designated Jerusalem as one of its sacred cities (the first version of the Dome of the Rock shrine on the Temple Mount was constructed at the end of the seventh century), but Muslim notables did not limit their activity to Jerusalem. For instance, at the start of the eighth century, they built a new town, Ramla, in the country's center, and within years, it was not only the capital of Jund Filastin, but actually the most important city in the country.[2] The Umayyads also invested heavily in creating a Muslim fleet, and in the renovation of the country's seaports. A little more than a decade after Yarmuk, Acre was already functioning as a naval base; for a time, before being supplanted by Tyre, it served as Jund Urdunn's harbor.[3]

The Muslim conquest of Palestine, writes Moshe Gil, "was in its essence the conquest of cultured countries by the Arab tribes." The Arab tribes, he adds, "both those who had formerly lived on the borders of Palestine and those who came to it within the framework of the Muslim army, were a separate entity of the population of the country." This Israeli historian's phrasing has an Orientalist ring, but his substantive point is that the demographics of the country did not change overnight, after the Byzantines were brought down to their knees at Yarmuk. Under Islam, he notes, "nomadism was considered the most natural and common state of the Arabs. . . . The Arabs were the military, the horsemen, and they had no responsibilities toward any other sectors of the population."[4] In short, his contention is that the Islamic conquest in Palestine was not settlement-oriented. "There is no reason to assume that the proportions in the structure of the population varied drastically in the period in question," Gil notes. He adds: "it seems probable that in this early period the Muslims did not implant real roots in the towns of Palestine, and certainly not in agriculture."[5] Heading up to the Crusader conquest at the end of the eleventh century, or at least up to the end of the Umayyad era, Muslims were not a majority in the country, Gil suggests. Up to the Crusades, the country's rural population was mainly Christian. In cities that served as, or were close to, centers of government, Jews had significant communities. Apart from Jerusalem, a complicated venue for Jewish settlement in this era (and others), these cities with noticeable Jewish presences in the early Islamic era included: Ramla, Tiberias, Tyre, Acre, Haifa, Ascalon, Gaza, Hebron, and Eilat.[6] Not all scholars have concurred with Gil's estimate about Christians remaining a majority in the country throughout the centuries of Islamic rule, before the Crusades; but his basic contention about how nomadic warrior tribesmen were not disposed to settle in Palestine has not been overturned. One scholar who has examined a number of demographic trends and questions pertinent to the Byzantine, Islamic, Mamluk, and Ottoman eras in Palestine and Syria writes: "The limited settlement of Arabs in southern Syria and Palestine immediately after the [Islamic] conquest is explained [partly] by the inclination of the nomad warriors to move towards new battlefields. . . . There are no records of any large scale migration of Arab tribesmen into Syria and Palestine in the decades after the conquest."[7]

Palestine played a pivotal role in disputes and battles connected to Islam's acute succession crisis, which centered upon Ali ibn Abi Talib, Muhammad's son-in-law and a figure of reverence in Shi'a Islam. Among renegades who refused to pledge allegiance to Ali, who served as the fourth Caliph from 656 to 661 CE, was Mu'awiya ibn Abi Sufyan, whose parents we met on the Yarmuk battlefield. At the time of Ali's great triumph near Basra in 656 CE (the Battle of the Camel), Mu'awiya had been appointed military commander in al-Sham by the Umayyads. For years, the politics of Palestine, Galilee included, pivoted around these circumstances—the head of what would be called in today's media the "anti-Shi'a" uprising happened to be the military ruler of Palestine. Tribal alliances sometimes shifted abruptly in this internecine Islamic struggle, but at least initially, Mu'awiya appears to have won support among important clans and clan leaders in the Galilee area. Abu'l A'war (Amr b. Sufyan al-Sulami), a leader of Urdunn tribes who was appointed army commander in the region by the Caliph Uthman, had renown for having accepted the Byzantines' surrender in Tiberias; with his son, he was a key fighter in Mu'awiya's struggle against Ali's followers. Another northern figure important in this connection was Abd al-Rahman b. Qays al-Qayni. Mu'awiya was supported by the Urdunn tribe, the Banu Quada'a, and its military leader Hubaysh b. Dulja.

The geography in tribal skirmishing which ensued within the frame of Islam's succession crisis is not constant, but in this mid-seventh century phase, it appears that Mu'awiya was buoyed by tribes in the country's north, whereas Ali's backers were mostly in the south. Mu'awiya became Caliph in 661 CE—whether ceremonies were conducted in Jerusalem in honor of his ascent before Ali's assassination is a matter of dispute—and he thereafter retained close ties in the country generally, and also, specifically, in Galilee. There was an economic rationale for this: tax collection in the country was effective, and Filastin produced annually 450,000 dinars, and Urdunn 180,000 dinars. Apparently because he felt safe among the northern tribes, Mu'awiya kept a residence in Galilee. This was on the southern tip of the Sea of Galilee, near the mouth of the Jordan, at al-Sinnabra, a site known as Khirbat al-Karak/BethYerah (House of the Moon).[8] About 450 years after Mu'awiya became Caliph, a Crusader battle would be fought where he had kept his palace. At the start of the twentieth century, Zionism's kibbutz movement started a few miles south of Khirbat al-Karak, at Degania. Nowadays, just southwest of al-Sinnabra, many thousands of Evangelical and other religious tourists annually visit the baptismal site at Yardenit.

After Mu'awiya's death in 680 CE, his son Yazid, heir to the caliphate, periodically took refuge in Tiberias because Galilee tribes, at least for the time being, remained loyal to his family. Also in 680 CE, Husayn, son of Ali ibn Abi Talib, was assassinated in Karbala. This sequence precipitated another blistering phase in the succession crisis, not centered on Yazid (who died in 683 CE) but rather on a bitter foe of the Umayyads, Abdallah ibn al-Zubayr. Now the Umayyads' strongest base of support in al-Sham came from the south of the country, owing to an alliance of tribes called the Banu Kalb; this alliance fought against al-Zubayr's champion in Syria (meaning also parts of Palestine), al-Dahhak b. Qays al-Fihri, who headed an alliance of "northerners," the Banu Qays. The geographical coordinates and composition of these alliances were not constant, however—some tribal leaders switched sides, and sometimes a regional leader's disposition was challenged by his followers (this happened in Urdunn, when the preeminent tribal leader, Hassan b. Malik, professed loyalty to Yazid, up to his death, but many in the region disliked Yazid's two sons, Abdallah and Khalid, whom Yazid had appointed to administer the region).[9] Complicatedly fluid, clan politics in Galilee in this era ultimately were shaped by the Umayyad's caliphate's ongoing connections with it, and by the general crisis of authority this caliphate faced, both vis-à-vis its Shi'a rivals, and also as a result of its own self-debilitating tendencies.

The latter issue—power rivalry and assassination within the Umayyad Caliphate—destabilized life in Galilee. In 744 CE, for instance, the region was in tumult about the blood-strewn, controversial path taken by the new Caliph, Yazid ibn al-Walid, as he moved upward in his ascent to power. Facing rebellion in Jund Filastin, Yazid sent a cousin, Sulayman ibn Hisham ibn Abd al-Malik, to command his forces there, and stifle the uprising. Sulayman preferred negotiation to war and apparently purchased quiet in the region by proffering cash and gratuities. Urdunn tribal leader Muhammad ibn Abd al-Malik demanded similar benefits for his own region and seems also to have been placated. But the official in charge of collecting taxes in Urdunn for this Caliph Yazid, Muhammad ibn Said ibn Hassan, faced resistance, and turned to Sulayman for armed help in his unpopular work. Sulayman balked; Muhammad obtained a written order from the Caliph. Soon a hefty force of 5,000 soldiers was discharged to Galilee, its men taking quarter by night in villages around its lake. Muhammad prowled Tiberias with some of the soldiers. That sufficed to stifle the rebellion. Newly loyal to Caliph Yazid, clansmen in Galilee redirected their frustration to two of the uprising's instigators, Yazid ibn Sulaymin and Muhammad ibn Abd al-Malik, seizing their horses and weapons, and robbing their homes. Now in control, Sulaymin marched with his forces to al-Sinnabra, where he arranged for Urdunn tribesmen to participate in a ceremonial show of loyalty to Caliph Yazid. Sulaymin and some others sailed from there to a mosque in Tiberias, for the Friday prayer service.[10]

GALILEAN JEWS AND CHRISTIANS IN THE EARLY ISLAMIC PERIOD

Jews in Palestine greeted the arrival of Islamic rule with cautious relief. An indication of their mood can be found in the aforementioned apocalyptic prophecy, *The Secrets of Rabbi Shimon ben Yohai*. The document was written a few generations after Byzantine rule collapsed, but scholars assume that this text preserves sentiments felt by Jews in the country at the moment when Islam took control of it.[11] Supposedly relaying secrets that were revealed to Rashbi during the period when he hid in the cave to escape Roman persecutors, this prophecy's contention is that Islamic rule, while far from ideal, has relieved the Jews of the malevolent Byzantines ("Edom"), and will not last for long. The Islamic conquest is thus a step in a messianic process. In the key passage, Rashbi contemplates meanings of *Numbers* 24:21, "He looked on the Kenites," and exclaims, despondently, "is it not sufficient, what the wicked kingdom, Edom, has done to us?" Why should we also suffer the rule of Ishmael, he cries. Matatron, the Prince of Being, responds: "Do not be afraid, mortal, for the Holy One, blessed be He, is bringing about the kingdom of Ishmael only for the purpose of delivering you from that wicked one," namely, Edom (Byzantine rule). The passage then prophesizes Jewish restoration in Eretz Israel and also "great enmity" between Christians and Muslims.[12]

Drawing on Daniel 7:8, Jews sometimes used "little horn" imagery to articulate their expectations in the new Islamic era. In Daniel, "horns" represent gentile kingdoms, and the little horn is the last one before the "ancient of days"—Muslim rule, in other words, was seen as the final stage before the messianic era.[13] Compared to suppression in the Byzantine period, the new Islamic regime symbolized for Jews a promise of religious toleration, and it was thus greeted with semi-messianic enthusiasm. Eleazar ben Kalir, a celebrated composer of liturgical piyyutim who lived during this transition to Arab rule, expressed these lofty expectations in Galilean terms: "the day will come when the Messiah from the House of David will come . . . and Tiberias and Samaria will be comforted, and Acre and Galilee will find mercy."[14] Jewish prophetic writing in the eighth century sometimes displayed detailed awareness of what the Muslims were doing in Palestine. *The Secrets of Rabbi Shimon*, for example, alludes to an Islamic government undertaking a canal project in Galilee: "He will bring far-away peoples from alien lands to excavate and build a canal to bring up the waters of the Jordan to irrigate the land."[15] In fact, Arab sources confirm that the Umayyad regime took up a canal project in Jund Urdunn, though specific details about the project are lacking.[16]

Did Jews in Galilee, or elsewhere, try to exploit the inexperience of Umayyad rulers so as to carry out vendettas against Byzantine Christians and take reprisal for old grievances? The context in which such a dynamic seems most plausible is the "iconoclasm" controversy, which reached a peak in the early 720s CE, when Caliph Yazid II (Yazid bin Abd al-Malik) issued decrees against icon worship. In his detailed archaeological-historical survey of Christian sites in Palestine in this period, Schick concludes that vandalism against images in churches and related holy sites "must have been done by the Christians themselves."[17] He believes that the encouragement for icon-bashing provided by Yazid II must have been a factor in the phenomenon, and also cites "striking" evidence of how twelve synagogues were also vandalized, the damage usually being done to stone reliefs.[18] For their part, relating to the anti-icon vandalism, patristic writers put the onus on Jews. One Christian writer blamed the leader of the Jews in Tiberias, the "leader of the mad Jews, a magician and seer, a tool of soul-destroying devils," named Tessarakontapekhys (the man of forty cubits).[19]

Basing his survey on documents uncovered in the Cairo Genizah, Moshe Gil reasons that through the Umayyad period, and for decades after it, Jews in rural Galilean areas often managed to maintain communal life, more or less as it had been lived in earlier, Byzantine and Roman, epochs. Using examples from the Banias, Gush Halav, and Dalton areas, he concludes that some Jewish villages in Galilee "retained their ancient character." Some Muslims entered and settled in the villages during the Umayyad period, "and then there were the Christians, of course, about whom we hear very little." He adds: "To such questions as what the relative numbers of the three elements were, how they lived alongside one another, and what was their livelihood, we have no unambiguous answers." Gil assumes that Galilee's rural Jewish population was "evidently gradually wiped out" in subsequent, Fatimid (909–1171 CE) and Crusader periods. He points to evidence of Jewish flight from Galilee in Geniza documents relating to the eleventh century in which Jews involved in transactions of some sort in central Palestine locales like Ramla identify themselves as having roots in Gush Halav, Dalton, or Amuka, near Safed.[20] In a separate, following, section, we will relate to how Jews and Christians in Galilean urban milieus, particularly Tiberias, fared after the Islamic conquest.

The Islamic conquerors were less violent toward Byzantine populations and sites in Jerusalem and Palestine than their Persian predecessors had been. "The Muslim invaders did not go out of their way to be destructive," concludes one study of the subject.[21] Christian pilgrimages to the Holy Land slowed during the early phase of Islamic rule in Palestine, but they did not stop altogether. Records exist verifying pilgrimages taken by Arculf and Epiphanius (both about half a century after Yarmuk), and later visits were made by pilgrims named Willibald (around 725 CE) and Bernard (870 CE). Such pilgrims demonstrated very little interest in the Muslims, who themselves mostly ignored the Christians once they reached Palestine. The problem, however, was getting to the vicinity of the Holy Land. Some of the Pilgrims, for example, Willibald and Bernard, reported that they were arrested when they first entered Muslim lands.[22] The ecclesiastical hierarchy was gravely damaged by the Muslim conquest, but it seems to have remained mostly intact. The Jerusalem Patriarch Sophronius, whose distraught bewilderment after Ajnadayn ("How is it that the incursions of the barbarians increase...") we have noted, survived for only a few years after Yarmuk, and his patriarchal post remained vacant for about forty years, when it was resumed without interruption. During the peak years of the Abbasid caliphate (775–861), a line of Armenian bishops was attested in Jerusalem in parallel with the Orthodox Patriarchate, and Monophysite bishops could be found in Tiberias, and elsewhere in the country.[23] Ecclesiastical contacts between church officials in Muslim-controlled Palestine and counterparts in the Byzantine empire were sporadic, sometimes quite sparse, but not extinguished. In the Abbasid period, contacts which persisted between these Christians related mostly to the controversy that erupted over the vandalism of iconic images in Palestine's Byzantine churches. The isolation of the Palestine churches is exemplified by the fact that important Byzantine chroniclers, such as Theophanes' in his ninth-century writings, were unsure about the identities of Jerusalem patriarchs after the Muslim conquest. Interestingly, the Palestine churches were able to establish contacts with Christians in the west during the Carolingian period, particularly Charlemagne's reign (Charlemagne was crowned in 800 CE). In 808 CE, a roster of Jerusalem Patriarchate churches, monasteries, and finances was prepared for Charlemagne.[24]

Archeologists who have searched for evidence of Christian presence in Palestine in the early Islamic period, 640–813 CE, are certain that church structures remained in Tiberias and suspect that elsewhere in Galilee, including the example of church of the Annunciation in Nazareth (in some form), and also at Kafr Kanna, Christianity kept some physical presence. They have also established that some Christian structures remained standing for some time after the Islamic conquest but apparently did not last into the Abbasid period—in the Galilee area, the relevant locales are Nazareth (for Saint Joseph), Hammat Gader, and Magdala.[25] The fate of Capernaum's St. Peter's House is uncertain, though archeologists suspect that it was out of use by the ninth century.[26] All told, in Palestine, concludes Robert Schick, "the evidence for the implementation of extensive anti-Christian policies in the Early Islamic period is slight. Christians could and did build and repair churches, in contradiction to what the legal theorizing of the Abbasid jurists would lead us to expect."²⁷

TIBERIAS IN THE EARLY ISLAMIC PERIOD

A major natural disaster rocked Tiberias and Jerusalem in 748 CE (or 749 CE). The earthquake caused the eastern and western sides of the Dome of the Rock shrine, then barely fifty years old, to collapse; apparently dozens of persons in Jerusalem were killed, and survivors fled the city and remained outside of it for forty days. The earthquake (if it was just one) reportedly wrecked Tiberias after it wrought this devastation in Jerusalem. Some sources date the Tiberias disaster as happening in early 749 CE, during a sabbatical *shmita* year; they relay that the city was annihilated, the one home left standing belonging to a man named Isa. Thirty synagogues crumbled to dust and Jewish bath-houses were also destroyed. Some reports imply that tens of thousands of persons in Palestine and beyond perished in the earthquake. It is assumed that a piyyut (liturgical poem), *yoser ra'ash shevi'i*, composed by Shmuel Bar, memorializes this earthquake, since the "seventh" (shevi'i in its title) ties the occurrence to a shmita year. The poem refers to chaos and terror in Tiberias, as well as flooding in Ramla (or the Sharon Valley)—"the capital, Tiberias, was shaken and convulsed with fear, and suddenly shrouded by darkness," records the piyyut.²⁸ Attaching a date to this disaster has been a topic of scholarly interest since 1941, when researcher M. Margolit reviewed a version of the piyyot found in the Cairo Genizah, and speculated about the earthquake's date based on references to a fast day. Nineteen years later, the same scholar published an update, based on another Genizah document which alludes to the disaster happening 679 years after the Second Temple *hurban*. Margolit was a little indecisive as to whether the relevant date was 748 CE or 749 CE, but in the early 1990s, archaeologists found coins and remains at a Beit Sha'an excavation which seemingly nail the date to January 18, 749.²⁹

The capital of Jund Urdunn, Tiberias' premier status in Galilee lasted beyond the Umayyad Caliphate, and up to the Crusades. Evidence indicates that as late as the eleventh century, Acre and Tyre remained, administratively, subordinate to Tiberias, and Genizah documents suggest that a significant Jewish community remained in this city at this late date.³⁰ Muhammad Ibn Ahmad Al-Muqaddasi, an influential Arab geographer and author who lived in the second half of the tenth century, composed an excellent description of Tiberias, capturing its communities' struggle with the blazing summer heat, and also the charm of its position on the edge of the Sea of Galilee. From the Islamic standpoint, Muqadassi exulted about Tiberias' *jami*, its main mosque, which boasted a gravel-covered courtyard,³¹ but his balanced portrait is notable for its non-sectarian description of the city's life as a whole. Written somewhat after the Umayyad period, it bears citation here as a glimpse of how life developed in this Galilee capital after the Islamic conquest. The geographer is far from a Tiberias public relations booster. In fact, Muqadassi's depiction opens by proclaiming that Tabariyyah (Tiberias) is "narrow, hot in summer, and unhealthy"—but despite its criticisms, the half-humorous portrait is embracing. "Of the people of Tiberias it is said that for two months they dance, and for two more they gorge; that for two months they beat about, and for two more they go naked; that for two months they play the reed, and for two more they wallow," Muqadassi recorded. He explained why this is so: "The explanation for this is that they dance from the number of fleas, then gorge off the Nabak fruit; they beat about with fly-laps to chase away the wasps from the meat and the fruits, then they go naked from the heat; they suck the sugar-canes, and then they have to wallow through the muddy streets." He also noted Tiberias' large marketplace, which ran between the city's gates, its eight natural hot baths, its palm trees by the lake, and the many boats on the water.[32]

The advent of Islamic rule coincided with an economic upsurge in Tiberias. The city's hot springs were appreciated as a soothing, therapeutic attraction for residents, the infirm and tourists. Agriculture around the city, and fishing on the sea, provided an economic base, and the city's population groups specialized in various trades, with the Jews, for instance, making headway in textile spheres and the weaving of religious mats out of reeds[33] (as early as the ninth century, Arab geographers visiting Tiberias were impressed by these prayer mats, which were sold for five dinars apiece[34]).

Through the ninth century, at least, Christians remained an identifiable presence in Tiberias. Arab chroniclers offer conflicting versions of the surrender of Byzantine Tiberias to the Muslims—one of them suggests that the city's Christians agreed to forfeit half of their assets. Whatever the arrangement, Christian inhabitants in Tiberias soon revolted, but the Muslims easily stifled this unrest. Bishop Willibald visited the city in 723 CE, the period of the iconoclasm controversy, and reported on the presence of many churches in Tiberias, as well as the city's suitably reverent attitude toward God. Rosters of Monophysite bishops in Tiberias, starting in 793 CE, are extant.[35]

For Muslims, Tiberias became in this Umayyad period the headquarters of Urdunn tribes, particularly the Banu Ash'ar. Scholars identify a number of prominent Muslim residents in Tiberias in this period. One, Abdallah b. Hawala, of the Banu Azd (died in 678 CE) lyricized about the salubriousness of living in al-Sham. Decades later, another Muslim from Tiberias, Abu Muhammad Salih b. Jubayr al-Suda'i al-Tabarani, also of the Banu Azd, won a strong reputation for organizing tax schedules and payment allowances to tribesmen and soldiers.[36]

With provisions, the Caliph Umar opened Jerusalem's gates to Jews, but Tiberias nonetheless remained the Jews' central city in *al-Sham* during the Umayyad period, and through the tenth century. Its famed Yeshiva did not really slow down during the turmoil of the Persian-Byzantine-Islamic power jockeying, and descendants of the fifth-century Amora, Mar Zutra, led it into the eighth century. The issue of whether Tiberias and Galilee, and Eretz Israel in general, retained the premier position in Jewish affairs for decades and centuries after the Islamic conquests merits clarification.

By and large, Jews in the early Middle Ages belonged to Muslim countries, essentially in the same places where they had been before Muhammad's warriors took up the sword—Palestine, Persia, Iraq, Syria, Egypt, North Africa. Jews outside of Islam's orbit dwelled mainly in the Byzantine empire, in Greece, Rome and south Italy, Constantinople and Anatolia.[37] During this Islamic period in Jewish history, communal leaders were yeshiva heads who had the title Gaon, which can be translated as "excellency," and apparently was an acronym referring to the head of the *yeshivat ge'on ya'akov*.[38] In addition to the Tiberias yeshiva, Babylonia (Iraq) had two great yeshivot, Sura, in the south, and Pumbedita further north, near the Euphrates. Scholars tend to emphasize decentralization of power in Judaism in this period, meaning that a kind of horizontal parity of authority persisted between the two Babylonian yeshivot, and the one in Palestine. At the same time, because of Byzantine oppression, followed by the chaotic turbulence of the early Islamic period, which continued after the Umayyad dynasty (as we will see), the Jews' religious culture in Palestine, after the Tannaim and the first generations of the Amoraim, was tarnished by some decline, relative to Mesopotamia. There is a tendency among scholars to suggest that the Babylonian yeshivot is where Jewish law was honed in the Middle Ages, whereas in Palestine the premium was put on *piyyut* liturgy, mysticism and midrash.[39] It bears mention that the three yeshivot in question here were far from identical to the more familiar *yeshiva* institutions which consolidated centuries later, continuing through modern times—these later institutions were essentially religious schools, whereas the Babylonian and Tiberias yeshivot played defined communal leadership roles, and carried out various judicial functions, in addition to being scholarly centers.[40]

In the ninth century, and parts of the tenth, Tiberian Jewry was led by Gaonim from the Ben-Meir family line.[41] One of them, Aaron ben Meir is remembered for having initiated, in 921 CE, a controversy about the dating of Passover in which his overseas rival, Saadia, Gaon of Babylonia, had the upper hand—the dispute was between the Tiberian designation of a Sunday as the start of the holiday, versus the Babylonian insistence on Tuesday. Technically, Aaron's father Meir was the Palestine Gaon at the time, but Aaron led the unsuccessful campaign for Sunday. "The fact that the Babylonians prevailed in the long run proves that their authority was greater than that of the Palestinian Geonim," concludes Gil; he also astutely points out that the dispute flared in the period (905–935 CE) when the Iraq-based Abbasid caliphate resumed control of Palestine, and this instilled "a larger degree of Palestinian dependence on Babylonia in all dealings with central authorities," to the detriment of Aaron in the dispute.[42] Yet it is a little misleading to regard Saadia Gaon, a renowned figure in Judaism from the Abbasid period who wrote in Arabic, as a diaspora spokesman in this debate: migrating slowly from Egypt to Babylonia, Saadia spent considerable time in Tiberias, apparently more than five years,[43] up to a year or two before the Passover date debate with Aaron.

Scholars speculate that the Palestinian yeshiva remained in Tiberias until the middle of the tenth century, or through the eleventh century.[44] Essentially, in the period between the Bar Kochba rebellion and a few decades before the Crusader conquest, Galilee, via Tiberias in the later part of this period, retained its paramount position in Jewish affairs. Syrian Christian sources confirm that the Palestine yeshiva was still located in Tiberias through the first decades of the ninth century. The Passover date dispute toward the middle of the tenth century proves that the yeshiva remained in Galilee at this date—we know this because in *Sefer ha-Mo'adim*, Saadia Gaon, the main Babylonian polemicist in this debate, refers to how the Palestine Gaon, presumably Meir Gaon, sent his son from Tiberias to Jerusalem, to inform Jews there about various calendric calculations. In Cairo Genizah documents from the start of the eleventh century, Gil notes, the Palestine Gaon is still called *al-Tabarani*, the Tiberian. As that century progressed, however, relevant Genizah materials indicate that Tiberias was no longer the home of the yeshiva.[45]

Before then, Tiberian Jewry set standards in the evolution of the Hebrew language, particularly its pronunciation, and for cantillation in Torah reading. Along with colleague-competitor *Masoretes* in Jerusalem and Babylonia, these Tiberian sages standardized Hebrew pronunciation and Torah reading by preparing external diacritical notes (*nikkud*) and by working out cantillation (*taamim*) patterns. Tiberian pioneers in this Masorete context were active by the end of the eighth century. Some two hundred years later, their accomplishment was recognized by Jonah ibn Janah, a prominent, Spain-based, Hebrew grammarian: Tiberians, he proclaimed, "have the purest Hebrew" in the Jewish world.[46] From the end of the eight century, the roster of prominent Tiberias masoretes includes Abraham b. Furat, Abraham b. Riqat, Pinhas "the head of the Yeshiva," Ahiyahu ha-Kohen, Asher b. Nehamia, and Moses Muha.[47] Supplementing this list is the five-generation Ben Asher family line, culminating in Aaron ben Moses ben Asher, often known simply as Ben Asher, who died around 960 BC. His contribution in the development of "Tiberian vocalization" and of Hebrew grammar was acknowledged (with some criticism) by Maimonides, medieval Judaism's preeminent figure.[48] Aaron's father, Moses, could be the author of one of the oldest extant manuscripts which contains substantive portions of the Tanakh. Some documents uncovered in the Cairo Genizah revived speculation about how this masorete family might have had Karaite roots or affiliation (as part of their criticism of rabbinical Judaism, Karaites often pointed to discrepancies in vocalization designations dividing the Tiberias school and its Babylonian counterpart; yet at least one Karaite writer praised the Tiberian masoretes, perhaps implying that Ben Asher was one of his group, or perhaps not[49]). The "Tiberian scribe," Abu Kathir Yahya b. Zakariyya, one of the most intriguing figures in the masorete movement, authored a groundbreaking translation of the Tanakh into Arabic. During his stay in Tiberias, on his journey from Egypt to Babylonia, Saadia Gaon reportedly studied with Zakariyya, who died in 932 CE.[50] Masorete scholars from Tiberias are said to have journeyed among Jewish communities in Palestine and overseas, teaching the city's renowned grammar and vocalization system. In the diaspora, Jews "beseeched these teachers to come, and teach their children to read [Torah] as it is done in Eretz Israel."[51]

Tiberias' masorete movement had a parallel in a flowering of Islamic letters in the city. The concurrence of religious culture trends among these two communities in Tiberias is quite suggestive. In the late ninth century, Tiberias became a "thriving center of Muslim scholarship."[52] A leading Arab grammarian, Abu'l-Qasim Abd al-Rahman ibn Ishaq al-Zajjaji al-Nihawandi, spent a prolonged period in Tiberias, dying in the city in 952 CE. Other Islamic intellectuals and spiritual leaders who lived in this period in Tiberias, as cited by al-Tabarani (himself a prominent scholar who was born in Tiberias), include Abd al-Wahid ibn Ishaq, Tahir b. Ali b. Abdus Abul-Tayyib, and Hamid b. al-Hasan al-Bazzar.[53]

An acutely poignant aspect of Jewish life in Tiberias in this period was its leper colony. The city's therapeutic and quarantining functions in this connection was an issue commanding much international Jewish attention—Moshe Gil, a meticulous scholar of Palestine Jewry in this period and an expert on Cairo Genizah materials, mentions that no less than seventeen documents in the Genizah relate to lepers in Tiberias.[54] Even before the Islamic conquest, as early as the late sixth century, disease sufferers were drawn to Tiberias to "get healed by the water and the air," as commentators put it. The springs at Hammat Gader were called the "baths of Elijah," and advertised as a cure for leprosy. Afflicted persons entered through a separate door, at night, carrying lamps and incense, and they stayed in the baths through dawn. Whether or not they were judged to be healed depended upon the contents of dreams they dreamed in the bathhouse. A leprosy inn at the site was apparently maintained by public funds. Through the eleventh century, overseas Jews maintained interest in leprosy curing at Hammat Gader, though it is likely that other springs, within Tiberias, also found use in this connection.⁵⁵ The Arab geographer Muqadassi alluded to "those who suffer from scabs, ulcers, sores and other suchlike diseases" who came to bath at Hammat Gader for three days—the identities of these treatment-seeking sufferers are not clear. After three days, on Muqadassi's description, the sufferer immersed in a cold spring—should Allah vouchsafe it, this treatment brought cure.⁵⁶

UP TO THE CRUSADES: SOCIOPOLITICAL INSTABILITY IN GALILEE AND PALESTINE

The rise of the Abbasid Caliphate in the mid-eight century transformed political affairs in Palestine. Umayyad leaders, it will be recalled, maintained close ties with Palestine, and the country's tribal leaders exerted some influence over policies enacted by the caliphs. Based in Baghdad, which was founded in 762 CE, the Abbasid rulers were remote from Palestine's life on many levels, social, geographic, political. From this point, Palestine's clans are nowhere to be found in records of political decision-making processes in the caliphate; their primary presence is in rebellions.⁵⁷ Anti-Umayyad propaganda circulated by the Abbasids cast a negative spotlight on Palestinian affairs; al-Sham became notorious as a hotbed of recalcitrant ingrates, as a place where no true Muslim could find peace. "A visitor coming to Baghdad can close his eyes quietly and sleep well," proclaimed one ode to the new city, "but in al-Sham no newcomer would dare do so." The poet explained that after the Abbasids regaled al-Sham residents with "favors and bounty," they responded only with "enmity and slander."⁵⁸

A brief suspension of this atmosphere of antagonism and suspicion occurred during the last quarter of the ninth century, after a Turkish strongman, Ahmad ibn Tulun, took power in Egypt, and nudged away the Abbasids. Within a few years, ibn Tulun had control of Syria and Palestine as well. Palestine was now ruled by the Egypt-based Tulunids, who (in contrast to the Abbasids) believed that they had much to gain by developing infrastructure in the country, and promoting trade with it. The downside in this development in the early Middle Ages is that it reverted macrolevel circumstances in Palestine to what they had been in ancient times. For a quarter millennium after Yarmuk, there had been a kind of locality in the country's politics whereby an engaged, and not distant, central government forged alliances with, or fended away, loyal or rebellious tribes in Palestine; but now, once again, the country became a pawn in a larger regional power game whereby armies in Egypt were in chronic conflict with other armies from the north. The identities and alignment of these forces was not constant (the Abbasids were not always a major player), but "the common element in all these wars was that Palestine appeared to be a vital defensive position to each of the sides, as well as a springboard from which to attack."[59]

The boost in Palestine's socioeconomic life provided by the Tulunid regime can be seen in Acre (pronounced today in Israel as Akko, and often, confusingly, given that spelling). From this mid-Islamic period, and then in the Crusader period, Acre becomes an indispensable gateway in Galilee history, even though (or, more precisely, *because*) it is, as a coastal harbor, perched on the western cusp of the region, not deeply within it. We have a striking record of how and when Acre comes onto the map of Galilee history in a description provided by Muhammad Ibn Ahmad Al-Muqaddasi, to whose work we have already referred. Born in Jerusalem, he was a traveler and a geographer who produced in 985 CE an extraordinary work, *Ahson at-Taqasim fi ma'rifat al-aqalim* (Best Classification for Knowledge of Regions). Arguably, while his life was blissfully devoid of the traumas and turnabout endured by his Jewish counterpart 900 years earlier, al-Muqaddasi is to Palestinian historiography what Josephus is to Jewish historiography. Coincidentally, his grandfather was the engineering demiurge of Acre's ascent, a fact that lends a compellingly personal character to Muqadassi's account of the city's rise.

In general, Muqaddasi's writing about Palestine and Galilee has in it more Herodotus than Thucydides, meaning that it is rife with anthropological-oriented detail, at the expense of politics. In one passage, for instance, he details cooking techniques and cuisine in Palestine. A *tabun*, he explains, is an oven for baking bread that is placed in the ground; pebbles line the pit-oven, and its fires are kindled with dry dung. He proceeds to describe a carob-based dessert called *Kubbait*, and a sugary butter-cake baked in the winter, called *Zullabiyyah*.[60] In general, Muqaddasi was not impressed with Islamic culture in Palestine, opining "it is seldom recorded that any legal authority in Syria propounds new doctrines, or that any Muslim here is the writer [of anything significant]." Tiberias, it bears mention, is a conspicuous exception in his account; Muqaddasi stresses that the city's Muslim scribes have long been "in repute."[61]

In 985, looking back at Acre's rise a century earlier, Muqadassi wrote that "the city had remained unfortified" until the time [in the 880s] when Ibn Tulun visited it, coming from Tyre, where he had been impressed by that harbor's protective walls. Resolved to construct in Acre a harbor fortification as impregnable as Tyre, Tulun summoned engineers, but "in those days nobody knew how the foundations of a building could be laid in the water." Tulun was referred to the author's grandfather, Abu Bakr, an architect who nonchalantly assured the sovereign that the fortification work could be easily accomplished with the use of large sycamore beams. "Those beams he

[Abu Bakr] set to float on the surface of the water, to prolong the town walls seawards, and then he roped them together," the grandson recorded. Weighed down with stones and cement, the beams sank downward; Abu Bakr order that work be suspended for a year, so that the "construction could consolidate itself." The architect then designed a pathway between the beams and Acre's ancient city walls; he also built a bridge at the western gate of the port, and every night, when ships entered the harbor, its managers "drew across the water a chain, as was done in Tyre."[62]

Abu Bakr earned 1,000 dinars for this achievement. His name was inscribed at a high mark in the harbor—Yaqut, a famed, learned geographer from the late Abbasid period, found the inscription honoring Muqadassi's grandfather when he visited Acre in the thirteenth century. More conscious than Muqadassi of Acre's prehistory, Yaqut noted that Umayyad Caliph Muawiyah conquered Acre and took steps to fortify it before setting out on a campaign in Cyprus; but the city had fallen into ruin before the Tulunids.[63] Other important reports of Acre prior to its transformation by the Crusaders are extant. For instance, the Persian traveler Nasir i-Khusrau visited the city in 1047 CE and lauded its central mosque, which was higher than all other buildings in the city, and adorned by marble columns and a courtyard which mixed stone pavement and green herbs (the latter due to the tradition that Adam had farmed in the area). Nasir visited a tomb ascribed to the town's presumed founder, Akkah, "a very pious and great personage." The town's most sacred attraction, both for Nasir and a roster of other chroniclers, was a site known as Ain al Bakar, the Ox Spring. Reached by descending twenty-five steps, the site was reputedly where Adam watered his oxen.[64] Some bits and pieces in the Genizah materials attest to Jewish communal life in Acre in this period, a generation or two before the Crusades. Some records suggest that Acre hosted a small "center of learning" in the mid-eleventh century, apparently comprised of Jews who had moved to the city from Tiberias.[65]

Ahmad ibn Tulun died in May 884, and his son and heir, Abu'l-Jaysh Khumarawayh quickly became locked in a wide-ranging power struggle against an Abbasid fighter, Abu'l Abbas ibn al-Muwaffaq, who was effectively regent in the caliphate. Armies from these sides clashed in a major battle, the Seven Mills, fought near Ramla. The Tulunid forces came out victorious, but as the Iraqi and Egyptian armies exhausted one another, the major consequence of these military developments was that they opened the door to new power brokers in the Islamic world.

In the last decades of the ninth century, Shi'ite extremism was on the rise. It drew inspiration, as Shiism has always done, from narrative accounts related to descendants of Ali ibn Abi Talib and Fatima, the Prophet Muhammad's daughter; supplementing these were various Hellenistic and Neo-Platonic accretions. The force which came from this, the Ismaili movement, was a new element in regional religion and politics, and it also proved to be fractious. Basically two Shi'ite sub-streams came from the Isma'ilis—the Qarmatis, an enigmatic and militarily imposing group which introduced principles of common ownership in agricultural work and other spheres, and the Fatimids, who consolidated power with blinding speed, starting as a kind of clandestine underground in North Africa and, within seventy years or so, becoming rulers of Egypt and Palestine.[66]

One of many factors that complicated Islamic politics in this era is that ideological affinity did not necessarily breed military-political alliances. The opposite was often the case, as though in illustration of the Freudian principle concerning narcissistic fixation with small differences. For instance, the Qarmatis and Fatimids regarded one another as mortal enemies, "perhaps just because" the two groups adhered to a similar religious-political philosophy.[67] Though it was not promoting trends of sociopolitical unification, Shi'ite Islam was nonetheless making strong inroads in al-Sham at the start of the tenth century. Ibn al-Faqih, a prominent Persian historian in this century, estimated that Shi'ites were a majority in Tiberias, Nablus, and Jerusalem, and other chroniclers noted significant Shi'ite presences in Tyre, Acre, Ramla, and Ascalon.[68]

In this atmosphere, the Qarmatis became a powerful military and political force in Galilee. In 906 CE they launched their first, astonishingly successful, raid in the north. In April–May they captured Tiberias, which had a major army base, and executed its emir, Ja'far b. Na'im. Residents in the city resisted, so the Qarmatis rampaged and plundered in it, reportedly killing many and also taking women captive. The Tulunid governor of Urdunn, Ahmad ibn Kayghalagh was forced to send two successive armies to Tiberias in order to dislodge the Qarmatis.[69] Two generations later, the Qarmatis again took hold of Tiberias for a spell. This occurred in May 964 CE. They held the city captive, demanding ransom payments in iron; a governor in Aleppo, Sayf al-dawla, who belonged to the Shi'ite Hamdanid dynasty, capitulated, ordering his soldiers to dismantle entry gates at the city of Raqqa, and to confiscate scales and other iron instruments from merchants. This odd story bears witness to the power wielded by the Qarmatis in Galilee.[70] In the tumbling dice character of Islamic politics in this era, Palestine was then ruled by the Ikhshidids, a dynasty based in Egypt and allied with the Abbasids—this dynasty had been founded by a Turkic soldier, Muhammad ibn Tugjh al-Ikhshidid. Nestled in Tiberias, the Qarmatis started to launch raids on Ramla, and gained temporary domination over Palestine as a whole. The Ikhshidid governor of the country, al-Hassan ibn Ubaydallah had to bribe the Qarmatis away by agreeing to pay them an annual tax.[71]

Using Galilee as their power base, the Qarmatis were not strong enough to hold al-Sham for any real length of time, but, arguably, their maneuvering in this period changed the course of regional history, and also of world history. Not blind to the damage wrought to Islamic power by ideological fracture and internecine warfare, the Byzantine empire was gearing up for a major onslaught on the Holy Land in 963–964 CE, exactly when the Qarmatis were engaged in their second, successful, foray in Tiberias. The Greek Christians began to stir during the reign (959–963 CE) of Romanus II, who supervised a successful invasion in Crete, used then by Muslims as a naval base. The commander of this Cretan campaign, Nicephorus Phocas, succeeded Romanus as emperor, and reigned until 969 CE. In those years, his army marched more than once on Aleppo, at one point installing a vassal (Abu'l-Ma'ali Sharif) to control it. Nobody doubts that Nicephorus' intention was to proceed to Jerusalem after conquering Antioch and Aleppo so as to restore Christian rule to it after a 300-year hiatus. Ultimately, what stopped Nicephorus was that he was assassinated—but, earlier, his campaign had picked up considerable momentum, culminating in the capture of Tripoli, where he reportedly seized 100,000 persons. From Tripoli, Nicephorus' plan was to march straight on to Jerusalem, but he was deterred by the Qarmatis, who were enjoying another phase as the toughest kid on the block in al-Sham, just having toyed with the Ikshidid governor, Hassan ibn Abdallah ibn Tughj.[72] In this way, militant Shi'ite Islam was the wild card in Palestine politics in the tenth century. Had it not spread forcefully in Galilee and elsewhere, largely via the Qarmatis, Byzantine Christians might possibly have retaken Jerusalem, thereby eliminating the casus belli of their western Christian brethren's holy Crusades in the Holy Land.

Murdered in his sleep by his nephew John Tzimiskes, Nicephorus II Phokas died as a result of Byzantine intrigue in the final days of 969 CE. John I went on to have an active seven-year reign, but, at this juncture, his uncle's demise nullified Christian aspirations in the Holy Land. Throughout November 969 CE, the Qarmatis had Ramla under siege. With the Byzantines sidelined, it was the Fatimids' turn in Palestine. Al-Sham basically staged a Shi'ite civil war in 970 CE, and Galilee was in the thick of it. In late spring 970 CE, Fatimid forces, led by Ja'far ibn al-Fallah, invaded the country, brazenly ignoring anti-Qarmati distress calls that had been sent out by a certain Hassan, the hapless Ikshidid governor of Ramla (Hassan was later executed, or exiled, by the Fatimids). After pacifying Ramla, Ja'far rumbled on to Tiberias, whose Ikhshidid governor was named Fatik. Ja'far's Fatimid army was comprised of Berbers (*maghariba*), and it recruited local allies from the Banu Murra and Banu Fazara tribes. Fatik was caught, duped into believing that he had been rewarded clemency, and then executed. The Berbers reportedly plundered Tiberias. Sources refer to Ja'afar then building a celebratory citadel on the Sea of Galilee, confusingly calling it a bridge.[73] From Tripoli, Nicephorus had dreamed of reconquering the Holy Land for Christianity;

now, from Tiberias, the Fatimids were dreaming of conquering the entire Muslim world. Both dreams, as it turned out, were delusional. The fact that they both came up short narrowed the distance on the road by which Pope Urban II launched the Crusades, a little over a century later.

Meantime, over the next several years, the fortunes of the Fatimids ebbed and flowed in Palestine. The truth is that besides being, somewhat oddly, perennial enemies with the Qarmatis, they were never really popular among Muslims in Palestine. In a few recorded instances, local leaders in Ramla and elsewhere in the country forged ad hoc alliances with the Qarmatis, so as to oust the Fatimids from their area.[74] The Fatimids' closest friends among local population groups in Palestine were probably the Jews. In the latter part of the 970s CE, they empowered a Jewish man, Fadl, son of a physician named Salih, to head a military unit. Fadl reasoned that the other Shi'ite group, the Hamdanids, might be amenable to joining an alliance; and so in winter 978–979 CE he traveled to Tiberias to negotiate with a Hamdanid leader, Abu Taghlib. Arrogantly, the latter refused for a time to conduct diplomacy with a Jew. The meeting finally took place at al-Sinnabra, the Sea of Galilee site where Caliph Mu'awiyah had kept a residence. It was an uneasy discussion, and Abu Taghlib would soon have reason to regret hitching his Hamdanid cart to the Fatimids—his forces became engaged in a disastrous skirmish in August 979 in Ramla, and Abu Taghlib literally lost his head.[75]

The Fatimids were looking for all the allies they could possibly find in this period because they faced an unexpected constellation of enemies. In the middle of the 970s CE, the Qarmatis had struck up an alliance with an impressive Turkish military leader, named Alptakin. After joining with the Qarmatis, Alptakin promptly harassed the Fatimids on the northern coast, besieging Sidon, and then dividing his forces for a coordinated dual attack on Acre and Tiberias. Alarmed, the Fatimid Caliph al-Mu'izz li-Din Allah tried to negotiate terms with Alptakin, but the Turk demurred. Soon Alptakin put one of his allies, from the Banu Uqayl tribe, in charge of Tiberias—wherever he went and conquered, Alptakin's men said prayers to the Abbasid Caliph, rather than to the Fatimid one. In order to regain Tiberias, the Fatimids had to pull out their big gun, Ja'far ibn al-Fallah.

The Fatimids had been scared and insulted by Alptakin, but worse was in store for them. In the mid-970s Byzantine Emperor John Tzimisces was on the march, conquering Hims and Ba'labakk and aiming for Damascus. In Syria, the emperor met with Alptakin, who showed off his horsemanship skills. Reports circulated that John Tzimisces sponsored Alptakin's conversion to Christianity (they are not verifiable). Despite this diplomatic gain, the Byzantine emperor never quite summoned the nerve to launch a campaign on Jerusalem—he seems to have been deterred by Fatimid fortresses on the Palestine coastline, and, more significantly, by internal challenges in

Byzantium.[76] John Tzimisces and the Byzantines were not sufficiently organized to overcome the political volatility of the era, and reassert Christian sovereignty in the Holy Land.

The Crusades are a confounding, almost unfathomable, phenomenon, but when viewed through this prism of Galilee history and local politics in Palestine, some measure of their mystery abates. More than a century before the Crusades' inception, two eastern Christian rulers had evinced intentions to reconquer Jerusalem and had also displayed ability in relevant areas of war and diplomacy. Anyone looking at the history of key Holy Land locales in this period, such as Tiberias, can see that they were up for the taking—a relative novice whose main asset was discipline, such as Alptakin, could go far in the country. There were many reasons for this, but surely the leading one was ideological: whereas at Yarmuk, Islam was a profoundly unifying force among scattered and otherwise mutually suspicious tribes, 350 years of succession challenges, and of roving caliphates between Syria, Egypt, and Iraq, had seemingly rubbed out of Islam its talent for cohesion and unity. Strikingly, the strengthening of Shi'ite movements in this period enhanced Islamic reputations of militancy, but they did nothing to enhance unity. As the Qarmati-Fatimid rivalry demonstrated, the opposite was probably the case: the rise of Shi'ism rendered areas under Islamic control more vulnerable, especially ones which were coveted by forces whose orientation had profound, long-standing, spiritual, and ideological roots.

Readers who are familiar with the works of the outstanding western scholars who wrote monumental works about the Crusades will recall how these Christian scholars, no matter how objectively detached and secularized they seem to be, become progressively disenchanted as they describe, from one Crusade to the next, in-fighting between the "native" Byzantine Christians and the western Crusaders, and also the sheer venality and rapaciousness displayed by many of the Crusaders. In fact, not just in our postmodern, politically correct, era, but also several decades earlier, important scholars such as the Hebrew University's Joshua Prawer used the pejorative-sounding term, "colonialism," to frame the Crusades, and it is hard to foresee any other rubric dominating study of this phenomenon for decades to come. But—setting aside moral judgments—our angle of analysis here, looking at events on the ground in a locale like Galilee, in decades well before the Crusader explosion, encourages a somewhat different way of looking at the issue. Hardly saints, the Crusaders were, by and large, an ideologically unified group. Until the era of Saladin and the battle at Hattin, Islamic politics were not that—not unlike the Jewish situation in the late Second Temple period, Islamic political circumstances were a fury of disorder waiting to be exploited by anything that had the requisite ideological motivation to do so. As the eleventh century advanced, Christian-Islam relations were in suspension, largely because of the logistical shortcomings and tactical indecisiveness of characters like Byzantine Emperor John Tzimisces. What injected a time-delay explosive device in this state of suspension was Fatimid recklessness. If anyone doubted that Christians had debts to close in the Holy Land, the reign of the sixth Fatimid Caliph (996–1021 CE), al-Hakim bi-Amr Allah settled the issue.

His reign has been described colorfully in many histories, and since its most provocative episode, the burning of the church of the Holy Sepulchre, occurred in Jerusalem, its details need not occupy us here. I assume that many western-oriented readers who, at this juncture, carry out an "al-Hakim" Google search will become acquainted with this Fatimid Caliph as a kind of al-Qaeda forerunner who, as a special supplementary indignity, harbored genocidal intentions toward dogs. It suffices to mention just a few points here. One is that scholars have identified an underlying rationale for the earlier phases of Hakim's career—he persecuted Christians as retribution for their anti-Fatimid orientations.[77] Second, in keeping with the Middle East's penchant for polarization, it is important to keep in mind that millions of people in the region totally ignore or dismiss the madman attributes which have long been attributed to al-Hakim in the west. They, in fact, regard al-Hakim as a prophet. For our Galilee purposes, the most important such group are the Druze. The Druze, historically, have made enemies, but they have everlastingly been considered an enigmatic, not extremist, group (in connotation, their name, when mentioned in Hebrew, and, I presume, other languages, is virtually metonymic for "enigma"); when viewed closely, and insofar as generalization can be permitted, the Druze personify a quite compelling, anti-sovereign, model of national survival and continuity. We will return to them in this study's second volume—for now, I defer the discussion because, from a historian's standpoint, the Druze become a fascinatingly intriguing group because of the way they re-worked memories of the Crusades, and not because of the controversial behavior of their inspirational prophet decades before the start of this western intervention in the Middle East. Third, following the suggestion of several scholars, I think it is correct to end our analysis of Galilee in this early Islamic period with al-Hakim's caliphate. The assault on the church of the Holy Sepulchre and other sacred Christian sites in al-Sham set unstoppable dynamics in motion, on the path to Pope Urban II's call at Clermont, in 1095. Among many other things, as soon as reports of the atrocity done to the Jerusalem church reached Europe, Jews were evicted from various locales. In the minds of many historians, of all the dynamics that al-Hakim provoked, not rampant anti-Semitism (which always found causes to latch onto), but rather the "idea of western intervention to protect the holy places in Palestine," was the most important one.[78]

PALESTINIAN VILLAGES IN GALILEE IN THE EARLY ISLAMIC PERIOD

Yet, drawing this early Islamic, Umayyad to Abbasid to Fatimid, period to a close, we still have a little work to do, but not as additional warm-up to the Crusades in Acre and Galilee. Instead, from the Arab point of view, we should set the stage for a still later catastrophe in Galilee, the 1948 Nakba.

When we define the early Islamic period broadly, not just as the Umayyad dynasty but rather as the entire, nearly 400 years, era preceding the Crusader invasion, aforementioned generalizations about Islamic settlement in Galilee remain more or less remain valid. When we hazarded the generalization about the Islamic conquest not being settlement-oriented, we were referring to the Umayyad period in which tribal organizations whose mobilization brought about the Byzantine defeat had a nomadic character, and did not therefore readily associate military triumph with land-grabbing, just as they were not habituated to the sort of agricultural work by which peoples plant roots in specific locales. Yet we have also seen factors in subsequent, Abbasid and Fatimid periods, which might have militated against Arab settlement in the country. Unlike the Umayyads, the Abbasids were stand-offish about al-Sham, in a number of ways. Now and then regimes arose which were inclined to invest in infrastructure development in the country and thereby create conditions for large-scale settlement—we recall the Tulunid investment in the Acre harbor as a good example. But, as a result of the chaotic turbulence of Islamic politics in the region, these regimes did not remain intact in al-Sham long enough to sustain a long-term settlement project of any sort, be it deliberately calculated or naturally flowing.

However much he exaggerated about figures, Josephus describes heavy Jewish settlement in Galilee in years ahead of the great rebellion against Rome. For the aforementioned reasons, nothing comparable, from a Palestinian (in our contemporary sense of the word) vantage point, can be said about Galilee's Muslim population a thousand years later. Insofar as the ongoing Palestinian-Israeli dispute boils down to the depth and veracity of competing land claims, this historical analysis, so far, sounds like bad news for the Palestinians.

That is not really the case, however. Much to the detriment of its potential as a democratic, morally just, state, Israel's propaganda machine has, over the decades, become so well-honed and aggressive that Nakba denial has become institutionalized in the country's mainstream political culture. Easily overcoming a passing, truth-telling, "post-Zionist" glitch at the end of the twentieth-century, right-wing Israeli politicians have campaigned effectively for years to out-law references to the 1948 Palestinian catastrophe, the Nakba, or to cut-off public funding for artistic or educational ventures which want to examine its realities and consequences.

The issue raised by this illiberal, anti-Nakba, campaign is whether any religious-national group has the right to maintain an exclusionist attitude toward a region like Galilee, where monotheism multiplied, claiming that the area really "belongs" to it, and to no other group. In terms of the Palestinian-Israeli conflict, this exclusionist attitude on the Jewish side revolves around an historical assessment holding that Palestinian claims as an indigenous population are artificial and disingenuous. The Palestinians, on this theory, are relative newcomers to the land, having largely arrived in it during the British Mandate period (due to the attraction of westernization benefits) or the late Ottoman period, just a few generations before, if before, European Zionists who immigrated to the country from the 1880s onward. In a cruelly misguided, and under-researched, 1984 volume,[79] the pro-Israel propagandist Joan Peters ridiculed Palestinian claims of indigenous rootedness in the country, mocking their proponents for imagining that Palestinians have been in the land "from time immemorial." Peters' minatory and duplicitous analysis was discredited by Edward Said and others, but in pro-Israel culture this exposure was only skin deep.

In a bizarre series of twists symptomatic of the pathology of global politics after one generation in the new millennium, strong-men politicians on Israel's political right, such as Avigdor Lieberman, who have for many years taunted and threatened Israel's non-Jewish minorities by talking about the imposition of political loyalty tests and by promoting Nakba denial laws, have become popular with Israel's *liberal-minded* elements. This can only have happened as a result of the failure in the way history is taught in Israel's educational system. It has happened because children in the country were never taught to distinguish between political realities, on the one hand, and historical truth, on the other hand, and then to find some creative compromise between these two, non-identical, phenomena. The political reality is that Galilee, and the rest of the lands upon which Israel asserted sovereignty before 1967, with solid (not unanimous, but solid) international backing, must remain under Israel's sovereign control, if our country is to survive. But the historical truth is that Galilee does not "belong" to us (Jews), just as it does not belong exclusively to Christians and Muslims. You are a citizen of one type (I daresay a liberal type) if you constantly and judiciously, not only with an open heart but also with an unflinching willingness to fight for your own survival, balance political realities and historical truths. You are a citizen of another type if you mistakenly believe that political realities are the historical truth.

Prominent scholars of the early Islamic era and the Crusader era, it bears mention, have never been in agreement about the basic demographic realities of these periods.[80] As one era turned its page, and the Crusader conquest began, the Christians remained a majority in Palestine's rural population, contended Gil. But Joshua Prawer, a Crusader authority, proclaimed that Muslims were a majority at this juncture, "certainly to the south of Lebanon." Both scholars concurred that these Muslims in the country were not predominately Arab nomads—Muslims in Palestine were mostly descendants of local converts, Christians, Jews, and Samaritans. This sole point of agreement between them inspired other researchers to examine how such a conversion process might have unfolded in late phases of the pre-Crusader, Islamic, period. In one careful examination of this topic, Nehamia Levtzion conceded that there is no real evidence of mass conversion to Islam by Christians or other groups in Palestine, in the pre-Crusader period. Islamic conversion, he suggested, is a longue duree process only perceptible in Palestine (and elsewhere) over centuries; it resulted as an Islamic infrastructure consolidated in the country, and also when Mamluk elites (in the post-Crusader period) sent out hostile signals about the value of non-Islamic cultures, both of these being long-term processes. There is no strong indication of episodes of compulsory conversion to Islam in Palestine or Syria, and though there is an array of scholarly opinion about how the *jizyah* poll tax imposed on non-Muslims might have incentivized conversion in the pre-Crusader period, Levtzion doubted that the jizyah was a determinative factor. Moreover, the conversion of Christians in Palestine in decades after the fall of Byzantine rule could not have been quick or massive, Levtzion reasoned, since most Christians in the country (he believed) were Jacobite monophysites who were estranged from Byzantine Orthodoxy, and sometimes welcomed Muslim conquerors. All told, Levtzion concluded, the one undeniable demographic trend in the country in centuries spanning between the Byzantine period and the onset of Ottoman rule in the sixteenth century is huge population decline, a drop from about one million persons to 300,000, over nine centuries. Islam took root in Palestine in a protracted process in which a concurrent, comparably significant, demographic trend of population flight unfolded. All of these points have to be kept in mind in discussions about the continuity of any group's population, Jewish, Muslim, or Christian, in Palestine from ancient and medieval times, through modernity.

Islamic settlers did not have a massive presence in Galilee one thousand years ago. But they had a substantive one. Palestinians who remained or left the country in 1948 may not have been here from "time immemorial" (nor, of course, were many Jews at the time indubitably rooted in the land for multiple, consecutive generations), but a significant number of these Palestinians lived in villages where their own forefathers, or Islamic brethren, had dwelled a very long time ago. Quite possibly, some Palestinians victimized by defeat in the Nakba were leaving villages where their families had lived for *one thousand years*.

A compilation of travel reports and geographical studies submitted by Arab medieval chroniclers conveys interesting, unequivocal information about this last claim of millennium-length Palestinian indigeneity in Galilee. The book was compiled in 1890 by an English Orientalist, Guy Le Strange, who is touted by Walid Khalidi, himself a tireless documentarian of the Nakba, as the greatest scholar of Islamic medieval geography to write in English.[81] Strange worked a decade before the advent of organized Zionism, and about a quarter century before his own country extended patronage to Jewish national settlement in Palestine via the Balfour Declaration and the assumption of Mandatory control—that is to say, he had no reason to fudge his work in any way attendant to what we today recognize as its political implications. As to the reports of the Arab geographers and travelers he collated: they had absolutely no incentive to embellish details of what we would now call "Palestinian" settlement in the region, from the eighth century through the first phases of the Crusader era. On the contrary, many of them display an animus of some sort toward the country's residents—we have, for example, already alluded to Muqaddasi's recoil from what he regarded as the low cultural level of Muslim residents in the country. Strange's volume is, in short, politics-free, at least with regard to political issues of import to us today.

Because the 1948 Nakba was primarily (though by no means exclusively) a Galilee event and because illiberal deniers of the catastrophe believe they have historical truth on their side, it is natural to wonder about the depth of Palestinian "roots" in Galilee. Specifically, heading to the High Middle Ages and the Crusader midpoint in our two-volume study, a juncture preceded by several centuries of Islamic rule, it is natural to wonder how many "Palestinians" might have lived in the region. The issue is not, I believe, quantifiable on an individual numerical level, but Strange's book allows us to reliably account for this "roots"/indigeneity sort of issue on a communal level. Through the first decades of Crusader rule, the Arab geographers document viable Islamic village life in some twenty-five Galilee locales—again, this might be indicative of the fact that the Islamic conquest in Palestine was not, throughout this long period, settlement-oriented, but it is nonetheless a substantive number, one easily large enough to rebut conclusively the Nakba denial school's thesis about shallow Palestinian roots in Galilee.

Some locales pleased the geographers because of their special attractions. Near Acre, in the coastal district, for instance, Muqaddasi was impressed by the village of Kabul, because of its sugar cane fields. "They make excellent sugar, better than anywhere else in Syria," he noted.[82] At the Ma'aliya village, in upper Galilee, the travel writer from Damascus known as "Dimashki" was impressed by musk pears grown in a valley. They are "incomparable for their exquisiteness of fragrance and flavor," he exuded. Ma'aliya had a "fine castle;" the Crusaders used it as a frontier fortress, but the Mamluk leader

Baibars had captured the locale before Dimashki composed his report, around 1300.[83] Another village which charmed Muqaddasi was Kadas (Kadesh Naphthali), near the Hula. "This is a small town on the slope of a mountain," Muqaddasi relayed. "It is full of good things—it has three springs for drink and there is a bath below the city." He warned, however, that weather at the village "is very hot."[84]

Muqaddasi regarded the Hula as Galilee's epicenter. He called its water source the "Lake of Kadas," and, ever the grandson of a gifted hydraulic architect-engineer, he was fascinated by the swampy area's transformation as this lake: "In order to form the lake, they have built a wonderful embankment of masonry along the river, confining the water to its bed." Reed found around the lake provided a livelihood for Kadas residents, who used it to weave mats. The lake was full of fish.[85] The Hula Lake, in Muqadassi's observations, is at the core of al-Sham's water grid. He wrote that the Jordan River descended from Banias, pouring into the Kadas Lake, and then flowed toward Tiberias and spilled into the Sea of Galilee. From there, it flowed through the Jordan Valley (the Ghaur Valley) into the Overwhelming Lake (the Dead Sea).[86]

Galilee, on Islamic interpretations, was filled with places important in the lives of the Biblical patriarch Jacob and his sons, and there were also supposed to be locales connected to Moses in the region. Many settled Galilee villages intrigued the chroniclers because of such presumed holy sites. Yaqut, for instance, visited Kafr Manda, in lower Galilee on the slopes of Mt. Atzmon, and reasoned that its name was derived from Maydan (Midian). He reported that he located the tomb of Moses' wife, as well as a "rock which Moses raised up in order to give himself and his wife water to drink." So, too, at Kafr Manda were the tombs of two sons of Jacob, Asher and Naphtali.[87] Also, Kasr Yakub, "between Tiberias and Banias," was where "Jacob wept for the loss of Joseph, and the pit where the latter was thrown is near here."[88] Chroniclers believed that another son of Jacob, Judah, was buried in Rumah, described as a "small village near Tiberias."[89] Visiting Irbil (Arbel), near Tiberias, Nasir i-Khusrau reported the existence of four graves on a mountain, on the village's south side (this citation precedes important Jewish references known to contemporary Israel excavators of an area memorably described by Josephus[90]). Almost 200 years later, Yaqut's writing verifies that there was a village at Irbil.[91]

At Ibilin, the Persian writer Nasir i-Khusrau found a site connected to the pre-Islamic history of Arabia, the tomb of the prophet Hud, as well as sites of significance in the Hebrew Bible, such as the tomb of the prophet Uzair (apparently Ezra).[92] Close to coastal Acre, Nasir visited a village named Damun, where he reported the discovery of the tomb of Dhul Kifl, the son of Job, in a small cave.[93] On this 1017 visit, Nasir stopped also at the Birwah village, located between Acre and Damun, where he reported that the tombs of Ish (Esau) and Sham'un (Simeon) could be visited.[94] Some 930 years later the Palestinian poet Mahmoud Darwish and his family fled from this village, which was destroyed in the Nakba.[95]

Another village visited by Yaqut was Aksal—the village neighbors Nazareth but, following his cultural coordinates, Yaqut mentioned only its distance from Tiberias.[96] Yaqut's writing verifies the existence of other villages around Tiberias and the Sea of Galilee, including Kafr Akib, Susiyah and Kafr Sabt (Yaqut also located Daburiyyah in Tiberias' vicinity).[97]

Nazareth was not totally ignored by these Muslim chroniclers. Masudi, a Baghdad native and the author of a popular history called *Meadows of Gold*, visited al-Sham in 926 CE, and reported on Nazareth, noting "I myself have seen in this village a church greatly venerated by the Christians. There are in it sarcophagi of stone." Yaqut noted that Nazareth is 13 miles from Tiberias. Dimashki called Nazareth a "Hebrew city," but mentioned that "it is a well-known place of pilgrimage for the Christians."[98]

Christian associations of some Galilee villages seemed to be unknown to some of these geographers and travel writers, and we can see how some locales which are hallowed in the New Testament became more or less Islamicized in the centuries between Byzantine and Crusader rule. Kafr Kannah, or Cana, the site of the wedding where Jesus turned water into wine (John 2:1–12), was visited by Nasir i-Khusrau in 1047 CE, whose interest in its Christian roots was exhausted by a glancing reference to a fine monastery overlooking the village. He seemed more interested in the village well, which held "sweet and good water." Later, Dimashki's report focused solely on the contemporary (circa 1300 CE) social situation in this village. "The chiefs of several tribes live here, and they are all turbulent and warlike" (he noted that the strongest tribe was called Kais al Hamra, the red).[99]

Political volatility stirred by the Crusader wars impacted on some travel reports. Ibn Jubair, a Spanish-Arab who traveled out from Granada in 1183 CE and visited Palestine two years later, authored a telling description of Beit Jan, located, he said, between Darayyah and Banias. Heading out from this village in the direction of Banias, he reported, one encounters a large, sprawling oak tree. He explained why locals called it the "tree of balance": if you were to pass it on one side, the Crusaders would surely catch you, but if you passed by the tree on the other side, you could proceed safely in your travels.[100] At the village of Hittin, Yaqut articulated his opinion on an ongoing debate, stimulated by a report filed by a previous visitor, Ali of Herat, as to whether the tomb of Shu'aib (Jethro) was located in it. When Yaqut visited this village, memories of fateful events of the 1187 CE battle, fought there some forty years earlier, were still relatively fresh. His recap of the battle at Hattin (discussed in the next chapter) warrants quotation: "Saladin gained a great victory here over the Franks . . . the kings of the Franks were all vanquished in this battle, and all the coast towns were freed from them. Their Pharaoah Arbat [Robert] was slain in this battle."[101]

Mesmerized in a Galilee stretch between the Hula and Banias, Muqaddasi wrote at some length about current events in the Banias village, which he located "near the border of the Hula, at the foot of Hermon," adding that it was blessed with "climate softer and pleasanter than that of Damascus." Muqaddasi visited this village in the period of Arab-Byzantine fighting, after Taurus had been captured by the Christians, and he reported that "the greater part of the Muslim inhabitants" in "frontier districts" around Taurus had migrated to this Upper Galilee village (the locale's reverential standing in Christianity, in Matthew 16, as the home of Peter's rock, has no echo here). The village river was "extremely cold" and refreshing, and also irrigated cotton and rice fields; fields around the village served as the "granary of Damascus." The village town, he concluded, "is pleasant to inhabit, being situated among lovely villages, and the sole drawback is that the drinking water is bad."[102]

After having been a powerful locus of Jewish cultural, religious, and political activity in Galilee for centuries, Sepphoris' presence became negligible in this early Islamic era.[103] Calling it Saffuriyah, Yaqut makes no more than a glancing reference to a "town in the Jordan [Urdunn] province, near Tiberias.[104] Today, scholars assume that Sepphoris was not "permanently abandoned" after Byzantine times, and they allude to a few coins found in the town's area which date from the period of the Islamic conquest. The Crusaders captured the town, called it Le Saphorie, and turned it into one of sixteen bourgs in the Kingdom of Jerusalem. Subsequently, during the Mamluk period, "it seems reasonable to assume that there was steady growth [in Sepphoris'] Muslim community up to the time of the Ottoman conquest of Palestine in 1516."[105]

Finally, the Arab geographers make no mention of Safed in reports composed before the Crusades. Galilee's entrancing hilltop city caught their eye because of engineering feats in it that were carried out by the Crusaders and then the Mamluks. Dimashki, circa 1300 CE, referred to a fortress at Safed maintained by "a unit of Franks [Crusaders] called Templars." Mamluk Sultan Baibars captured the fortress in 1266, Dimashki reported, and, on a hill adjacent to the town, he executed everyone who had fought in the fortress. He then tore down the Crusader structure and built a *Kullah* castle tower in its stead. The structure amazed Dimashki, who detailed how five horses could, side-by-side, climb up the castle's wide winding passageway, where there were no stairs. Mamluk forces drew water from a well called As Saturah—the pulley system, replete with ropes, wooden casks, mule power, and iron levers shaped like human hands, thrilled this chronicler, who raved about it as "one of the wonders of the world." He related how he had stood at the mouth of As Saturah, and hollered.

After what seemed like a minute his words had hit the water at the well's surface and returned to him, exactly as he had said them.[106] Dimashki would be far from the last person in Safed to hear what sounded like wondrous echoes.

NOTES

1. Moshe Gil, *A History of Palestine, 634-1099* (New York: Cambridge University Press, 1992), 111–113.
2. Ibid, 106.
3. Ibid, 107.
4. Ibid, 134–135.
5. Ibid, 170.
6. Ibid, 169–171.
7. Nehamia Levtzion, "Conversion to Islam in Syria and Palestine and the Survival of Christian Communities," in Michael Gervers, Ramzi Jibran Bikhazi (eds.), *Conversion and Continuity: Indigenous Christian Communities in Islamic Lands, Eight to Eighteenth Centuries* (Toronto: Pontifical Institute of Medieval Studies, 1990), 293.
8. Gil, 76–78.
9. Ibid, 79–80.
10. Ibid, 85–86.
11. Ibid, 61–62.
12. "Secrets," https://pages.uncc.edu/john-reeves/research-projects/trajectories-in-near-eastern-apocalyptic/nistarot-secrets-of-r-shimon-b-yohai-2/.
13. Gil, 63–64.
14. Oded Avissar, *Sefer Tiveria* (Jerusalem: Keter, 1973), 91.
15. Secrets.
16. Gil, 108–109.
17. Robert Schick, *The Christian Communities of Palestine from Byzantine to Islamic Rule* (Princeton: Darwin Press, 1995), 218, 223.
18. Ibid, 202.
19. Gil, 83.
20. Ibid, 216–217.
21. Schick, 83.
22. Ibid, 109.
23. Ibid, 108.
24. Ibid, 101–107.
25. Ibid, 112–117.
26. Ibid, 280.
27. Ibid, 179.
28. Avissar, 92; Gil, 89–90.
29. Yoram Tsafrir, Gideon Foerster, "The Dating of the 'Earthquake of the Sabbatical Year' of 749 C.E. in Palestine," *Bulletin of the School of Oriental and African Studies, University of London* 55, no. 2 (1992): 231–235.

30. Gil, 175.
31. Gil, 175.
32. Guy Le Strange, *Palestine Under the Moslems: A Description of Syria and the Holy Land from A.D. 650 to 1500* (Beirut: Khayats, 1965), 334–335.
33. Avissar, 92.
34. Le Strange, *Palestine,* 357.
35. Schick, 464–465.
36. Gil, 125.
37. Ibid, 491.
38. Ibid, 494.
39. Ibid, 504.
40. Ibid, 499.
41. Avissar, 92.
42. Gil, 564–565.
43. Gil, 177, 563–568.
44. Avissar, 92.
45. Gil, 500.
46. Avissar, 92.
47. Gil, 179.
48. Avissar, 93.
49. Gil, 181. There is no evidence of a Karaite community in Tiberias in this period (Gil, 178, 182).
50. Gil, 177.
51. Ibid.
52. Ibid, 329.
53. Ibid.
54. Ibid, 183.
55. Ibid, 185.
56. Le Strange, *Palestine,* 335.
57. Gil, 279.
58. Ibid.
59. Ibid, 307.
60. Le Strange, *Palestine,* 23.
61. Ibid, 21.
62. Ibid, 328–329.
63. Ibid, 332–333.
64. Ibid, 329–330.
65. Gil, 190.
66. Ibid, 310.
67. Ibid, 348.
68. Ibid, 312.
69. Ibid, 313.
70. Ibid, 321.
71. Ibid.
72. Ibid, 323.

73. Ibid, 337.
74. Ibid, 353.
75. Ibid, 355.
76. Ibid, 345.
77. S. D. Goitein, *A Mediterranean Society: The Jewish Communities of the Arab World as Portrayed in the Documents of the Cairo Geniza* (Berkeley: University of California Press, 1967–83), vol. 2, 283–284.
78. Ibid, 379.
79. Joan Peters, *From Time Immemorial: the Origins of the Arab-Jewish Conflict over Palestine* (New York: Harper and Row, 1984).
80. This discussion summarizes the main points of Levtzion, "Conversion to Islam."
81. Le Strange, *Palestine* (preface by Walid Khalidy).
82. Le Strange, *Palestine,* 467.
83. Ibid, 495.
84. Ibid, 468.
85. Ibid, 68.
86. Ibid, 52–53.
87. Ibid, 470.
88. Ibid, 482.
89. Ibid, 521.
90. Eilan, *Arbel,* 7–15.
91. Le Strange, *Palestine,* 457–458.
92. Ibid, 382.
93. Ibid, 435.
94. Ibid, 423.
95. Reuven Snir, introduction to *Mahmud Darwish, Hamishim shenot shira* (N.P.: Keshev, 2015), 42–53.
96. Le Strange, *Palestine,* 390.
97. Ibid, 427, 468, 471, 540.
98. Ibid, 301–302.
99. Ibid, 469.
100. Ibid, 412.
101. Ibid, 451.
102. Ibid, 418.
103. For a survey of references to Sepphoris by Arab writers in this era: Strange, *Excavations,* 24.
104. Le Strange, *Palestine,* 525.
105. Seth Ward, "Sepphoris in Sacred Geography," in Meyers, *Galilee Through,* 393–395.
106. Le Strange, *Palestine,* 424–425.

Chapter 6

Crusader Galilee

INTRODUCTION: WHY STUDY THE CRUSADES IN GALILEE?

Jerusalem was the focus of the Crusader movement in the Middle East, which lasted from Pope Urban II's call at Clermont in 1095, to the final defeat of the Franks' Second Latin Kingdom in the Holy Land at the hands of the Mamluks in 1291. The First Crusade's capstone was the conquest of Jerusalem, an event scarred by gruesome brutality, not only when measured by contemporary yardsticks, but also one which, when viewed by its own standards, was distinguished by physical courage, astounding stamina, and religious idealism.

During the Crusades, Galilee, including its port outlet of Acre, figured as a supporting actor. Galilee, to be sure, was important, but it was nonetheless a consolation prize. Its subordinate status is exemplified by the fact that the most dramatic event in this two hundred year Crusader epoch, which occurred at its midpoint in 1187 at Hattin, near Tiberias, was perceived in Europe as a horrendous catastrophe because it led to Islam's seizure of Jerusalem—but Hattin was nonetheless never thought of as total obliteration. That is because the Latin Kingdom regrouped in the north, at Acre, for its second incarnation. In this, and many other examples, Galilee's function in the Crusades is indeed comparable to what understudies are supposed to do, holding the stage for a while when the star of the show has the flu.

The same dynamic can be identified on a biographical level. For reasons which we will examine, Tancred, an Italo-Norman and the most outstanding character in the First Crusade, was unable to climb to the pinnacle of the new Latin regime, and become its king. As a sort of second prize, he became Prince of Galilee, while others, starting with Godfrey of Bouillon (who modestly declined the formal title, "king") won fuller glory by becoming Crusader rulers in Jerusalem. Many decades later, France's King Louis IX, widely regarded as the preeminent figure in the Crusader period as a whole, regrouped in Acre after a devastating experience in Egypt of military defeat and captivity. In his case, Galilee was a sorrowful consolation prize, a venue for soul-searching penitence symbolic of the impending end of the Crusader movement in the Holy Land. Had he reached Jerusalem, this phase of his career would have been written in an utterly different, optimistic, hue.

Such points are not open to dispute. Nonetheless, the thesis of this chapter is that many aspects of the Holy Land Crusader movement are better elucidated if we remain in the country's north, in Acre and Galilee, in lieu of Jerusalem. This is what historians call a "revisionist" contention, challenging a huge corpus of writings on the Crusades whose center is Jerusalem.

In general, Crusader historiography has developed richly in recent decades, to the point where enveloped within it are well-defined interpretive schools. An ongoing debate focuses on the motives of the Crusader knights. One line of interpretation, associated with the scholar J. Riley-Smith, emphasizes the Franks' religious piety,[1] whereas Steven Runciman, the twentieth century's most influential English-writing scholar on the Crusades, adopted a much harsher view of the Crusaders' orientations and impulses (Runciman famously defined the Crusades as "one long act of intolerance in the name of God which is the sin against the Holy Ghost"[2]). Scholars of the Crusades are sometimes divided into four groups: "generalists," who emphasize how Crusader phenomena emerged out of Christian warfare trends which preceded 1095, "popularists" who stress roots of popular piety in the Crusades, "traditionalists," who insist on the centrality of Holy Land and Jerusalem, and "pluralists" who focus on issues of papal directives, canon law, and pious motivations and doubt whether the warfare was directed at one overriding destination.[3]

In terms of this nomenclature, my impression is that in popular discussions about the Crusades, the "traditionalists" have the upper hand. Witness, for example, Karen Armstrong's influential 1988 volume on the topic, which insists on a "triple vision" (Muslim, Christian, and Jewish) perspective honed to past and present events in the Middle East, particularly involving Israel and the Palestinian Authority. Armstrong assertively draws analogies between the Crusades and recent developments in the Arab-Israeli conflict.[4] If most of us are, to some extent, "traditionalists" attuned to crusading in the Holy Land, why, then is our geography within this country so tilted and limited? What happened in Galilee during the Crusades?

Remarkably, to my knowledge, there is no single, comprehensive study of Frankish Galilee. There are some important specialized studies which undergird many passages in this chapter.[5] But there is no master study of

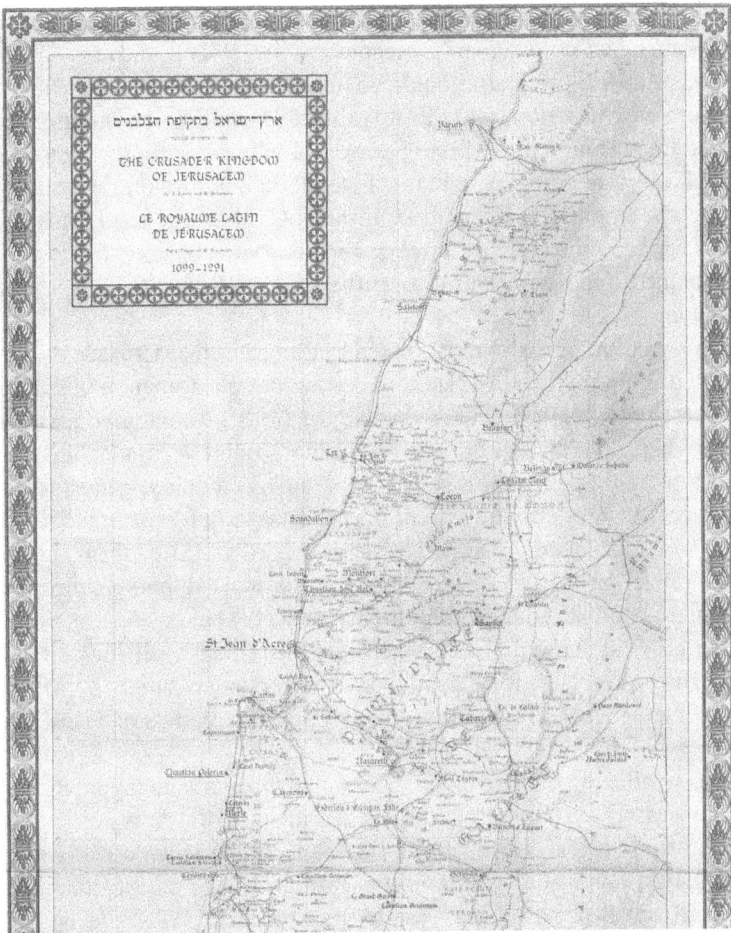

Figure 6.1 Map of Galilee in Crusader Times, based on work of J. Prawer and M. Benvenisti. *Source*: Courtesy of Tel-Hai College Historical Maps Archive.

the Crusades and Galilee, one which integrates knowledge of what was happening on a global level in this medieval period, the biographies of several non-politically correct but nevertheless (forgive me) thrilling or inspiring personalities like Tancred or Louis IX, and on-the-ground details of military battles or rural settlement processes in Galilee. This makes little sense for three reasons, one numerical, another colonial, and the third military.

On a simple, quantitative level, and relying on this volume's methodological premise that Galilee has a special place in world culture dating from the period of Jesus' lifetime, the region has a two-thousand year history, meaning that the Crusades constitute a rather durable phenomenon, 10 percent of the total, and not just a blip on its radar screen.

Second, without getting into contentious subtleties of what counts as colonialism or as colonialism's precursors, the Holy Land crusade movement constitutes a fascinating and provocative example of overseas or far-off settlement expansion, and the ways it built itself up on the ground, and imagined that it might have staying power, obviously warrant serious consideration. From this colonial settlement standpoint, Jerusalem, as a holy city, is distinctive and not representative. Instead, Galilee, the first lordship in the country, founded by Tancred, provides a fuller view of how this experiment in transplanted feudalism unfolded at the time, and whether it was possibly sustainable.

Being "traditionalists," most people associate the Crusades with the Holy Land, but they were in fact a wide-ranging phenomenon which spread north, west, and south in Europe, in key regions of contemporary Turkey, and elsewhere. So there were many, on-the-ground, Crusader feudal lordships. However much such discoveries strained credulity, relics associated with Jesus' life kept cropping up in many of these fiefdoms, including areas located well outside of Palestine's historic borders. Still, from this settlement colonization standpoint, Galilee was the most important rural area to be conquered and administered by the Crusaders. That is because, outside of Jerusalem, it was the only place where the movement's self-perception as a sacred effort to reclaim for Christianity lands "contaminated" by Muslim or pagan elements was indisputably rooted in gospel accounts of Jesus' life and mission.

Third, Galilee was the venue of epochal military engagements in the Crusader era. They transpired at a medieval midpoint between late antiquity's fateful battle at Yarmuk, and the later, dramatic events of Zionism's Independence War victory and the Palestinian Nakba catastrophe in 1948. In each of these battle phases, Yarmuk, Crusades, 1948, the geography, demographics, and cultural character of the world's monotheistic faiths were determined and reshaped on battlefields in the heart of Galilee, or on its perimeter.

Of these three instances, the Crusader period is unique in that one of its two great battles featured an outside, menacing, presence, the Mongols, thereby teasing or prodding monotheistic rivals toward a scenario that is well known among devotees of science fiction films. On this scenario, circumstances encourage long-standing foes to consider whether they should set aside their mutual animosity in order to survive against a shared threat. At the end of this chapter, closing this volume and half of our study of Galilee's history, we will consider whether the challenge posed by the Mongols in the mid-thirteenth century is rightly framed as such a science fiction-like scenario posed by an incomprehensibly dangerous foe from afar. Less debatably, Crusader warfare in the Galilee region had a lasting and troubling normative meaning. The Crusades showed how monotheism may promote its claims by shedding blood.

By medieval times, Christianity had no cause to regard Judaism as a vibrant sociopolitical presence capable of putting up a fight. In late antiquity, at Yarmuk, a Byzantine leader such as Heraclius, whose lifetime was coterminous with that of the Prophet Muhammad, could not really have grasped how Islam was transforming itself into a powerful monotheistic presence and rival. When they are put on such a timeline, the Crusades can be seen for what they were, a noticeably bloody exercise in historical game-changing. The Crusades were, of course, preceded by a long series of bellicose episodes involving Christian and Muslim soldiers, and Jewish victims; nevertheless, they were, on the level of human consciousness, transformative. The Crusades proved that "Holy War" was not an oxymoronic notion, but rather a defining experience in the world created by monotheism.[6]

In Galilee, this reality was especially sobering and poignant. The region where Jesus' Sermon on the Mount dared human morality to embrace values of forgiveness, compassion, and love is the one where Christians and Muslims and Jews staged life-or-death battles in the name of their own most cherished values, or physical survival, wielding swords, trebuchet siege machines and Czech rifles. On one level or another, that cannot be coincidence.

From the Christian standpoint, the roots of Holy War doctrine can be traced to the searing ambiguity of the Book of Matthew, the gospel which has inspired images of a militant Jesus, just as its Sermon on the Mount hallowed "turn the other cheek" pacifism. From the First Crusade onward, knights who viewed themselves as "milites Christ," warriors of Christ, quoted Matthew (16:24): "whoever wants to be my disciple must deny themselves and take up their cross and follow me."[7] Read in its gospel context, Jesus' preaching in this and other passages can be interpreted as referring to a *spiritual* crusade, either of an eschatological character, as preparation for the world to come, or as "Born Again," moral revivalism. The road to the Holy Wars of the Crusades was paved once theologians and preacher activists started insisting that such gospel passages had a second meaning, that Jesus' stricture to "follow me" could also entail actual warfare. This is exactly what Bernard of Clairvaux, the most prominent recruiter for the Second Crusade, had in mind when he referred to a "double fight." Upon the establishment of the Templar order, Bernard welcomed "a new sort of knighthood, fighting indefatigably a double fight against flesh and blood as well as against the immaterial forces of evil in the skies. . . . The knight who puts the breastplate of faith on his soul in the same way as he puts a breastplate of iron on his body is truly intrepid and safe from everything."[8]

Early church fathers, explains Crusader scholar Christopher Tyerman, interpreted the "charity texts of the New Testament [which] insisted on forgiveness" as being "applicable to the behavior of private persons, [and] not the behavior of public authorities." In Jerome's Latin version of the New Testament, which became canonical in the medieval west, "the exclusive word for enemy . . . is *inimicus*, a personal enemy, not *hostis*, a public enemy"—on this translation, turning the other cheek applied to conflicts between individual persons, not between countries or religious cultures. Also, Tyerman adds, the medieval church relied heavily on the Old Testament, on its moral stories and prophecies. For anyone interested in justifying Holy War concepts, the Hebrews' Old Testament "supplied rich pickings," he writes—Moses recruits the Levites to slaughter followers of the Golden Calf (Exodus 32: 26–28), God commands Saul to decimate the Amalekites, "men and women, infant and suckling" (I Samuel 15:3), and so on. When Augustine of Hippo developed a just war theory, based on ideas of justifiable cause, legitimate authority and rightful intents of participants, he used Old Testament wars as precedent. Sometimes drawing on such Hebraic sources, other times inspired by various contemporary calculations of sociopolitical expedience, a culture of religious warfare consolidated gradually after the fifth century, particularly in Germanic successor states of the Roman Empire. In short, when Urban II issued his call for what became known as the First Crusade, the concept of Holy War seemed viable and cogent to many of his listeners, and it was readily processed by them.[9]

Why Europeans of varying class and regional backgrounds answered his call is not germane in our study, nor is the chronicle of their experiences on their journey to the Holy Land and their surprising capture of Jerusalem in early summer 1099. We have, though, an excellent representation of how these motivations and unusual, dramatic experiences reached Galilee on the First Crusade—the story of Tancred. Our history of Crusader Galilee begins with him.

TANCRED, PRINCE OF GALILEE

The best, insider, account of Tancred was authored by Ralph of Caen sometime before 1118.[10] Like Tancred, Ralph was a Norman, and he was ordained for priesthood in 1106, under the direction of Arnulf of Chocques, Ralph's lifelong mentor who became Patriarch of Jerusalem in 1099 and served intermittently in that role until 1118. In 1106, Ralph became chaplain in the entourage of Bohemond, son of Robert Guiscard, a Norman swashbuckler famed for capturing Sicily; Bohemond became ruler of Antioch during the First Crusade, and he was also Tancred's uncle. At some uncertain point before Bohemond's death in 1111, Ralph left his service and became a staff-worker for Tancred, who stood in for Bohemond as Prince of Antioch. Ralph came to know Tancred well, and acquired valuable information from him. After Tancred's death in late 1112, Ralph drifted from Antioch to Jerusalem, where Arnulf had his protégé installed as a canon of the cathedral church, and actively supported Ralph's preparation of the *Gesta Tancredi*, also titled *A History of the Normans on the First Crusade*. Though it is the least well known of some five or six Latin accounts of the First Crusade which were composed either by participants, or by authors who had direct access to these early Crusaders, Ralph's memoir is an invaluable record of one of Galilee's most memorable characters, the Crusader who became Prince of the region (Tancred's formal title in Galilee warrants parenthetical mention—as Crusader historian Joshua Prawer explains, Tancred took the title *princeps*, a classification which exempted him from vassal dependence on the Crusader king in Jerusalem, and is therefore a token of Tancred's outstanding, independent, status in the First Crusade narrative[11]). Apparently for technical reasons, Ralph's memoir ends with telegraphically incomplete passages relating to latter years of the twelfth century's first decade, and it leapfrogs over Tancred's actual administration of Galilee.[12] This lacuna can be filled by gleaning information from specialized studies published in past decades, and which relate to an array of topics in the Galilee lordship which Tancred established.

As supplementary sources, there is a dissertation on Tancred, published in 1940,[13] and a number of hagiographic biographies which were published through the nineteenth century,[14] in the age of colonialism when there was renewed fascination with medieval times and its Crusades. Drawing partly on *Gesta Tancredi*, these adulatory biographies of Tancred convey semi-reliable anecdotes about his adventures. The epic poem, *La Gerusalemme liberate*, written by the Italian poet Torquato Tasso in 1581, is filled with legendary depictions of Tancred's exploits on the First Crusade which have no basis in fact, just as Disraeli's 1847 novel, *Tancred; or, the New Crusade* uses the Norman knight's name, but describes a nineteenth-century character whose life is not that of the Crusader. Though they have little to do with the "real" Tancred, such literary texts attest to how powerfully Tancred's chivalric image radiated over time.

His life generated innumerable gems of apocrypha. For instance, one legend, circulated by credulous Crusader historians through the nineteenth century, held that Tancred was the son of a Muslim emir named Makrizi. The basis for this fable is Crusader era coins which bear an imprint of Tancred wearing a turban. The turban itself has inspired sedulous but inconclusive discussion among experts. Prawer, the Hebrew of University of Jerusalem scholar who depicted Crusaders as non-integrated colonizers in the Middle East, dismissed speculation about how Tancred's headdress betokened a fair measure of European assimilation in an Arab region. Prawer soberly wrote that this Crusader, a "typical Norman mixture of craftiness and adventurism," put on a *keffiyeh* because he found it to be a useful way of dealing with the blazing Levantine sun (Prawer conceded, though, that Tancred spoke Arabic).[15] Nicholson, the Tancred dissertation author, argued that the Crusader had coins printed bearing his likeness in Saracen dress for political reasons, out of a desire to rally support among local inhabitants subordinate to him in Antioch. A prime magnet of Crusader myth, wholly heroic by the European standards of his time, no less than half monstrous by the politically correct measures of our own era, Tancred is an undeniably intriguing figure. What do we really know about him, and his relation to Galilee?

Tancred was the son of Marquis Odo the Good. Odo's region of rule is unknown, but popular accounts of Tancred refer to an estate called Santa-Agata, located in Calabria.[16] All accounts of his life refer to the animosity harbored in his Norman milieu toward Muslims ("Saracens"), and also toward Greek Christians; his great uncle Guiscard (Bohemond's father) spent his days driving members of these groups out of parts of Italy, or chasing them here and there in Byzantium. Tancred's inherited malice toward Byzantine Christians warrants comment. The biographical writings are so immersed in contempt for these eastern Christians—"the arrogance" of Byzantine Christian leaders was "equaled only by their cowardice and degradation," comments one such text[17]—that is sometimes difficult in their battle descriptions to ascertain whether Tancred and his men are warring against non-European Christians, or against Muslims from Turkey or Syria. Ralph depicts Tancred as being torn in his youthful years between New Testament values of charity and forgiveness, and the ethic of Holy War valor: "The Lord had commanded that after one cheek had been struck, the other was to be offered as well. But a secular military life did not even permit the sparing of a relative's blood."[18] In the biographies, after Tancred forges an alliance with Bohemond for journeying on the First Crusade, the first military report we receive of him is as a killing machine in Macedonia, on the Vardar River, where his victims are Greek Christians ("Half-dead bodies filled the banks on both the right and left, with a middle channel of blood"[19]).

Tancred's entry into Byzantine lands on the First Crusade led to the first, formative test of his chivalric honor. When the Norman Crusaders entered his jurisdiction, Byzantine Emperor Alexios I Komnenos began to wonder whether the main strategic threat he faced was posed by Muslim infidels, or by the Latin Crusaders. Wasting no time, the emperor demanded that the Normans take an oath of loyalty to him. Tempted by the lure of treasures offered to him by Alexios, or realizing pragmatically that he needed Byzantine materiel for his army's march toward Antioch and Jerusalem, Bohemond relented, and formally paid homage to the emperor. Balancing his loyalty to his uncle against his disdain for the Greek Christians was, for Tancred, tormenting. Tancred dodged repeated invitations sent by

Alexios. When circumstances finally hoisted him into the emperor's court in Constantinople, Tancred preserved his honor by announcing provisional support for the emperor, rather than proclaiming no-strings-attached homage. "If you wish to rule, strive to serve and you can be certain of [my] service when you have made clear that the army of Christ is your own," Tancred defiantly proclaimed to Alexios. "If you are the common leader, in the interest of everyone I will not refuse to serve you."[20]

Not long thereafter, Tancred taunted the Byzantine emperor, calling him an enemy. This happened when Alexios invited Tancred to choose a gift, expecting that he could purchase the Norman Crusader's loyalty by dishing out gold, silver, and gems. Instead, Tancred demanded that the emperor furnish him with a kind of portable palace tent, one which "looked like a city with a turreted atrium" and which required twenty beasts of burden for transport.[21] Alexios withdrew the gift offer, and the two men never saw one another again.

Tancred's biography grotesquely recalculates the obligations of feudal Christianity in crusading warring terms. Not everyone would find humor in its anecdotes, but there are hints of cheekiness in Ralph's accounts of Tancred's honor and courage. For instance, during one skirmish in the Franks' prolonged siege on Antioch, Tancred, according to the chroniclers, slayed 700 Turks, and then decapitated seventy of them so that their heads could be delivered to Bishop of Le Puy—in this tale, the one-tenth proportion mimics the ratio of tithes owed by Christians to local parish churches.[22] In another Antioch incident, Tancred impulsively set out on a patrol, under-equipped and accompanied only by his arms bearer. With daring commando finesse, as in an action film, he skewered three Turks who tried to ambush him.[23] The incident entered his chivalry repertoire because of its denouement—Tancred compelled his arms bearer not to tell anyone of the triple kill.[24]

Something of a loner, Tancred forged no lasting political alliances. His only ongoing relationship was with Bohemond, but this was a testy connection, one marred by Tancred's mostly unstated disdain for his uncle's cringing self-abasement in Constantinople, as well as by episodes in which Bohemond stole battlefield glory from his nephew. As the First Crusade chronicle unfolds, Bohemond becomes self-interestedly derailed at Antioch, allotting himself a plush lordship there, thereby divesting himself of the whole enterprise's objective of recapturing Jerusalem for Latin Christianity. A foil to his uncle in all these respects, Tancred nonetheless remained loyal to the unreliable Bohemond in years after the Crusade, at one point substituting for his wayward uncle at Antioch in a disadvantageous arrangement. It is hard, in these depictions, to identify any warmth between uncle and nephew. Tancred's behavior generates out of an abstract ideal of familial loyalty. In fact, basing our profile of Tancred solely on Ralph's real-time documentation, the First Crusade figure most famed for chivalric romance comes across as an automaton who mechanically demonstrates battlefield bravery and brutality, and mechanically dispenses Christian charity. Perhaps precisely because something seems missing in this portraiture, subsequent, legendary, accounts of Tancred lavish him with romance. The half-believable biographies dwell on his real-life marriage with Cecile, daughter of France's King Philip I, sprinkling it with Hollywood, happily-ever-after, details.[25] Going far further in an imaginary direction, Torquato Tasso's poem invents a relationship between Tancred and Clorinda, and then develops it as a romantic parable of Christianity's conquest of Islam.

Tancred's contingent reached Jerusalem's outskirts, via Bethlehem, and, characteristically, he broke away from his men to scout the city before its siege. He climbed up the Mount of Olives, hoping that his reconnaissance work would find inspiration at this locale, one where "Christ, the son of God, had gone to meet his father."[26] Unexpectedly, he encountered a "learned hermit," a sagacious, eccentric war counsellor for Tancred whose background invited speculation over the ages. Ralph relays that the hermit hailed from an area in Byzantium which had been terrorized by the Guiscardians, and so the encounter, in Ralph's chronicle, becomes a vignette of Christian reconciliation. Later, less reliable, versions imply that the hermit shared Tancred's Norman background.[27] These variations are attempts to find logic in what was, I believe, an actual occurrence and strange twist in Tancred's career: he collated valuable intelligence about what was to be found within Jerusalem's walls from a lonely crank he met on the Mount of Olives, and this reconnaissance accident enabled him to keep a step ahead of other Crusaders, who were rivals and comrades in a race for glory and booty in the Holy City. As a loner, and as having some relation to prior Norman conquests, the hermit can be seen, on some level, as a projection of Tancred himself, and the Mount of Olives encounter reinforces the idea that the worthiest knowledge, sacred or military, is accrued by individuals. In this way, Tancred on the First Crusade should be seen as a transitional figure, one who brought with him the private disposition of Christian pilgrims on a Holy Land journey, even as he was a pioneer patron of actual Christian settlement in the country and a symbol of a Christian communal quest for restored sovereignty.

During the assault on Jerusalem, Tancred positioned himself on the northwest side of the city's walls, at a site later known as Tancred's Tower (Ralph calls it the Tower of David[28]). He appears to have been the first Crusader who scaled the Jerusalem wall, utilizing a tower and bridge propped up by Godfrey. Tancred was the Crusader who, from the Frankish standpoint, liberated Solomon's Temple, the hallowed Jerusalem structure which, at the time, was not the Jews' Temple but rather the Islamic shrine, the Dome of the Rock. Ralph reports that multitudes of deliriously frightened city residents had taken refuge within the building's iron gates; Tancred's sword slaughtered some of them, but he was distracted by his aim of ransacking the heathen temple and so did not finish this massacre. There were gem-encrusted walls, extremely heavy devotional objects to Muhammad cast out of precious metal, and much other treasure to pillage. Taking nothing for himself, Tancred ordered his men to divide the valuables among themselves. "The soldiers had never carried out an order as willingly as this one," Ralph giddily relays.[29]

Soon enough, the division of spoils from the supposed Temple of Solomon instigated controversy among Crusaders, and also tested the chronicler Ralph of Caen's powers of rhetorical finesse. His mentor, Arnulf of Chocques, who became patriarch of Jerusalem, challenged Tancred. The patriarch devised a series of ingenious arguments whose gist was that Christianity had empowered the Crusader triumph, and so the spoils of its ultimate triumph belonged to the church. Tancred held fast to what was, for the Crusaders, a rival holy principle: when it comes to the spoils of war, first come, first serve. Ralph stages this dispute as a formal debate between his two heroes, Tancred and Arnulf, which was decided by the embryonic *Haute Cour*, the Crusader ruling council—he claims that a payment of 700 marks for the Temple's Christian renovation amicably settled the affair.[30] Ralph's writing about this compensation to Arnulf has a saccharine feel, and his memoir thereafter loses its analytic momentum.

When we wonder how Tancred turned himself into the Prince of Galilee, we are asking a larger question about how the Crusaders' Latin Kingdom became chopped up into rural lordships. On Prawer's influential interpretation, this transformation was by no means inevitable. He believed that the establishment of feudal lordships in the Middle East constituted an atavistic, foreign import needlessly wrought out of the imitative and unimaginative character of the Franks. At the time of the Latin Kingdom's establishment, Prawer contended, the Crusaders "continued the local Near Eastern tradition of a money economy." The first Crusader lordships were really "money fiefs," and had the first two kings, Godfrey de Bouillon and his brother Baldwin I, followed these initial precedents, the Latin Kingdom would have become a bureaucratic-feudal state with a "salaried nobility," essentially modelled on the example of neighboring Muslim countries. Things did not develop that way, Prawer explained, partly because of technical-logistical issues faced by all feudal regimes, challenges which hedged against effective control of large areas. Yet he also emphasized the Franks' "unchanging rigidity," and their "blind clinging to the past." Everyone in the kingdom expected that a knight who provided loyal service on the Crusade would be rewarded with a landed fief, simply because that was the way the world worked.[31]

Much in Prawer's prolific scholarship has been reexamined by new generations of researchers,[32] and this view of "rigid" and "blind" Crusader monarchs coopting cooperation among egoistic and unruly knights by land grants is one such contested point. One monograph reverses this chain of causality, contending that Crusader rulers exploited the lordship system with resolve and prudence. The conferral of fiefdoms, argues Steve Tibble, was an extension of monarchic *policy*. The Crusader kings created smaller fiefdoms within larger lordships, appointed loyal confederates as fiefdom managers as counterpoise against local barons who were acting too independently, and kept portions of lordships as their own royal properties. In other words, the kings used land allotments as a form of social control, and the lordships should therefore **not** be seen as emblems of decentralization and power instability in the Outremer settlement movement wherein local lords did whatever they wanted, and the monarchy was a purely a symbolic affair.[33] As in many other issues connected to myths and realities of the First Crusade, where he is seen in different ways by different people, Tancred looms as a bridge between these two scholarly interpretations.

In August 1099, Tancred moved north via Beit Sha'an (Beisan), using it as a base for forays in the Galilee. He commanded a militia of some eighty knights in this period. In the north, the Crusaders' antagonist was a Turko-Persian regime, the Seljuk Empire, and its Damascus-based ruler, Duqaq (mockingly called the "fat peasant" by the Crusader knights). Godfrey controlled Tiberias through September; Tancred and his Italian Norman *Wiscardides* appear to have temporarily been engaged in a power rivalry with Godfrey in the north.[34] In his bid for lordship rights over Tiberias and its outlying region, Tancred's bargaining leverage wedged out of his skirmishing in Syria. In spring 1100, Tancred boldly staged a direct showdown with Duqaq, at one point sending six men to Damascus to demand that the Seljuk ruler surrender the city and profess Christianity (Duqaq promptly beheaded five of these messengers). Tancred launched a devastating two-week siege on Damascus, forcing the Seljuks to pay tribute. Tancred relayed a portion of this booty to Jerusalem, so the conferral of the Galilee benefice can possibly be understood as a reward.

Tancred's daring raids in Syria had important diplomatic consequences, compelling "the rulers of Damascus to recognize that a new power was rising in the Middle East and was determined to stay."[35] The Seljuks were forced into negotiations with the Franks, and eventually the Damascenes and the Crusaders worked out an unusual condominium arrangement whereby lands east of the Sea of Galilee (the Golan Heights), and also south of Damascus, would be demilitarized, and revenue generated in them would be divided into thirds, with equal portions going to Damascus, to the Crusaders, and to fellahin (peasants) who worked the land. According to Prawer, this was the Franks' most lasting diplomatic agreement, and it remained intact up to the Hattin debacle in 1187.[36]

Tancred, Prawer estimates, "probably did not intend to rule a fief dependent on the Crown of Jerusalem, but rather [wanted to] carve out an independent state in the north of the country." This state would have Tiberias and the Sea of Galilee at its center, and it would extend to Damascus in the east, to the Yarmuk River in the north, and also, as a window to the Mediterranean Sea, to Haifa in the west. This city, Haifa, located beyond Galilee and called Caiphas by the Crusaders, became the thorn in Tancred's ambitions.[37]

The establishment of the first Latin Kingdom lordship, in Galilee, resulted from the daring and energy of a single individual, Tancred, but this does not mean that the country's frontier was free for any strong-willed Crusader to operate as he pleased. Godfrey appears to have promised Haifa to Tancred, but he backtracked and detached the coastal town from the lordship, and pledged it to Galdemar Carpenel. As it turned out, Godfrey was dead before Haifa was captured by the Crusaders, but Godfrey's maneuver set a precedent, as an assertion of the monarch's ability to control the size and character of lordships in the Latin Kingdom.[38]

Intending to use the coastal city as his Galilee princedom's port, Tancred attacked Haifa in late July 1100. The young kingdom had earlier set its eyes on the much larger port, Acre, and, before he died in the middle of the month, Godfrey forged a military pact with leaders of a Venetian fleet, who were keenly aware of Acre's value for trade, but, in summer 1100, the new kingdom's wherewithal was limited, and so the Franks settled for an attack on the smaller port prize, Haifa. Tancred's main naval ally in the attack was a Pisan patriarch, Daimbert, who coordinated with the Venetian ships.[39] The three-and-a-half week battle in Haifa ensued at a time of political turmoil in the fledgling Crusader Kingdom that was provoked by Godfrey's death. Tancred was infuriated by disclosure of Godfrey's deathbed conferral of Haifa as a benefice to Galdemar, but intense negotiations coaxed and revived Tancred's fighting resolve, and he returned to vanquish the coastal town.

Unexpectedly, the Haifa siege turned into a pivotal, defining moment for Jews in the Holy Land's Crusader period. The country's Jewish population at the time was small, but Tancred's new Galilee lordship as a whole contained some fifteen Jewish villages, largely clustered around Tiberias, and Safed. Their identification is tricky since key documents are reports composed by visiting Jewish travelers and pilgrims in the early thirteenth century, decades after the inception of Crusader rule. One such text was written by Samuel ben Samson, whose pilgrimage was undertaken in 1210 and who mentions having celebrated Purim at Gush Halav, and also a Shabbat in Safed, and we also have the famous travel log furnished by Benjamin of Tudela in the twelfth century (Benjamin refers to twenty Jewish families in Gush Halav, and fifty families in Alma). Scholars believe that many of the Galilee villages cited in such reports—Birya, Ain al-Zeitun, Alma, Gush Halav, and Dalton—were well established when Tancred proclaimed his lordship, and, in some cases, had roots stretching back to Roman and Byzantine times.[40]

Not in these villages, but rather in Haifa, Jews make a strong, albeit brief, appearance in the early military history of the Latin Kingdom. Their courageous defense on the city's ramparts, fighting against the Crusaders, is documented by a twelfth-century Crusader chronicler, Albert of Aix. Albert depicts Jews and Muslims fighting side by side, hurling oil and burning straw at Tancred and his fellow Crusader attackers. "Citizens of Jewish origin who inhabited the place by a grant and consent of the King of Babylon [meaning Egypt, in Crusader parlance] . . . rose armed on the walls, putting up a very strong resistance," noted Albert. The Crusaders unsuccessfully besieged Haifa for fifteen days, this being the period during which Tancred's motivations fluctuated; they used a huge siege tower and seven stone-throwing mangonels in attacks against Haifa's citadel (*turris*).

His fighting spirit reinvigorated, Tancred and twenty warriors wielded double-edged axes and iron mattocks in a furious blitz against the citadel. On Albert's report, Tancred put aside his bitterness, and, in the name of Christ, "sounded the trumpets," exhorting his warriors to "resume the interrupted attack on the city, [and] fight the Jews who had so valiantly defended it." For two days, as oil and flaming flax poured down on Tancred's men, this new surge was deflected, but eventually the Crusaders exploded past the city gates, killing "whoever was found," and reportedly confiscating an immense fortune of gold, silver, clothes, horses, mules, and wheat.[41]

Haifa's Jewish community was devastated by Tancred's massacre and does not appear to have revived throughout the subsequent Crusader period. Also, for Tancred, the thrill of victory was fleeting. Following Godfrey's death, Tancred aspired to rule the Latin Kingdom, but he was ousted in a power struggle by the late ruler's brother, Baldwin. Antagonizing his rival, the new Crusader ruler supported Galdemar's control in Haifa, and, at the end of 1100, the Crusader *Haute Cour* ratified Galdermar's claim.[42] Subsequently, in 1102, with Tancred relocated in Antioch, as a regent stand-in for his restless uncle Bohemond, Baldwin reorganized political arrangements in the Galilee district. Tancred regained the Galilee lordship in 1109, but he does not appear to have returned to it for this second term.

In fact, control over the lordship, through 1120, was arranged by kingly appointment, rather than being a matter of hereditary seigneurial ownership. The first four Crusader princes of Galilee—Tancred, Hugh de St Omer, Gervaise de Bazoches, and Joscelyn de Courtenay—were not related, and the principality appears to have reverted to the royal domain upon their deaths.[43] The second prince, Hugh of Falkenberg died in battle in Hauran in 1106. His two daughters were too young for anyone to consider hereditary right as the ruling principle in the lordship, so Baldwin relayed the lordship to a comrade from Picardy, Gervais, in September 1106.[44] In 1108, Gervais was captured in Syria by the Turkic leader, Toghtekin, who demanded Haifa, Acre, and Tiberias. Baldwin balked, and instead offered a ransom of 30,000 gold bezants and the release of several hundred prisoners. The Atabeg declined his offer and gave the Galilee prince a choice of conversion or death. Gervais refused the apostasy offer. Toghtekin had his skull customized as a chalice.[45]

Tancred's term was short, but he managed to change Galilee's landscape in a strikingly charitable way, conveying a hefty portion of the region's properties to the church. In fact, amidst the rowdy disorder of Crusader reality, he leaves our story in this distinguished key. What else, besides killing Saracens, was a Crusader knight really supposed to do? Acknowledging a job well done in Galilee, the influential Crusader chronicler, William of Tyre, became a major Tancred booster, lavishing praise upon him for his generosity to the church at Tiberias, Nazareth, and Mount Tabor.[46] Insofar as the two sides of Matthew's Gospel, the Christian militant and the forgiving charitableness of the Sermon of the Mount, could ever be reconciled, Crusader historians like William believed that Tancred accomplished this synthesis on the First Crusade, and in the Galilee lordship. Their approbation helps explain why his name fanned legend for centuries.

The monastery on Mount Tabor became the Galilee lordship's largest landowner. Its holdings became capacious by 1103, when Pope Pascal II confirmed the monastery's holdings of forty-seven properties throughout Galilee. This papal registry refers to the church's control of twenty-two small rural villages, what the Crusaders called *casalia*, on the western side of the Sea of Galilee, and a bloc of five casalia on the western edge of the lake, and another bloc of four or five casalia on its southern shore. This document also recognizes casalia called "Alme," one near Saphet and the other near Banias. Many of these properties seem to have been bestowed by Tancred's hand, or by his vassals, though some monastery holdings seem to have been arranged after he had moved on to Antioch. By 1103, at any event, the church had gained massive land-holdings in Galilee, and Tancred's munificence toward it set a precedent for the church's expansion in the region, up to the 1187 turning point.[47]

FIRST KINGDOM CRUSADER SETTLEMENT IN GALILEE

Before the Crusader catastrophe at Hattin in 1187, the Franks established other, smaller, lordships in Galilee, or in outlying regions located in today's Southern Lebanon. These include[48]

Toron (today, Tebnine). This South Lebanon castle site was built-up by Tancred's successor, Hugh de St Omer, in 1106, owing to military calculations related to Muslim fortifications in Tyre. It was detached from the principality of Galilee and became an independent lordship after Hugh's death. There is evidence that a smaller Crusader castle, Qalat Doubal, was also constructed at this time.

Banias. The Muslim Assassins sect delivered Banias to Crusader King Baldwin II in 1128. The principality might have been allocated to a Frank named Renier Brus in 1132, though the evidence is not definitive. At some point before 1157, Baldwin's son-in-law, Humphrey II, Lord of Toron, gained control of this lordship.

Chastel Neuf, in the Upper Galilee Panhandle, apparently established by Hugh in 1105–7. After Hugh's death, Baldwin II apparently split northern lands, creating the two lordships, Toron and Chastel Neuf. The castle in this lordship was refortified both during the Crusader period, and also by the Mamluk sultan, Baibars. The Palestinian village, Hunin, which sprouted on this Crusader site, was destroyed in the 1948 war.

Nazareth. The town became an independent lordship no later than 1121.

Crusader era settlement in Galilee was variegated, and so it is misleading to summarize it only by providing such a roster of lordships. According to Israeli scholar Ronnie Ellenblum, the Franks enacted an agricultural colonization plan via a number of different settlement forms. He prefers not to use the term "casalia," objecting to its overly loose usage as a rural village,[49] and stresses that Franks sometimes implanted settlement forms such as the "castrum" which had well-developed analogues in medieval Europe. A castrum involved a specific number of residential dwellings, wall fortification, religious institutions, and agricultural field placement in keeping with a sophisticated planning blueprint. Other Frank settlement forms in Galilee (and elsewhere in the country) included seigneurial homesteads, farming villages owned by a noble but operated by a designated administrator, and royal domains. Ellenblum believes that Crusader era Christian settlement in Galilee had a substantive agricultural orientation, and was not simply a case of military-minded entrenchment whereby European colonizers prop up some dwellings in strategically plotted villages proximate to one of their castles. Evidence in support of this view is the fact that farmers in Frank settlements paid tithe requirements in kind (i.e., a portion of their agricultural produce) rather than via coin currency—this "in kind" mechanism, he reasons, "necessitates the construction of storerooms and a network of rural roads, and the acquisition of greater expertise concerning seasonal cultivation and the quality of crops."[50]

In general, Ellenblum believes, Crusader era settlement had a civilian character. He distances himself from earlier scholars like Prawer who thought of inhabitants of rural settlements in a region like Galilee as veteran knights of the crusading wars, or their descendants or vassal dependents. By examining extant rosters of inhabitants in these villages, Ellenblum finds that they came from areas in southern France and northern Spain, which are not the same as the native grounds (e.g., northern France) of the Crusader fighters themselves. European work migration in the twelfth century had a kind of randomly sprawling character (the distinguished historian Marc Bloch branded this "Brownian movement"). Quite possibly, the same sort of small tradesmen and farmers who drifted in this era to Languedoc, Gascony, Catalonia, or Sicily also flowed to Galilee and elsewhere in the Holy Land, once the country was under Christian Crusader rule. Decades passed before these sort of migrants discerned disadvantages in the Outremer option—these, in Ellenblum's view, included "difficulties of working the land, the need to contend with a technology unknown to many of the settlers of storing water and bringing it from a source to the fields, the frequent droughts and locust plagues."[51] In the view of these European lower-class farmers and workers, the pros and cons of laboring in Galilee under the banner of the Crusades were weighed on such civilian scales. At least in the period preceding the 1187 cataclysm at Hattin, security calculations were probably not determinative for them.

This civilian character influenced Galilee settlement on several levels. These European migrants who settled in Galilee villages had social assumptions and preferences that were unlike those of the knights who fought the Crusader wars. By keeping this distinction in mind, we reach a clearer picture of social patterns of settlement in Frankish Galilee.

As exemplified in Tancred's biography, Crusader knights with specific backgrounds (Norman, in Tancred's case) often carried violent grudges against Byzantine Christians as they journeyed east (a reader who has doubts or questions in this regard can peruse accounts of the Fourth Crusade, which, in lieu of its express goal of regaining Jerusalem by first destroying the Ayyubid caliphate in Egypt, turned into a Christian civil war wherein the western Christians, the Crusaders, sacked the capital of eastern Christianity, Constantinople). Farmers and tradesmen may not have shared this anti-Greek Christian animus, however. When scholars like Ellenblum look at the Crusader era from the bottom up, that is, in terms of what was actually happening on the ground rather than legends that swirled around the famous Crusader knights, they shatter long-standing shibboleths.

One myth maintains that Franks like the kefiyyeh-clad Tancred sometimes mingled in the Levant with Muslims, whereas they consistently shunned, or killed, Greek Christians. In actual fact, this realm of Holy Land social interaction in the Crusader era is a complicated subject, one filled with mild surprise, or at least inconsistency wrought by expedience, and it is not accurately described by pejorative generalizations such as "colonialist apartheid."

Attesting to this complexity, Tyerman writes: "Where necessary, Frankish rulers occasionally extended patronage to Muslim settlers, doctors and merchants, while at the same time showing no qualms about using Muslim slave labor. A few shared sites of religious worship survived, such as in the suburbs of Acre in the 12th century." Outremer, he explains, featured demographic diversity, "but no deep cultural synthesis." The Franks' "clothes (such as the fashionable turban or the prudent loose garments and surcoats), food, domestic architecture (even the rugged Hospitallers seem to have installed bathrooms at their castle of Belvoir), personal hygiene, and medicine were adapted to the environment. Franks learnt Arabic."[52]

On a settlement level, broad patterns in the Crusader era seem to have been less nuanced. Whereas the swords of Frankish noble elites often clashed against those of the Byzantines, in rural Galilee villages these two groups of Christians, western (Frank) and eastern (Greek), seem to have lived and worked together. A clear majority of Frankish settlements in Galilee were located in its western parts, precisely the areas where there was a preexisting layer of Christian Byzantine settlement, as (it will be recalled) archaeology work supervised by Moti Aviam has proven. The migrant workers who, in Ellenblum's interpretation, drifted to the Levant after the Crusader conquest, appear to have settled and farmed in Galilee in areas where there were preexisting, familiar, Christian symbols and elements, albeit of the Byzantine variety—a small church, Christian neighbors, among others. Earlier, we noted that Eastern Galilee, in the Byzantine and the pre-1099 Islamic eras, hosted Jewish and Muslim populations: by and large, Ellenblum argues, Jews left the region during the Crusader epoch, and the Muslim population remained nomadic. From the Franks' standpoint, this East Galilee region was unstable, a hotbed of violent banditry, and not subordinate to the Latin kingdom's administrative machinery; so far fewer Frankish villages are to be found in this eastern part of Galilee. In the Crusader era, in short, western Christians settled where Byzantine Christians had prepared the ground, and sometimes continued to live, primarily in western Galilee.[53]

There are no reliable estimates of the size of Frankish settlement in Galilee. One chronicler, a Latin biographer of Bishop Benoit of Marseille, refers to 260 Frankish villages in the proximity of Safed (about a quarter century before the 1291 collapse of the Latin Kingdom as a whole, Bishop Benoit was instrumental in the construction of the Templar fortress in Safed). Basing his extrapolative reasoning on more reliable demographic estimates of Galilee in later, Mamluk and Ottoman periods, Ellenblum concludes that this 260 village figure actually relates to the total number of Frankish settlements in Galilee as a whole, not just in Safed's area.[54] If each settlement had some 200 Christian inhabitants, this would total as roughly 50,000 Christian settlers in Galilee in the Crusader era. Ellenblum corroborates this tally by referring to another figure cited by Benoit's anonymous biographer—this text refers to 10,000 Christians "armed with bows and arrows" in Galilee. Reasoning that each fighter had a support crew of five, "we conclude that in the rural areas of Galilee there were at least 50,000 Christian inhabitants who had been absorbed into the Frankish network and protected it," writes Ellenblum.[55] These are little more than population guesses, however.

Suggestive information about seigneurial holdings in Galilee can be gleaned from a roster composed in 1265 by one the Latin kingdom's foremost aristocrats, Jean of Ibelin (the Old Lord of Beirut). This document lists noblemen in the country who were obliged to contribute knights to the Crusader army. The list purportedly relates to nobles up to 1187, the year when realities in the kingdom convulsed and contracted because of Hattin.[56] By the time Jean drafted this roster, many of the Galilee territories were under control of military orders (the Seignuerie of Count Joscelyn, whose fiefs were large, from 50 to 150 square kilometers in size, was owned by the Teutonic Order, whereas the Seignuerie of Acre's properties were divided between the Templars, the Hospitallers, and also Acre's Italian communes).[57] Before Hattin, the properties were mostly owned by individual notables, or were administered by the king's officials, and, confusingly, their names were sometimes not the same as ones in use at the time the military orders took possession of them. For our Galilee purposes in the pre-1187 era of the Jerusalem-based kingdom, one notable entry in this ledger refers, atypically, not to the name of a particular nobleman, but rather to a kind of cluster fief called "Castellum Regis," which owed four knights to the Kingdom's army.[58] Castellum Regis typifies what Ellenblum describes as the Frankish "castrum" settlement pattern. This agricultural settlement bloc was based in the heart of Western Galilee, in today's Christian village of Mi'ilya, located about six miles northeast of Acre. As decades passed in the Latin Kingdom, up to a mid-thirteenth-century period after Hattin when the Teutonic Order (as we will see) became active in Galilee, this "castrum" model consolidated at Castellum Regis. In addition to showing a castle adjoined to a rural *burgus* settlement, the documents allow identification of thirty-seven Frankish landlords and farmers who apparently lived in the cluster, and also "fields, vineyards, gardens, a mill, the church, the old curia," and even a leprosy facility which was located, as was the custom, outside of the settlement walls.[59] The road network grid in this castrum, running between Tarshika in the south and Fassuta in the northeast, includes sites established by the Teutonic Order well after 1187, including the important Montfort fortress in the northwest. Yet, in addition to the site's appearance in the Old Lord of Beirut's registry of pre-Hattin nobility, scholars have found evidence indicating that the castrum's infrastructure pre-dates 1187. One is references to an "old curia" in the Frankish village. A few remains of the village castle, originally built several decades before Hattin, can be seen today in Mi'ilya. Castrum residences serving the archbishop of Nazareth, and the bishop of Acre have been identified. Several elements—for example, the way two rows of the seventeen identified residences are aligned, and the complex vineyard allotments—have persuaded researches that this Galilee castrum was built according to a preconceived plan.[60]

Jean of Ibelin's roster describes other pre-1187 fiefdoms in Galilee. One such Frankish settlement in Western Galilee of special interest is the lordship of St. George de La Baena. That this was an important fiefdom can be inferred from the citation in John's list saying that it owed ten knights—fairly prominent lordships in the region, in today's Israel and Lebanon, such as ones in Haifa and in Scandalion (in the Tyre region) were obliged to send a lesser number of knights.[61] The center of this St. George lordship was located in today's Muslim Arab village of Deir al-Assad. Details about the origins of the St. George de La Baena lordship are sketchy, but we know that it was functioning generations before Hattin. The fief belonged to a certain Henricus Bubalus, the son of Guido de Miliaco, a knight from Champagne. After Henricus passed away, the fief was divided between his three daughters; in 1161, one of his heirs, Phillip de Milli designated the Crusader king "seignior" of the lordship, even though the family continued to live in it.[62] Philip de Novare, an admirer of Jean of Ibelin who wrote a partisan history of the Ibelin family's feud with Emperor Frederick II,[63] describes another de Milli, Henry, as a "rich man," which probably means that he belonged to the kingdom's prospering "middle class," a stratum below barons.[64] Henry bequeathed the St. George fief, some 150 square kilometers in size, to his daughters. Four of the seven villages in the portion allotted to one of them, Beatrice von Henneberg, have been identified (Arket, Yanot, Cabra, and Meblie—the first two are today Druze villages, Yarka and Yanoh).[65] After Hattin, when the region was still under Muslim rule, the Lordship at least nominally was controlled by Pisans, in an arrangement brokered by Conrad of Montferrat. Subsequently, descendants of Henricus Bubalus regained brief control of it, and then, for the last decades of the Crusader era, St. George de La Baena was controlled by the Teutonic Order. Many of these Western Galilee sites that ended up under Teutonic control are known: Beitegen (Beit Jann), Seisor (Sajur), Nef (Nahaf), La Hasenie, Mergelcolon (Madjel-Kurum), and Gelon.[66]

Archaeologists have worked on the Frankish building at the center of Deir al-Asad, and identified it as a Carthusian abbey. Researchers also identified a domicile used by Henricus or his descendants, located in al-Ba'ina[67] (a village that is physically joined to Deir al-Asad, but has, through today, separate municipal recognition on account of relationship dynamics among the extended Arab families which took possession of the area after the Crusader period). St. George, incidentally, is an iconic figure in Islamic culture, as well as in Christianity. The Galilee lordship in Crusader times was established at George's presumed birthplace and attracted pilgrimage trade.

One of the more scenic, enjoyable stretches of Galilee's contemporary coastline, located eight and a half miles north of Acre, within Nahariya's municipal borders and quite close to Lebanon, the Achziv area hosted another Frankish settlement in Crusader times, called Casale Imbert.[68] Operated as early as the 1120s by a Frankish notable for which it was named, Humberti de Pace, the settlement formally belonged to a Jerusalem-area institution, the abbey of St. Mary Josaphat, which held other properties in Galilee as well.[69] Up to the mid-twelfth century, Casale Imbert functioned as an ecclesiastic settlement of moderate proportions and status, with dwellings provided to ranking church officials from Acre and Nazareth. Sometime before 1154, its status and activities were ambitiously revamped, and it was redesignated as a settlement for free farmers. The Crusader king had seigniorial rights to the settlement, and imposed tithing duties on its farm workers, including a demand for 40 percent of produce from the settlement's olive grove. The monarch also took one-fifteenth of bread baked in the village oven, and 10 percent of revenue generated by its bathhouse. These tithes may look steep, but the truth is that the kingdom incentivized settlement at this Galilee village, exempting its farmers from tax payments due on wine, meat, and other products sold in Acre's markets. These Galilee settlers in Crusader times received preferential terms, compared to farmers who made their residence at villages in the Jerusalem area, such as Nova Villa. Settlers at this Judean village received plots of land from its owner (the Church of the Holy Sepulchre) but were compelled to pay for their own houses, whereas at Casale Imbert settlers received work plots and free housing. Apart from the noticeably high impost on Galilee olives, the Casale Imbert farmers were obliged to tithes and taxes for agricultural produce and other items at rates quite lower than their Judean village counterparts. Some scholars, including Prawer, viewed this discrepancy as an expression of deliberate Crusader policy designed to encourage Frankish settlement in peripheral areas, such as Galilee, much as the state of Israel after 1948 has used taxes and other mechanisms to incentivize Jewish settlement in Galilee in the north, and the Negev on its southern periphery, but other researchers insist that the divergence in tax schedules stemmed from free market dynamics, not settlement policy planning.[70]

A final settlement form relevant to Frankish Galilee was a royal domain leased to a trusted servant of the king, the camerarius regis. Ellenblum identifies such a settlement cluster in a Galilee stretch running between Acre and Nahariya, next to contemporary Israeli kibbutz and moshav settlements, Ivron and Amqa.[71] These Frankish villages are called, in the sources, Lanahia (next to Ivron), and Ancra (near Amqa), along with Casale Album, whose location remains unidentified. The documents indicate that the villages were functioning in the camerarius regis framework by the mid-twelfth century. The responsibilities and privileges accorded to the chamberlain (camerarius) in these fiefs are not entirely clear. After Hattin, some of the fiefs were sold by the Crusader king to Joscelyn III, the Count of Edessa, and the terms of this transaction hint that this village cluster was about half as large and prestigious as Castellum Regis. Lanahia's distinguishing emblem was its sugar mill production—sugar products thrilled the Franks and their chroniclers, including sweet-toothed William of Tyre, but scholars continue to debate whether the Crusades brought about global innovations in sugar production and trade.[72]

HOLY WAR AT HATTIN IN HISTORICAL PERSPECTIVE

The Battle of Hattin, fought in Galilee on July 3–4 1187, precipitated the decline of the Crusaders' Latin Kingdom in the Holy Land. At Hattin, located close to Tiberias and the Sea of Galilee's western shore, Muslim fighters led by Saladin routed a large Crusader force headed by King Guy of Lusignan, and the Arab victory set the stage for the Crusaders' loss of Jerusalem, after eighty-eight years of Christian rule in the sacred city. After Hattin, the shrunken Crusader Kingdom, based in Acre, never fully recovered, though it lasted for another century, and Saladin, founder of the Ayyubid dynasty, became a figure of renown in world culture, as a mujahid warrior and as a chivalrous conqueror.

Hattin's impact should be kept in perspective, and its results were not unambiguous. Saladin's crushing victory at Hattin by no means spelled the end of the Crusader phenomenon, not only because the Latins maintained a viable, albeit constricted, kingdom on the Holy Land coast for another century. Historians in past decades have amplified our understanding of the Crusades, arguing that this European Christian practice of Holy War was not limited to the Middle East, and lasted well beyond the late thirteenth century, virtually until the early modern period.[73]

Nor is it entirely accurate to view Hattin as the climactic moment of unadulterated animosity between fully separated Christian and Muslim civilizations. Crusader barons and Muslim chieftains frequently forged tactical alliances and sometimes maintained non-bellicose social contacts. For a few years before Hattin, Saladin and the Latin Kingdom maintained a truce, and the fact that one Crusader baron, Raymond III of Tripolis, the Prince of Galilee, temporarily hatched a controversial and ill-fated pact with Saladin[74] shows that players in the Hattin drama did not always view themselves as representatives of implacably antagonistic religious civilizations. Often, their relations proceeded on a footing of passing political calculation or self-interest, and did not really express the spirit of Holy War.

Also, after his impressive triumph at Hattin, Saladin did not win instant, unqualified acclaim in the Arab world as Islam's champion against the invading Franks. His ascent in the Middle East had been complicated by the ongoing Sunni-Shi'ite rift in Islam and by political rivalry, and so chroniclers sympathetic to the vanquished Shia Fatimid Caliphate in Egypt, or to Nur al-Din's Zengid dynasty in Syria-Iraq, viewed Saladin with suspicion as a rival or enemy, and this tarnished the Hattin hero's historical reputation for some time.[75]

Nonetheless, as an indispensable marker of world cultural geography, Hattin is the event in the Middle Ages which exposed the vulnerability and ephemerality of the Crusader Kingdom in the Holy Land. No less than other signposts (such as the Battle of Ayn Jalut, discussed at the end of this chapter, and the Ottoman conquest of Constantinople in 1453), Hattin clinched the perception, and the reality, of the Middle East as a Muslim region.

Though there were always skeptics, Saladin became revered in the Muslim world as the defender of the faith against western encroachment, and his reputation soared higher than that of any Arab hero in eras subsequent to Islam's original seventh and eighth century conquests. Despite aforementioned sources of friction, this reputation developed rather steadily after his death in 1193, as Muslims mourned him as a holy mujahid (Abd al-Latif al-Baghdadi, a contemporary writer, noted that Muslims grieved for Saladin "as they grieve for prophets"), and it resonated subsequently in fascinating and provocative permutations.[76]

One study of Hattin, published in 2015 as part of an Oxford University Press series on Great Battles in history, follows Saladin's enormously powerful and complex reputation.[77] The process includes softening in European perception of the Crusaders' enemy, starting with a mid-thirteenth-century French poem, *Ordene de chevalrie,* and continuing through the Enlightenment period when writers such as Voltaire and Gotthold Ephraim Lessing celebrated the Hattin hero as a model of enlightened chivalry. However, Saladin and Hattin's legacy has reverberated "even more deeply" among peoples of the Middle East, this new study notes. True, some groups have been ambivalent about Saladin, most notably the state-less Kurds, who have reasons both to be proud of the Ayyubid warrior, since Saladin was a Kurd, and also to resent the way his record has been Arabized.

Though there is some evidence that Saladin's memory was neglected in some parts of the Middle East in the early modern period (his grave in Damascus was neglected through the nineteenth century), late colonial controversies in the region, and then, with comparable or greater force, Israel's establishment in 1948, generated new interest in Hattin. Among Muslims, over the past century, the efforts of a number of Arab leaders who violently opposed Israel and Western forces or symbols, including Gamal Abdel

Nasser, Saddam Hussein, and Osama Bin-Laden, have been associated with Saladin. In this mythology, Jewish Zionists from the late nineteenth century become identified as Western colonialists comparable to Christian Crusaders who invaded Palestine in the twelfth century, and Hattin becomes an instructive blueprint of how the Muslim world must organize to annihilate the Jewish state of Israel. While this Crusader-Zionism analogy has fueled hatred of the Jewish state in the Arab world,[78] contemporary Jewish commentators have not one-sidedly condemned Saladin, owing to their awareness of Crusader violence against Jews.[79]

From the Western-Christian point of view, little could be done to mitigate the perception of Hattin as a demoralizing Crusader debacle. Since some traditions locate Hattin as the site of the Sermon on the Mount, a few Christian institutions have adopted the name, as in the case of a certain Mount Hattin church in Baltimore,[80] but there could never be a quarrel about the devastating result of the 1187 battle.

There is unanimity of opinion among western commentators about the cause of the Crusader defeat: Hattin's outcome has been seen largely as a result of disunity in the Latin kingdom, and not as solely the product of Muslim battlefield tactics, or the demographic realities of the region.[81]

Debate among western commentators on Hattin has focused on the apportionment of blame for political fracture among the Crusaders. Some scholarly schools have blamed the loss on King Guy,[82] a relative newcomer in the kingdom who was not a capable and inspiring military figure, whereas others have pointed to Raymond's inconsistent behavior,[83] and there has been discussion about the validity of analyzing this issue of disunity in terms of a "court faction" loyal to Guy and consisting of Crusader immigrants committed to an aggressive military strategy of campaigns for glory and spoils, and a baronial faction of native-born, second- or third-generation Crusaders, who were familiar with regional realities and who were relatively cautious and conservative in their military instincts. Lack of factual clarity has dogged this debate from the start because important Crusader chroniclers, most notably William of Tyre (who owed his archbishopric to Raymond and admired him[84]), were partisan defenders of one side, or the other.

PRELUDE TO THE BATTLE

Less than half a century after the Crusader seizure of Jerusalem, the Muslim world remobilized. In 1144, Zengi of Mosul captured one of the four Crusader states, Edessa in the north, thereby provoking the Second Crusade (despite the eloquent preaching of the Pope's spokesman, Bernard of Clairvaux, and the participation of two kings, this crusade dissipated with disappointing result). Intermittently, the Latin Kingdom displayed foreign policy ambition—one such assertive phase was the reign of King Amalric (1163–1174), when the Crusaders launched attacks on Egypt. Overall, however, the Latin Kingdom became ever less socially and politically cohesive as decades went by. During Amalric's decade-long reign, one telling sign of this growing disunity was the unwillingness of the Catholic military orders, the Hospitallers, and the Templars, to support the Crusader monarch's foreign policy (after getting no help from such potential Christian allies, Amalric made no headway in complicated negotiations with the extremist Islamic Assassin sect for a joint campaign against Zengi's son, Nur al-Din).

This trend of Crusader erosion continued when Amalric's leprous son, Baldwin IV, took the throne in 1174. His coronation plunged the Latin Kingdom into a leadership-succession crisis from which it never recovered before the showdown at Hattin. In this same period, starting with Saladin's rise to power in Egypt in 1169, an opposite trend of political unification picked up momentum in the Arab world. In 1174, when Amalric passed his crown to his incapacitated son, Saladin gained traction because his rival Nur al-Din died. Nine years later, in 1183, Saladin conclusively ousted the Zengid family by capturing Aleppo. Syria and Egypt were now under Ayyubid control.

What was propelling Saladin into action in this period? Citing a letter Saladin sent to his brother and son after Hattin, shortly before his death, the pro-Zengid historian Ibn al-Athir argued that land lust, family interests and personal glory motivated this Muslim hero. Formulating an agenda seemingly devoid of spiritual intents, Saladin's letter envisioned continuing eastward campaigns, with a final aim of extending the Ayyubid empire through Persia. Rejecting this realpolitik interpretation, Muslim multitudes came to believe that Saladin experienced an Islamic rebirth relatively late in his life. In years between Nur's death and Hattin, Saladin survived two Assassin attacks and also fell gravely ill. These life-threatening experiences are understood to have purified his perspective, bringing him to focus on a holy jihad campaign to drive the Franks from Jerusalem.[85] Whatever his innermost intentions, early in the 1180s Saladin was pinching the Latin Kingdom top and bottom, attacking it east of the Jordan in Galilee, and also in the south, on the edge of Egypt.

A crucial dress rehearsal for Hattin occurred in fall 1183. As regent to ailing King Baldwin, Guy assembled a huge Crusader contingent at Sepphoris (called le Saforie in Crusader chronicles), and then at al-Fula. William of Tyre recorded a mobilization of 1,300 knights and 15,000 foot soldiers, one of the largest Frank military assemblies anyone could remember. In mid-September, Saladin and his men camped at the Ayn Jalut springs, tantalizingly close to the Crusaders. However, despite the superior size of his own Crusader forces, and despite the fact that Saladin had encroached in his own kingdom and was now in close range, Guy chose not to engage the Saracens in battle. After some minor skirmishing, Saladin's army disappeared from the scene, via Tubania, by mid-October.

Guy, a Potevin knight, was a relative newcomer in the Latin kingdom whose military record in France did not go beyond a dubious incident wherein he ganged up with his brothers to kill an English pilgrim, the first Earl of Salisbury. He unexpectedly rose to prominence in Jerusalem by catching the eye of the ailing leper king's sister Sibyl. Regarded as a lucky upstart by the barons, Guy lacked the stature in 1183 to give authority to a defensive or offensive strategy vis-à-vis the Saracens. He had, at this stage, few allies in court—in fact, during and after the 1183 standoff, the kingdom's barons threw Guy under the bus. As battle neared at al-Fula, the barons acted inertly, leading Guy to believe that they were not enthusiastic about a fierce assault on Saladin, and then after the Arabs departed, the Crusader notables shamelessly and opportunistically excoriated Baldwin's heir apparent for not leading them into battle.

Assessed strictly in military terms, this criticism was not judicious. Four years later, at Hattin, when Guy opted for the opposite, offensive, tactic he lost his kingdom, so it is far from clear that he really erred in 1183. At least one historian, R.C. Smail, argues strongly that Guy's defensive tactic in 1183 was prudent. Most European residents in the Crusader settlements lived around fortresses and walled towns, and so an aggressive strategy of sending the Franks' warriors far from these protected places ran the risk of leaving the outnumbered European population dangerously vulnerable. Since such vulnerability was precisely the result of the disastrous Hattin campaign a few years later, the Crusader barons did their kingdom a real disservice by lambasting Guy for choosing a cautiously prudent route in 1183, Smail suggests.[86]

That said, almost all commentators on Crusader military history have suggested that the Latin Kingdom shot itself in the foot by granting Guy the reins of command, rather than Raymond. Guy's main power rival in the kingdom, Raymond III of Tripolis was a much more discerning and efficient warrior whose conservative instincts were molded out of years of trial and error in the region (in his youth, Raymond had been held captive for a decade). Not just William of Tyre, who was indebted to Raymond, but Arab commentators such as Ibn al-Athir and Baha al-Din, categorically identified the Prince of Galilee as the most able Crusader military and political leader in the kingdom.[87]

The pre-Hattin crisis in the Latin Kingdom was not limited to the fact that a militarily inexperienced knight, Guy, ended up on the throne, in lieu of the far better qualified Raymond. Guy's authority was compromised on another level as well. There was no clear constitutional reason for Raymond and his followers to have given Guy the benefit of the doubt, and to have regarded him as a rightful heir apparent to the leper king, rather than a usurper.

Via their *Haute Cour* assembly mechanism, the barons retained a measure of veto or ratification control over the policy decisions of any Jerusalem sovereign. As Crusader historian Prawer averred: "More than any other institution, the *Haute Cour* characterizes the Latin Kingdom… By imperceptible degrees, the legitimacy of royal decisions became dependent on the agreement of the *Haute Cour,* which could thus paralyze a king's plans and policies."[88] Under normal circumstances, a baron such as Raymond, who headed the independent Crusader state of Tripolis (in addition to his lordship of the Galilee, within the Latin Kingdom) would not have had a particularly obedient attitude toward an interloper like Guy, and the years of constitutional crisis in the Crusader Kingdom during the disabled Baldwin's rule were not normal circumstances. With family ties to the leper king, Raymond had plausible claims to the throne, and he prosecuted them with renewed vigor after Guy's perceived blunder at al-Fula in 1183. Baldwin, who was losing his sight and use of his limbs in the final phase of his afflicted life, validated the barons' self-interested dismissal of Guy as an incompetent coward. The king nullified Guy's status as his heir, and even took steps to separate his now humiliated brother-in-law from his sister, Guy's wife Sibyl.

At this stage, Raymond gained effective control of the kingdom as procurator. On paper, his *bailliage* was supposed to last a decade, until the leper king's son, Baldwin V, reached the age of fifteeen. Under explicitly formulated terms, Raymond's control as procurator was shielded: should both Baldwins die during this decade, he would remain procurator until an elite committee, comprised of the pope and the kings of England and France, reached a decision about the succession. In particular, this committee would decide whether rule should devolve upon the family of one of Amalric's daughters, Sibyl or Isabel (of the two half-sisters, Sibyl was better positioned, being the daughter of a major player in the Jerusalem court intrigues, Agnes of Courtenay, who was also an inveterate enemy of Raymond's).

A year after his father succumbed to disease, young Baldwin V passed away in 1186, and his death triggered what was essentially a palace coup. Blatantly violating the agreed-upon procedure for ending Raymond's term as procurator, the Lusignan camp rallied hastily to crown Guy (one participant in this coup, Gerard of Ridefort, was motivated by an old grudge,[89] and his poisoned attitude toward Raymond was later fateful at Hattin). Since William of Tyre was no longer alive, there is no detailed record of how the barons were outmaneuvered by Guy's faction, but the appended *Continuation* of William's chronicle, possibly written Ernoul, squire of Balian of Ibelin, depicts Raymond as being flatly outwitted, allowing the intriguers to persuade him to stay away from Jerusalem in the interval slated in their plot for Guy's coronation.

Raymond's stumbling performance in this court drama brings to mind an earlier, comparable incident. As Prince of Galilee, Raymond was a latter-day successor to Tancred, who, in the kingdom's first days, suffered an equally humiliating setback in a court power struggle, being bested by Baldwin I after Godfrey's death.

After the August 1186 coup, Guy had practical means and the ritual authority of coronation on his side, forcing almost all of the barons to acquiesce to this fait accompli. Raymond's position was badly compromised. Things looked especially bleak when the newly crowned and confident ruler, Guy, informed Raymond's emissary, Balian of Ibelin, of his intention to lay siege to Tiberias, the Galilee capital to which the defeated Raymond had fled.

For Raymond, all bets were off. He had been betrayed, and, under the chivalrous ethics of the day, he could hardly have submitted to the usurper, Guy, and retained his honor.

As noted, at an earlier stage in his career, Raymond had forged a defense pact with Saladin, and, formally, in autumn 1186, this years-long truce was still in effect. Now, pressured in Tiberias, the Prince of Galilee viewed options that are best characterized as a devil's dilemma. On the one hand, he could choose the unbearable humiliation of submission to Guy, or, on the other hand, he might hatch a temporary alliance with the Saracens, in order to stave off his dangerous, and newly empowered, Crusader rival, Guy. For Raymond, the choice of the latter option would have had the backing of family precedent; almost forty years before, his father, Raymond II, had deployed the same tactic, striking an agreement with Nur al-Din to outflank a Frank rival (Bertram of Toulouse).[90] Viewed from the standpoint of the Crusades' overall normative-strategic purposes, however, the second option could only have paid Pyrrhic dividends for Raymond. Choosing it would have consigned him to political-cultural isolation. The entire rationale of the Crusader settlement in the Holy Land was to expulse the Saracens, not to rely on them to gain an advantage in a power rivalry with a fellow Crusader.

As it turned out, Raymond staggered in Tiberias and imprudently tried to square the circle by choosing both options. Saladin demanded that Raymond grant him passage through his Galilee domain, so as to exact revenge against Reginald of Krak and other Franks who had raided and robbed an Arab caravan in which Saladin's sister had happened to be travelling. To avoid the optics, or substance, of treasonous behavior, Raymond warned Reginald's group about Saladin's thirst for vengeance, but the Prince of Galilee also granted passage to the Ayyubid ruler. So, in the warm-up to Hattin, this is where the Latin Kingdom inauspiciously stood: in Galilee, its most capable warrior, Raymond, was busy trying to square circles of honor and self-protection, while the kingdom's formidable enemy, Saladin, followed superior, mathematically precise, principles of military and political preparation.

THE BATTLE OF HATTIN

Our knowledge of what happened at Hattin in 1187 is imperfect because only one medieval account was actually composed by an eyewitness to the battle. Nonetheless, historian Joshua Prawer managed in 1964 to reconstruct the event vividly, using information about the topography of the Galilee area which he collated from Talmudic sources and from explorations of the area.[91]

The truce with the Saracens having ruptured, King Guy ordered a general mobilization of Crusader forces. Repeating the 1183 procedure, the Crusader contingent gathered at Sepphoris, right where Judah HaNasi and the Tannaim had composed the Mishnah, a millennium before. For this round, the expanded Crusader army consisted of 1,200 knights and some 18,000 foot soldiers. For his part, Saladin recruited a large force of 12,000 horsemen. This Islamic army moved from Tel Ashtara to a point on the southern edge of the Sea of Galilee, where it encamped until July 1.

This situation prompted the most fateful series of Christian consultations in the Holy Land during the Middle Ages.

The first discussion was staged on June 30, after the Crusaders received intelligence of an impending Arab attack on Tiberias. Raymond basically advised Guy to concede the Galilee capital to Saladin, urging the king to wait patiently for aid to come from Antioch; in the meantime, Raymond advised, Guy should fortify other strategic Crusader locales. Drawing on knowledge of what happened during Saladin's previous campaigns, particularly in 1183, Raymond argued that the Arab commander would not be able to hold his troops in the region for a protracted period. Many Arab soldiers came to Galilee from far-off regions in the hope of winning riches. Booty from Tiberias would not suffice for Saladin's men, and many of them would return to their homes at the end of the summer, Raymond insisted.

This counsel had enhanced credibility because Raymond was conceding the key city of his own Galilee lordship, and was also putting at risk his own wife, Eschiva, who was trapped in Tiberias. However, the Galilee prince's inveterate rival, Gerard of Ridefort, cast suspicion on this reasonable piece of advice by playing the trump card of Raymond's recent traitorous alliance with Saladin. Together with Reynald of Chatillon, Gerard informed Guy that Raymond's "counsel was not good . . . and mingled with the hair of the wolf." What is striking about this war council, John France observes, is its "bitterness."[92] Even a leader with more savvy and experience than Guy would have had no way of knowing who in this debate was evaluating a battle strategy on its own merits, and who was inspired by old grudges and egoistic self-interest.

The next day, on July 1, Saladin himself appeared before Sepphoris, hoping to bait the Crusaders into military entanglement. The Frank army did not move, but Saladin's provocation irked its warriors, and then the arrival of the "True Cross" further piqued their fighting mood (this holy item, discovered in the aftermath of the Crusader conquest of Jerusalem in 1099, was brought to the Crusader's Galilee camp by the bishops of Acre and Ramla). Almost unanimously, the Franks believed that they should set out at dawn, "accompanied by the Lord's cross, to fight the enemy" (as the medieval accounts attest). Against the grain, Raymond continued to lobby for a defensive strategy, telling Guy that should Saladin take Tiberias, the Crusaders could effectively concentrate their army on the coast, at Acre.

The following day, July 2, Muslims grabbed Tiberias, whose European residents fled into its citadel, directed by the fearless Countess Eschiva. Circumstances and tactical calculations were now altered, providing leeway to the cautious Raymond. In another tempestuous war council, the Prince of Galilee managed to win the debate: Raymond persuaded the Crusaders to stay put at Sepphoris and "watch events" as they unfolded.[93] So resolved, the war council adjourned and the barons went to bed.

That night, however, the future of their kingdom turned dark. In an "astonishing reversal of policy,"[94] Guy ordered his troops to leave camp, and move eastward to war. The medieval chronicles explain that after the war council disbanded, Gerard took Guy into a corner, imploring him to ignore the treasonous Raymond and lead the Crusaders to a glorious victory. "Sire, do not trust the advice of the count for he is a traitor, and you well know that he has no love for you and wants you to be put to shame and lose the kingdom. I advise you to move off immediately together with the rest of us, and let us go and defeat Saladin," implored Gerard. "If you do not leave this camp Saladin will come to attack you, and if you withdraw at his attack the shame and reproach will be all the greater for you."[95]

Just as the Crusaders awoke on July 3 to learn of Guy's fateful decision in favor of an attack, the ever alert Saladin shrewdly moved heavy equipment from his Sea of Galilee camp to a point called Kafr Sabt, located around the midpoint of the Crusaders' proposed trek on the mountain plateau from Sepphoris. Saladin was thinking astutely about ways to box his Christian antagonist and about how to move supply lines with practical efficiency.

In contrast, Guy, Saladin's counterpart, had been distracted by the necessity of sifting through the innermost motivations and emotional dispositions of his advisers. His war decision was manifestly impacted by issues not germane to the immediate emergency, including the matter of Raymond's past loyalty to the kingdom. Historians continue to wonder whether the preoccupied Guy even managed to articulate a coherent war objective, other than smashing Saracens, as the Crusaders decamped from Sepphoris—presumably the idea was to liberate Tiberias first of all, but if that goal were fulfilled, then what were the Franks going to do?

Fatefully, Guy and his advisers had neglected the crucial matter of supply for their proposed 30 kilometer hike eastward in hilly Galilee, to be undertaken in the scorching summer heat. Incomprehensibly, Guy had no plan for guaranteeing the provision of water to his soldiers and horses after they left the ample spring at Sepphoris. The destiny of the Crusader Kingdom turned on this one mistake.

The Franks rumbled off on the main eastwest road, Darb al-Hawarnah (road of the inhabitants of Hauran) which had apparently lasted in Galilee from Roman times. On the western, Mediterranean Sea, side, the road emerged from Wadi Rummanah and moved through the Beit Netofa Valley before forking, with one branch heading northward up to the Horns of Hattin (*Karnei Hittin*), and the other continuing straight through Kafr Sabt before twisting northeast to reach Tiberias.

Having left camp an hour or two before dawn, the Crusaders marched in three columns, with the vanguard led by Raymond. This formation accorded with a tradition holding that the ranking local knight should be the point man in an attack. The mounted knights were flanked by archers and crossbowmen who marched on foot, as well as by mounted archers, called Turcopoles, locally recruited archers who mastered the Turkish war art of firing their weapons while riding horseback.

Coming out of Kafr Sabat, Saladin personally commanded the Arabs' central column, with his right and left wings commanded by Taqi al-Din 'Amr and Muzaffar al-Din. Saladin's forces included some heavy shock cavalry, but depended mainly on light-armed horsemen. These fighters tortured the Franks by firing a shower of arrows—the weapon was far too light to penetrate a Crusader knight's armor, but the Arab archers fired in the air, hoping that some arrows would land on enemies' heads, or, more realistically, would destroy their horses. After a volley, the Arab archers could retreat on their horses to rearm for another shower of arrows, but, when the moment was right, they were trained to sling their arc bows over their shoulders, and charge the enemy on horseback, swords in hand. After decades of warfare in the region, the Crusaders had learned to use the Arabs' own war tactics against them, as exemplified by the deployment of the Turcopoles. Nonetheless, on the road from Sepphoris, historians suggest, the Crusader style of warfare was slow and inefficient, compared to Saladin's skilled and quick-mounted archers.[96]

After several hours of harassment by Muslim showers of arrows, and of parching torment in the scorching summer heat, the Crusaders reached Wadi Rummanah. Their arrival had been shielded by a hilltop, Mount

Turan, on their left wing. Moving past this peak at about 10:00 a.m., the thirsty Crusaders were unable to fight their way to a spring in this area. By noon, after they had progressed some fourteen kilometers from their camp at Sepphoris, Raymond ascertained that the army was log-jammed in the rear, and also dangerously extended in the front. The speediest Crusaders had reached a point at Meskenah where the northern fork of the main Darb al-Hawarnah road itself branched into subtributaries, with the northern mini-branch heading through Hattin (the other, southern, sub-fork ran through Lubiyah before it reconnected with the southern part of the main road, and led to Tiberias). In other words, the most advanced part of Raymond's vanguard had traversed some 18 kilometers, perhaps a little more than half the distance between Sepphoris and the Sea of Galilee. This was not a pace sufficient to reach the lake after a single day of skirmishing and marching, and so Raymond faced a decision.

Foregoing hopes, at least for the time being, of reaching the Sea of Galilee, not to mention the citadel at Tiberias where his wife was imprisoned, Raymond decided to lead the Crusader troops up the northernmost route, to the village of Hattin, where water was plentiful, and where the Crusaders could bivouac for the night, and re-group. Because of Raymond's inherently controversial status in the Latin kingdom, this decision was subsequently second-guessed by detractors who imagined that a full assault on the Arabs staged from Meskenah would have been a better plan, but Prawer, who meticulously reconstructed the battle's stages, concludes that "Raymond's plan to reach these springs [at Hattin] was reasonable."[97]

The truth is that the Crusaders might have already become so debilitated by thirst and Arab arrows that they might not have been rescuable under any plan. By the time Christian soldiers behind Raymond's vanguard reached Meskenah, where they were to turn left en-route to Hattin, the Crusader formation had already disintegrated. Mounted knights in the front raced toward the springs in the village, leaving vulnerable, demoralized foot soldiers in the rear (Templars were among those who suffered the most excruciating torment).

Knowing that enemy blood, war spoils, and spiritual glory were within reach, Saladin's better-provisioned soldiers moved quickly, and managed to block the path to the Hattin village. The battle was effectively decided, though much of the carnage of the Crusader loss was still to come.

Guy reached a typically uninspired decision, ordering beleaguered Crusaders to camp where they were, at Meskenah, even though there was no water in range of this site. Taqi's column held the entrance to gorges in the Hattin area, whereas Saladin had his other Arab contingents pitch camp at Lubiyah, located at an extremely short, diagonal distance from Meskenah, to the southeast.

If it is possible to rip from the pages of history a genuine image of the "clash of civilizations," this was the scene. In their two camps, the night before the final round of the Battle of Hattin, the warring Christians and Muslims were so excruciatingly close to one another that, as the chroniclers inform us, a cat could not have exited the Crusader compound without being noticed by Saladin's men. Ordering that provisions be brought up from Kafr Sabt, Saladin taunted and intimidated the thirsty, doomed Crusaders. Their lungs dried out, the Franks could not even gasp as camels carried water-filled goatskins, and hundreds of loads of arrows to the enemy's camp.

Battle tactics and technologies had changed, and monotheism had multiplied, but the plain facts of warfare in Galilee remained in 1187, some 1,100 years after Josephus had first disclosed them. Whoever won the big battle stayed on and whoever lost might receive a few decades of grace to regroup and then leave. Raymond's situation at Hattin is uncannily similar to Josephus' at Jotapata. Both men, Josephus and Raymond, were tragicomically conflicted military generals in Galilee. In the earlier siege, the Jews were thirsty and doomed, but managed for over a century to restore a Tannaitic principality of sorts, in Galilee, under Judah HaNasi and successor patriarchs, after the devastating rout at Jotapata; then their Jewish sovereignty in the Holy Land would be gone for over 1,500 years. Now, at Meskenah, the Crusader Franks were thirsty and doomed, and all that awaited them was to restore for a century a kingdom, of sorts, in Acre, after the devastating rout on the Horns of Hattin; then their Christian sovereignty in the Holy Land would be gone.

The next morning, July 4, the Crusaders broke camp at dawn, and Saladin let them march to their fate for a few hours on the mountainous plain. The Franks' main force reached Nimrim, just on the edge of Karnei Hittin. These Crusaders were at the start of two paths in a gorge which funneled, each on its own route, to a water source at Hattin village. But the Franks had little hope of quenching their thirst because Saladin's men were destroying the rearguard and right-wing of their army. The Crusaders were in panic, and a better commander than Guy would not have been able to calm them. The Latin king ordered his soldiers to set-up at the foot of Karnei Hittin, but the Crusaders managed to pitch just three tents (and these were engulfed and incapacitated by enemy smoke, as Arab soldiers lit fires by the side of the mountain and fanned havoc among the Europeans).

Raymond, on his own initiative, decided to lead the few men who remained by his side on a desperate full frontal charge at the gorge entry to Hattin. Cleverly, like a bullfighter raising his cape, Taqi al-Din allowed Raymond and a few of his knights to keep riding straight through Hattin, and just keep going, into oblivion. The kingdom's most impressive Crusader survived ignobly for another few weeks; circumstances never allowed him to rescue

Eschiva from the Tiberias citadel, and, the medieval chroniclers tell us, Raymond soon died of grief at Tripolis[98] (in an ironic twist, of all defeated Crusader veterans of Hattin, it was Guy who later distinguished himself—he rebuilt his reputation in Cyprus, becoming the first sovereign in a three-hundred year line of Lusignans on the island).

With Raymond out of the way, the Arab forces closed ranks before the village. Some berserk Christians scrambled up the summit at Hattin village, about 30 meters above the bloody plateau—at Yarmuk, some five hundred and fifty years earlier, defeated Christian soldiers threw themselves off a cliff, whereas here, at Hattin, they deserted the battle by climbing up a hill. Their escape, as Prawer phrased it, symbolized how the Crusaders' spirit was broken at Hattin: "This massive desertion of the infantry marked the beginning of the end. Repeated royal orders were of no avail. The foot soldiers who reached the summit no longer thought of battle. Nothing, not even death, could bring them back into the whirlwind of Muslim and Christian horsemen at their feet."[99]

The battle ended when Saladin's force seized King Guy's red tent and the True Cross. The Crusader loss at Hattin meant the end of their Jerusalem-based kingdom, eighty-eight years after the Franks conquered the Holy City. Less than forty years after the battle, decades before the collapse of the Crusaders' second, Acre-based, kingdom, the eminent Arab geographer, Yakut, visited Hattin, and spoke clearly and accurately about its import: "Saladin gained a great victory here over the Franks. All the Frank princes were beaten in this battle, and as a result of it, all the coast towns were freed from [the Crusaders]."[100]

THE THIRD CRUSADE

Europe raged. Its Crusader movement was all but obliterated. Legend has it that Pope Urban III died from shock. Acre fell to the Muslims straight after Hattin, and Saladin's men captured many other towns and castles in the Holy Land. The only important towns held by the Franks were outside its borders—Tyre, Tripoli, and Antioch. Guy remained imprisoned for months, and so there was a leadership vacuum among the Crusaders (Saladin eventually released Guy, probably calculating that the release of an incompetent king would do the Franks more harm than good; Guy, for his part, did not redeem his pledge to the Ayyubids and continued to fight them).

Right after Hattin, the most authoritative Crusader figure in the Holy Land was Conrad of Montferrat, uncle of Baldwin V who had been in the country for two years, and had a power base in Tyre. Conrad and other remaining Latin Kingdom notables bombarded the west with appeals for a campaign to restore Jerusalem—one report claimed that Conrad circulated a picture of a Turkish soldier allowing his horse to urinate in the Church of the Holy Sepulchre.[101] Not much propaganda was needed to outrage and engage the Christian West, however. Preparing the Third Crusade, Joscius, archbishop of Tyre (successor to William, the historian), negotiated a military alliance between Europe's monarchs.

One, England's Henry II, instituted a "Saladin Tithe," commandeering a tenth of the income and movable property, of everyone in his realm, and France's ruler, Philip II Augustus, enforced a similar tax. France and England were, in this period, embroiled in a prolonged dispute (England held France's maritime areas, from Boulogne to the Pyrenees), and Henry had lost control of a power struggle between his sons, Richard and John. In weeks before Henry died, Richard brazenly defied him by doing homage to Philip for fiefs held in France—later, as the Third Crusade unfolded, the fact that Richard the Lionheart was formally a vassal of Philip II's seemed ironic, since Richard, who was ten years older than his French counterpart, proved to be a much better financed, and militarily assertive, Crusader.

Preparations for the Third Crusade were marred by setbacks and delays, foremost among them the death of Holy Roman Emperor Frederick Barbarossa, who drowned in the Goksu River (Calycadnus) in June 1190. That summer, Richard and Philip were at sea with their own separate contingents, whose size continues to be debated by scholars (Philip signed a contract with the Genoese for the transport of 650 knights and 1,300 squires, but his chroniclers insisted that his army was three times that size; Richard's chroniclers tally his fleet as 180 ships and 39 galleys).[102] There were mishaps in the sea journeys, and Richard's troops were exercised in Cyprus, whose ruler, Isaac Commenus, called himself emperor of Byzantine, but Richard turned the Cypriot sideshow to his advantage, conquering the island, which has strategic proximity to Palestine's coast, and reportedly talking half of the fungible property from every inhabitant as booty. In early July, exactly four years after Hattin, his force joined the siege on Acre.

Richard's arrival was preceded by Guy, who had marched out of Tyre the previous summer with a small force, and launched an attack on Acre. Conrad also besieged the key coastal harbor, but refused to cooperate with Guy, a rival for the crown of a restored Latin Kingdom; scholars hazard contradictory estimates about whether Guy's early attack on Acre had any military value.[103] Philip had reached Acre in April 1191, a few months before Richard, at a time when Saladin's troops were seriously depleted, partly because one his deputies, a nephew, Taql-ad-din a-Muzaffar Umar, invested manpower and resources at this time for his own purposes, in Syria's Hamah region. Some scholars believe Philip and his men could have successfully scaled Acre's walls at this point,[104] but the French king was distracted by a number of issues, including the factious rivalry between Conrad and Guy, and his own claim maintaining that his alliance agreement with Richard entitled him to half of the booty which the English ruler had commandeered in Cyprus.

Reaching its climax in July with Richard's arrival, the Crusader siege on Acre was a tumultuous, consequential affair whose outcome was the establishment of a second Crusader kingdom, based in the northern city, on Galilee's western, coastal edge. From the Frankish standpoint, only the conquest of Jerusalem on the First Crusade, more than ninety years before, displayed greater triumphant resolve. Viewed from the Ayyubid vantage point, the siege exposed the hypocrisy of European norms of chivalry, owing to Guy's double-dealing and, more importantly, the way Richard, in victory, reneged promises about the protected egress of two or three thousand defeated soldiers from the Acre garrison (Richard slaughtered these Saracens outside the city, in full view of Saladin's command).[105]

Before this surrender, when enduring the Crusader attacks, Muslim warriors used smoke signals and carrier pigeons to communicate between parts of the Acre garrison. Muslims mutilated and scorched Christians by using state-of-the-art combustibles ("Greek Fire"), while the Franks built rolling siege towers—the Crusaders were better engineers, while Saladin's men were superior chemists.[106] Christopher Tyerman, a Crusader scholar who ordinarily eschews provocative generalizations and analogies, opens one of his books with an image of the Acre siege, presenting it as an exercise in torment comparable to the most miserable experiences of the twentieth century: "Between 1189 and 1191, a cosmopolitan army of western invaders besieged the Palestinian coastal city of Acre, modern Akko. Their camp resembled the trenches of the Western Front during the First World War, fetid, disease-ridden and dangerous."[107]

The summer 1191 siege says much about Christian Europe's determination not to lose its kingdom in the Holy Land. It also attests to Acre's strategic value, and to its rise in the economics, culture, and politics of the Middle Ages.

Today, Acre retains some of its seaside charm, but its souk, mesmerizing to many western visitors (though repugnant to others), and its historical sites, do not have a grand feel commensurate to Acre's centrality 900 years ago. The mixed, Arab-Jewish, town provides shabby, insufficient municipal services to its residents, and Israel's investments in its tourist infrastructure are inconsistent, poorly planned and not worthy of Acre's ranking as one UNESCO's world heritage sites. At the height of the Middle Ages, Acre was a global trade center and cultural crossroads comparable to London and Paris in the nineteenth century, but you wouldn't know that on a visit to the city today, due to Israel's ultra-nationalist policy of neglecting historical sites not clearly connected to Jewish narratives.

Figure 6.2 View of Acre Today. *Source*: Courtesy of Adi Lam.

With Tancred being diverted to Haifa, Acre had remained out of the First Crusade's reach for a few years, before being conquered by the Franks, with assistance from the Genoese fleet, in a twenty-day siege in May 1104. A dress rehearsal for Richard the Lionheart's bad faith occurred in this first siege, when the Genoese violated the terms of the Muslim surrender, and executed 4,000 souls. As the twelfth century progressed, Acre was governed directly by the Crusader king, and, though Jerusalem remained the Frank capital up to 1187, Acre frequently hosted sensitive *Haute Cour* deliberations, such as an 1123 meeting convened to discuss responses to King Baldwin II's capture. Acre's palace was more opulent than Jerusalem's, and it was a wealthier city, as evidenced by the fact that it was required to furnish eighty knights to the king, whereas Jerusalem only supplied sixty-one. Visitors reported that the town's upper classes were, in the twelfth century, dining and dressing in relatively luxury, compared to the austere style of European towns.[108] On the eve of the battle at Hattin, Acre's population was 40,000 persons, twice the size of Jerusalem's.

The city's Jewish population did not scatter when the European Christians claimed Acre. Twenty years or so before Hattin, Benjamin of Tudela reported that there were 200 Jewish households in Acre, which translates to perhaps 800 persons. Acre became "the [country's] most important Jewish center under Crusader rule."[109] In 1165, just as Benjamin was setting out on his long journey, Maimonides, medieval Jewry's preeminent figure, spent five months in Acre. In past eras, Acre was, for Jews, a foreign and morally dubious town, but now it was gaining recognition as belonging to the historic land of Israel—as Benjamin put it, Acre was the "beginning of Eretz Israel."[110]

At the end of July 1191, days after Saladin's surrender of the Acre garrison, Philip returned to France, and the Franks' course for the rest of the Third Crusade was determined by Richard. Arrogant and imprudent as a ruler, and also rash and reckless as a fighter, Richard proved to be an astute military commander. "Few captains in history have been as difficult to understand as Richard the Lionhearted," writes one historian of this Crusade. "He would risk his own life with complete nonchalance, but nothing could persuade him to endanger his troops more than was absolutely necessary."[111] Autumn 1191 witnessed one of history's intriguing military chess matches, between Saladin and Richard, with three main pieces, Jaffa, Ascalon, and Jerusalem being moved around the playing board.

By the start of 1192, Richard decided that he could not meet his objectives in these first two locales, and also hold Jerusalem for any length of time in the event that the Franks captured it. So he decided to abandon plans of attacking Jerusalem, which, while not a popular decision among many knights, was a smart one. Based in Ascalon in spring 1192, Richard kept himself busy with raids against Saladin's logistical lines with Egypt, including an operation in Darum (Deir el-Baluh), on the Gaza Strip, in which the Franks freed some Christian prisoners. These forays irritated Saladin and probably strengthened the Crusaders' negotiation position, but, as it was reestablishing itself at its new Acre base, the Latin kingdom incurred a self-inflicted wound, owing to its inability to solve its ongoing succession crisis. Conrad had the upper hand in this succession contest, but he was killed at the end of April by the Assassin sect. Fairly or not, that incident cast suspicion on Richard, who had, many months before, met with Conrad's rival, Guy of Lusignan, in Cyprus.

The Third Crusade was unraveling toward an outcome which would not really be satisfying to either side, Christian or Muslim. Another successful Crusader raid in June, this time halfway between Darum and the Dead Sea, in which Richard and some French and English knights captured 6,000 camels and horses, and 500 human prisoners, was for the Franks, consolation, but not a game changer. His troops restive, Saladin made one last lunge for Jaffa over the summer, but it was inconclusive. In early September, the two sides forged an agreement, nominally a three-year truce. Richard, ailing, left for England in October.[112]

For the Europeans, this was not a glorious outcome, but Richard and his comrades reestablished the kingdom, which ran along the Mediterranean coast, from Tyre in the north to Jaffa in the south, with bustling Acre at its capital. A few European pilgrims won entry to Jerusalem under the terms of the truce.

From our Galilean standpoint, Richard and the Third Crusade completed about a third of the work of Christian restoration. Frank rule jutted three to five miles inward from the coast, along Galilee, leaving key historical sites like Sepphoris and Nazareth within view, but just outside, of this Second Latin Kingdom (Monfort, Galilee's most dramatic Crusader castle, would later be built almost exactly on the line of the Saladin-Richard truce). The next two phases, more or less restoring the historically defined area of Galilee to the Second Latin Kingdom before its dissolution, occurred in 1229 as a result of Frederick II's campaign in the Holy Land, and then in 1240–1241 under an agreement signed by Richard of Cornwall and Egypt's Sultan as-Salih Aiyub—these later two phases expanded Crusader Galilee eastward, to the Sea of Galilee and the Jordan, thereby including Tiberias, Safed, and Mount Tabor.[113]

THE ACRE KINGDOM

Rule in this Second Kingdom was more baronial than monarchical. Some kings were relatively authoritative figures, as exemplified by Guy's brother, Amalric II, who united the Cypriot and Acre kingdoms, and extended Crusader sovereignty northward, through Sidon and Beirut, before his death in 1205. As Guy's pre-Hattin career illustrated, succession rights in the kingdom were often claimed by convenient marriage, but this mechanism caused upheaval in the Acre kingdom in 1225, when Queen Isabella II was wed, by proxy, to German King Frederick II, whose departure on the Sixth Crusade was much awaited. As nominal head of the Acre kingdom, Frederick, a versatile, multilingual and learned ruler who could also be maddeningly obstinate, never won backing among knights who were born and bred in Outremer, particularly from the powerful noble family, the House of Ibelin. The ensuing War of the Lombards (1228–1243), fought between backers of the "foreign" Hohenstaufen ruler (who were largely from Lombardy and are also called "imperialists" in this context), and the Ibelin family and its confederates,[114] largely eliminated centralized, monarchic rule during the last quarter of the 200 year-long Crusader period in Palestine.

Even before Frederick II, monarchic regents, under the title bailli, sometimes ruled the kingdom. With quite mixed results, Frederick utilized this bailli mechanism, sending (for instance) Riccardo Filangieri, from Naples, to take the reins of the kingdom. Thus, in some periods, these regents held a measure of power in the kingdom, grudgingly sharing it with the three military orders (Templar, Hospitaller and, from the end of the twelfth century, the Teutonic), with visiting, powerfully charismatic monarchs from Europe (as in the example of King Louis IX's four-year stint in Acre, discussed below) and also with the Italian traders, who dwelled in mini city-state boroughs in Acre, and who periodically feuded with one another (most uproariously in the mid-thirteenth century, in a Venetian-Genoese clash[115]).

Most scholars conclude that under these decentralized, semi-chaotic, circumstances, the core power institution in the Acre Kingdom was not the king, but rather the high court, the *Haute Cour*.[116] This assembly by no means operated in judicial realms alone. It had important legislative and administrative powers in areas such as tax collection, and it assembled to reach political and strategic decisions of paramount import to the kingdom's future. Originallyconstituted of nobles who owned lands awarded to them directly by the king, and who were therefore his vassals, the *Haute Cour*'s composition broadened over time. It came to include the bulk of nobles in the kingdom and also delegates from the military orders. Apart from a dozen years (1231–1243) when the brunt of the kingdom's notables reorganized in what they called Acre's "commune," essentially to carry out the Ibelin-fueled power struggle against Frederick's bailli, Filangieri, the *Haute Cour* governed the Second Latin Kingdom.

This was an oligarchic system, heavily tilted to the protection of well-defined religious, commercial, and military interests. The *Haute Cour* operated on the basis of meticulously documented regulations and precedents; in this sense, it reflected the Crusaders' quasi-mania for the law. In view of the chronic, sometimes mortal, danger posed by the kingdom's Muslim enemies

Figure 6.3 Crusader Acre. *Source*: Courtesy of Adi Lam.

and also by (as the thirteenth century progressed) Mongol outliers, this legalism has been regarded by modern historians as bizarre Frankish self-distraction. Prawer, for instance, referred quizzically to "legalistic hair-splitting" as the Franks "favorite pastime."[117] Undeniably, the legal penchant had prestige: John of Ibelin, count of Jaffa and Ascalon and nephew of the other John (Jean), the "Old Lord of Beirut," whose lifetime (1215–1266) spanned the key years of the Acre Kingdom, attained fame for his legal treatise composition. On a cultural level—at least in the eyes of historians like myself who have lived most of their lives in a second country and region—there is nothing really puzzling about this legalism, since it reflects the existential need of newcomers, and their direct descendants, to establish order in what started as an unknown world. At any event, the *Haute Cour* was a functioning body, and the demise of the Acre Kingdom at the end of the thirteenth century cannot be related to the obsessive legalism of its members. The "foreign policy" decisions it faced—whether, for instance, to lean toward the Mongols or the Mamluks before the Battle of Ayn Jalut,[118] as discussed below—were of bewildering complexity, and the high court's decisions on these matters were reasonable enough. If anything distracted this second Holy Land Crusader era, to its strategic detriment, it was the intervention of papal delegates in war-or-peace decisions faced, on the ground, by European rulers and knights who arrived on the later Crusades; and the most questionable strategic decisions reached on these later Crusades, particularly ones pertaining to the pros and cons of campaigns in Egypt, were really out of the purview of the *Haute Cour*.

In short, Acre was governed with some efficiency in the thirteenth century—and, Galilee's gateway was one of the best places on the globe to be, for most of this period. To be sure, our view of its daily life is filtered through the upper class, and Orientalist, orientations of medieval chroniclers, and Acre was hardly utopia. Lower classes lived in crowded city neighborhoods, and there is no paucity of reference to slave-trading and other abuses, but these ills were not ubiquitous (for instance, most of the ships that went to and fro in Acre's harbor were galleys, and their rowers were not slaves). Also, it bears mention that the city's prosperity waned in the later decades of the century, largely because the Mongol incursions changed trade routes in the Middle East, along with many other places.

From our "politically correct" standpoint, Acre's main calling card in this high medieval period is the prerogative it gave to commerce. For most of the Second Kingdom, economics trumped Holy War in Acre. Christian and Muslim traders, Crusader knights and Italian merchants, Arabs and Turks, went on with their daily business. Curious as it seems to us, this norm of business activity held even at times of warfare over the fate of Jerusalem, the Egyptian campaigns, and related life-or-death issues in the late Crusades.[119]

Muslim traders were, by and large, treated reasonably in Frankish Acre. The town's large mosque was converted into a church, but a prayer area for Muslims was allotted in it.[120]

Acre was hardly a politically neutral, placid sanctuary. The War of the Lombards was fought largely in Cyprus and other places outside of Palestine, but its violence sometimes spilled onto streets in Acre, and Italian traders sometimes mangled one another in these neighborhoods. Nonetheless, throughout the thirteenth century, the city magnetized the Franks, drawing them as a luxurious haven, sometimes in a way which compromised, in fact or imaginatively, the religious piety of the Crusades (chronicles of the later Crusades are punctuated with innuendo about knights who drifted northward toward the Acre fleshpots, instead of carrying on campaigns in the south; in this way, Acre's luxuriousness was sometimes blamed for the fact that the Cross was not planted atop Jerusalem's Church of the Holy Sepulchre).

As a trade crossroads, a dizzying array of products streamed into Acre, on camel caravans or on ship, from the west and from the east. Items from the west included licorice (used often for medicinal purposes), resin, hazelnut and tin, and from the east came Pernambuco wood, ammonia, arsenic, ginger, and lavender.[121] International trade in such products yielded more income in Acre than did the pilgrimage market. Spices and perfumes dominated the list of products which came from Asia. When shipped out to Europe, black pepper (as a meat preservative) and cinnamon were particularly popular, and the Venetians were known for trading these products. Out of Acre flowed agricultural produce that had been cultivated and harvested in the Latin Kingdom. Europeans craved sugar imported from Acre. The city also exported locally produced paint products, glassware (produced mainly in the city, and also from Tyre), indigo from the Jordan Valley, and a variety of textile products, including cotton cloth, silk, and brocade.[122]

At home in the city,[123] Frank knights kept their hair long and, in contrast to Greek Christians and Muslims, shaved off their beards. They wore colorful clothes and gold jewels; their wives kept their hair bundled, and, in winter, wore jackets not unlike what the men wore. Meals, among the Frank nobility, were heavy in meat—venison, rabbit, quail, wild boar. Peas, rice carobs, and olives are cited as side dishes. Fruit stewed in sugar was a popular desert. References to oranges on dining tables make their Holy Land debut in this Crusader period. In general, the diet was not very healthy, and scholars refer to a high incidence of digestive ailments, and also relatively short life spans, in this Acre setting.

Franks, and Muslims, are reported as having sought treatment offered by Jewish physicians when they were ill. Muslim chroniclers ridiculed the Franks' belief in therapeutic charms; they affirmed that their own, Islamic, culture supported a much more sophisticated, medicine-based, treatment system. Among the Franks, the Hospitallers worked to improve medical services in this period, both for locals in Acre and also for visiting pilgrims.

Frankish elites had time for leisure—games of cards and dice, chess, and also, reportedly, horse racing in the Na'aman River, just outside the town. A thriving extracurricular activity in Second Kingdom Acre was prostitution. Famously, the Muslim historian Imad a-Din reported on a cargo of 300 prostitutes shipped to Acre in 1191, at the time of the Third Crusade and the siege. His description of the women is detailed and, for the time, unusually lascivious.[124] That sex work was a major issue in Acre is indicated by the church's work in establishing a Mary Magdalene convent for former prostitutes (apparently located near the city's Jewish borough, in Mont Musard). Acre's seamy underside in this Crusader period had some notoriety. Chroniclers vented their frustration about the city's pickpockets and bandits—one complainer was Jean de Joinville, Louis IX's biographer, whom we will meet below.

The rejuvenation of Acre's Jewish community in the Second Kingdom bears witness to the city's centrality and heterogeneity in this period. Far from its reputation among Jews in earlier times as a profane locale detached from Eretz Israel, Acre "became the undisputed center of Jewish life in the thirteenth century," in the country.[125] There is no strong reason to believe that during the brief, 1187–1191, period of Ayyubid rule in Acre, harm befell the city's several hundred Jews whom Benjamin of Tudela had observed. In fact, quite reminiscent of stirrings animated by the collapse of Byzantine rule 500 years before, apocalyptic Jewish writers expected that the temporary ascendance of Islam would spell the end of Edomite (Christian) rule in the Holy Land, as a stepping stone to Jewish restoration in it—one Genizah fragment actually refers to the Third Crusade siege on Acre ("The Edomites and Ishmaelites will fight each other in the Valley of Acre until their horses will sink in blood and neigh").[126] However, when the Franks rebounded, and "Edomite" rule returned to Acre, Jewish hopes were not shattered. In sharp contrast to the fate of European Jewish communities during the Crusades, Acre Jewry retained a certain measure of positive acknowledgment and rights in this period (Jewish testimony, for instance, was recognized in the Franks' intricate legal system).[127] The worst hardship occurred at the start of the Second Kingdom, when Jews were removed, apparently by legal fiat, from Acre's old city to a new, lower status, suburb, Mont Musard, where they neighbored Eastern Christians and Muslims. Not directed specifically at Jews, this policy stemmed from a passing phase of property upheaval in Acre—Crusader heroes of the 1191 siege quickly claimed dwellings abandoned by Muslim fighters, but the rights of the new tenants were contested by Christians who had lived in the houses before 1187, and now reclaimed rights to them.[128]

Starting in the second decade of the thirteenth century, this relocation to Mont Musard did not deter overseas Jews from settling in Acre, a prospering city conveniently located as the port of entry to the Holy Land. Jews, many of them known Talmudic scholars, came to Acre from Italy, Spain, and Central Europe. In the 1230s, Acre ranked as a center of Jewish learning, largely owing to a sub-community of French Tosafists that was led by a respected immigrant rabbi, Samson of Sens (Tosafist refers to Talmudic commentators who "added," as the Hebrew term implies, explicatory glosses).[129] In general, this influx of scholarly European Jewish immigrants, called Ashkenazim, in Acre set precedents because of their interaction with local, eastern (Mizrahi) Jews. Frankish Palestine, and Acre in particular, was the first period in the country's history when this west-east, Ashkenazi-Mizrahi (or Ashkenazi-Sephardic) dynamic is readily discernible in communal affairs. And Acre Jewry in the thirteenth century is also unusual for the impact exercised in it by Ashkenazi immigrant newcomers—no such Ashkenazi impact would occur again until the late eighteenth and early nineteenth centuries, when Hasidic and Perushim immigrants from eastern Europe settled in the country, mostly in Galilee until a series of calamities ravaged the region in the 1830s[130] (sixteenth-century Safed filled with Sephardic Jewish refugees). Samson of Sens' sub-community simultaneously enriched and convulsed Acre Jewry's cultural life. Its convulsive effects stemmed from the fact that the French Tosafists imported to the Holy Land their animus against Maimonides—Samson endorsed many of Maimonides' halachic rulings, but he was outraged by signs of the great philosopher's ambivalence about the resurrection of the dead. In addition to its religious aspects, the dispute took on familial and sub-ethnic qualities because Maimonides' son, Abraham Maimuni, became connected to it, and because the non-Ashkenazi Jews in Acre unreservedly admired Maimonides. For better or worse, through the early 1230s, this Maimonides dispute became a kind of brand logo for Jewish life in Acre, its level of acrimony ebbing and flowing in tune with the anti-Maimonides campaign waged in Montpellier and Saragossa, where the philosopher's books were burned, or where he was excommunicated. Affairs settled down as the second quarter of the thirteenth century unfolded, and, according to Prawer, Acre's Jewish community was molded increasingly by Ashkenazi culture.[131]

In terms of Acre Jewry's rising self-confidence, the turning point transpired in the early 1230s. In this period, a dispute about communal authority first flared in Alexandria, Egypt. It was provoked by a patriarch (nasi) named Hodaya ben Jesse, who claimed ancestry from the house of David—Hodaya proclaimed that he had authority to impose a *herem* excommunication ban on Jews who lived in far-off countries and regions. Hodaya's opponents in this dispute were Maimuni, who headed the Jewish court in Alexandria, and one of its *dayan* judges, Joseph ben Gershom.[132] Gershom subsequently moved to Acre, where the dispute about Hodaya's brazen assertion of patriarchal authority entered its second round. Basing their view on a responsum drafted by Maimuni and calling themselves the "Sons of the Community of Acre Inside the Boundaries of the Tribe of Asher," Acre's communal leaders issued a set of regulations (*takkanot*), negating the right of an overseas nasi to excommunicate a member of their own local community, so long as the Jew in question had the support of three of its notables.[133]

As we have seen, this sort of dispute about calendar designation or communal authority, in which a Babylonian patriarch vied against delegates from a Galilean community such as Tiberias, had occurred periodically in past centuries. Interestingly, in Crusader times, the honor of Palestine Jewry in this sort of dispute was represented by the community in Acre, of all places. A thousand years before, in the Roman era, a Tannaitic rabbi who paid a dodgy visit to a bathhouse in the city was thought of as tempting sin, in a locale, then called Ptolemais, which did not really belong to ancestral Eretz Israel. Now Acre was the capital of Galilean Jewry, and of Eretz Israel as a whole.

TEUTONIC GALILEE

Frankish development of Galilee in the Second Kingdom period became indelibly connected to the Teutonic Order. The other orders were active in the north, of course (as exemplified by the well-excavated Hospitaller complex in Acre, one of the worthy tourist projects undertaken in the city in past years), but the Teutonic Order differs from its older Templar and Hospitaller counterparts in that it came into existence as a result of the post-Hattin crisis and the Third Crusade, and its leading figures became deeply involved in the diplomacy of the later Crusades.

The Montfort Castle built by this Germanic order is the lodestar of the Crusader period in Galilee. You reach it after an invigorating trek on a rocky, rolling path that leads straight into Galilee's breathtaking green solitude. It is impossible not to climb up this castle without contemplating history's somersaults, how noblemen and commoners, men and women[134] came to erect such a statement of Christian European power in the region where Jesus preached love and fellowship.

The Teutonic Order emerged out of a small naval contingent organized in Bremen and Lubeck on the Third Crusade. It arrived in Acre in September 1189 and created a small hospital in the city in the name of the "Hospital of St. Mary of the Teutons in Jerusalem." This name faithfully reflected the ultimate goal of the Third Crusade,[135] but it exudes irony in retrospect, since the order, after this start in Acre, became rooted in Galilee.

As earlier Christian warriors in the Holy Land had done, Teutonic knights on the Third Crusade imagined themselves as superseding ancient fighting Israelites, and the order's founding documents brim with references to imagined predecessors such as the Maccabees. From its start, the order had three pillars of support—the Hohenstaufen emperors, the papacy, and Frankish magnates in Outremer. Its calling card, in this formative period, was the medical support it offered to pilgrims, who resumed their flow into the Holy Land, via Acre, when the Third Crusade accomplished some of its goals and established a new kingdom. The order also established cemeteries and offered burial services for pilgrims. Reports of its good works spread throughout Europe and "noblemen began to offer alms to the brethren even though they had not embarked for the East themselves."[136] By 1215, the Teutonic Order had an established presence, one symbolizing the commitment of Germanic Christians to Frank settlement in the Holy Land. It had property in Palestine, and also in Armenia and the Peloponnese, Italy and the German empire, and it had the approval of the Pope. A quarter century after its inception, it combined military and medical work, and was beginning to carve out enclaves in Europe, starting with Hungary, whose King Andrew had in 1211 allotted it the Burzenland province.[137]

Despite this impressive growth, the Teutonic Order was at this time still a relatively small operation in the Holy Land that mainly supported pilgrims in the Latin East. It was the Fifth Crusade (1217–1221) which turned it into a powerful player, and, for some years, medieval Christianity's most impressive presence in the region where Jesus grew to age. This transformation was largely due to the diplomatic finesse and political acumen of the order's Master, Hermann of Salza. "Just as the Council of Troyes in 1129 and the advocacy of Bernard of Clairvaux drew attention to the Templars," ahead of the Second Crusade, "so too did the work of Herman von Salza during the Fifth Crusade raise awareness of the Teutonic Knights," writes one historian of the order.[138]

The Fifth Crusade was, above all, a papal Crusade.[139] Calling Europe to action in 1215, Pope Innocent III claimed that the fortress on Mount Tabor, recently built by Ayyubid Sultan al-Adil, endangered the security of the Second Kingdom as a whole. Innocent III, and after his death, Honorius III, deployed a number of preachers, but none was more effective than James of Vitry, who had won the papacy's attention due to his preaching for the Albigensian Crusade, in southern France. On the eve of the Fifth Crusade, James was Bishop of Acre, and disconsolate about how the second generation of Franks in Outremer, the so-called "poulains," had assimilated in the region in a fashion which made them, he thought, corrupt and unmanly. "In Acre, the key city of the Latin kingdom, where women of the street accepted the favors of the clergy . . . the eloquent James of Vitry restored something of the spiritual ardor of the early crusading era," writes a historian of this Crusade.[140]

In Europe, recruiting for this new Crusade had mixed success. The papacy demanded that clergy and religious orders surrender one-twentieth of their income for three years, to finance the campaign; this, and other, demands exhausted, rather than inspired, many in the church. Hungary's King Andrew was the first monarch to answer the call, but he proved to be an easily unnerved and ineffectual leader in the Holy Land. In September 1217, Andrew and a few other overseas rulers and high nobility, King Hugh I of Cyprus, Duke Leopold of Austria, convened with the local Frank leadership, at a kind of extended *Haute Cour* assembly in Acre (some chroniclers hyperbolically reported that 20,000 knights and 200,000 foot soldiers congregated under a big tent!). Hermann of Salza and masters of the other two orders attended this meeting; they had earlier conferred with the land's ranking Frank, King John of Brienne, an experienced and astute field commander, about the possibility of launching a major Crusader invasion on Damietta, as a launching pad for a Frank conquest of Egypt and Syria.

The huge Acre assembly balked at this idea. In autumn, Crusader forces rummaged in areas south of the Sea of Galilee, at one point (November 10) crossing the Jordan some miles south of the lake. This foraging frightened Sultan al-Adil, but the Crusaders, at this stage, lacked a plan and a leader. Andrew ignobly returned to the comforts of Acre, and some Crusaders launched, in early December, attacks on the enemy fort on Mount Tabor. Though these were military failures, the Sultan's son, al-Muazzam, decided that there was no point in holding on to the fortress, a magnet of Crusade ire, and ordered that the garrison be set afire. The Crusade languished in the Holy Land over Christmas.

It was rejuvenated, surprisingly, by a lowly preacher, named Oliver, a scholasticus who reached Acre in early 1218 with knights from northwestern Germany and Frisia. Oliver applauded King John when the Frank ruler took the Damietta plan out of the desk drawer. Conveniently, James of Vitry was also on hand, furnishing arguments about why this Egypt campaign was preferable to an assault on Jerusalem. The Holy City was hot and lacked water in spring, warned Acre's bishop. Egypt had associations with Jesus' childhood, and a number of Christians were being persecuted there by the Saracens, James added. More than anything, preachers like James and Oliver stressed that the unwelcome Muslim presence in the region as a whole, including Jerusalem at its heart, could be undone should the Crusaders capture Damietta.[141]

The Damietta siege on the Fifth Crusade has notoriety for many reasons. From engineering and military standpoints, it is a hypnotically interesting episode centered around the Franks' dealings with a chain tower (Burj as-Silsilah) located on an island, opposite the city. In terms of strategic objective, the operation wafts confusion and megalomania. As would happen with Napoleon at the end of the eighteenth century, the Crusaders viewed the conquest of Egypt, a huge undertaking, as a means to achieving other goals, and ended up paying a steep price for this hubris. Morally, the result of the campaign speaks for itself—for a brief spell, the Crusaders conquered Damietta, and marked their victory (according to their own chroniclers) by killing all but 3,000 of the city's 80,000 inhabitants.[142] Such strategic and normative issues can be viewed on another level, one which threads together Crusader experiences in the Middle East. Twice the Franks waged major campaigns in Egypt, and exactly what derailed them in Damietta on the Fifth Crusade, the Muslims' superior knowledge of Nile tributaries and back channels, is what later snared France's Louis IX, on his Crusade.[143] This arrested development in the military-strategic realm was not recapitulated on an ethical-education level, however. The Franks learned absolutely nothing from the Fifth Crusade, whereas, as we will see, Louis IX's period of self-reflection in Galilee's Acre after his debacle in Mansourah can, with some important reservations, be connected to Europe's lost faith in Holy Land crusading, a trend which gave the world cause to sigh with relief. Finally, the turn of events at Damietta on the Fifth Crusade shows how a leadership crisis foiled the Franks in this period, and why newcomers in Latin Kingdom politics like Hermann of Salza and the Teutonic knights were able to exploit this breakdown, and promote projects like Galilee settlement.

The Franks' seizure of Damietta rattled and unnerved the already fractious world of Muslim politics. On repeated occasions, the Crusader camp received truce proposals from the enemy whose acceptance would have fulfilled the original strategic intentions of King John and his Acre-based comrades. More than once, Egyptian Sultan al-Kamil offered the Franks practically the full restoration of their pre-Hattin kingdom, including the return of Jerusalem, Tiberias, and Ascalan, in exchange for their departure from Egypt. The problem was that the pragmatism of John of Brienne was overruled by the on-site papal delegate, Pelagius, cardinal of Albano. "Imperious, proud, headstrong and dogmatic," Pelagius at Damietta imagined that he "personified the church triumphant: he was Joshua before the walls of Jericho."[144] Expecting that the Franks would decimate Saracen power once and for all, this papal interloper repeatedly caused the Crusaders to miss opportunities to leverage their temporary conquest of Damietta and secure the return of Jerusalem to Christian rule. After al-Kamil's forces regrouped and trapped the Franks on the Nile, the Crusaders settled for a demoralizing, status quo ante-bellum, sort of arrangement—under an eight-year truce agreement forged in late August 1221, the Muslims allowed them to flee from Egypt, tails between their legs, and they freed some prisoners but gave the Franks nothing else. "The Fifth Crusade ended in colossal and irremediable failure."[145]

For the Teutonic Order, nothing succeeded like failure.[146] During the Fifth Crusade, pilgrim traffic in the Holy Land rose exponentially, and tens of thousands of troops entered the country, many of them from the German empire. Johnny-on-the-spot, Hermann seized opportunities to strengthen the order. Knights were invited to join the order; one famous recruit was a Crusader named Litot, who joined the Teutonic brotherhood after having stormed the chain tower at Damietta. Another mechanism used to bolster the order was the conferral of formal association on a *confratres* basis, one which did not entail monastic vows. Quite possibly indigent fighters might have become *confratres* as a way of remaining with the army on the Crusade. This sort of affiliation with the Teutonic Order was evidently widespread—desperate to keep the Crusade in swing, Pope Honorius III avidly supported the Germanic order by offering a number of special privileges to *confratres*, including the right of burial in the Holy Land. As was customary with the other two orders as well, the pope also offered Teutonic *confratres* remission for sin—after the Fifth Crusade, this incentive played a part in the order's construction of the Montfort fortress. The most important papal concession won by Hermann and his order during the Fifth Crusade was Honorius' decision to accord it status equivalent to that of the older, better-established, Templar and Hospitaller orders. This newfound status allowed Teutonic brothers to claim exemption from the one-twentieth tithe, among other things.

Teutonic knights were active in military events of the Fifth Crusade, helping the Templars construct their fortress at Atlit, and participating in the various, attack and retreat, phases of Damietta. Chroniclers highlight Teutonic fighters who fell in Egypt, perhaps exaggerating their numbers. But the main lever propelling the order forward in the Holy Land and Galilee during this Crusade was not battlefield activity, but rather Hermann's diplomacy. The Teutonic Master participated in the fateful Acre war councils in 1217. He wisely advocated for acceptance of al-Kamil's offers to return the Holy Land to the Franks in exchange for their removal from Egypt, and, after the Franks' humiliating surrender, Hermann was one of the two dozen Franks who became hostage guarantors of the Crusaders' fulfillment of their agreement with the sultan. In order to be selected as a hostage, the Teutonic master "must have been viewed by both the Christian and Muslim forces to be a man of considerable ability and consequence."[147]

In the 1220s, the papacy turned to Hermann and the Teutonic order, as part of its effort to rejuvenate Holy Land crusading, following the debacle at Damietta. In 1227, Honorius' successor, Pope Gregory IX, appealed to Teutonic master Hermann of Salza, writing that "for the aid of the Holy Land ... you should seek to gather crusaders from the Teutons, and others, whoever you are able [to recruit], according to the wisdom given to you by God."[148] Scholars have debated about the Teutonic Order's goals in this period. It was on the move, it bears mention, both in Europe and in Outremer.[149] Before its eviction from Hungary, the order possibly intended to carve out an independent mini-state; invited to colonize Prussia, by dictate of the emperor in 1126, the Teutonic order might also have worked there with the same intention. In fact, some scholars have viewed the Teutonic Knights' settlement expansion in Galilee as being part of a far-flung state-building campaign.[150]

Whatever its exact intentions on the Galilean rolling hills, the Teutonic Order's ability to move ahead with its settlement program depended upon the disposition and success of the charismatic emperor, Frederick II. Called the "first European" by Nietzsche, Frederick II is one of history's formidable figures. He spoke multiple languages, cultivated serious interests in sciences and mathematics, had benumbing knowledge about the culture of the Arab east, made friends and foes wherever he went, and startled everyone. On his own belated Crusade, Frederick negotiated with a brilliant representative of Sultan al-Kamil, named Fakhr ad-Din—Frederick stumped the envoy by posing learned questions about geometry and numbers theory, which were eventually referred to the foremost mathematicians in Egypt.[151] As it turned out, Frederick negotiated the restoration of Frankish sovereignty in Jerusalem by working out access arrangements for Muslims whose ingenuity and daring set a standard far higher than anything that has subsequently been reached on the Temple Mount, through the various phases of the Israel-Arab conflict, to our present-day. Even though he regained Jerusalem for the Franks—something that neither his illustrious predecessors, like Richard the Lionheart, nor successors, like Louis IX, the Crusades' greatest figure, ever did—his enemies never forgave Frederick for negotiating terms with Muslims, and offering limited concessions to them. In our own contemporary parlance, they accused him of being an Arab lover. In medieval times, such accusations were quite literal. Frederick was suspected of keeping a harem, and innuendo spread about his alleged sympathy and association with Islam. In short, from the standpoint of Hermann of Salza and his comrades in the Teutonic Order, Frederick was not only the most promising of all possible allies but also an inestimably complicated one.

Frederick II's assistance was needed by them for specific purposes. In a 1220 agreement reached on the Fifth Crusade, the Teutonic Order acquired, in Galilee, lands which were in the estate inheritance granted to Otto, count of Henneburg, by his father-in-law, Joscelyn III of Courtney. Otto and his wife Beatrix, Joscelyn's daughter, carried out the sale after they decided to leave the Latin Kingdom and resettle in Franconia. The lands included the aforementioned Castellum Regis. One problem with this transaction, the order's first estate acquisition in the Latin Kingdom, was that many of the lands in the Joscelyn inheritance were, in 1220, controlled by Muslims.[152] The second issue is that Beatrix had sisters who apparently had rights to the inheritance (one of them later brought the Teutonic Order to court). To mitigate this second problem, the order relayed to John of Brienne formal ownership control over some of the inheritance lands—by making the Crusader king a stakeholder in this Galilee property, the order apparently estimated that John would suppress lawsuits initiated by the sisters.[153] But to solve its Muslim problem, and thereby gain access to its newly acquired Galilee lands, the Teutonic Order needed a new Crusade, one with power and effect greater than anything local Frank rulers like John, pinned in their scaled-down, coastal Second Kingdom, had been able to muster. That is where Frederick II enters on Teutonic Galilee's stage.

Most of the military standoffs during Frederick's Crusade, and in its aftermath, occurred offshore, particularly in Cyprus, and the adversaries were not Muslims, but rather disaffected local nobility, particularly from the House of Ibelin. The War of the Lombards germinated out of Frederick's assertion of authority in Beirut and Cyprus, which was detrimental to the Old Lord of Beirut, Jean of Ibelin, and his confederates. The 1229–1233 skirmishing had one notable spill-off in Galilee. This occurred on the night of May 3–4, 1232, at Casal Imbert, where the Ibelin forces were caught by surprise by the pro-Frederick "imperialists," led by Filangeiri, who launched their attack from Tyre. The event sent a shiver down the spine of the anti-imperialists because some of the prominent figures in their faction, including Jean of Ibelin's three sons (Baldwin, Guy, and Hugh), and the fourteen-year-old King Henry of Cyprus, were in the camp at Casal Imbert. Henry, half-naked, was thrown up on a horse, which fled to Acre while the three sons, according to pro-Ibelin historian Philip de Novare, fought valiantly ("Never did men so surprised better defend themselves . . ."), before scampering off into the Galilee hills. Casal Imbert was a setback for the anti-Frederick camp (twenty-four Cypriot knights were taken captive, and "a few" were slain, Philip wrote),[154] but within a number of months, the imperialists were expelled from Cyprus. When Philip composed his memoir, in intermittent stages between 1247 and 1259, a generation before the collapse of the Acre Kingdom,[155] he thought of the War of the Lombards as a glorious demonstration of how the fortitude and righteousness of the Frankish nobility triumphed over Frederick, whom he regarded as an immoral tyrant.

For Frederick, the Cyprus sideshow yielded a disappointing outcome, one which became fully apparent long after he had returned to Europe. No better, Frederick's status as an excommunicate during his period in the Holy Land was awkward. Frederick, who was an excommunicate owing to his broken promises and ongoing arguments with the papacy, turned into a divisive figure on this Crusade, almost to the point of parody. In May 1229, when he hastily left the Holy Land in hopes of staving off John of Brienne's rebellion in Apulia, Frederick was reportedly sneaked out to the Acre harbor at dawn, hoping to avoid detractors. This stratagem failed, and he was trailed down the Street of the Butchers by haters who pelted him "most scurrilously with tripe and bits of meat."[156] Several weeks before this degrading departure, on March 17, Frederick and his soldiers and jubilant German pilgrims marched into Jerusalem, and the next morning Frederick entered the Church of the Holy Sepulchre for a coronation ceremony to validate his status as ruler of a kingdom significantly enlarged and enriched by his Crusade. He had won for it the land's three holiest Christian sites, Jerusalem, Bethlehem, and Nazareth. Nonetheless, kingdom notables boycotted the ceremony. There was nobody to crown him. Before the ceremony, Hermann of Salza had lobbied vociferously with Jerusalem Patriarch Gerald, to no avail; Gerald decried Frederick's behavior and intentions. Frederick was an excommunicate whose entry to the vaunted Jerusalem church was an outrage, and to make matters worse, he had negotiated with the Saracens and granted them mini-autonomy on the Temple Mount, objected the patriarch. In the ceremony, Frederick took the crown and put it on his own head. Herman loyally read aloud, in German and French, Frederick's account of his connection with the Crusades.[157]

None of this sounds like material of a successful Crusade story, and, in truth, Frederick made nothing of himself as a Frankish warrior. Yet, as it happens, he was the most successful diplomat in the history of the Crusades.

This happened partly by default. In the period of the Fifth Crusade, in an Arab parallel to the way John and Pelagius bickered about who should get the glory for the Franks' temporary seizure of Damietta, three Ayyubid brothers, sons of sultan al-Adil, feuded between themselves about fruits of triumph, after the Crusaders were routed and sent back to Acre. Of the three, Egyptian sultan al-Kamil decided to outmaneuver his sibling rivals by hatching an alliance with Frederick—in 1226, many months before Frederick's Crusade, he sent the aforementioned emir, Fakhr ad-Din, to curry favor with the German emperor. Then, after Frederick reached Acre, al-Kamil lavished him with gift bribes (an elephant, ten horses, ten camels, silk). Frederick, for his part, amazed al-Kamil and Fakhr ad-Dinwith by displaying his familiarity with Arab diplomatic protocol, not to mention his knowledge of science and math.[158]

Al-Kamil did not want to fight. Hence, Frederick barely had to raised his sword, in harmless and token demonstrations of Crusader strength, before Egypt's sultan sent him an agreeable peace treaty. The sultan relinquished Jerusalem and villages around it, Nazareth, Toron, parts of the Sidon district, and more. The accord included the provision awarding unarmed Muslims control and prayer rights on what we today call the Temple Mount, with assurance of Christian prayer access in this area as well. As mentioned, this shared space provision in Jerusalem's sacrosanct Temple Mount area proved controversial among some Franks and papal delegates, no matter that the accord allowed the Crusader kingdom "to rebuild the city of Jerusalem in as good a state as it has ever been," as Frederick put it.[159] These Christian reservations paled in comparison to howls of outrage about al-Kamil's unwarranted concession generosity emitted by Arab chroniclers, who called the agreement "one of the most disastrous events in the history of Islam."[160]

For the Teutonic Order, Frederick's accomplishments were a windfall. Historians of the order have, for decades, debated whether Hermann of Salza ought to be viewed as a kind of Crusade consigliore to Frederick, or whether he and the order maintained neutrality regarding the emperor's tempestuous relationship with the papacy (one recent study sensibly refers to Hermann's activity as a careful "balancing act"[161]). This debate might be overly nuanced, however. Hermann of Salza stood firmly with Frederick during the emperor's most controversial or vulnerable moments, when prelates like Gerald contemptuously ostracized the German emperor. Indeed, the Teutonic Order won the heart of central Galilee, dozens of settlements radiating 10 or 15 kilometers on all sides of its Montfort castle, as a result of Hermann's acuity. The Teutonic Master's achievement is imprinted in the diplomacy of Frederick's Crusade. Frederick inserted in the agreement with Egypt's Sultan al-Kamil clauses awarding the Galilee properties, including Toron, to the Teutonic Order, and protecting its right to fortify Montfort.[162]

Scholars have identified 118 Teutonic Order holdings in the northern part of the Second Latin Kingdom, roughly half of them in the central-western Galilee area (four or five hug the coast, north of Acre), and the other half in today's Lebanon, north of Beaufort.[163] Some areas in the Joscelyn estate acquired by the order have been examined in detail by Haifa University archaeologist Rafael Frankel. These include a 75 square kilometer holding listed by Jean of Ibelin as "the land of Phillip le Rous" in the Sakhnin Valley, presumably separated from the St. George fief by the Hilazon Valley, and fiefs in northern parts of the Joscelyn inheritance, including Chastiau de Roi and also Manuet (located to the east of Chastiau de Roi and to the west of Casal Imbert; Manuet had a press for sugar production).[164] On another scholar's reading, in 1234, two villages and three gastinas were acquired in the lower Galilee, east of Acre; also, in April 1249, the Lord of Caesarea sold the order six villages, also east of Acre, and in November 1261 "vast possessions" were purchased by the order from Jean of Ibelin, on the coast north of Acre. By 1291, the Teutonic Order had paid in Galilee land acquisitions the hefty sum of 101,098 bezants.[165]

The crown jewel of Teutonic Galilee is the Montfort fortress, called Mezudat Monfort, in Hebrew, Qal'at al-Qurayn in Arabic and, in Crusader time, Starkenberg. The castle has, in recent years, been the subject of extensive excavation and study sponsored by Haifa University's Zinman Institute of Archaeology.[166] Adrian Boas,[167] one of the project's directors, aptly describes the fortress as "one of the most remarkable Crusader remains surviving in the Holy Land." He explains that Montfort was a "spur" castle, one of the two dominant forms built by Crusaders in the country in the post-Hattin period, once they had progressed beyond the simple fortified tower and enclosure castle model which they had used when they were still struggling to establish a presence in the country (the Franks built some seventy-five such towers in the First Kingdom period, throughout the twelfth century). The spur model has that name because such a castle "occupies the end of a mountain spur, above two converging river valleys," Boas writes.

Though it is easily identifiable as such a spur castle, Montfort has various anomalies, including the lack of a courtyard. Generally, the fortress' extremely isolated location has mystified modern explorers since the end of the nineteenth century, when British surveyors from the Palestinian Exploration Fund,[168] and others, came upon the Teutonic castle. Boas speculates that the Teutonic knights might have chosen such an isolated spot to keep a safe distance from the two other, Templar and Hospitaller, orders, but the records of Teutonic Order experiences in the era of Hermann of Salza and Frederick II do not really project consistent rivalry and animosity vis-à-vis these two older orders, and so this explanation is open to debate. Even once we try to imagine how perceptions of space, and how the lay of the Galilee landscape, were quite different in the thirteenth century, it seems reasonable to assume that this fortress' current "end of the world" ambiance was also palpably felt during the era of its construction; and, it should be borne in mind, located a fairly exhausting fifteen-mile journey from the temptations and vice dens of Acre, the structure was used for mixed, living, administrative, and security purposes by a monastic order. Prominent order brothers lived periodically in the fortress, and this suggests that Montfort's rationale may have been perceived in terms of soulful retreat and expiation, among many other things.[169] Scholars have not clarified whether the fortress contained a treasury vault,[170] but this seems like a logical line of inquiry when wondering about Montfort's oddly removed location—the Templars were in this period becoming Europe's global banking house, but other orders and interests in Outremer might have lacked secure places to store assets.

At any event, the Teutonic fortress was built in two stages, the first being the tower structure on its east side, and the next stage being the construction of a three story administrative center, including a ceremonial hall. Boas' team believes that building work on Montfort might have proceeded right up to its destruction by the Mamluks in 1271. Despite this dismantling, much of the fortress' physical infrastructure and overall character survived, and so

Montfort became (and remains) an arrestingly inviting symbol of Frankish Galilee.

As such, in past centuries and decades, Montfort attracted a roster of professional researchers, curious laymen, and eccentrics who, with good reason, apprehended it as a token of what Holy Land crusading must have looked and felt like. An excellently produced 2016 volume, edited by Boas and Rabei Khamisy, includes amusing discussions of an American museum official who sponsored a 1926 research trip to Montfort hoping to find, of all things, Crusader armor,[171] as well as articles on Mamluk perceptions of the fortress site,[172] and new research findings regarding Galilee's prime Crusader site. Akin to what Sepphoris was to Tannaitic Galilee in the era of Judah HaNasi, and to what Safed would later become in Galilee in the early modern period of Isaac Luria and the Kabbalah, Montfort, in this intermediary medieval juncture, looms as the preeminent symbol of Crusader Galilee in its Teutonic Order, post-Hattin, phase.

THE CONTRITE SPIRIT OF SAINT LOUIS

Louis IX (1214–1270)[173] led the Seventh Crusade[174] (1248–1254), a calamity whose nadir featured the capture of the Capetian monarch and his men in Mansourah, Egypt. He died of disease in Tunis shortly after embarking on another failed Crusade, idiosyncratically aimed at North Africa. He was canonized posthumously, thanks partly to campaigns launched by the Dominican and Franciscan orders.[175] Louis IX is a towering medieval figure, one whose idealistic striving compels some commentators to wonder about his contribution to the rise of individuality at this phase of the Middle Ages,[176] while others regard his administrative reforms as important precedents in the subsequent consolidation of the modern state.[177]

Laden in some biographical discussions of this majestic Capetian figure is a hypothesis holding that Louis would have better served history had he not embarked on the Seventh Crusade. On this view, the cutting-edge aspects of his legacy remained *despite* his six-year period in the Acre kingdom. This argument receives sustained backing in Jacques Le Goff's monumental biography, where the Crusade is regarded as a regrettable abomination, insignificant in every respect other than the function it played in Louis' mind as a kind of boiler plate demonstration of one thing an ideal Christian ruler had to do. Le Goff's work divides into three parts, one devoted to a factual chronicle based on all known facts of Louis' life, and the latter two written in a vein of self-conscious historiographic meditation about the production of images and myths in the drive to sanctify Louis, and about the extent to which biography can treat this subject as a human individual as opposed to an ideal type of a certain kind of religious ruler. Le Goff's lengthy work comes across as an encyclopedic compilation of all extant information regarding Louis' "real" life, and its subsequent mystification—the exception being that this biographer judges that Louis' crusading did not matter.

Le Goff is candid about this omission, stating, "I have chosen not to recount Louis IX's crusade and stay in the Holy Land in any detail."[178] Later, this biographer is explicit about his judgment that the Crusades were morally problematic, at least when viewed by latter-day standards, and also generative of destructive responses and trends such as Islamic holy war *jihad* (this moralistic view is, of course, familiar in popular works such as Karen Armstrong's book on the Crusades).[179] Moreover, Le Goff asserts, the Crusades were simply a waste of time, when viewed in non-normative, socioeconomic, and settlement terms. "Materially, there were no significant results," he writes. "For all their efforts, the crusaders ultimately left only the ruins of imposing monuments, notably in Jerusalem and Acre."[180] The only "actual result" of the Crusades, he concludes, involved changes in medieval elite structures, stemming from the fact that Outremer adventurism "decapitate[d]" the lineage of various noble families.[181]

Le Goff's dismissive attitude is not shared by Crusader historians, needless to say. In fact, it is the antithesis of these specialists' viewpoint, by which Louis IX is presented, on many levels, as the acme of the Crusader movement. Christopher Tyerman's overview of the Crusades, titled "A Very Short Introduction," necessarily affords little detail about any specific subject, but its snapshot of Louis IX suggests that he must be the paramount subject worthy of more study than any other, in this Crusader context. "Louis IX's Crusade proved the best prepared, most lavishly funded, and meticulously planned of all. It was also one of the most disastrous, its failure matching its ambition," writes Tyerman, teasing the reader to learn more about it.[182]

Outside of this circle of Crusader experts, some researchers do not downplay the impact of Louis' Crusade in Egypt and his subsequent stay in the Acre kingdom, but their measuring rods are set to considerations of France's sociopolitical development, or to representations of Louis' career as a kind of middle ground between secular sovereignty and divine rule. Notable in this connection is William Chester Jordan's 1979 study,[183] which argues that preparatory arrangements and fund-raising for Louis' 1248 departure on his ill-fated Crusade necessitated new types of monitoring and deployment of *baillis* and other representatives or processes in local government, and also altered relations between the crown and the church, and between the crown and various smaller groups, including the Jews (Louis' punishments of Jews for usury and other perceived faults are a smear on his legacy[184]).

Lacking in these stimulating yet contradictory arguments is attention to the ongoing moral narrative of Galilee. Louis' four-year period of contrition and self-renewal in the Acre Kingdom is a stellar example of Galilee's continuing function in a meta-didactic narrative of human history. Whether the authors from all periods, including our own, are aware of it or not, Galilee is unquestioningly viewed in their writing as the place where one historical era comes to an end, and the suffering of transitional figures is viewed as adumbration of an impending, new historical period.

Galilee is a powerful crossroads of faiths because of this myth of the region as host to end-of-an-era, tormented, figures. It hosts personalities symbolic of a new period in the earthly history of humanity *precisely because* they never reached Jerusalem and opened a messianic era beyond human time. The myth is so deeply impacted in the way the history of contrite holy figures (Christian, Jewish, and Muslim) is told that nobody seems to notice how the needle is stuck in the same, ever-revolving, record.

Much as contemporary historians treat the canonization campaign for Louis as a feature in the public relations history of a much earlier period, essentially the message imprinted in aforementioned, recent biographical accounts of this French Crusader king is the same as that promoted in the late thirteenth-century hagiographic texts. That is, the moral didacticism in their view of history has more in common with these bygone hagiographers than these contemporary writers realize. The myth of Galilee has conquered them, even as they posture in a guise of historiographic sophistication, protesting that the Crusades meant nothing to Saint Louis. In actual fact, writers like Le Goff are saying that *everything* changed in history as a result of Louis' years in the Acre Kingdom, just as Jesus' followers changed everything 1,200 years earlier, by developing a new creed by which masses could move emotionally in history to some place beyond debasing subjugation to smug, venal Roman rulers.

Everyone agrees that Saint Louis became a more devoted Christian, and a more solicitous ruler of subjects in lands of France, as a result of his harrowing Crusade experiences, and period of self-examination in the Acre kingdom. Laden in this conventional view is the idea that the contrite spirit of Saint Louis in Galilee led to the decolonization of the Crusades, to the distillation of their essential Christian message, to the replacement of Holy War by moral suasion, and, in the end, to a new historical era.

A crucial link in the chain of this thinking is the basic historical fact that Jerusalem was closed to Louis IX, a generation after Frederick II's stunningly successful agreement. Khwarazmian troops took control of the Holy City in 1244 (sixteen years later, the Egyptian-based Mamluk regime gained power in Jerusalem, and subsequently the city passed onto Ottoman rule, meaning that just under five hundred years passed, following Frederick's restoration, before Christian power reasserted itself in Jerusalem with Britain's Field Marshall Allenby's conquest of it during World War I). After he paid a king's ransom to release himself from captivity after the Egyptian disaster, had Louis IX returned to Frankish Jerusalem, the whole dynamic of his Crusade would have been different. Its penitent quality, and its subtext of a semiconscious European recognition of the failure and futility of Holy Land crusading, resulted from his several years in Acre, on the edge of Galilee, where Christianity originated as a spiritual movement, declaratively contemptuous of profane political power.

This image of the Galilee as the lever for a precocious penitent's passage from one historical era to the next leans heavily on the Jesus narrative, but is not entirely rooted in it. Jesus' followers shaped tales of the Christian savior's Galilee's upbringing in tune with the objective of enlightening themselves and others about the necessity of thinking in new spiritual terms, or in terms of some new historical era divorced from the Jewish zealotry which brought about the unspeakably calamitous rebellion against the Romans. Of course, Christian penitents like Louis IX in the Acre Kingdom always had Jesus on their minds, but they were not beholden to one single martyrological narrative. Viewing his staggering defeat at Mansourah as punishment for his sinful aggrandizement of church resources in preparation for the Crusade, Louis was apparently sometimes thinking of the Old Testament story of Joshua's conquest of Jericho, and the sacrilegious behavior of the plunderer Achan.[185]

Inspired by the Jesus narrative, among other things, Galilee has a continuing moral geography, based on its simultaneous proximity and separation from Jerusalem. Since the messianic option of escape from historic time in Jerusalem is not available to agonizing penitents, such as the saintly Christian King Louis IX, or the Jewishly saintly mystics of Safed Kabbalah (who will open our next volume), they are compelled to ruminate in Galilee about the transition to another era of improved spiritual or national orientation, in this world.

It is impossible to ascertain what portion of Louis' years in the Holy Land were "really" spent in the Galilee's coastal gateway, in Acre. The authoritative text, a famous biography of Louis IX written by Jean de Joinville, a nobleman from Champagne who accompanied the king on the Crusade, suggests that the ruler of the rump kingdom spent some of his time outside of the Holy Land's northern region, fortifying crusader settlements in Caesarea and Jaffa,[186] and also engaging limited military operations in Lebanese locales, Sidon and also Sajetta (the site of a Saracen massacre of Crusader defenders). In fact, the most telling details in Joinville's memoir about what life was like in Acre, the Crusader capital, in these years refers to the author's own lifestyle (Joinville had been captured in a boat during the Mansourah debacle and lost all his possessions, so he originally depended upon a stipend from King Louis, but he became a figure of means in Acre, and his memoir includes details as to how he would stock up with a hundred casks of wine, and how he would take his meals with ten of the fifty knights allotted to him by Louis, all of the diners "sitting on mats on the ground, according to the custom of the country"[187]).

Yet the geography of Louis' Seventh Crusade combines religious myth with vivid empirical detail of thirteenth-century travel, and so the issue of how long Louis "really" dwelled in Galilee is not entirely an empirical question. His mind was not always where his body was. On the one hand, Louis' journey reflected considerable investment, attention to real-life detail, and innovation. He commanded an army of some 15,000 troops, a figure regarded by historians as "sizable."[188] His journey on the Mediterranean featured "imposing" feats of engineering, construction, and navigation, including port construction work undertaken under Louis' direction[189] (Louis' courageous disregard for dangers of sea travel was lauded as part of his saintly, heroic ledger[190]). However, literally and figuratively, the Capetian king set out on this Crusade without a reliable map. His interest in the Orient was limited to Christian sites, and information about them was garnered primarily from oral accounts of former Crusaders who had returned to their homes in Europe.[191] When members of his entourage displayed interest in important natural landmarks in the region, outside of Christian space, they exhibited considerable credulity; in this connection, scholars cite Joinville's description of the Nile, a wonderfully complicated mix of empirical observation and bizarre approbation of legend.[192] In other words, had anyone asked the French king where he "really" was, when he settled in Acre after his ransom was effectuated, he could only possibly have answered, "in the Holy Land;" if pressed, he would have referred to his proximity to the Jesus narrative of Nazareth and other parts of Galilee.

In August 1250, King Louis sent to his subjects, from Acre,[193] a letter explaining the circumstances of the Crusader defeat at Mansourah, and the terms of his own, and his comrades', release from captivity. The letter also announced Louis' decision to remain in the Acre kingdom, and it ended with a call promising rewards to subjects who joined the effort to fortify the Crusader presence in the Holy Land. Louis battle report detailed problems that had arisen when traversing the Nile tributary (called the River Thanis), and it mentioned that his troops were crippled by hunger and contagious disease. Yet, in its overall explanatory thrust, the report maintained that the stunning defeat came as punishment for Crusader impiety. "Because the paths of man do not lie in himself but in He who guides his steps and arranges everything according to his will," Louis wrote, "the Saracens gathered all their forces and attacked the Christian army and, with God's permission, because of our sins, we fell into the enemy's hands."[194]

Louis' one-month captivity was a turning point in his career and in the history of the Crusades. Of course, being compelled to purchase his own freedom, and also the release of relatives, loyal knights and thousands of Christian prisoners, Louis was taught a lesson in humility. But the lesson also had a pragmatic cultural component. The negotiation hinged on the premise that Saracens would listen to reason and its successful conclusion apparently changed the French king.

Implicit in accounts of the Mansourah debacle is the assertion that Louis learned how to reach terms with Arabs only after his army was devastated. Joinville's laudatory biography conveys this interpretation in a sharply pointed way. Prior to the army's climactic defeat in battle, it was effectively ruined by disease. Owing to the "unhealthiness" of Egypt, where "there never falls a drop of rain," Joinville recorded, "we were stricken with the 'camp-sickness,' which was such that the flesh of our limbs shriveled up, and the skin of our legs became all blotched with black, mouldy patches, like an old jack-boot, and proud flesh came upon the gums of those who had the sickness, and none escaped from this sickness save through the jaws of death."[195]

Louis' army was manifestly outmaneuvered, relying on dubious intelligence provided by mercenary Bedouin. The King was shuffling his men back and forth futilely between strategically worthless crossings of the Thanis Tributary, when he received an incredibly lucky truce offer from his Muslim antagonists. Basically, the Arabs offered Louis the restoration of Jerusalem to Crusader control in exchange for the return of the recently captured Damietta to the Sultan.[196] Under the circumstances, this would have been a remarkably fortuitous trade, but Louis rejected it because the enemy demanded that he himself serve as collateral, remaining as a hostage until the Arabs witnessed the Crusaders' full evacuation from Damietta.[197]

Joinville inserts a gruesome image which implicitly criticizes the Crusader king's inability at this stage to communicate with Arabs, at this pre-captivity stage. Had Louis been less belligerently disposed to Muslims before the debacle, he might have finessed the Damietta evacuation negotiation, and avoided the catastrophic defeat of the Seventh Crusade, Joinville suggests. This opportunity was missed because the king was inflicted by moral ailments and Crusader arrogance. We have seen the latter, European arrogance, in the narrative of the Fifth Crusade, and Pelagius' self-defeating extremism in Egypt. But, starting with Tancred and his transformation as Prince of Galilee, we have not witnessed turns in Crusader self-perception like the ones Joinville is now taking in his chronicle of Louis' failures in Egypt. Galilee, for Saint Louis, will play a completely different role. In Joinville's image, the Crusader sickness at Mansourah becomes a metaphor for sin and divine punishment, and the illness' result is excruciating silence, and cultural deafness. Louis' refusal to negotiate intelligibly with the Saracens, even when the ultimate objective of the Crusade, Jerusalem's restoration, was on the table for the taking, becomes the metaphorical equivalent of his speech-afflicted soldiers having their gums extracted. Here is where Joinville's narrative turns immediately after it records Louis' rejection of the Damietta-for-Jerusalem trade: "The sickness began to increase at such a rate in the camp, and so much dead flesh came upon the gums of our people, that the barbers were obliged to remove it, to enable them to chew their flesh and to swallow. A most piteous thing it was to hear through the camp the screams of the people from whom they were cutting the dead flesh."[198]

The inexpressive agony of the sin-afflicted, gum-sore Crusaders serves as a foil to Joinville's earlier description of the terrifying din unleased by the sultan's soldiers on the battlefield of Damietta: "The noise that they made with their kettledrums and their Arabian horns was dreadful to hear."[199] That is to say, Holy War was unnegotiable, consisting of one side's brute cacophony, and the other's inexpressive lockjaw.

Louis acted with unimpeachable honor during his month-long captivity. His stoic refusal to be intimidated by threats of torture, and his pious physical comportment,[200] constitute a vignette of Christian composure and discipline, and a dignified contrast to reports of his captors being debilitated by regicide and continuing power struggle in the Ayyubid-Mamluk conflict.

The chronicles do not specifically refer to a contrast between Louis' honorable behavior, and the brutal depravity indulged by Richard I, the Crusader king who, it will be recalled, perpetrated a massacre of hundreds of Saracen prisoners in a desert stretch, Ayyadieh, outside of Acre in 1191—but this contrast is implicit. Louis' scrupulous handling of concessions offered to the Muslims seems evocative of a new norm of Crusader behavior, if not a retreat from the Holy War ethos itself.

In terms of that ethos, it would have made sense for Louis to renege any concession promised to the Arabs, whenever he could get away with it. Following a different logic, the chronicles highlight an episode in which King Louis proactively seeks full financial restitution for his captors after he discovers that his own handlers had managed to shortchange the Muslims out of about 10 percent, 20,000 pounds, of the negotiated ransom.[201] Joinville attested to Louis insistence upon this full restitution in the context of the deceased king's canonization inquiries, and this episode came to be regarded as important evidence of Louis' saintliness.[202]

During his imprisonment, Louis reportedly engaged banter with his Arab captors, at one point joking with an emir about how it had been a little crazy to risk crossing the sea.[203] He also is said to have admired the sultan's library, which was stocked with religious works, albeit blasphemous ones. Influenced by this example, Louis IX became the first monarch in France to create his own library of religious (i.e., Christian) manuscripts.[204]

In his letter from Acre, Louis justified his unconventional decision to remain in the Holy Land by citing Saracen infringement of truce agreements regarding helpless Crusader prisoners. He suggested that this was a consensual decision, reached in consultation with local Crusader barons. Originally, these confidantes had recommended that the king return to France, but reports of Arab malfeasance regarding captive prisoners turned the tide in favor of his remaining to defend the Acre kingdom, Louis attested.[205]

Joinville told a different story. His chronicle diverges from this testimony, suggesting that Joinville himself stood alone among the king's high advisers, lobbying for Louis to remain in Acre. Joinville was impugned by his native French peers. He was accused of acting as though his sensibilities belonged not to a real French patriot, but rather to the second-generation Frankish residents in the Holy Land, the poulains.[206] Meantime, Louis admired Joinville's fortitude and originality, privately praising him for standing his ground against "all the great men and wise men of France."[207] According to Joinville, Louis deliberated for a week before he gathered his advisers to announce that his mother, Blanche of Castile, was eminently capable of maintaining order and protecting France, whereas were he to leave Acre, the Crusader kingdom would be lost.[208]

Despite discrepancies in these accounts, they share an emphasis on passing, relatively technical, considerations about Saracen treaty compliance, and the balance of power in the region of the Acre kingdom. Eventually, however, such on-the-ground sort of explication was eclipsed by a more ethereal interpretation of Louis' residence in the Acre kingdom as a form of penance.

The chronicler who most insistently depicted the king's decisions and actions in the aftermath of the Mansourah debacle as evidence of Louis' moral growth was Matthew Paris,[209] but there is also quite a bit of anecdotal evidence in Joinville's more reliable account pointing to the self-improvement, educational effects of Louis' years in Galilee. Joinville casts Louis in Acre as an endearingly complicated human being, not as a flat, two-dimensional, portrait of Christian piety. For instance, when he renewed his agreement with Louis to remain in Acre after his first year's stipend ran out, Joinville negotiated a surprising term with the king. Joinville told Louis that while he did not need more money, he would only remain in Acre on condition that the king swore never to get angry with him. "You always get angry when anyone asks you for anything," Joinville recorded, using this retrospectively recorded (or invented) dialogue to insist that Louis should not be thought of as a submissive pushover during his years of contrition in the Holy Land, and instead remained a complicated character. After Joinville made this request, Louis "burst out laughing heartily."[210]

Louis' period in Galilee forced him to develop a more discerning attitude toward the region's populations. Accounts of his semi-jocular relations with captors during his captivity in Egypt might be tainted by hagiographic distortion, if not Stockholm syndrome dynamics, but, ruling the Acre Kingdom,

Louis needed to assess Muslim subgroups with cool realism, and the record of his diplomacy in this period reflects empirical prudence.

Joinville's memoir attests to how the Crusaders' spiritual cartography, focused solely on sacred Christian sites, proved to be a strategic liability. Prior to the disaster at Mansourah, Louis assented to the extortion of a Bedouin mercenary, who promised to lead the Crusaders to a secure spot where the Thanis could be crossed.[211] Such dubious intelligence was a prelude to disaster, and Louis and his confidantes subsequently reasoned that the rump kingdom's defense depended upon a lucid assessment of Bedouin.

To this end, Joinville's text includes a sustained discussion about Bedouin culture, apparently based on lessons learned during the Acre Kingdom period. His account conflates aspects of Bedouin society, Shiite Islam, and the order of the Assassins,[212] and it is, of course, prejudicially biased ("they wear napkins twisted round their heads and passing under their chins, so that they are a loathsome people and hideous to behold"),[213] but it also includes a measure of empirical commitment sufficient to warrant an overall evaluation about moral growth in Louis' personality, and in his camp, as a result of the king's four-year reign in the Acre kingdom. A ruler celebrated and sanctified for his other-worldly piety learned how to draw a map of non-Christian locales in Galilee and elsewhere in the kingdom, owing to strategic considerations and the thirteenth-century equivalent of due diligence in governance. "In Palestine," Le Goff observes, "Saint Louis learned how to identify the actual differences" between groups like the Assassins and Bedouin.[214]

Joinville described Bedouin fatalism and fearlessness with evident unease, mentioning that Muslims who entered the battlefield with nothing but swords and spears were contemptuous of the armored Crusaders, viewing their knightly accoutrements on the battlefield as cowardly evidence of their enemies' fear of death.[215] His comments attest to how Louis and his men were watching their Galilee neighbors with considerable attention: "The Bedouin dwell neither in towns nor cities nor castles, but lie always in the open fields. . . . The Bedouin have great pelisses of sheepskin, called 'Damascus hides,' which cover their whole body, legs and feet and all," Joinville recorded. On rainy or cold nights, he added, the Bedouin wrap themselves up in their pelisses. "When morning comes, they spread out their pelisses again in the sun, and dress them, and there is not a trace to be seen of the night's wetting."[216]

Joinville's memoir features a dramatic scene wherein emissaries of the Assassin order's leader, the Old Man of the Mountain, arrive at the Acre court, and demand tribute from Louis. The Crusader king surrounds himself with intimidating soldiers from the military-religious orders, and they bully the Assassin envoys. The Old Man on the Mountain subsequently sends a gold ring and articles from his own wardrobe, to signify how the Crusader ruler is "closer to his heart than any other king."²¹⁷ This propagandistic vignette accentuates Louis' boldness by implicitly comparing him favorably to the most renowned, courageous rulers in the region's history, including Saladin, who spent their days and nights fearing Assassin hit men sent by the Old Man on the Mountain.

In fact, the scene's "we won't submit to terrorists" logic is reminiscent of the way western leaders, many centuries later, have related to Al Qaeda or ISIS figures whom they view as latter-day successors to the Old Man on the Mountain. Such an analogy is admittedly problematic, but we raise it here in order to question non-nuanced accounts of the Crusades which mechanically assume that the end of this European intervention in the Middle East before the fourteenth century, as a result of the turbulent events in the period of Louis' adventure, was necessarily a welcome development. Louis and his comrades were testing diplomatic and strategic approaches in the field and developing a more realistic view of the region's political and cultural circumstances. Who can possibly say that the unwitting reapplication of these approaches by Western powers today, after an interruption of centuries, is history's preferred outcome? Had Crusaders remained in the region, Christian and Muslim representatives would have honed new networks of relations (while continuing to plunder and kill one another); some measure of religious enthusiasm which expressed itself violently in Europe during its religious wars would have been exported, for better or worse, and the "collateral damage" wrought by the Crusades in the depredation (among other things) of European Jewish communities would have continued, thereby possibly exhausting anti-Semitic energy in a less technologically empowered age. These counterfactual considerations can be turned and parsed in innumerable directions, but my point is to contest uni-directional, and dogmatically sanctimonious, interpretations of the Crusades. If I myself had to choose between the hagiographic adulation of Crusaders in Western historiography through the age of colonialism and the twentieth-century world wars, and the monochromatic preachy condemnation of the Crusades in our current politically correct environment, I would choose the latter. But neither outlook constitutes an interesting way of thinking about history.

"Louis changed" as a result of his experiences in the Acre Kingdom, writes historian William Chester Jordan. "Everyone, from his intimates to his enemies to the pope who would eventually canonize him, recognized and either criticized or praised the change."²¹⁸ Campaigning for Louis' sanctification, the king's confessor, Geoffrey of Beaulieu, highlighted this transformation. "After his return to France," Geoffrey wrote, "those who observed his comportment" were astonished by "how devoutly he acted toward God," how "justly" Louis treated his subjects, and how "mercifully" he related to those in need.²¹⁹ Geoffrey proceeded to detail Louis' post-Crusade efforts to ban blasphemy, and how he strove to ameliorate suffering in France by (among many other things) touching those afflicted by scrofula.[220]

How, exactly, are we to judge the contrite spirit of Saint Louis in Galilee? Whether the king developed a cogently expressible interpretation identifying specific transgressions in his preparations for the Seventh Crusade, sins which were subsequently punished at Mansourah, is debatable. Louis' overall feeling of having failed the Cross was emotive, and probably non-analytic. Insofar as it hitched to specific details and criticisms, Louis was probably troubled by the knowledge that much of this pre-Crusade preparation preyed upon church resources that were later squandered by his own inept command of troops in Egypt—one passage in Joinville's memoir drops a suggestive hint as to how Saint Louis' Crusade had relied upon the clergy's funds and resources.[221] In Galilee, this alluring medieval figure grieved the way he had taken from the church, and then betrayed its trust.

However he identified the character and cause of his sins, Louis returned from Acre as a penitent king. "His face and mind disturbed," wrote Matthew Paris, Louis "would not accept any consolation." Louis, on this account, was convinced that his fallibility had exposed all of Christendom to humiliation. "If I were the only one to have to put up with the shame and adversity," Louis reportedly exclaimed, "I would bear them more serenely. But, unfortunately for me, it is all Christendom that has been exposed to embarrassment because of me."[222]

Similarly, Joinville paints a somber portrait of Louis in France after the Crusade. The king would water down his wine, and apathetically eat whatever his cooks put on his plate. For his wardrobe, he shunned furs or "Siberian squirrel or scarlet or golden spurs." Instead, he wore only garments of rough cloth.[223]

The humiliation at Mansourah, and years of contrition in Galilee, did not cure Saint Louis of his Crusader fever. He died in 1270 at the onset of another ill-advised exercise in Holy War.

Nonetheless, the images of a publicly penitent Louis after his return to France in the mid-1250s can be seen as a retreat from the dangerous arrogance which brought European princes, knights, and clergymen to believe that they could use the sword to rearrange spiritual realities in the Holy Land. Too humble to deliver imperious orders to anyone, not even willing to tell his cooks what he wanted to eat, Louis emerged from the Acre Kingdom as a more discursively open figure. Scholars have stressed unwitting details in Joinville's memoirs and other chronicles wherein Saint Louis is seen (for instance) conducting royal business while sitting under a tree.[224] Such details, they argue, constitute evidence of a developing populism in Louis' personality, a trait which, to some extent, withdrew from the overbearing, even genocidal, arrogance of Crusader culture. For these reasons, Saint Louis' years of contrition in the Acre Kingdom reflect a transition away from the Crusades and toward a more individualized, dialogic Christianity, one oriented toward suasion and conversion of indigenous peoples rather than the slaying of Saracens.[225] The Crusades began in Galilee when Tancred, a thoroughly admirable character when viewed by the political morality of his own time and milieu, brought with him the rough and militant side of the Book of Matthew. The Crusades end in Galilee when Saint Louis, an admirable character when viewed by the political morality of our own time, and when viewed by the morality of God, searched for the other, forgiving and charitable, side of Matthew, no matter whether he found it, or not.

AYN JALUT

During Saint Louis' invasion of Egypt in 1250, the tide turned against the Franks because of the enemy's deployment of a special Mamluk shock unit, the Bahriyya regiment.[226] The Mamluks were slave-soldiers, mostly Turkish in origin, who had, as children, been brought to Egypt from the wilds of the Asian steppes. As youngsters, they were converted to Islam, trained intensively until they became skilled mounted archers, manumitted, and then mobilized in the army. They became a one-generation military elite, since the sons of Mamluks could not become Mamluks—the Egyptian regime replenished its army by bringing in new child slave recruits each generation. The last Ayyubid ruler of Egypt, al-Salih Ayyub, whose reign ended in 1249, did not trust his army's non-Mamluk soldiers, and so, slave acquisition being a buyer's market, he stepped up Mamluk recruiting and established the Bahriyya regiment. Ironically, the regime's Mamluk strategy backfired, as the former slaves became the masters of Egypt; the Bahriyya were instrumental in the 1250 founding of the Mamluk sultanate.

The climactic battle of Ayn Jalut, waged in 1260 on the southern edge of Galilee, fourteen miles from Nazareth, was fraternal in the sense that the two foes came from the Asian steppes. The two sides, Mamluks and Mongols, had other interconnections. Ferocious, almost unstoppable, warriors, Mongol forces marauded in many areas, including southern Russia. Their triumphs in this Russian region created a huge market for child slaves plucked from the Mongols' vanquished enemies, and, as it turned out, many of these captive young males from the Qipchaq Turkish tribes were purchased by the Ayyubids, and became Mamluks. When the Mongols attacked Mamluks at Ayn Jalut, some of their foes were former slaves whose transformation as Muslim warriors had been initiated by the Mongols themselves.[227]

The first pieces of the Mongol Empire were put in place by Genghis Kahn at the end of the twelfth century, and by the end of the first decade of the thirteenth century, his forces busily conquered areas in China. Mongol offensives against Islam began about a decade later. In 1219, Genghis Khan launched a huge attack on the Khwarazm-shah, who held power over most of the eastern Islamic world.[228] Over ensuing decades, Mongol forces extended their rule slowly but steadily in Muslim lands; the strategic turning point in this Mongol offensive came in the mid-1250s, when one of Ghengis Khan's sons, Mongke, newly elected as supreme ruler, ordered his brother, Hulegu, to accelerate conquests in what we call the Middle East. Around 1256, Hulegu had a battle plan, aiming first at the Ismaili sect in eastern Iran; after Iran, his Mongol troops were to head into Iraq, and suppress rebellious elements like the Kurds; then, as circumstances evolved, Hulegu would decide what to do with the Caliph.[229]

Mongol military formidability is best attributed to the fighters' nomadic background and culture, rather than to any technological innovation or to ideological indoctrination.[230] At least from the point of view of sedentary enemies,[231] the Mongols brought improbably large number of horses to the battlefield—Marco Polo claimed that the average Mongol warrior had from six to eight horses, and that some had as many as eighteen. Across continents, this horsepower advantage enabled Mongol fighters to outmaneuver and surround enemies. Mongol weaponry was hardly state-of-the-art by thirteenth-century standards. Relatively few warriors wore armor, or had swords, and the Mongol soldiers were responsible for making their own weapons, mainly arrows. Marco Polo reported that each soldier brought sixty arrows into battle, half of them light ones for piercing, whereas the other thirty had broad heads and were used to kill the enemy at close range. Undoubtedly, the second, larger, variant was the key Mongol weapon; these heavy arrows were deadly when fired at targets within a 30-yard range, and they had a maximum range of 150 yards. Mongol attack tactics sounds deceptively simple: a rider would fire three or four arrows, and then circle back and wait his turn for the next round. Nothing in war worked more efficiently in this medieval period. The Mongols' nomadic warfare style was as deadly and nearly invincible in its era as was the Ottoman Turks' introduction of gunpowder centuries later, or Napoleon's mobilization of a mass army heading into the nineteenth century.

In early 1258, Hulegu's men overcame an enemy Islamic force of 20,000 men subordinate to Caliph Mustas'im, and conquered Baghdad. The end of the nearly five-hundred-year Abbasid caliphate, and the terrifying devastation of the city, was widely regarded as the worst calamity ever endured by the Islamic world.[232]

Hence, when Hulegu's forces invaded Syria in winter 1259–1260, the Frankish knights in Acre had cause to worry. For centuries, commentators have speculated about whether the Crusaders might have panicked at this undeniably nerve-wracking juncture, and chosen the wrong strategy. Their critics hypothesize that the Franks missed an opportunity to ally with the Mongols, and share the benefits of a thorough drubbing of Muslim forces that might have been wrought by the Mongols, with Crusader assistance. Records of events preceding the fateful Mamluk-Mongol battle on the southern edge of Galilee are rife with evidence of Mongol readiness for such a strategic alliance, these critics allege.

Years before Ayn Jalut, this theory points out, Mongol leaders tested the waters with the Franks, trying to see if some sort of cooperation was possible. One such feeler involved Louis IX. In late 1248, many months before his invasion of Egypt, when the French Crusader was, in Cyprus, preparing his men, Louis received one such overture from a Mongol general, Eljigidei. In this decade, it bears mention, prominent Christians, prelates and explorers sponsored their own diplomatic-religious contacts with the Mongols. Inspired by rumors that Nestorian or other Christian influences had penetrated among this strangely ferocious Asian people, these delegates hoped that some military or spiritual gain could be accrued by visiting the Mongols in their own home territory. These errands accomplished nothing, other than colorful travel memoir writing,[233] but they, at least, reflect ongoing European hopes that the Mongol menace could be turned into an advantage for Christianity. In fact, Nestorianism had made inroads among Mongols, many of whom were, from the Frankish perspective, well placed. The commander entrusted with the portion of Hulegu's forces which remained in Syria ahead of Ayn Jalut, Ketbuqha, was a Christian, being a member of the Naiman tribe within which Nestorianism had been popular for centuries.[234]

A final point in this conjecture about a possible Crusader-Mongol alliance features the fate of Franks who, in this tension-filled 1259 juncture, chose on their own to ally with invading Mongol troops. In 1246, the Frankish ruler of Antioch, Bohemond V, became a tributary of the Mongols, and this allegiance passed on to his son.[235] One report held that when Ketbuqha conquered Damascus in 1259, Bohemond VI was by his side and was allowed by the Mongols to destroy mosques, and even turn one into a church.[236] From the Franks' standpoint, all of these apparent indications of Mongol readiness for an alliance pivoted around one basic point: the Crusaders had come to the Holy Land to rid it of Saracens, so why shouldn't they lean toward a proven scourge of Islam, the enemy of their enemies?

This theory, historian Peter Jackson demonstrates, does not hold water. The Crusaders in Acre had no hopes of such an alliance, he argues, adding that "letters sent to the west by the leaders in Acre in 1260, appealing for help against this unprecedented menace, give absolutely no indication that the Mongols were prepared to act as heaven-sent auxiliaries against Islam."[237] Looking at the issue the other way, evidence of genuine Mongol interest in an alliance with the Christian Franks turns out to be flimsy. Jackson shows that the Mongols had rather exaggerated concerns about the Franks' ability to replenish their fighting forces with recruits sent from Europe, and their overture to Louis IX should be seen in this connection, as deceptive tactics (and the French king identified the Mongols' insincerity). The Franks drew no inspiration from reports of the behavior of the Antioch prince in Damscus (historians have doubts about this story of Bohemond attacking mosques, with Mongol backing, though they concede it might have a "grain of truth"[238]). In fact, *Haute Cour* consultations in Acre in 1260, ahead of the Mongol-Mamluk Ayn Jalut showdown, proceeded on a line of thought antithetical to what is assumed in this speculation about the possibility of a Mongol-Crusader alliance. The Franks viewed the Mongols as a credible and worrisome threat. They imagined themselves, on a scenario of a Mongol victory, being pinned down and isolated in Acre, and one or two other coastal strongholds. For instance, Templar Master Thomas Berard, one of the senders of the emergency appeals to Europe, believed that a Mongol conquest of the Holy Land would leave the Franks standing only in Acre and Tyre. All that would be left of the Crusades would be in these two cities, as well as his own order's castles in Safed and Atlit, and the Teutonic Order's Montfort, warned Berard.[239]

Master Berard and others were beating the drums of emergency in March 1260 for good reason. Sometime around the conquest of Damascus, Ketbuqha send a detachment into Palestine, where it marauded in Beit Jibrin, Hebron, Ascalon, Jerusalem, and Nablus. By April 1260, these raiders were back in Damascus, hauling with them captives, livestock, and other types of booty.[240] In this period, incidentally, the Mongols had one client ally in Galilee, al-Sa'id Hasan, at Banias.[241]

The Haute Cour's most fateful strategic decision in the late phase of the Acre kingdom was reached in mid-to-late August 1260. The Mongols had sacked Sidon; busily stockpiling wood by chopping down trees in orchards, and pilfering stones from city cemeteries, residents of Acre were visibly frightened about being next in line.[242] The Crusader consultation proceeded on the assumption that Egypt's Mamluk military regime was not particularly formidable and that the Mongols were the real problem. Should Mongol forces remain in the country, they would postpone a much awaited, and expected, Crusader restoration of the full, original Jerusalem kingdom.

Seen in retrospect, this thinking was incorrect. The Mamluk victory at Ayn Jalut strengthened the Franks' Islamic enemies. Throughout the next few decades, the Mongols and Mamluks continued to skirmish, but on the Mamluk-Frank axis, everything went downhill for the Crusaders, and their Acre kingdom was annihilated in 1291, just three decades after Ayn Jalut. This, however, is unfair hindsight. Up to the moment in question, August 1260, Ayyubid rulers in Egypt had hardly been imposing, and the Franks had no reason to think that the new Mamluk sultan, Qutuz, would be different. They certainly could not have expected that Qutuz, who fought valiantly at Ayn Jalut, would be assassinated within months, and replaced by a new Mamluk sultan, Baibars, another veteran of Ayn Jalut, who would hold the throne for seventeen years, unifying and intensifying Islamic power in that time.[243]

In August 1260, the *Haute Cour* adopted an officially neutral policy, one which was, de facto, mildly pro-Mamluk. The Mamluk forces were granted unfettered passage through Frankish territory, on their march to Ayn Jalut. This however, was limited support. Teutonic Master Anno von Sangerhausen articulated the Acre assembly's position, arguing that is was "unwise to spend the lives of Christians in a victory which might well simply encourage the Egyptians to turn next upon [the Franks]." The Crusaders should "conserve their resources."[244]

Ayn Jalut is an all-year spring located on the northwest corner of Mt. Gilboa, just west of the contemporary Israeli village, Gidona. In Arabic the name Ayn Jalut means "Goliath's Spring," and the site is known today in Israel as Ma'ayan Harod (it is well-maintained as a national park by Israel's Nature and Parks Authority, but local and overseas visitors who visit the site have absolutely no way of knowing that one of the climactic battles of the Middle Ages was fought in it). Mamluk forces arrived first for the battle, which was staged on September 3. In the hot summer,[245] they were probably attracted to the area for its strong grazing and water resources. The Mongols surely hoped to ambush Mamluk soldiers who were expected to march from Megiddo on the Esdraelon plain, but thanks to the Crusader *Haute Cour* decision, the Mamluk force might well have unexpectedly moved behind Mt. Carmel, and slipped by Mongol scouts. Reports about numbers on both sides are virtually unverifiable, but scholars dismiss partisan accounts that circulated over the centuries, suggesting that one side or the other had a decisive manpower edge at Ayn Jalut. Amitai-Preiss estimates Ket-buqa's force as about 10,000–12,000 men,[246] whereas John Masson Smith tallies a similar number for the Mamluks, 12,000 or so, basing his reasoning partly on logistical calculations and manpower choices reached by earlier commanders of stunning Islamic triumphs, especially Saladin (who, it will be recalled, brought 12,000 men to Hattin).[247]

One point about the Battle of Ayn Jalut which is not in dispute, and which impinged upon its outcome, is that the Mongol contingent could have been much larger. After the Mongols' successful siege on Aleppo, in January 1260, Hulegu abruptly left the scene with the vast majority of his soldiers, eventually setting camp with them in Azerbaijan. The Mongols left in Syria just a small remnant of Hulegu's army, perhaps 10 percent or 12,000 men, under the command of Ketbuqha. The traditional explanation for this sequence highlights the death, in August 1259, of Hulegu's brother Mongke, who had been supreme ruler, and a subsequent succession struggle for rule of the Mongol empire. Scholars, however, have chipped this account by referring to a variety of other motives which might have inspired Hulegu's decision, both on a logistical level (e.g., a desire to camp in a better pasture area) and in the realm of politics (e.g., concerns about Mongol control in Iran).[248] At any event, the Mongols lacked a manpower advantage at Ayn Jalut owing to a decision reached by Hulegu months before the battle.

The Mongols' nomadic style of battle was neutralized in the showdown. The Mamluks came to the Springs of Goliath with helmets, body armor, lances, javelins, swords, axes, maces, and daggers—but most of this equipment proved useless against the Mongols' hit-and-run warfare. If they had relied on it, the Mamluk weaponry would have made their force too heavy, and unable to keep up with the Mongols' horse-based, galloping, style of warfare. Instead, what turned the tide in the battle was the Mamluks' superior skills in archery. "Where the Mongols made the most of their horses, the Mamluks made the most of their archery," writes Masson Smith. "If nomads can produce more horses than sedentaries, sedentaries can make more and better bows and arrows, and spend more time learning to use them."[249] Drilled in accuracy and also (no less impressively) shooting speed,[250] Mamluks were highly trained archers.

Accounts of what actually happened on the battlefield at Ayn Jalut suggest that the Mongols had an early advantage, and even managed to break one Mamluk wing. Qutuz, the soon-to-be-overthrown Mamluk sultan, fought hard in the center, inspiring his troops with battle cries (*wa-islamah*, For Islam!), and he is often credited as the hero of the unexpected Mamluk triumph.[251] The prevailing image of the battle has Mongols racing on horses, up to the point of exhaustion, while the Mamluks hunker down, conserve their horses, and fire arrows faster, and more lethally, than the enemy. By battle's end, Mongol survivors scrambled away in many directions, some climbing up a hilltop with Baibars in hot pursuit; others apparently fled all the way to the Antioch region, where their herds and families had remained (Baibars reportedly found and killed these survivors, as well). Some chroniclers claim that "almost all" the Mongol fighters who started the battle did not survive it, while others cite Mongol losses of 1500.[252] No record of Mamluk losses is anywhere to be found, appropriately enough, because Ayn Jalut was a stunning Muslim victory.

In late antiquity and medieval times, three fateful battles were fought on Galilee's northern edge, its center, and its southern rim. The first, Yarmuk, ended Christianity's growth as a more or less consecutive presence in the Middle East, one which started with Jesus in Galilee, endured Roman persecution, and then developed, after Constantine, in the Byzantine framework.

Yarmuk inculcated what could only have then been an unsettling, if not incomprehensible, message: the region where Judaism begat Christianity could now become Muslim. Or put differently, while monotheism had multiplied by two in Galilee in the time of Jesus and his followers, now, because of Yarmuk, there was suddenly a third factor, Islam. The second battle, Hattin, dampened the Christian messianic utopianism of the First Crusade. It cast serious questions about the durability of the Crusader project, about the long-term restoration of Christian power in the land of Jesus, and about whether the theory of the supersession of the land's promise to the Jews could be effectuated, for centuries to come, as the political fact of Christian sovereignty in the Holy Land. In the short term, the Battle of Hattin, fought on the edge of Lake Kinneret and in the heart of Galilee, spelled the contraction of the Crusader kingdom, and its relocation, to Acre, but the long-term implications of this second Galilee battle were more voluminous. Hattin showed that after Catholicism resettled in Europe, in Rome, it could never readily support a movement for the restoration of its power in the region of Jesus. The Crusades effected such restoration, but they were an exhausting, costly, and relatively short-lived project (just as would be the British Mandate in Palestine in the twentieth century, a project whose religiosity was, of course, not stressed or necessarily determinative). The consequences of the third Galilee area battle at Ayn Jalut were still more encompassing and monumental. The Mongol invasion of the Middle East was the last time when Islamic consolidation in it might conceivably have been undermined or forestalled on a wide level. Simply put, Ayn Jalut meant that the land believed by the Jews to have been promised to them, and the land where Christians believe that the Son of God sacrificed himself for humanity, would ever hereafter be located in a Muslim region. The common denominator in all three Galilee battles is obvious: they were well-executed and decisive Muslim victories. They set an example of military valor and communal (*umma*-level) Islamic resolve which makes the Palestinians' 1948 Nakba defeat in Galilee so overwhelmingly difficult for them, and the Arab world as a whole, to accept.

To my mind, the fact that the Crusaders decided to grant the Mamluks free passage for the fight at Ayn Jalut says something about the overarching interdependence of the monotheistic faiths, but many others would contend that the Franks' *Haute Cour* decision was based on contingent reasoning, and was by no means ecumenically sympathetic to Islam. On any interpretation, the import of Ayn Jalut cannot be downplayed. We will give the final word to J.J. Saunders, a scholar of medieval Islam and the Mongol conquests. The Battle of Ayn Jalut, he wrote, was "a turning point in history." The Mongol advance in the West was never seriously renewed. "Egypt was saved and rose in consequence to the status of a Muslim Great Power." Following their victory, the Muslims "opened a great counter-offensive against the Mongols and their Christian allies, and the dream of a Christian restoration in the Near East was dispelled forever."[253]

NOTES

1. J. Riley-Smith, "The Motives of the Earliest Crusaders and the Settlement of Latin Palestine, 1095–1100," *English Historical Review* 98 (1983): 721–36.
2. Steven Runciman, *A History of the Crusades*, vol. 3 (Cambridge: Cambridge University Press, 1954), 480.
3. Christopher Tyerman, *The Crusades: A Very Short Introduction* (Oxford: New York, 2005), 145. Tyerman follows classifications suggested by Giles Constable.
4. Karen Armstrong, *Holy War: The Crusades and their Impact on Today's World* (New York: Anchor Books, 2001).
5. See, for instance: Steven Tibble, *Monarchy and Lordships in the Latin Kingdom of Jerusalem 1099–1291* (Oxford: Clarendon Press, 1989), 153–69; Adrian Boas (ed.), *Montfort: History, Early Research and Recent Studies of the Principal Fortress of the Teutonic Order in the Middle East* (Leiden: Brill, 2017); John France, *Hattin* (New York: Oxford University Press, 2015).
6. This is the main point in Karen Armstrong's exploration of the Crusades and their impact, *Holy War*.
7. Tyerman.
8. Ibid, 65.
9. Tyerman, 64–85.
10. The following information about Ralph relies on: Bernard Bachrach, David Bachrach (eds.), *The Gesta Tancredi of Ralph of Caen: A History of the Normans on the First Crusade* (Burlington: Ashgate, 2005), translators' introduction, 1–19.
11. Joshua Prawer, *The Crusaders' Kingdom: European Colonialism in the Middle Ages* (London: Phoenix Press, 2001), 127.
12. According to a co-translator and editor of the *Gesta*, the most plausible explanation for this omission is that parts of Ralph's manuscript were lost. E-mail communication with David Bachrach, September 1, 2020.
13. Robert Lawrence Nicholson, *Tancred: A Study of His Career and Work* (Ann Arbor: dissertation, 1940).
14. For instance: *Tancred: Prince of Tiberias, a Tale of the Eleventh Century* [N/A] (Baltimore: John Murphy & Co., 1884).
15. Prawer, *The Crusaders'*, 519.
16. *Gesta*, 21 (n. 7); *Tancred*, 8. In reported dialogue in Ralph's *Gesta* chronicle, Tancred is referred to as a student of warfare from Calabria (28).
17. *Tancred*, 28.
18. *Gesta*, 22.
19. Ibid, 26.
20. Ibid, 41.
21. Ibid, 42.
22. Ibid, 77 [n. 105].

23. Ibid, 78.
24. *Tancred*, 110.
25. *Tancred*, 165–79.
26. *Gesta*, 130.
27. *Tancred*, 130–31.
28. *Gesta*, 143.
29. Ibid, 144.
30. Ibid, 148–53.
31. Prawer, *The Crusaders'*, 126–29.
32. Sophia Menache, "After Twenty-Five Years: Joshua Prawer's Contribution to the Study of the Crusades and the Latin Kingdom of Jerusalem Reconsidered," in Adrian Boas (ed.), *The Crusader World* (New York: Routledge, 2016), 675–88.
33. Steven Tibble, *Monarchy and Lordships in the Latin Kingdom of Jerusalem 1099–1291* (Oxford: Clarendon Press, 1989).
34. Riley-Smith, "Motives," 726–27.
35. Prawer, *The Crusaders'*, 18.
36. Ibid.
37. Ibid, 127.
38. Tibble, 11–12.
39. Joshua Prawer, *The History of the Jews in the Latin Kingdom of Jerusalem* (Oxford: Clarendon Press, 1988), 34–36.
40. Ibid, 54–56.
41. Ibid, 37–39.
42. H. Pirie-Gordon, "The Reigning Princes of Galilee," *The English Historical Review* 27/107 (July 1912): 446.
43. Tibble, 12.
44. Pirie-Gordon, 447.
45. Ibid, 448.
46. Tibble, 153.
47. Ibid, 156.
48. Information from Tibble, 13–23, 28–29, 96–98.
49. Ronnie Ellenblum, *Frankish Rural Settlement in the Latin Kingdom of Jerusalem* (Cambridge: Cambridge University Press), 200.
50. Ibid, 213.
51. Ibid, 80.
52. Tyerman, 113–15.
53. Ellenblum, 213–21, 253–76.
54. Ibid, 215.
55. Ibid, 217.
56. Ibid, 159.
57. Rafael Frankel, "Topographical Notes on the Territory of Acre in the Crusader Period," *Israel Exploration Journal* 38, no. 4 (1988): 262.
58. Ellenblum, 166.
59. Ibid, 43.
60. Ibid, 41–53.

61. Ibid, 166.
62. Ibid, 167.
63. Philip de Novare, *The Wars of Frederick II Against the Ibelins in Syria and Cyprus* (New York: Columbia University Press, 1936).
64. Ellenblum, 167. Frankel (253) says that Henry originally controlled three fiefs (St. George de la Beyne, Bouquiau and Saor), but these were consolidated as one bloc by the time of his death.
65. Frankel, 254.
66. Ibid.
67. Ellenblum, 167–68.
68. Ibid, 65–68.
69. Tibble, 156–57.
70. Ellenblum, 69–72.
71. Ibid, 175–78.
72. Anat Peled, "Sugar in the Crusader Kingdom," http://www.antiquities.org.il/Article_eng.aspx?sec_id=17&sub_subj_id=472&id=1252.
73. Jonathan Riley-Smith, "History, the Crusades and the Latin East," in Maya Shatzmiller, *Crusaders and Muslims in Twelfth-Century Syria* (Leiden: Brill, 1993), 1–18.
74. Marshall Baldwin, *Raymond III of Tripolis and the Fall of Jerusalem, 1140–1187* (Princeton: Princeton University Press, 1936), 83–93.
75. For instance, due to his preference for the Atabeg Nur al-Din's Zengid dynasty, the historian Ibn al-Athir resisted a hagiographic view of Saladin in his multivolume *Chronicle of Ibn al-Athir for the Crusading Period*. On the other hand, Saladin kept close to him writers who celebrated his efforts, including the poet Ibn Sana al-Mulk, and two biographers, Imad al-Din al-Isfahani and Baha ad-Din Ibn Shaddad. See: Carole Hillenbrand, *The Crusades: Islamic Perspectives* (Edinburgh: Edinburgh University Press, 1999), 179–93.
76. Hillenbrand.
77. France, *Hattin*, 132–69.
78. Emmanuel Sivan, *Radical Islam: Medieval Theology and Modern Politics* (New Haven: Yale University Press, 1990).
79. See, for instance, France's discussion of Dahlia Ravikovitch's poem "The Horns of Hittin," 144.
80. France, 142.
81. Peter Edbury, "Propaganda and Faction in the Kingdom of Jerusalem: The Background to Hattin," in Shatzmiller, *Crusaders and Muslims*, 173–89. France's book follows this tradition, extensively detailing sociopolitical dynamics in the Crusader kingdom.
82. For attempts to revise this negative perception of King Guy: Edbury, "Propaganda," and R.C. Smail, "The Predicaments of Guy at Lusignan, 1183–1187," in B.Z. Kedar, H.E. Mayer, and R.C. Smail (eds.), *Outremer: Studies in the History of the Crusading Kingdom of Jerusalem* (Jerusalem: Yad Ben Tzvi Institute, 1982), 159–77.
83. Baldwin, *Raymond II of Tripolis*.

84. Baldwin, 45–46; Edbury.

85. Highlighting the effects of Saladin's illness, al-Ishfahani wrote this experience was sent to the great Mujahid by God to "wake him from the sleep of [religious] forgetfulness." Hillenbrand.

86. Smail, "The Predicaments."

87. Baldwin, 60–61.

88. Prawer, *The Crusaders'*, 113–14.

89. Years earlier, Gerard, a knight errant, had expected to solidify his status in the Crusader north via marriage to an heiress, the daughter of William Dorel, lord of Botron, but Raymond allowed Gerard's marital ambition to go unconsummated, probably because he was bribed by an Italian merchant. Baldwin, 40–41.

90. Ibid, 8.

91. Prawer originally published his account of Hattin in French, in the *Israel Exploration Journal* 7 (1964). The description above relies on his extended version of this original article, published as, Joshua Prawer, "The Battle of Hattin," in Prawer, *Crusader Institutions* (Oxford: Oxford University Press, 1980), 484–500.

92. France, 84.

93. Ibid, 86.

94. Ibid.

95. Ibid, based on *De Expugantione Terrae Sanctae Libellus*.

96. Baldwin, 97; Prawer, "The Battle," 492, 497.

97. Prawer, "The Battle," 495.

98. Baldwin, 136–38.

99. Prawer, "The Battle," 499.

100. Strange, 451.

101. Sydney Painter, "The Third Crusade: Richard the Lionhearted and Philip Augustus," in Kenneth Meyer Setton et al. (eds.), *A History of the Crusades,* vol. 2 (Philadelphia: University of Pennsylvania Press, 1962), 47.

102. Ibid, 57.

103. Painter, 51–53, doubts that Guy's early siege was effectual, but the author of an Israeli history of Acre believes that these early attacks raised the Franks' morale: Nathan Schur, *Toldot Ako* (Tel Aviv: Dvir, 1990), 69–72.

104. Painter, 67.

105. Ibid, 72.

106. Schur, 76–77.

107. Tyerman, *Introduction*, 1.

108. Schur, 63.

109. Prawer, *The History of the Jews*, 61.

110. Schur, 64.

111. Painter, 73.

112. Ibid, 82–85.

113. See the map: Schur, 84.

114. A colorful, partisan (pro-Ibelin) account of the War of the Lombards is Philip de Novare, *The Wars of Frederick II Against the Ibelins in Syria and Cyprus* (New York: Columbia University Press, 1936).

115. Schur, 98–99.
116. For a description of the *Haute Cour*'s powers: Prawer, *The Crusaders' Kingdom*, 112–21; also, Schur, 87–89.
117. Prawer, *The Crusaders'*, 76.
118. Peter Jackson, "The Crisis in the Holy Land in 1260," *English Historical Review* July 1980, 481–513.
119. Schur, 107.
120. Ibid, 108.
121. Ibid (table).
122. Ibid, 109.
123. This description of Acre's trade, daily life, and society relies on Schur, 117–19.
124. Hillenbrand; Adrian Boas, "On Immorality in the Holy Land" (blog, 14/12/2018), https://www.adrianjboas.com/post/on-immorality-in-the-holy-land.
125. Prawer, *The History of the Jews,* 258.
126. Ibid. L. Ginzberg, who published this fragment, erroneously believed that such references applied to the Crusaders' 1104 capture of Acre.
127. Schur, 101.
128. Prawer, *The History*, 259–62.
129. Ibid, 266–68.
130. Schur, 102.
131. Prawer, *The History*, 273–74.
132. Arnold Franklin, *This Nobel House: Jewish Descendants of King David in the Medieval Islamic East* (Philadelphia: University of Pennsylvania Press, 2013), 47–48.
133. Prawer, *The History,* 270–71.
134. Consideration of what happened to Frankish women, including the question of whether they were on battlefields, is a developing field. Here are two references: Helen Nicholson, "Women on the Third Crusade," *Journal of Medieval History* 23, no. 4 (1997): 335–49; Helen Nicholson, "Women's Involvement in the Crusades," in Boas, *The Crusader World*, 54–68.
135. The name might also refer to the order's origins in a Jerusalem hospital founded some forty years before Hattin, but this possibility is murky. Kristjan Toomaspoeg, Montfort Castle and the Order of the Teutonic Knights in the Latin East, in Adrian Boas and Rabei G. Khamisy (eds), *Montfort: History, Early Research and Recent Studies of the Principal Fortress of the Teutonic Order* (Leiden: Brill, 2016), 16.
136. Nicholas Morton, *The Teutonic Knights in the Holy Land, 1190–1291* (Rochester: Boydell Press, 2012), 19.
137. This background information is taken from Morton, 9–30, and also: Shlomo Lotan, *Tevtonim b'mamlekhet yerushaliyim ha'tzalbanit* (Tel Aviv: Ofir, 2012), 23–41.
138. Morton, 32.
139. Thomas C. Van Cleve, "The Fifth Crusade," in Setton et al. *A History*, 378.
140. Ibid, 382.
141. Ibid, 396.
142. Ibid, 418.
143. Ibid, 425–26.

144. Ibid, 403, 421.
145. Ibid, 428.
146. This analysis draws from Morton, 33–43.
147. Ibid, 33.
148. Ibid, 49.
149. Lotan, 109–14.
150. Morton, 49. Toomaspoeg (18) doubts whether it is possible to speak of a "Teutonic state in the Holy Land."
151. Thomas C. Van Cleve, "The Crusade of Frederick II," in Setton et al., *A History*, 453.
152. For a detailed examination of these land ownership issues: Rabei Khamisy, "The Region of Monfort and Land Ownership in the Frankish Period," in Boas and Khamisy, *Monfort*, 26.
153. Morton, 53.
154. Philip de Novare, 138–40.
155. See John La Monte's introduction, *The Wars of Frederick*, 16.
156. Van Cleve, "The Crusade," 460.
157. Ibid, 458.
158. Ibid, 453.
159. Ibid, 455.
160. Ibid.
161. Morton, 60–84.
162. Morton, 68.
163. See the map in Morton's appendices, 196–97.
164. Frankel, 255–60.
165. Toomaspoeg, 18.
166. Adrian Boas, "Introduction," in Boas and Khamisy, *Montfort*, 11.
167. Except where noted otherwise, this summary relies on Boas' introduction.
168. C.R. Conder, H.H. Kitchener, *The Survey of Western Palestine* vol. 1 Galilee (London: Committee of the Palestine Exploration Fund, 1881), 186–90.
169. Toomaspoeg, 18.
170. Ibid.
171. Boas, "The Metropolitan Museum of Art Expedition to Montfort (1926)," in Boas and Khamisy, 75–92.
172. Rabei Khamisy, "Montfort Castle (Qal'at Al-Qurayn) in Mamluk sources," in Boas and Khamisy, 28–40.
173. The king's exact birthdate is unclear. Jacques Le Goff, *Saint Louis* (Notre Dame: University of Notre Dame Press, 2009), 3.
174. The numbering of the Crusades has been debated, the issue revolving around whether Frederick II's expedition should count as the Sixth Crusade. If so, Louis IX's misadventure in Egypt was the Seventh Crusade. Tyerman, *A Very Short Introduction*, 18.
175. For this sanctification process: M. Cecilia Gaposchkin, *The Making of Saint Louis: Kingship, Sanctity and Crusade in the Later Middle Ages* (Ithaca: Cornell University Press, 2008).

176. Le Goff, 366–419.

177. Jordan strongly argues for the precedent-setting character of Louis' administrative, political, and socioeconomic reforms, both in the pre-Crusade phase of his career, and after his return in 1254. He admits that many of these reforms lost their luster after Louis' death, but adds that the *"imago* of an ideal kingdom, one that had existed briefly on this earth, endured as a constant theme in royal propaganda and in both popular and learned criticism of future kings." Jordan, 181.

178. Le Goff, 134.

179. Ibid, 148.

180. Le Goff, 144.

181. Ibid, 145.

182. Tyerman, 8.

183. William Chester Jordan, *Louis IX and the Challenge of the Crusade* (Princeton: Princeton University Press, 1979).

184. This particular topic is studied in detail in: William Chester Jordan, *The French Monarchy and the Jews* (Philadelphia, 1989).

185. M. Cecilia Gaposchkin, "Louis IX, Crusade and the Promise of Joshua in the Holy Land," *Journal of Medieval History*, XXXIV (2008): 245–74.

186. Jaffa particularly benefited from Louis refortification work. Some twenty-four watchtowers were installed, along with three gates, and Louis admitted to Joinville that he had invested a prodigal sum (30,000 pounds) in the erection of a defense wall at Jaffa. Jean Joinville, *The Memoirs of the Lord of Joinville* [translated by Ethel Wedgewood] (London: John Murray, 1906), 288.

187. Joinville, 265.

188. Jordan, *Louis IX*, 65.

189. Ibid, 71–75.

190. Le Goff, 435–38.

191. Ibid, 439.

192. Ibid, 447–48. "Before the river [the Nile] reaches Egypt," Joinville wrote, experienced residents would throw nets into it in the evening. The following morning, they would find in these nets "ginger, rhubarb, aloe and cinnamon." Such things "come from earthly Paradise," Joinville noted. He added that if warm water from the Nile was properly mounted in pots of white clay, "it would become cold as water from a fountain" in the middle of the hot day. Joinville, 88.

193. "Louis IX's Letter to His Subjects from the Holy Land (1250)," reprinted in Le Goff, 739–46.

194. Ibid, 742.

195. Joinville, 145.

196. Ibid, 149.

197. Ibid, 150.

198. Ibid.

199. Ibid, 66.

200. Whenever left alone in his cell, Louis would "stretch himself cross-wise on the ground," and repeatedly make the sign of the cross. Joinville, 182.

201. Ibid, 194–95.

202. Le Goff, 138.
203. Ibid.
204. Ibid. The library was established in the Sainte-Chapelle.
205. "Louis IX's Letter," 744–45.
206. Joinville, 223.
207. Ibid, 222.
208. Ibid, 224.
209. Jordan, 127.
210. Joinville, 264.
211. Ibid, 101.
212. "The Bedouins do not believe in Muhammad, but they follow the law of Ali, who was Muhammad's uncle, and so obey the Old Man of the Mountain, the same who maintains the Assassins." Ibid, 125.
213. Ibid, 127.
214. Le Goff, 439–40.
215. Joinville, 127.
216. Ibid, 126–27.
217. Ibid, 235–36.
218. Jordan, *Louis IX*, 127.
219. Geoffrey of Beaulieu, *Here Begins the Life and Saintly Comportment of Louis*, in Cecilia Gaposchkin and Sean L. Field, *The Sanctity of Louis IX: Early Lives of Saint Louis by Geoffrey of Beaulieu and William of Chartes* (Oxford: University Press, 2013), 109.
220. Ibid, 109–11.
221. "Only part of the considerable expenses for the crusade fell on the Royal Treasury," writes Le Goff (145). Joinville's memoir substantiates this authority's judgment. The telling detail is included in the memoir section detailing Joinville's controversial recommendation in favor of Louis and the Crusaders remaining in Acre following the rout in Egypt—one of Joinville's arguments is that the Crusade did not cost the king very much, and had been conducted mostly at the church's expense. "It is said, Sir, whether truly or not I do not know, that the King has not yet spent any of his own money; [all the funding has come from] the money of the clergy." Joinville, 219.
222. Quoted in Le Goff, 156.
223. Joinville, 347; Le Goff, 156–57.
224. William Chester Jordan, *Ideology and Royal Power in Medieval France* (Burlington: Ashgate, 2001).
225. Le Goff (149 and passim), who downplays the impact of crusading on Louis' development and career, emphatically depicts him as a transitional figure in this respect.
226. The description here relies on: Reuven Amitai-Preiss, *Mongols and Mamluks: The Mamluk-Ilkhanid War, 1260–1281* (Cambridge: Cambridge University Press, 2009), 18.
227. Ibid, 18.
228. Ibid, 8.
229. Ibid, 11–12.

230. J.J. Saunders, *The History of the Mongol Conquests* (Philadelphia: University of Pennsylvania Press, 1971), 18–21.

231. This description relies on John Masson Smith, "Ayn Jalut: Mamluk Success or Mongol Failure," *Harvard Journal of Asiatic Studies* 44, no. 2 (Dec. 1984): 315–20.

232. Jackson, 481.

233. As exemplified by the intoxicating record penned by Giovanni Carpine: Giovanni diPlanno Carpino, *The Story of the Mongols Whom we Call Tartars* (Wellesly, MA: Branden Books, 2014).

234. Jackson, 493.

235. Amitai-Preiss, 24.

236. Ibid, 31.

237. Jackson, 487.

238. Amitai-Preiss, 31.

239. Jackson, 492.

240. Amitai-Preiss, 31–32.

241. Ibid, 33.

242. Jackson, 506.

243. Jackson, 507.

244. Jackson, 506.

245. Unless noted otherwise, this description of the battle relies on Smith's article, "Mamluk Success or Mongol Failure?"

246. Amitai-Preiss, 40.

247. Smith, 311–12.

248. Amitai-Preiss, 28–29.

249. Masson Smith, 322.

250. Mamluk training manuals refer to shooting three arrows in one and a half seconds, a rate not matched by contemporary archers. Ibid.

251. Amitai-Preiss, 41.

252. Ibid, 43.

253. Saunders, 115.

Bibliography

(ONLY WORKS CITED)

Adler, Rachel. "The Virgin in the Brothel and Other Anomalies: Character and Context in the Legend of Beruriah." *Tikkun* 3 (Nov. 1988).

Amitai-Preiss, Reuven. *Mongols and Mamluks: The Mamluk-Ilkhanid War, 1260-1281.* Cambridge: Cambridge University Press, 2009.

Armstrong, Karen. *Holy War: The Crusades and their Impact on Today's World.* New York: Anchor Books, 2001.

Aviam, Mordechai. "Christian Galilee in the Byzantine Period." In *Galilee Through the Centuries: Confluence of Cultures,* edited by Eric M. Myers, 285–94. Winona Lake: Eisenbrauns, 1999.

Aviam, Mordechai. "First Century Jewish Galilee: An Archaeological Perspective." In *Religion and Society in Roman Palestine*, edited by Douglas Edwards, 7–28. New York: Routledge, 2004.

Avissar Oded. *Sefer Tiveria.* Jerusalem: Keter, 1973.

Avi-Yonah, M. *The Jews of Palestine: A Political History from the Bar Kokhba War to the Arab Conquest.* Oxford: Basil Blackwell, 1976.

Avi-Yonah, M. "The Missing Fortress of Flavius Josephus." *Israel Exploration Journal* 3 no. 2 (1953): 94–98.

Bachrach, Bernard, David Bachrach, eds. *The Gesta Tancredi of Ralph of Caen: A History of the Normans on the First Crusade.* Burlington: Ashgate, 2005.

Baldwin, Marshall. *Raymond III of Tripolis and the Fall of Jerusalem, 1140-1187.* Princeton: Princeton University Press, 1936.

Becker, Hans-Jurgen Serge Ruzer, eds. *The Sermon on the Mount and its Jewish Setting.* Paris: J. Gabalda et Cie Editeurs, 2005.

Beecher, Henry Ward. *The Life of Jesus, the Christ.* New York: J.B. Ford and Company, 1871.

Be'eri, Nurit. *Yatsa le-tarbut ra'ah: Elisha ben Avuyah, Aher.* Tel Aviv: Yedioth Aharonoth Books, 2007.

Bellah, Robert et al, eds. *Habits of the Heart: Individualism and Commitment in American Life.* Berkeley: University of California Press, 1995.

Ben-Yehuda, Nachman. *The Masada Myth: Collective Memory and Mythmaking in Israel.* Madison: University of Wisconsin Press, 1995.

Boas, Adrian, ed. *The Crusader World.* New York: Routledge, 2016.

Boas, Adrian, ed. *Montfort: History, Early Research and Recent Studies of the Principal Fortress of the Teutonic Order in the Middle East.* Leiden: Brill, 2017.

Boyarin, Daniel. *Carnal Israel: Reading Sex in Talmudic Culture.* Berkeley: University of California Press, 1993.

Boyarin, Daniel. *Unheroic Conduct: The Rise of Heterosexuality and the Invention of the Jewish Man.* Berkeley: University of California Press, 1997.

Boyarin, Daniel, Jonathan Boyarin. *Powers of Diaspora.* Minneapolis: University of Minnesota Press, 2002.

Buchler, Adolf. *The Political and Social Leader of the Jewish Community of Sepphoris in the Second and Third Centuries.* London: Jews College, 1909.

Carenen, Caitlin. *The Fervent Embrace: Liberal Protestants, Evangelicals and Israel.* New York: NYU Press, 2012.

Carpine, Giovanni. *The Story of the Mongols Whom we Call Tartars.* Wellesly, MA: Branden Books, 2014.

Chancey, Mark. *The Myth of a Gentile Galilee.* New York: Cambridge University Press, 2002.

Clarke, Howard. *The Gospel of Matthew and its Readers: A Historical Introduction to the First Gospel.* Bloomington: Indiana University Press, 2003.

Cohen, Shaye. *Josephus in Galilee and Rome.* Leiden: Brill, 2002.

Cohen, Shaye. "Masada: Literary Tradition, Archaeological Remains and the Credibility of Josephus." *Journal of Jewish Studies* 33, nos. 1–2 (Spring–Autumn 1982), 385–405.

Cohen, Shaye. "The Place of the Rabbi in Jewish Society." In *The Galilee in Late Antiquity*, edited by Lee Levine, 157–74. Cambridge, MA: Harvard University Press 1992.

Cohen, Yehezkel. *Prekim b'toldot ha'tekufah ha'tana'im.* Jerusalem: Ministry of Education and Culture, 1977.

Conder, C.R., H.H. Kitchener. *The Survey of Western Palestine*, vol. 1 Galilee. London: Committee of the Palestine Exploration Fund, 1881.

Craffert, Pieter F. *The Life of a Galilean Shaman: Jesus of Nazareth in Anthropological-Historical Perspective.* Eugene: Cascade Books, 2008.

Davies, Stevan. *Jesus the Healer: Possession, Trance and the Origins of Christianity.* New York: Bloomsbury, 1995.

Davies, W.B. *The Setting of the Sermon on the Mount.* Atlanta: Scholars Press, 1989.

Edbury, Peter. "Propaganda and Faction in the Kingdom of Jerusalem: The Background to Hattin." In *Crusaders and Muslims in Twelfth-Century Syria*, edited by Maya Shatzmiller, 173–89. Leiden: Brill, 1993.

Edwards, Douglas, C. Thomas McCollough, eds. *Archaeology and the Galilee, Texts and Contexts in the Graeco-Roman and Byzantine Periods.* Atlanta: Scholars Press, 1997.

Eilan, Zvi, Avraham Ezderkat. *Arbel*. Tel Aviv: Kibbutz Movement Yediat Haaretz Department, 1988.

Ellenblum, Ronnie. *Frankish Rural Settlement in the Latin Kingdom of Jerusalem*. Cambridge: Cambridge University Press.

Esposito, John. *The Oxford History of Islam*. New York: Oxford University Press, 1999.

Fenton, J.C. *Saint Matthew*. London: Penguin Books, 1963.

Fiensy, David, James Riley Strange, eds. *Galilee in the Late Second Temple and Mishnaic Periods*. Minneapolis: Fortress Press, 2014.

Fine, Lawrence. *Physician of the Soul, Healer of the Cosmos: Isaac Luria and His Kabbalistic Fellowship*. Palo Alto: Stanford University Press, 2003.

France, John. *Hattin*. New York: Oxford University Press, 2015.

Frankel Rafael. "Topographical Notes on the Territory of Acre in the Crusader Period." *Israel Exploration Journal* 38 no. 4 (1988): 249–72.

Franklin, Arnold. *This Nobel House: Jewish Descendants of King David in the Medieval Islamic East*. Philadelphia: University of Pennsylvania Press, 2013.

Frey, Jorge. "The Character and Background of Matt 5:25-26." In *The Sermon on the Mount and its Jewish Setting*, edited by Hans-Jurgen Becker and Serge Ruzer, 3–39. Paris: J. Gabalda et Cie Editeurs, 2005.

Freyne, Sean. *Galilee: From Alexander the Great to Hadrian, 323 BCE to 135 CE*. Edinburgh: T&T Clark, 1980.

Freyne, Sean. *Galilee, Jesus and the Gospels: Literary Approaches and Historical Investigations*. Philadelphia: Fortress Press, 1988.

Friedman, D. A. *Rabbis of Ancient Times: Biographical Sketches of the Talmudic Period*. Indianapolis: Hollenbeck Press, 1921.

Gaposchkin, M. Cecilia. "Louis IX, Crusade and the Promise of Joshua in the Holy Land." *Journal of Medieval History*, XXXIV (2008), 245–74.

Gaposchkin, M. Cecilia. *The Making of Saint Louis: Kingship, Sanctity and Crusade in the Later Middle Ages*. Ithaca: Cornell University Press, 2008.

Gaposchkin, Cecilia M, Sean L. Field, eds. *The Sanctity of Louis IX: Early Lives of Saint Louis by Geoffrey of Beaulieu and William of Chartes*. Oxford: University Press, 2013.

Gardner, Richard. *Matthew*. Scottdale PA, Herald Press, 1991.

Geiger, Abraham. *Judaism and its History in Two Parts*. New York: Bloch, 1911.

Gervers, Michael, Ramzi Jibran Bikhazi, eds. *Conversion and Continuity: Indigenous Christian Communities in Islamic Lands, Eight to Eighteenth Centuries*. Toronto: Pontifical Institute of Medieval Studies, 1990.

Gil, Moshe. *A History of Palestine, 634-1099*. New York: Cambridge University Press, 1992.

Goitein, S.D. *A Mediterranean Society: The Jewish Communities of the Arab World as Portrayed in the Documents of the Cairo Geniza*. Berkeley: University of California Press, 1967.

Goodblatt, David. "The Beruriah Traditions." *Journal of Jewish Studies* 26 (1975): 68–85.

Goodman, Martin. *Josephus's The Jewish War*. Princeton: Princeton University Press, 2019.
Goodman, Martin. *State and Society in Roman Galilee, A.D. 132-212*. London: Valentine Mitchell, 1983/2000.
Goranson, Stephen. "Josephus of Tiberias Revisited." In *Galilee Through the Centuries: Confluence of Cultures*, edited by Eric M. Myers, 335–44. Winona Lake: Eisenbrauns, 1999.
Gordon, Milton. *Assimilation in American Life*. New York: Oxford University Press, 1964.
Goshen-Gottstein, Alon. *The Sinner and the Amnesiac: The Rabbinic Invention of Elisha ben Abuya and Eleazar ben Arach*. Stanford: Stanford University Press, 2000.
Graetz, Heinrich. *History of the Jews (from the Reign of Hyrcanus to the completion of the Babylonian Talmud)*, vol. II. Philadelphia: Jewish Publication Society of America, 1893.
Halivni, David Weiss. "The Reception Accorded to Rabbi Judah's Mishnah." In *Jewish and Christian Self-Definition: Aspects of Judaism in the Graeco-Roman Period*, vol. 2, edited by E. P. Sanders, 204–12. London: SCM Press, 1981.
Harkabi, Yehoshafat. *The Bar Kochba Syndrome: Risk and Realism in International Politics*. Chappaqua, NY: Rossel Books, 1983.
Harnack, Adolf. *Luke the Physician*. New York: G.P. Putnam's Sons, 1907.
Heschel, Susannah. *Abraham Geiger and the Jewish Jesus*. Chicago: University of Chicago Press, 1998.
Heschel, Susannah. *The Aryan Jesus: Christian Theologians and the Bible in Nazi Germany*. Princeton: Princeton University Press, 2008.
Hillenbrand, Carole. *The Crusades: Islamic Perspectives*. Edinburgh: Edinburgh University Press, 1999.
Hirschfeld, Yizhar. "The Anchor Church at the Summit of Mount Berenice Neat Tiberias." *Qadmoniot: A Journal for the Antiquities of Eretz Israel*, no. 3–4 (1993): 120–27.
Hobsbawn, Eric, Terence Ranger, eds. *The Invention of Tradition*. Cambridge: Cambridge University Press, 1992.
Holzman, Iris Brown. "Forgotten and Revived: The Bruria Incident in Contemporary Orthodox Discourse." *Daat: A Journal of Jewish Philosophy and Kabbalah* 83 (2017): 407–42.
Hoof, Anton van. *From Autothanasia to Suicide: Self-Killing in Classical Antiquity*. London: Routledge, 1990.
Horbury, William, W.D. Davies and John Sturdy, eds. *The Cambridge History of Judaism*. Cambridge: Cambridge University Press, 1999.
Horsley, Richard. *Archaeology, History and Society in Galilee: The Social Context of Jesus and the Rabbis*. Valley Forge: Trinity Press International, 1996.
Horsley Richard, with John Hanson. *Bandits, Prophets and Messiahs*. Harrisburg: Trinity Press, 1999.
Ilan, Tal. "The Search for the Historical Beruriah, Rachel and Imma Shalom." *Association of Jewish Studies Review* 22, no. 1 (1997): 1–17.

Jacobs, Andrew. "Visible Ghosts and Invisible Demons." In *Galilee Through the Centuries: Confluence of Cultures,* edited by Eric M. Myers, 359–76. Winona Lake: Eisenbrauns, 1999.
Joinville, Jean. *The Memoirs of the Lord of Joinville.* London: John Murray, 1906.
Jordan, William Chester. *The French Monarchy and the Jews.* Philadelphia: University of Pennsylvania Press, 1989.
Jordan, William Chester. *Louis IX and the Challenge of the Crusade.* Princeton: Princeton University Press, 1979.
Josephus. *The Jewish War.* Oxford: Oxford University Press, 2017.
Kaegi, Walter. *Heraclius: Emperor of Byzantium.* Cambridge: Cambridge University Press, 2003.
Kaell, Hillary. *Walking Where Jesus Walked: American Christians and the Holy Land Pilgrimage.* New York: NYU Press, 2014.
Kampen, John. *Matthew within Sectarian Judaism.* New Haven: Yale University Press, 2019.
Kasher, Aryeh. *Jews and Hellenistic Cities in Eretz-Israel.* Tubingen: J.C.B. Mohr, 1990.
Kedar, B.Z., H.E. Mayer, and R.C. Smail, eds. *Outremer: Studies in the History of the Crusading Kingdom of Jerusalem.* Jerusalem: Yad Ben Tzvi Institute, 1982.
Kimelman, Reuven. "*Birkat Ha-Minim* and the Lack of Evidence for an Anti-Christian Jewish Prayer in Late Antiquity." In *Jewish and Christian Self-Definition: Aspects of Judaism in the Graeco-Roman Period*, vol. 2, edited by E. P. Sanders, 226–44. London: SCM Press, 1981.
Kimelman, Reuven. "Identifying Jews and Christians in Roman Syria-Palestine." In *Galilee Through the Centuries: Confluence of Cultures,* edited by Eric M. Myers, 301–34. Winona Lake: Eisenbrauns, 1999.
Kimelman, Reuven. *Lekhah dodi ye-ḳabalat Shabat: ha-mashma'ut ha-misṭit.* Jerusalem: Magnes Press, 2002.
Kosman, Admiel. *Masekhet gevarim: Rav ve-hakatsav ve-od sipurim al gavriyut ahave ve-otentiyut be-sipur ha-agadah uva sipur ha-hasid.* Jerusalem: Keter, 2002.
Lau, Binyamin. *Hakhamim: tekufat Ha-galil.* Tel Aviv: Yedioth Aharonoth Books, 2008.
Le Goff, Jacques. *Saint Louis.* Notre Dame: University of Notre Dame Press, 2009.
Le Strange, Guy. *Palestine Under the Moslems: A Description of Syria and the Holy Land from A.D. 650 to 1500.* Beirut: Khayats, 1965.
Levine, Lee, ed. *The Galilee in Late Antiquity.* New York: The Jewish Theological Seminary, 1992
Levine, Lee. "R. Simeon b. Yohai and the Purification of Tiberias: History and Tradition." *Hebrew Union College Annual* 49 (1978): 143–85.
Leyerle, Blake. "Pilgrims to the Land: "Early Christian Perceptions of the Galilee." In *Galilee Through the Centuries: Confluence of Cultures,* edited by Eric M. Myers, 346–53. Winona Lake: Eisenbrauns, 1999.
Lotan, Shlomo. *Tevtonim b'mamlekhet yerushaliyim ha'tzalbanit.* Tel Aviv: Ofir, 2012.

Luz, Ulrich. *The Theology of the Gospel of Matthew*. Cambridge: Cambridge University Press, 2012.

Magness, Jodi. *Masada: From Jewish Revolt to Modern Myth*. Princeton: Princeton University Press, 2019.

Malinowski, F.X. *Galilean Judaism in the Writings of Flavius Josephus*. Ph.D. thesis, Ann Arbor, 1973.

Mason, Steve, ed. *Flavius Josephus: Life of Josephus*. Leiden: Brill, 2003.

Memmi, Albert. *The Colonizer and the Colonized*. Boston: Beacon Press, 1991.

Merrill, Sellah. *Galilee in the Time of Christ*. London: The Religious Tract Society, 1885.

Miller, Stuart. "The *Minnim* of Sepphoris Reconsidered." *Harvard Theological Review* 86 no. 4 (October 1993): 377–402.

Miller, Stuart. "New Perspectives on the History of Sepphoris." In *Galilee Through the Centuries: Confluence of Cultures*, edited by Eric M. Myers, 145–60. Winona Lake: Eisenbrauns, 1999.

Morton, Nicholas. *The Teutonic Knights in the Holy Land, 1190-1291*. Rochester: Boydell Press, 2012.

Myers, David. *Re-Inventing the Jewish Past: European Jewish Intellectuals and the Zionist Return to History*. New York: Oxford University Press, 1995.

Myers Eric M., ed. *Galilee Through the Centuries: Confluence of Cultures*. Winona Lake: Eisenbrauns, 1999.

Nagy, Rebecca Martin, Carol Meyers, Eric Meyers and Zeev Weiss, eds. *Sepphoris in Galilee*. Winona Lake: North Carolina Museum of Art, 1996.

Neusner, Jacob. *From Politics to Piety: The Emergence of Pharisaic Judaism*. Englewood Cliffs: Prentice Hall, 1973.

Neusner, Jacob. *In the Aftermath of Catastrophe: Founding Judaism, 70 to 640*. Montreal: McGill-Queen's University Press, 2009.

Neusner, Jacob. *A Life of Yohannan ben Zakkai*. Leiden: Brill, 1962.

Neusner, Jacob. *The Mishnah: A New Translation*. New Haven: Yale University Press, 1988.

Nicholson, Helen. "Women on the Third Crusade." *Journal of Medieval History* 23, no. 4 (1997): 335–49.

Nicholson, Robert Lawrence. *Tancred: A Study of His Career and Work*. Ph.D. Thesis, Ann Arbor, 1940.

Nickelsburg, George. "Enoch, Levi and Peter: Recipients of Revelation in Upper Galilee." *Journal of Biblical Literature* 100, no. 4 (Dec. 1981): 575–600.

Nicole, David. *Yarmuk 636 AD: The Muslim Conquest of Syria*. London: Osprey Military, 1994.

Oppenheimer, Aharon. *The Am Ha'aretz: A Study in the History of the Jewish People in the Hellenistic-Roman Period*. Leiden: Brill, 1977.

Oppenheimer, Aharon. *Between Rome and Babylon*. Tubingen: Mohr Siebrook, 2005.

Oppenheimer, Aharon. *Ha-galil be'tekufat ha-Mishnah*. Jerusalem: Shazar Center, 1991.

Oppenheimer, Aharon. "Roman Rule and the Cities in Talmudic Literature." In *The Galilee in Late Antiquity*, edited by Lee Levine, 115–25. Cambridge, MA: Harvard University Press, 1992.

Oppenheimer, Aharon. *Yehuda Ha-nasi*. Jerusalem: Shazar Center 2007.

Overman, J. Andrew. *Matthew's Gospel and Formative Judaism: The Social World of the Matthean Community*. Minneapolis: Fortress Press, 1990.

Painter, Sydney. "The Third Crusade: Richard the Lionhearted and Philip Augustus." In *A History of the Crusades*, vol. 2, edited by Kenneth Meyer Setton et al., 45–87. Philadelphia: University of Pennsylvania Press, 1962.

Peters, Joan. *From Time Immemorial: The Origins of the Arab-Jewish Conflict over Palestine*. New York: Harper and Row, 1984.

Philip, of Novare. *The Wars of Frederick II Against the Ibelins in Syria and Cyprus*. New York: Columbia University Press, 1936.

Pirie-Gordon, H. "The Reigning Princes of Galilee." *The English Historical Review* 27/107 (July 1912): 445–61.

Prawer, Joshua. *Crusader Institutions*. Oxford: Oxford University Press, 1980.

Prawer, Joshua. *The Crusaders' Kingdom: European Colonialism in the Middle Ages*. London: Phoenix Press, 2001.

Prawer, Joshua. *The History of the Jews in the Latin Kingdom of Jerusalem*. Oxford: Clarendon Press, 1988.

Rajak, Tessa. *Josephus*. London: Duckworth, 2004.

Rajak, Tessa. "Justus of Tiberias." *The Classical Quarterly* 23, no. 2 (Nov. 1973): 345–68.

Rappaport, Uriel. *Yoḥanan mi-Gush ḥalav: me-hare ha-Galil el ḥomot Yerushalayım*. Jerusalem: Shazar Institute, 2006.

Reed, Jonathan. "Instability in Jesus' Galilee: A Demographic Perspective." *Journal of Biblical Literature* 129, no. 2 (2010): 343–65.

Remus, Harold. *Jesus as Healer*. Cambridge: Cambridge University Press, 1997.

Renan, Ernest. *The Life of Jesus*. London: Watts, 1935.

Riley-Smith, Jonathan. "History, the Crusades and the Latin East." In *Crusaders and Muslims in Twelfth-Century Syria*, edited by Maya Shatzmiller, 1–18. Leiden: Brill, 1993.

Riley-Smith, Jonathan. "The Motives of the Earliest Crusaders and the Settlement of Latin Palestine, 1095-1100." *English Historical Review* 98 (1983): 721–36.

Rokeah, D. "The War of Kitos: Towards the Clarification of a Philological-Historical Problem." *Scripta Hierosolymitana* XXIII (1972): 79–84.

Rubinstein, Jeffrey. "Elisha ben Abuya: Torah and the Sinful Sage." *The Journal of Jewish Thought and Philosophy* 7 (1998): 139–225.

Runciman, Steven. *A History of the Crusades*, vol. 3. Cambridge: Cambridge University Press, 1954.

Safrai, S. "The Relations between the Roman Army and the Jews of Eretz Yisrael after the Destruction of the Second Temple." Tel Aviv University, *Roman Frontier Studies 1967*, Tel Aviv, 1971, 224–30.

Saldarini, Anthony. *Matthew's Christian-Jewish Community*. Chicago: University of Chicago Press, 1994.

Sanders, E.P. *Jesus and Judaism.* Fortress Press: Philadelphia, 1985.

Sanders, E. P., ed. *Jewish and Christian Self-Definition: Aspects of Judaism in the Graeco-Roman Period*, vol. 2. London: SCM Press, 1981.

Saunders, J.J. *The History of the Mongol Conquests.* Philadelphia: University of Pennsylvania Press, 1971.

Schafer, Peter. *Jesus in the Talmud.* Princeton: Princeton University Press, 2007.

Schick, Robert. *The Christian Communities of Palestine from Byzantine to Islamic Rule.* Princeton: Darwin Press, 1995.

Schiffman, Lawrence. "Was there a Galilean Halakhah?" In *The Galilee in Late Antiquity*, edited by Lee Levine, 143–55. Cambridge MA: Harvard University Press 1992.

Schur, Nathan. *Toldot Ako.* Tel Aviv: Dvir, 1990.

Schwartz, Joshua, Peter Tomson. "When Rabbi Eliezer was Arrested for Heresy." *Jewish Studies Internet Journal* 10 (2012): 145–81.

Schwartz, Seth. "How Many Judaisms Were There?" *Journal of Ancient Judaism* 2, no. 2 (May 2011): 208–38.

Schwartz, Seth. *Imperialism and Jewish Society: 200 B.C.E. to 640 C.E.* Princeton: Princeton University Press, 2001.

Schweitzer, Albert. *The Quest of the Historical Jesus: A Critical Study of its Progress from Reimarus to Wrede.* London: Adam and Charles Black, 1910.

Setton, Kenneth Meyer et al, eds. *A History of the Crusades*, vol. 2. Philadelphia: University of Pennsylvania Press, 1962.

Shatzmiller, Maya. *Crusaders and Muslims in Twelfth-Century Syria.* Leiden: Brill, 1993.

Shenhar, Aliza. "Le-Ammiyutah shel agudat beruria eshet rabbi meir." *Mehkari hamerkaz le-heker ha-folkore* (Jerusalem: Magnes Press, 1973) 3 (1973): 223–27.

Sivan, Emmanuel. *Radical Islam: Medieval Theology and Modern Politics.* New Haven: Yale University Press, 1990.

Smail, R.C. "The Predicaments of Guy at Lusignan, 1183-1187." In *Outremer: Studies in the History of the Crusading Kingdom of Jerusalem*, edited by B.Z. Kedar, H.E. Mayer, and R.C. Smail, 159–77. Jerusalem: Yad Ben Tzvi Institute, 1982.

Smith, John Masson. "Ayn Jalut: Mamluk Success or Mongol Failure." *Harvard Journal of Asiatic Studies* 44, no. 2 (Dec. 1984): 315–20.

Snodgrass, Klyne. "Matthew and the Law." *SBL Seminar Papers 1988*, 536–54. Atlanta: Atlanta Scholars, 1988.

Sofer Arnon, et al. eds. *Ertzot Hagalil.* Haifa: Israel Ministry of Defense, 1983.

Spector, Stephen. *Evangelicals and Israel: The Story of American Christian Zionism.* Oxford: Oxford University Press, 2009.

Steinberg, Milton. *As a Driven Leaf.* New York: Behrman House, 1939.

Strange, James, Thomas R.W. Longstaff and Dennis Groh. *Excavations at Sepphoris*, vol. 1. Leiden: Brill, 2006.

Strange, James. "First Century Galilee from Archaeology and From the Texts." In *Archaeology and the Galilee, Texts and Contexts in the Graeco-Roman and*

Byzantine Periods, edited by Douglas Edwards, C. Thomas McCollough, 39–49. Atlanta: Scholars Press, 1997.

Taylor, Joan. *Christians and the Holy Places: The Myth of Jewish-Christian Origins.* Oxford: Clarendon Press, 1993.

Tibble, Steven. *Monarchy and Lordships in the Latin Kingdom of Jerusalem 1099-1291.* Oxford: Clarendon Press, 1989.

Trifon, Dalia. "Did the Priestly Courses Moves from Judea to Galilee after the Bar Kokhba Revolt?" *Tarbiz* 59 (1990): 77–93.

Tsafrir, Yoram, Gideon Foerster. "The Dating of the 'Earthquake of the Sabbatical Year' of 749 C.E. in Palestine." *Bulletin of the School of Oriental and African Studies, University of London* v55 no. 2 (1992): 231–35.

Tyerman, Christopher. *The Crusades: A Very Short Introduction.* Oxford: New York, 2005.

Van Cleve, Thomas C. "The Fifth Crusade." In *A History of the Crusades,* vol. 2, edited by Kenneth Meyer Setton et al., 377–428. Philadelphia: University of Pennsylvania Press, 1962.

Vermas, Geza. *The True Herod.* London: Bloomsbury, 2014.

Vonder Bruegge, John M. *Mapping Galilee in Josephus, Luke and John.* Leiden: Brill, 2016.

Wachsmann, Shelley. "The Excavations of an Ancient Boat in the Sea of Galilee." *Atiqot,* XIX (1990).

Ward, Seth. "Sepphoris in Sacred Geography." In *Galilee Through the Centuries: Confluence of Cultures,* edited by Eric M. Myers, 391–406. Winona Lake: Eisenbrauns, 1999.

Weiss, Johannes. *Jesus' Proclamation of the Kingdom of God.* Philadelphia: Fortress Press, 1892/1971.

Wilson, John Francis. *Caesarea Philippi: Banias, the Lost City of Pan.* London: I.B. Taurus, 2004.

Wisse, Ruth. *If I am Not for Myself: the Liberal Betrayal of the Jews.* New York: Free Press, 1992.

Ya'ari, Abraham. "History of the Pilgrimage to Meron." *Tarbiz* 31 (1961): 72–101.

Zeitlin, Solomon. "Who were the Galileans? New Light on Josephus' Activities in Galilee." *Jewish Quarterly Review* 64, no. 3 (January 1974): 189–203.

Index

Aaron ben Moses ben Asher (Ben Asher, masorete), 219–20
Abbasid (caliphate), 215–16, 219, 221, 223–24, 226, 229, 305
Abdallah ibn al-Zubayr, 212
Abdallah ibn Hawala, 217
Abd al-Latif al-Baghdadi, 261
Abd al-Rahman b. Qays al-Qayni, 211
Abd al-Wahid ibn Ishaq, 220
Abraham b. Furat (masorete), 219
Abraham b. Riqat (masorete), 219
Abu Bakr (architect-engineer, grandfather of Muqaddasi), 222–23
Abu Bakr (caliph), 198, 203
Abu Kathir Yahya b. Zakariyya, 220
Abu'l Abbas ibn al-Muwaffaq, 223
Abu'l A'war (Amr b. Sufyan al-Sulami), 211
Abu'l-Jaysh Khumarawayh (Tulunid ruler, son of Ahmad ibn Tulun), 223
Abul-Qasim Abd al-Rahman ibn Ishaq al-Zajjaji al-Nihawandi, 220
Abu Sufyan ibn Harb, 202
Abu Unays al-Dahhak b. Qays al-Fihri, 212
Achziv, 104, 166, 259
Acre, 2, 6, 166, 187; Byzantine era, 172; Crusader period, 239–40, 251, 253, 256–60, 268, 271–83, 290–92, 294–310; early Islamic era, 209–10, 213, 216, 222–24, 226, 229, 232–33; harbor construction, 223; Persian invasion, 193–94; Tannaitic era, 101, 104, 142
Adler, Rachel, 113
Agrippa (II, client-king from Herod's family), 15, 43–44, 85–86
Ahiyahu ha-Kohen, 219
Ahmad ibn Kayghalagh, 224
Ahmad ibn Tulun (Tulunid founder), 221–23
Ahmad Pasha al-Jazzar, 2
Ajnadayn (battle), 200, 215
Akiva (ben Yosef, Tanna, rabbi), 105, 107, 115–16, 123, 128, 135, 150, 152–53, 178
Al-Adil (Ayyubid sultan), 290
Al-Ba'ina, 258
Albert of Aix, 252
Alexander (Alexander the Great), 5
Alexios I Komnenos (Byzantine emperor), 246–47
Al-Fula, 263–64
Al-Hakim bi-Amr Allah (caliph), 228
Ali ibn Abi Talib (caliph), 211–12
Alkabetz, Shlomo Halevi, 82
Al-Kamil (Ayyubid sultan), 286–88, 290–91

Alma, 251
Al-Masudi (historian), 234
Al-Mu'izz li-Din Allah (caliph), 226
Alptakin, 226–27
Al-Sa'id Hasan, 307
Al-Salih Ayyub (Ayyubid sultan), 304
Al-Sinnabra (Beit Yerah), 211–12, 226
Amalric (of Jerusalem), 263, 265
Amalric II (King of Cyprus, King of Jerusalem), 277
amei ha'aretz, 64–65, 88, 105, 120–23, 143, 167, 173
Amitai-Preiss, Reuven, 308
Amoraim, 123, 147, 167, 169–71, 187, 218
Amr ibn al As, 200
Ananus ben Ananus (high priest), 28–29
Ancra (Amqa), 259
Andrew II (King of Hungary), 285
Antigonus (Mattathiah, Hasmonean King of Judea), 13, 17
Antioch, 17, 172, 187, 192, 225, 244–47, 252–53, 267, 272, 306–7, 309
Antipas (tetrarch, son of Herod), 65–68, 73, 176, 189
Antipater (father of Herod), 9–10, 12
Aramaic (use of language), 25, 71, 102, 146, 189
Arav, 103
Arbela, 9, 14–18, 233
Arket (Yarka), 258
Armstrong, Karen, 240, 294
Arnulf of Chocques (Patriarch of Jerusalem), 244–45, 249
Asher b. Nehamia (masorete), 219
Aslan, Reza, 33, 66, 68, 73–74, 80
Assassins (sect), 254, 263, 276, 301–2
Atlit, 287, 307
Augustine (Saint, of Hippo), 79, 244
Aviam, Mordecai, 65, 67–68, 182, 189, 256
Avi-Yonah, M., 21, 118, 165, 186, 192–93
Avodah Zarah (Mishnah tractate), 113, 144

Avot (Mishnah tractate), 104, 135, 150–52
Ayn Jalut (battle), 190, 261, 279, 304–11; battle description, 308–9; battle significance, 309–11; *Haute Cour* deliberations before battle, 307–8; Mongol strength before battle, 305–6
Ayyubid (dynasty), 255, 260–61, 263, 266, 272, 274, 281, 284, 290, 299, 304, 307

Bagatti, Bellarmino, 183–84
Baghdad, 221, 234, 261, 305
Baibars, Rukn al-Din (Mamluk sultan), 233, 235, 254, 308–9
Baldwin I (of Jerusalem), 249, 252–53, 266
Baldwin II (of Jerusalem), 254, 275
Baldwin IV (of Jerusalem, the leper), 263–65
Baldwin V (of Jerusalem), 265, 272
Banias, 82–87, 101, 172, 214, 233–35, 253–54, 307. See also Muhammad ibn Ahmad Al-Muqaddasi
Banu Ash'ar (tribe), 217
Banu Azd (tribe), 217
Banu Fazara (tribe), 225
Banu Kalb (tribe), 212
Banu Murra (tribe), 225
Banu Qays (tribe), 212
Banu Quada'a (tribe), 211
Banu Uqayl (tribe), 226
Bar Kochba revolt, 42, 96–102, 104, 106–7, 109, 115–18, 121–22, 124–27, 129, 132, 148, 154, 164–66, 168, 186, 193, 196, 219
Beatitudes, 75
Be'eri, Nurit, 134
Beit Jan, 234, 258
Beit Natif, 200
Beit Netofa (valley), 130, 269
Beit Sha'an, 119, 171–72, 200, 209, 216, 250
Beit She'arim, 103, 116, 119

Benjamin (Tiberias Jewish notable, Byzantine era), 197–98
Benjamin of Tudela, 251, 275, 281
Ben Meir, Aaron (nasi, rabbi), 218–19
Benoit of Marseille (bishop), 256–57
Berard, Thomas (Templar Master), 307
Berdichevsky, Mica Josef, 134
Berenice (sister of Agrippa II), 85
Bernard of Clairvaux, 243, 262, 284
Beruria (sage, wife of Rabbi Meir), 110–15, 137–38. *See also* Meir
Bethany, 77
Bethlehem, 13, 16, 87, 186, 200, 248, 290
Bethsaida, 69, 72, 84
birkat ha-minim (prayer), 173, 180–82
Birwah, 233
Bloch, Marc, 255
Boas, Adrian, 292–93
Bohemond (of Antioch, of Taranto), 244, 246–47, 252
Bohemond V (of Antioch), 305
Bohemond VI (of Antioch), 306
boule (municipal council framework), 119, 166–67
Boyarin, Daniel, 32, 42, 112–15
Bruegge, M. Vonder, 82
Buchler, Adolf, 120–22, 177

Cabra, 258
Caesar, Sextus Iulius Caesar (governor of Syria), 12
Caesarea, 10, 85, 119, 167–68, 170, 172, 183, 188, 192, 296
Caesarea Philippi. *See* Banias
Cairo Genizah, 101, 180, 214, 216, 219–20
calendar designation (ibur hashanah), 106–9, 219, 283
Capernaum, 59–60, 63, 69, 71–74, 107, 171–72, 174, 184, 186, 189, 215
Caracalla (Marcus Aurelius Severus Antonius Augustus, emperor), 118
Casale Album, 259
Casale Imbert, 259, 289, 291

Case, Shirley Jackson, 62, 175
Castellum Regis, 257, 260, 288
Cestus Gallus (governor of Syria), 36, 39
Chalcedonians, 188
Chancey, Mark, 60, 62–64
Chastel Neuf, 254
Chastiau de Roi, 291
Chorazin, 72
Christianity, 1, 3, 5–6, 9–10, 24, 37, 51–55, 58–62, 71, 96–97, 103, 110, 121, 132, 144, 215, 225–26, 235; Byzantine period, 163–65, 168–90, 196–200; Crusader period, 240–43, 246–50, 259, 284, 295–96, 304, 306, 309–11; Evangelicalism, 188–89; and Islam, 190–204, 227–28
Chrysostom, John, 180, 186
Clarke, Howard, 78, 80–81
Cleitus (prisoner), 44–45
Cohen, Shaye, 19, 23, 35
Cohen, Yehezkel, 122
Conrad of Montferrat, 258, 272–74, 276
Constantine (emperor), 132, 163–65, 167–68, 171–72, 183–87, 192, 198, 309
Constantinople, 186, 192, 194–95, 200, 218, 247, 255, 261
Constantius II (emperor, son of Constantine), 186–87
Craffert, Pieter, 69
Crusades, 1–3, 9, 86, 134, 164, 190, 201, 210–11, 214, 216, 219, 221–28, 239–311; Acre Kingdom, 277–83; end of Crusader era in Galilee, 296–311; Galilee lordship established, 252–60; Hattin turning point, 260–72; historiography, 239–42; political background before First Crusade, 221–29; Teutonic Order, 283–92; Third Crusade, 272–77
Cyprus, 171, 192–93, 223, 272–74, 276, 280, 285, 289, 306

Dabarittha, 35, 40, 42–45

Dalton, 214, 251
Damascus, 192–93, 200, 202, 209, 226, 232, 235, 250–51, 301, 306–7
Damietta, 285–87, 290, 298–99
Damun, 233
Darb al-Hawarnah, 269
Darwish, Mahmoud, 234
Davies, Stevan, 70
Dead Sea, 22, 198, 233, 276
Dead Sea Scrolls, 57, 79
Decapolis (cities), 43, 188
Deir al-Asad, 258. *See also* St. George de La Baena
Dimashki (Shams al-Din al-Ansari al-Dimashki), 232, 234–35
Dinur, Ben Zion, 184
Diocletian (emperor), 165–66
Dome of the Rock. *See* Jerusalem
Druze, 2, 6, 228, 258

Edessa, 197, 262
Eleazar ben Judah (of Bartota, Tanna, rabbi), 110
Eleazar ben Kalir, 213
Eleazar ben Pedat (rabbi), 121, 170–71
Eleazar ben Shimon (Rashbi's son), 129–30, 168
Eliezer ben Dama (rabbi), 179
Eliezer ben Hyrcanus (rabbi), 178–79
Elisha ben Abuyah (aher), 115, 134–38. *See also* Meir
Ellenblum, Ronnie, 254–57, 259
Epimenides (philosopher), 133
Epiphanius (bishop), 132, 171
Eschiva (Countess of Tripoli, wife of Raymond III), 267–68, 272
Essenes, 23–24, 57, 122
Eusebius (bishop, historian), 172
Eutychius (Melkite patriarch), 193
Ezekias (Hezekiah, Jewish rebel), 12–17

Fatimids, 214, 224–29, 261
Filangieri, Riccardo, 277–78
Fox, George, 81
France, John, 267

Franciscans, 172, 183, 293
Frankel, Rafael, 291
Frederick II (Holy Roman Emperor), 258, 277, 288–89, 292, 295
French Revolution, 2
Frey, Jorge, 79
Freyne, Sean, 5, 57, 176

Gabara, 11, 39
Gafni, Isaiah, 177–78
Galileans (term used by Josephus), 9, 11–12, 25, 27, 30, 32–35, 40, 44, 54, 95–96, 122
Galilee of the Gentiles, 34, 57, 59–68, 121, 174–75
Gallus Caesar (Constantius Gallus), 186–87; anti-Gallus revolt, 187
Gamaliel II (nasi, rabbi), 104, 108–9, 142
Gamaliel VI (nasi), 188
Gamla (Gamala), 11, 28, 31
Gandhi, Mahatma, 81
Gaza Strip, 3, 99, 172, 198, 210, 276
Geiger, Abraham, 64, 88
Gelon, 258
Genghis Khan, 304–5
Geoffrey of Beaulieu, 302–3
Gerard of Ridefort, 265, 267–68
Gervaise de Bazoches (Prince of Galilee), 252–53
Ghassanid (clan), 188, 195, 200, 203
Gil, Moshe, 210, 214, 219–20, 231
Gischala, 26–28, 31. *See also* John of Gischala
Godfrey of Bouillon, 239, 248–52, 266
Golan Heights, 11, 28, 71, 190, 195, 201–2, 250
Goodblatt, David, 114
Goodman, Martin, 20, 22–23, 33, 41, 100–101, 129, 140, 143
Graetz, Heinrich, 64
Gregory IX (Pope), 287
Groh, Dennis, 174
Gush Halav (Gish), 27, 214, 251
Guy of Lusignan (King of Jerusalem), 260, 262–64, 276; biography, 264;

court intrigues, 265–66; Cyprus dynasty, 272; Hattin deliberations, 268–69

Hadrian (emperor), 98, 101, 104, 106, 129, 166
Haifa, 210, 251–53, 258, 275, 291–92
Hamid b. al-Hassan al-Bazzar, 220
Hammat Gader (springs), 215, 220–21
Hanania ben ahi R. Joshua (rabbi), 107–8
Hanina ben Dosa (rabbi), 103
Hanina ben Teradion (rabbi), 103, 112
Harkabi, Yehoshafat, 99
Hasmoneans, 10, 13–14, 17, 38
Hassan b. Abdallah b. Tughj, 225
Hassan b. Malik, 212
Hattin (battle), 190–91, 203, 227, 234, 239, 250, 253, 255, 257–58, 260–72, 308–10; battle description, 267–72; Crusader politics before battle, 262–67; historical significance, 260–62
haute cour, 249, 252, 265, 275, 278–79, 285, 307–8, 310
haverim (religious members, Tannaitic era), 98, 122, 145–46
Henricus Bubalos, 258
Henry I (of Cyprus), 289
Henry II (of England), 273
Henry de Milli, 258
Heraclius (Byzantine emperor), 191–203, 243; after Yarmuk, 203; biography, 191–92; Persian confrontations, 191–96. *See also* Yarmuk
Hermann of Salza, 284–88, 290–92. *See also* Teutonic
Herod, 5, 9–10, 12–18, 22, 67, 82
Herzl, Theodor, 5
Hilazon Valley, 291
Hillel (the Elder), 103, 151
Hillel II (Amora, rabbi), 188
Hind bit Utba, 202
Hippos-Susita, 189
Hirschfeld, Yizhar, 189

Hiyya bar Abba (rabbi, Amora), 170–71
Hodaya ben Jesse (nasi), 282–83
Holocaust, 2, 10, 32, 58, 73, 80, 124, 173
Honorius III (Pope), 284–87
Horsley, Richard, 12, 61, 68, 70
Hospitaller (order), 256–57, 263, 281, 283, 287, 292
House of Hillel (Tannaitic interpretive school), 140, 143–44, 146, 153–54
House of Shammai (Tannaitic interpretive school), 105, 144, 146, 153–54
Hubaysh b. Dulja, 211
Hugh I (King of Cyprus), 285
Hugh de St Omer (Prince of Galilee), 252–54
Hula Valley, 27, 233, 235
Hulegu Khan, 303, 305–6, 308–9
Humberti de Pace, 259. *See also* Casale Imbert
Huntington, Samuel, 201
hurban (Temple destruction), 96–97, 117, 124–25, 134, 137, 145–46, 150, 168, 173, 216
Husayn ibn Ali ibn Abi Talib (son of Ali), 212

Ibilin, 233, 256–57
Ibn al-Athir (historian), 263–64
Ibn Jubair, 234
Idumaeans, 10, 14, 29
Ikhshidids, 224–25
Iksal (Aksal), 234
Innocent III (Pope), 284
Isaac Commenus, 273
Islam, 1–3, 6, 9–10, 81, 163–65, 169, 190, 239, 243, 248, 256, 258, 261, 263, 281, 288, 291, 304–10; and Christianity, 190–204; consolidation in Galilee, 209–36; Rise of, 194–95, 199
Ismailis, 223–24, 305
Israel (modern state), 5–6, 9, 23, 27–28, 30, 33, 39, 41–42, 52, 63, 65, 81, 84,

89, 99, 106, 120, 127–28, 131, 144, 169, 173–74, 177, 182, 184, 202, 222, 229–30, 240, 258–59, 261–62, 274, 288, 308
Itureans, 84, 86

Jabala b. al-Ayham (Ghassanid leader), 195, 203
Jackson, Peter, 306
Ja'far b. al-Fallah, 225
Jafar b. Na'im, 224
James of Vitry (Jacques, Bishop of Acre), 284–85
Japha, 39
Jean of Ibelin, 257–58, 291
Jerusalem, 1, 3, 5, 9–14, 17–20, 22–32, 35–43, 51–55, 72, 82–83, 87–90, 95–98, 100, 107–08, 111, 116–17, 122, 124, 127, 129, 134–37, 141, 146–49, 169, 172, 177, 184–88, 192–94, 196, 198, 200, 210–11, 214–18, 222–28, 230–42, 245–51, 255, 257–68, 272–76, 279–83, 288–91, 294–98, 300; and Dome of the Rock, 210, 216, 248; and Second Temple, 1, 5, 10–11, 13–14, 18, 22–25, 27–38, 42, 51–54, 60–61, 67, 72, 77, 79, 82–83, 86, 88, 90, 96–104, 107, 110, 115, 117, 120–26, 137–39, 145–54, 173–74, 185–88, 196, 216, 227, 248–49, 288
Jesus Christ, 1–2, 5, 6, 9–11, 13, 16, 27, 32–34, 37, 39, 42, 51, 95–97, 99, 102–03, 110, 141, 145, 151, 163, 169, 172–72, 182–84, 186, 188–89, 234, 242; Book of Matthew, 52–58; Caesarea Philippi, 82–87; Capernaum, 71–74; Crusades, 242–43, 283–85, 295–97, 309–10; Galilee of the Gentiles, 59–68, 175–77; Jerusalem, 87–90; medical healing and miracles, 68–71; Sermon on the Mount, 74–82; Talmud, 178–80
Johanan ben Zakkai, 19, 103–4, 148

John (of Gischala), 19–22, 26–35, 37, 40, 42
John of Brienne (King of Jerusalem), 285–86, 289–90
John of Ibelin (nephew of John, jurist), 279
John Tzimiskes (Byzantine emperor), 225–28
Joinville, Jean, 281, 296–301, 303; memoir descriptions of Galilee life and society, 300–301
Jordan, William Chester, 294, 302
Jordan River, 15, 28, 89, 100, 102, 170, 183, 188, 209, 211, 213, 233, 263, 277, 285
Joscelyn de Courtenay (Prince of Galilee), 252
Joscelyn III (Count of Edessa), 260, 288–89, 291
Jose ben Kisma (rabbi), 104, 132
Joseph, (count, apostate from Tiberias), 132, 171–72, 184, 186, 198
Joseph ben Gershom, 282–83
Josephus, 5–6, 9–45, 51–55, 57, 62, 64, 72, 82, 85–88, 95–97, 119, 122–23, 131, 138, 189–90, 201, 213, 222, 229, 233, 271; *Antiquities*, 12, 24–25, 35, 40, 64–65, 131, 182; *Jewish War*, 13–30, 33–41, 43, 45; *Life*, 11–12, 14, 20, 23, 25–28, 30, 34–36, 38–45; upbringing, 23, 38
Jotapata, 11, 15, 19–20, 23, 27–28, 31, 34–35, 38, 40–45, 54, 67, 90, 201, 203, 271
Judah bar Ilai (rabbi), 104–6, 108, 120, 129–30, 142, 145, 147, 152, 167
Judah ben Bava (the Hasid, rabbi), 106
Judah HaNasi, 99–99, 102, 105, 108, 120–21, 151, 159, 165–68, 170–71, 187, 267, 271, 293; biography of, 115–20; dream legends, 118–19
Judah II (Nesi'ah, Judah HaNasi's grandson), 167, 169–71
Judaism, 1, 10, 19, 24, 30, 34, 36–37, 42, 51–56, 72, 79–80, 82, 96–97,

164–64, 167–69, 172–77, 185, 191, 196, 218, 220, 243, 310; and Christianity, 56–61, 63, 96, 163, 179–84; Reform movement, 64; Tannaitic period, 3, 6, 98–154
Judas (Galilean rebel extremist), 24
Judham (clan), 202–3
Julian (the Apostate, emperor), 126, 187–88, 193, 196
Justinian I (Byzantine emperor), 189
Justus (of Tiberias), 26–27, 40

Kabbalah, 2, 3, 6, 9, 74, 81–82, 117–18, 124–25, 127, 131–35, 139, 185, 293, 296
Kabul, 232
Kaegi, Walter, 197
Kafr Akib, 234
Kafr Kanna, 215, 234
Kafr Manda, 233
Kafr Sabt, 234, 268–69, 271
Kampen, John, 57, 72
Karaites, 220
Kasr Yaqub, 233
Kennedy, John F., 81
Ketbuqha (Kitbuqa), 306–8
Kfar Hananiah, 66, 141
Khalidi, Walid, 232
Khalid ibn al-Walid, 199–200, 203–4
Khamisy, Rabei, 293
Khusrau II (Khosrow, Sassanid ruler), 192, 195–96
Kilayim (Mishnah tractate), 140
Kimelman, Reuven, 179–81
Kitos War, 99
Kosman, Admiel, 170
Kursi, 189

Lag B'Omar (holiday), 127, 133
Lakham (clan), 202–3
Lanahia (Ivron), 259
Lau, Benny, 128, 138
Lebanon, 27, 101, 193, 209, 231, 253–54, 258–59, 291
Le Goff, Jacques, 293–95, 301

Lekha Dodi (liturgical prayer), 82
Lessing, Gotthold Ephraim, 261
Le Strange, Guy, 232
Levine, Lee, 129, 132–33
Levtzion, Nehamia, 231
Lilienblum, Moshe Leib, 134
Locke, John, 81
Lod (Lydda), 113, 115, 170, 187
Longstaff, Thomas R.W., 174
Lord's Prayer, 76–82
Louis IX (saint, King of France), 240–41, 277, 281, 286, 288, 293–304, 306–7; Acre, 299–304; historiography, 293–95; Seventh Crusade, 297–300
Lubiyah, 270
Luke (Gospel of), 55, 58, 69, 75, 82
Luria, Isaac (Ari), 128, 131, 293
Luz, Ulrich, 53, 59, 76, 78, 83

Ma'ayan Harod, 191, 308
Magdala, 70, 215
Maimonides (Moses ben Maimon), 220, 275, 282
Maimuni, Abraham (Abraham ben Moses ben Maimon), 282–83
Mamluks, 5, 134, 210, 231–32, 235, 239, 254, 256, 279, 292–93, 295, 299, 304–10
Mansourah, 286, 293, 296–98, 300–301, 303
Manuet, 291
Marco Polo, 305
Mariamne (Herod's second wife), 14
Mark (Gospel of), 55, 57–58, 68–69, 83
Mary (of Bethezuba), 17–19
Mar Zutra (Amora, rabbi), 218
Masada, 13–15, 22–23, 28, 42, 45
Mason, Steve, 42–43
Masoretes (scribes), 219–20
Matthew (Gospel of), 16, 18, 32–34, 52–90, 96–97, 110, 145, 151, 172, 176, 179, 235, 243, 253, 304
Meblie, 258
Megiddo, 101, 166, 308

Meir (Tanna, rabbi), 104–5, 108–10, 140, 152; and Beruria, 110–15; and Elisha ben Abuya, 134–38
Memmi, Albert, 36
Mergelcolon (Majdel-Kurum), 258
Meron (hilltop site), 127, 131, 133–34
Meskenah, 270–71
Mi'ilya, 257–58
Miller, Stuart, 169, 175, 182–83
minim (heretics), 173, 175, 178–84
Mishnah, 9, 51, 54, 97–98, 101–5, 107, 110, 114–16, 120–21, 124–27, 129, 132, 134, 137, 166–67, 184, 267; Galilee geography, 141–43; moral outlook, 150–53; non-historical character, 139, 149–50; political outlook, 146–49; sexuality, 144–45; social strata, 143; women, 145–46
Mongke Khan, 305, 309
Mongols, 1, 191, 279, 304–10
Monophysites, 188–89, 231
monotheism, 1, 4, 9, 13, 17, 34, 51, 54–55, 81, 95–97, 144, 163–64, 169, 173–75, 190–91, 197, 201, 230, 243, 271, 310
Montfort (castle), 257, 277, 283, 287, 291–93, 307
Mont Musard (Acre neighborhood), 281–82
Moses, 43, 52, 74, 76, 87, 233, 244
Moses ben Asher, 220
Mount Hermon, 85, 183, 235
Mount of Olives, 116, 248
Mount Tabor, 42, 65, 253, 277, 284–85
Mount Turan, 270
Mu'awiya ibn Abi Sufyan (caliph), 202, 209, 211–12, 226
Muhammad (prophet), 190–91, 194, 196, 198–99, 202, 211, 218, 223, 243, 249
Muhammad ibn Abd al-Malik, 212
Muhammad ibn Ahmad Al-Muqaddasi, 216, 222, 232–33, 235; Acre harbor, 222–23; Banias, 235; Hula, 233; Tiberias description, 216–17

Muhammad ibn Said ibn Hassan, 212
Muhammad ibn Tugh al-Ikhshidid, 224
Muzaffar al-Din, 269
Myers, Eric, 66

Nahaf, 66, 258
Nahariya, 182, 259
Nahman (of Breslov, rabbi), 128
Nakba (Palestinian catastrophe), 3–4, 86, 229–34, 242, 310
Napoleon, 2–3, 6, 9, 286, 305
Nasir i-Khusrau, 223, 233–34
Nazareth, 11, 59–60, 62, 66, 171, 175–78, 186, 193, 215, 234, 253–54, 258–59, 277, 290, 297, 304
Nebe Samuel, 134
Nero (emperor), 38, 85, 109
Neusner, Jacob, 24, 124, 139, 149
Nicephorus Phocas (Byzantine emperor), 225
Nicholson, Robert Lawrence, 246
Nimrim, 271
Nur al-Din, 261, 263, 266

olives (cultivation and trade in Galilee), 11, 27–28, 101, 140, 142, 167, 189, 191, 259, 280
Oppenheimer, Aharon, 101, 118, 120, 122
Overman, J. Andrew, 56–57

pardes (orchard legend), 135
Paris, Matthew, 300, 303
Parthians, 13, 17
Pascal II (Pope), 253
Patricius (rebel leader in 351 CE), 187. *See also* Gallus Caesar
Paul (Saint, Saul of Tarsus), 76, 179, 202
Pelagius (cardinal, of Albano), 286, 290, 298
Penn, William, 81
Peter (Saint, Simon Cephas), 71, 80, 83, 86, 186
Peters, Joan, 230

Pharisees, 18, 23–24, 32, 35–36, 51, 54, 56, 58, 77, 80, 82–83, 87–89, 122
Phasael (brother of Herod), 9
Philip (son of Herod, tetrarch), 84
Philip II (Philip Augustus, of France), 273, 276
Philip de Novare, 258, 289
Phillip de Milli, 258
Phoenicians, 62, 64
pilgrimage (in Galilee), 127, 164, 186, 189, 198, 214–15, 234, 251, 259, 280
Pinhas (head of Tiberias Yeshiva), 219
Prawer, Joshua, 227, 231, 241, 245–46, 249–51, 254, 259, 265, 267, 270, 273, 279, 282

Qarmatis, 224–26
Qutuz (Mamluk sultan), 308–9

Rajak, Tessa, 19
Ralph of Caen, 244–49
Ramla, 210, 214, 216, 223–26, 268
Rappaport, Uriel, 27, 32–33
Rashbi, 104–5, 124, 136–38, 152, 168, 213; biography of, 127–29; cave episode, 129–31; grave hillula, 133–34; Tiberias purification, 131–33
Rashi (Shlomo Yitzhaki, rabbi, commentator), 113–14
Raymond III (of Tripoli, Prince of Galilee), 260, 262, 264–72; at Hattin, 267–72; rivalry with Guy, 265–66
Reagan, Ronald, 81
Reginald of Krak, 266
Remus, Harold, 68–69
Renan, Ernest, 37
Richard I (of England, Richard the Lionheart), 273–77, 288, 299
Richard of Cornwall, 277
Riley-Smith, J., 240
Romanus II (Byzantine emperor), 225
Rome, 2, 5, 10–11, 13, 17–22, 36, 38–44, 51, 55, 62, 67, 70, 86, 95–96, 99, 103–06, 117–18, 123–24, 130, 144, 148, 154, 163–65, 168, 175, 180–81, 184–87, 197, 218, 229, 310
Rumah, 233
Runciman, Steven, 240

Saadia Gaon, 218–20
Sadducees, 23–24, 150
Safed, 2, 6, 81–82, 117, 124–28, 131–34, 139, 184, 214, 235–36, 251, 256, 277, 282, 293, 296, 307
Said, Edward, 230
Sakhnin (Sikhnin), 103, 112, 165, 178, 291
Saladin (Salah ad-Din), 9, 227, 234, 260–73, 276, 302, 308; command at Hattin, 267–72; reputation before and after Hattin, 261–62; rise to power, 263
Saldarini, Anthony, 56
Salih b. Jubayr al-Suda'I al-Tabarani (Abu Muhammad), 217, 220
Samaritans, 183, 231
Samson of Sens (ben Abraham), 282
Samuel ben Samson, 251
Sanders, E.P., 70, 176
Sanhedrin (Jewish council), 12, 19, 57, 100, 108–10, 116–19, 148, 153, 169, 171
Sassanid Empire (Neo-Persian), 164, 167–68, 192, 194, 196
Saunders, J.J., 310–11
Sayf al-dawla, 224
Schick, Robert, 193, 214–15
Scholem, Gershom, 135
Schwartz, Seth, 29
Schweitzer, Albert, 33, 70, 73, 78–79, 180
Sea of Galilee (Lake Kinneret), 14, 20, 37, 39–40, 44, 60, 65–66, 71, 81, 102, 189–90, 202, 209, 211, 216, 225–26, 233–34, 250–53, 260, 267–68, 270, 277, 285, 310
Second Temple. *See* Jerusalem
Secrets of Rabbi Simeon ben Yohai (apocalyptic text), 133, 213

Seisor (Sajur), 258
Sepphoris, 11, 14, 26, 57, 62–68, 73, 100–101, 103, 119, 121–22, 132, 141, 165–66, 168–72, 174–78, 182, 192, 209, 235, 263, 267–71, 277, 293
Septimius Severus (emperor), 119
Shahrbazaz (Sassanid army leader), 192, 194–96, 201
Shavei Tzion, 182
Shfaram, 104, 106, 119
Shimon Bar Yochai. *See* Rashbi
Shimon ben Gamaliel II (nasi, rabbi), 108, 120; biography of, 108–10
Shimon ben Lakish (Resh Lakish, Amora), 170–71
Shlomi, 182
shmita (fallow year), 105, 117, 130, 140–41, 216
Shurahbil ibn Hasana, 200
Sibyl (Queen of Jerusalem, sister of Baldwin IV), 264–65
Sidon, 57, 226, 277, 290, 296
Simon (son of Gioras), 20, 34
Smail, R.C., 264
Smith, John Masson, 308–9
Social Gospel (Protestant movement), 80
Sophronius (Patriarch of Jerusalem), 200, 215
Sotah (Mishnah tractate), 148
Steinberg, Milton, 136
St. George de La Baena (lordship), 258, 291
Strange, James, 66–67, 174
Strauss, David Friedrich, 69
Sulayman ibn Hishman ibn Abd al-Malik, 212
supersessionism, 32, 52–53, 59–60, 71–72, 74, 76, 82–83, 86–87, 172, 183

Tahir b. Ali b. Abdus Abul-Tayyid, 220
Talmud, 1, 3, 6, 9, 36, 42, 51, 97, 99, 101, 104–19, 121, 123, 127–31, 134–39, 163–66, 169–70, 173–74, 178–79, 182, 282; Babylonian Talmud (Bavli), 105, 108–9, 112, 117, 121, 129, 132, 135, 170, 179; Jerusalem Talmud (Yerushalmi), 107–08, 135, 137, 169
Tancred, 239, 241–42, 244–55, 266, 275, 298, 304; biography, 244–46; First Crusade, 246–49; Haifa, 252; Prince of Galilee, 249–51
Tannaim, 19, 97–115, 120–29, 131–54, 164, 166–68, 173, 175, 178–80, 184–85, 190, 196, 218, 267, 271, 283, 293
Taqi al-Din 'Amr, 269, 271
Tarichaeae, 20, 37, 39, 43–44
Taylor, Joan, 172, 183–84
Tel Ashtara, 267
Templar (order), 235, 243, 256–57, 263, 270, 277, 283–84, 287, 292, 307
Testa, Emmanuele, 183–84
Teutonic (order), 257–58, 277, 283–93, 307–8; background, 283–84; Fifth Crusade, 284–87; Galilee settlement, 288–89, 291–92; Monfort, 291–93
Theodosius I (emperor), 188
Thucydides, 20, 222
Tibble, Steve, 250
Tiberias, 2, 14, 57, 100, 132–33, 138, 166–71, 200; Byzantine era, 171–72, 182, 184, 186–89, 196–98; Crusader era, 239, 250–53, 260, 266–70, 277, 283, 286; early Islamic era, 209–26, 233–35; earthquake, 216; establishment of, 65, 67–68, 73; Mishnah references to, 141; New Testament, 66; Persian invasion, 192–93; Rashbi's activities in, 129–33; Second Temple era, 11, 20, 26–27, 39, 42–44, 62, 132; Tannaitic era, 101, 103–4, 118–19, 135–37; Yeshiva in, 170–71, 218–19
tithing (Temple devotions), 105, 120, 125, 143, 145, 147
Titus (emperor), 22, 25–26, 33, 37–39, 85–86
Tolstoy, Leo, 79
Toron (Tebnine), 254, 290–91

Tosefta (oral law compilation), 102, 108, 135
Tulunids (of Egypt-based dynasty), 221, 223
Tyerman, Christopher, 243–44, 256, 274, 294
Tyre, 27, 57, 166, 185, 193–94, 209–10, 216, 222–24, 253–54, 258, 260, 272–73, 276, 280, 289, 307

Umar ibn al-Khattab (caliph), 199, 203, 218
Umayyad (caliphate), 185, 202, 209–12, 214, 216–18, 221, 223, 229
Urban II (Pope), 226, 228, 239, 244
Urban III (Pope), 272
Usha (Galilee assembly), 100, 103–4, 106, 108–10, 119, 121–23, 129, 165
Uthman ibn Affan (caliph), 211

Vahan (Byzantine military commander), 201–3
Vatican, 10, 82, 87
Vespasian (emperor), 19, 22, 25, 33–34, 38–40, 85
Voltaire, 261

Wadi, Rummanah, 269
Wadi Ruqqad, 202–3
War of the Lombards, 277, 280, 289
Wesley, John, 75
William of Tyre, 253, 260, 262–65, 273
Willibald (bishop, pilgrim), 215, 217
Winthrop, John, 81

World War I, 2, 126, 274, 295

Ya'akov ben Karshi (Tanna, rabbi), 109
Ya'ari, Abraham, 134
Yanot (Yanoh), 258
Yaqusah, 202–3
Yaqut al-Hawami, 203–4, 223, 233–35, 272
Yarmuk (battle), 190–204, 210–11, 215, 221, 227, 242–43, 272, 309–10; army sizes, 202; Byzantine weaponry, 199; course of battle, 202–3; diplomacy options, 201; Heraclius before battle, 197–98; Islamic strategy and weaponry, 199–200
Yavne, 19, 36, 82, 100, 103–7, 122, 142, 145, 170, 173
Yazid ibn Abd al-Malik (Yazid II, caliph), 213
Yazid ibn al-Walid (Yazid III, caliph), 212
Yazid ibn Mu'awiya ibn Abi Sufyan (caliph), 212
Yazid ibn Sulaymin, 212
Yishmael ben Elisha (rabbi), 128
Yohanan bar Nafha (rabbi), 170
Yose ben Hanina (Amora, rabbi), 167

Zahir, al-Umar al-Zaydani, 2, 6
Zarrar ibn al Azwar, 200, 203
Zengi of Mosul, 262
Zionism, 2–4, 6, 23, 41–42, 126–27, 134, 140, 168, 184, 190, 211, 229–30, 232, 242, 262

About the Author

M. M. Silver is Professor of Jewish History and World History at the Max Stern Yezreel Valley College and at the University of Haifa in Israel. He has published books in Hebrew and English that include *Louis Marshall and the Rise of Jewish Ethnicity in America*, and *Zionism and the Melting Pot: Preachers, Pioneers and Modern Jewish Politics*. He lives in Safed, Galilee, and is the father of four children.

www.ingramcontent.com/pod-product-compliance
Lightning Source LLC
Chambersburg PA
CBHW071359300426
44114CB00016B/2119